Takane & Hana

12

STORY AND ART BY
Yuki Shiwasu

Takane & Hana

12

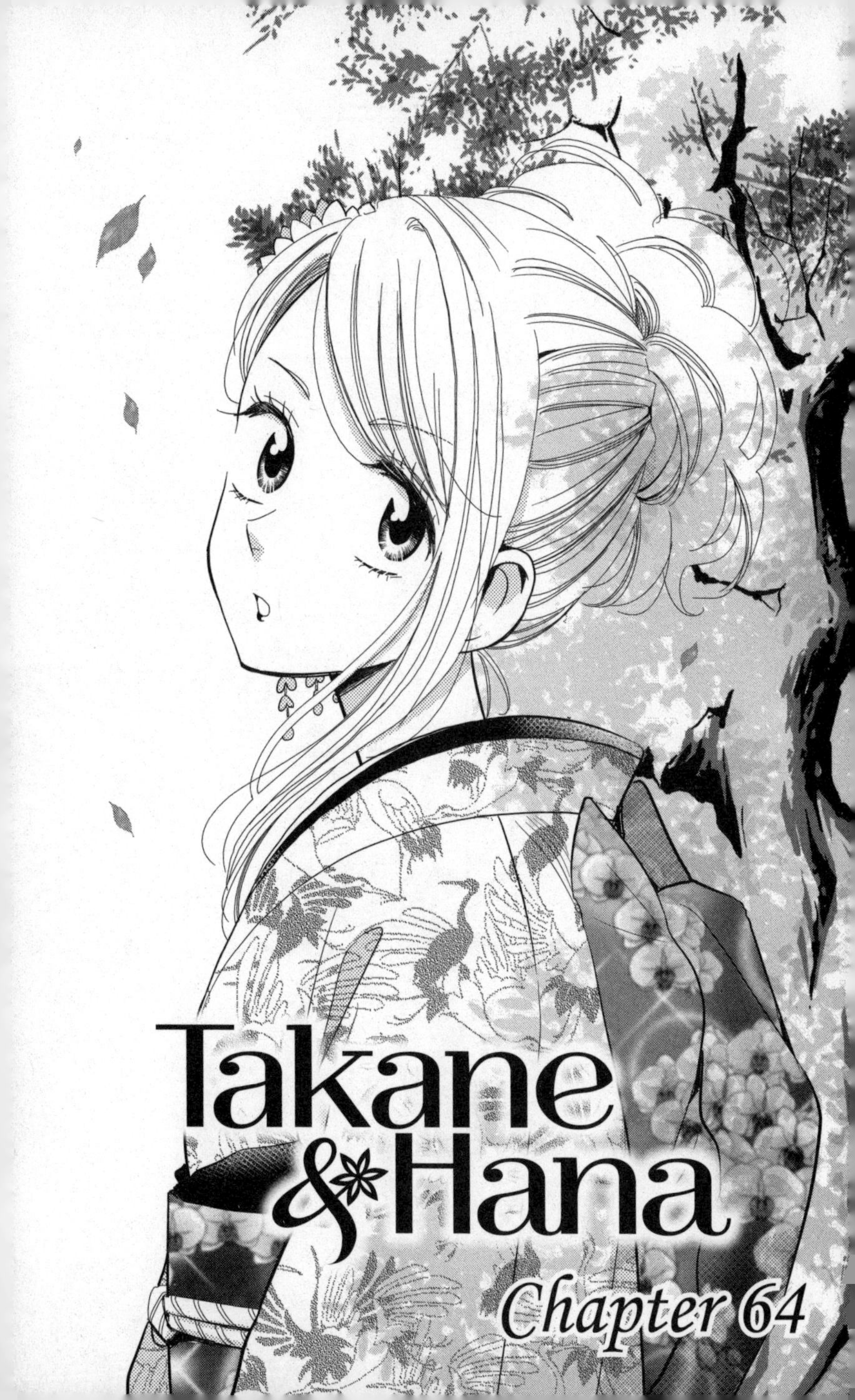
Takane & Hana
Chapter 64

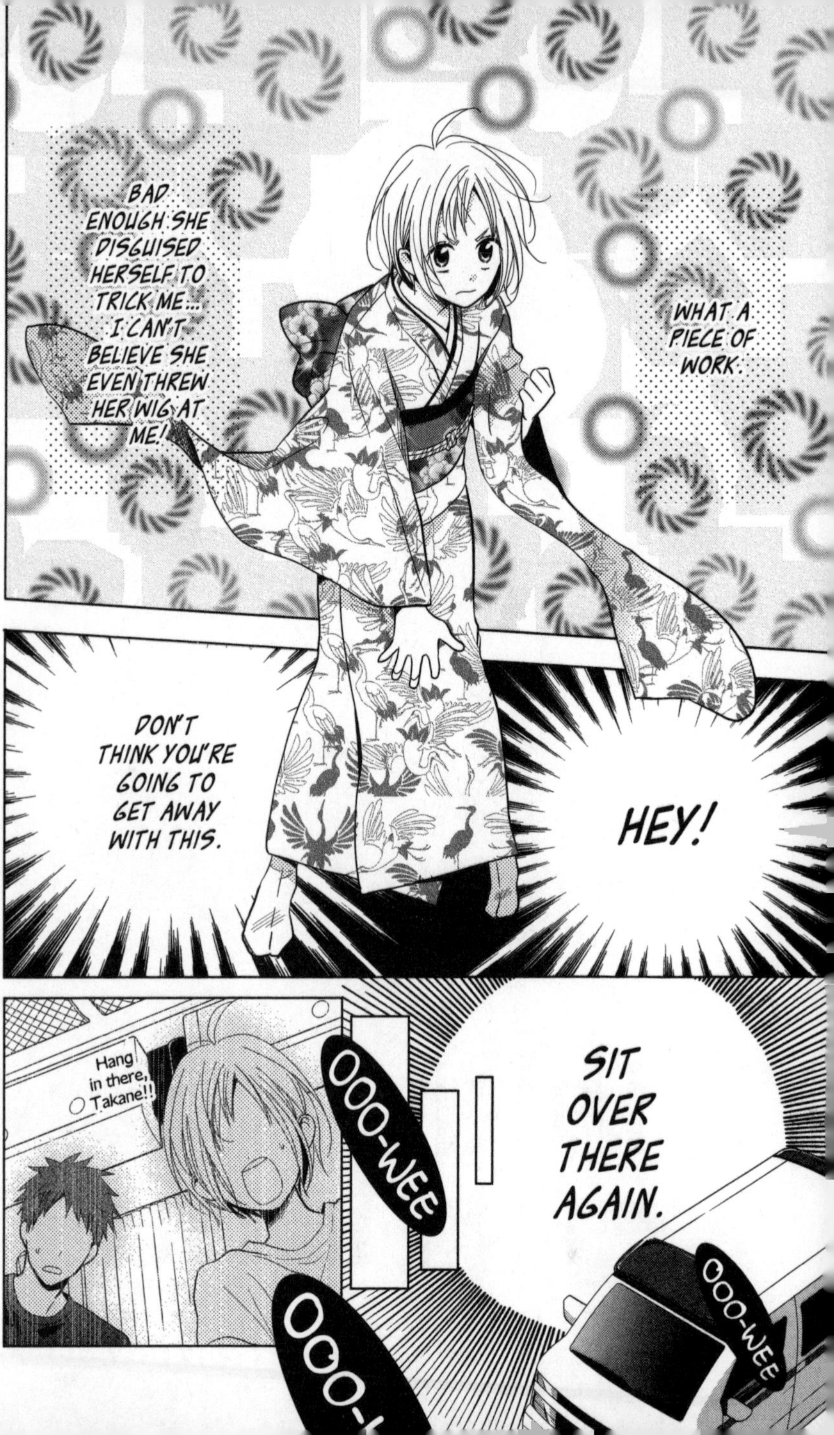
WHAT A PIECE OF WORK.
BAD ENOUGH SHE DISGUISED HERSELF TO TRICK ME... I CAN'T BELIEVE SHE EVEN THREW HER WIG AT ME!
HEY!
DON'T THINK YOU'RE GOING TO GET AWAY WITH THIS.
SIT OVER THERE AGAIN.
OOO-WEE
OOO-WEE
Hang in there, Takane!!
OOO-WEE
OOO-

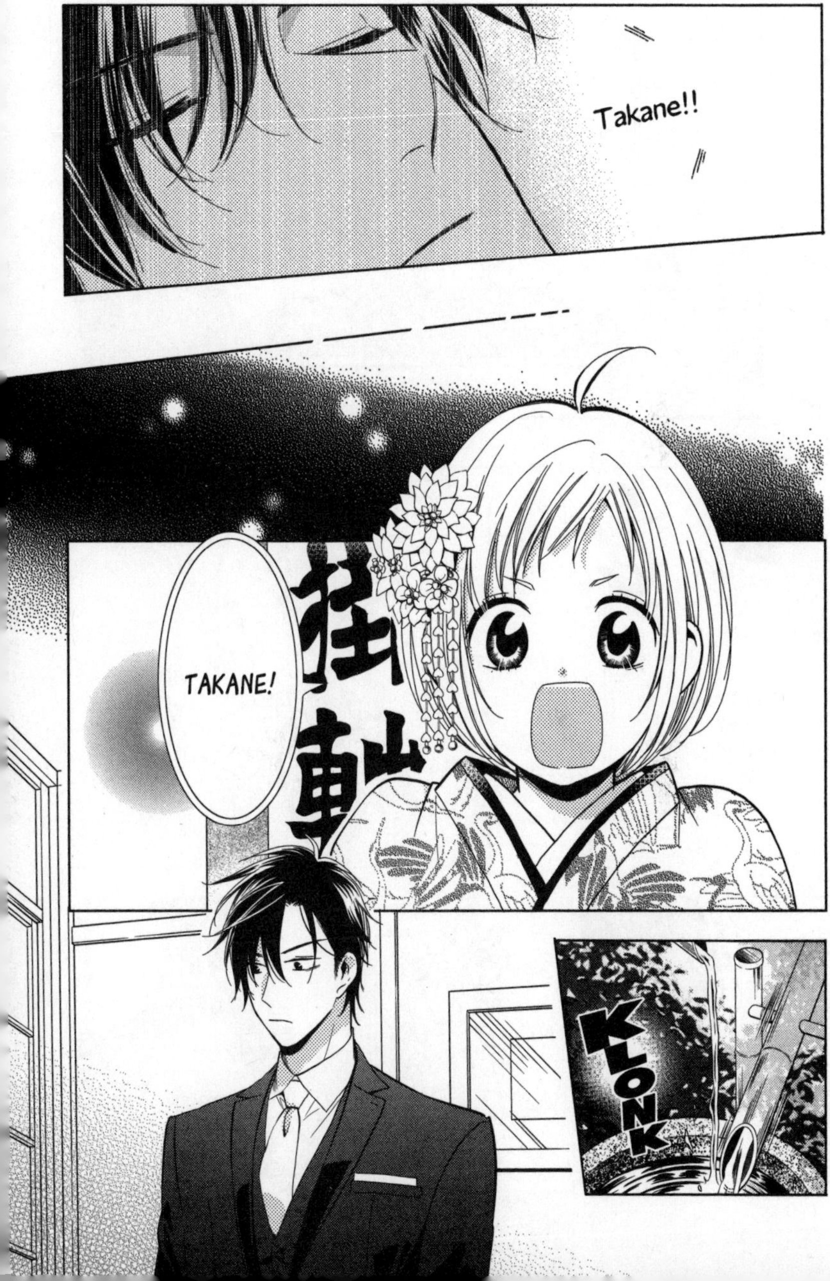
Takane!!
TAKANE!
KLONK

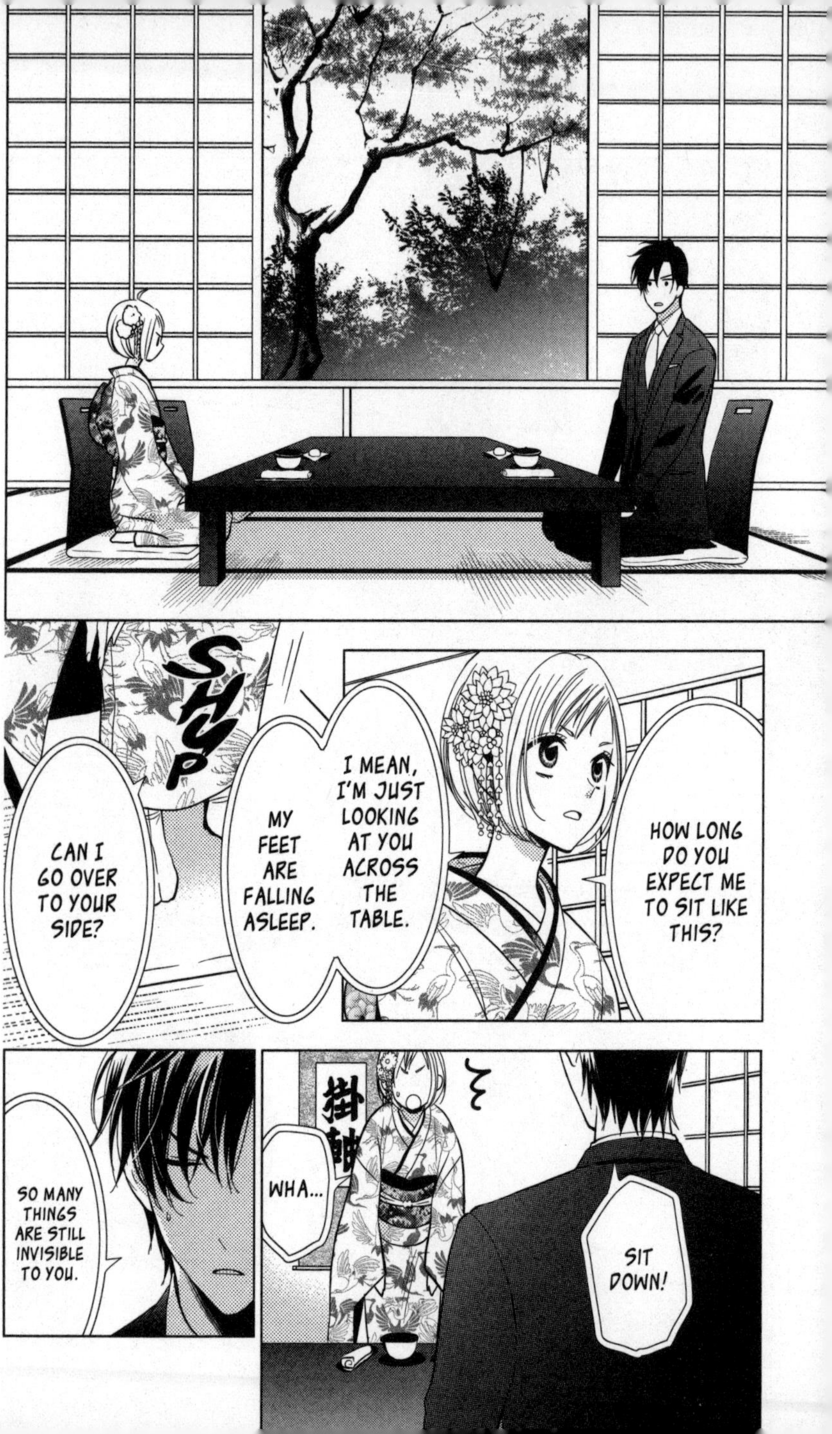
HOW LONG DO YOU EXPECT ME TO SIT LIKE THIS?
I MEAN, I'M JUST LOOKING AT YOU ACROSS THE TABLE.
MY FEET ARE FALLING ASLEEP.
SHUP
CAN I GO OVER TO YOUR SIDE?
SIT DOWN!
掛軸
WHA...
SO MANY THINGS ARE STILL INVISIBLE TO YOU.

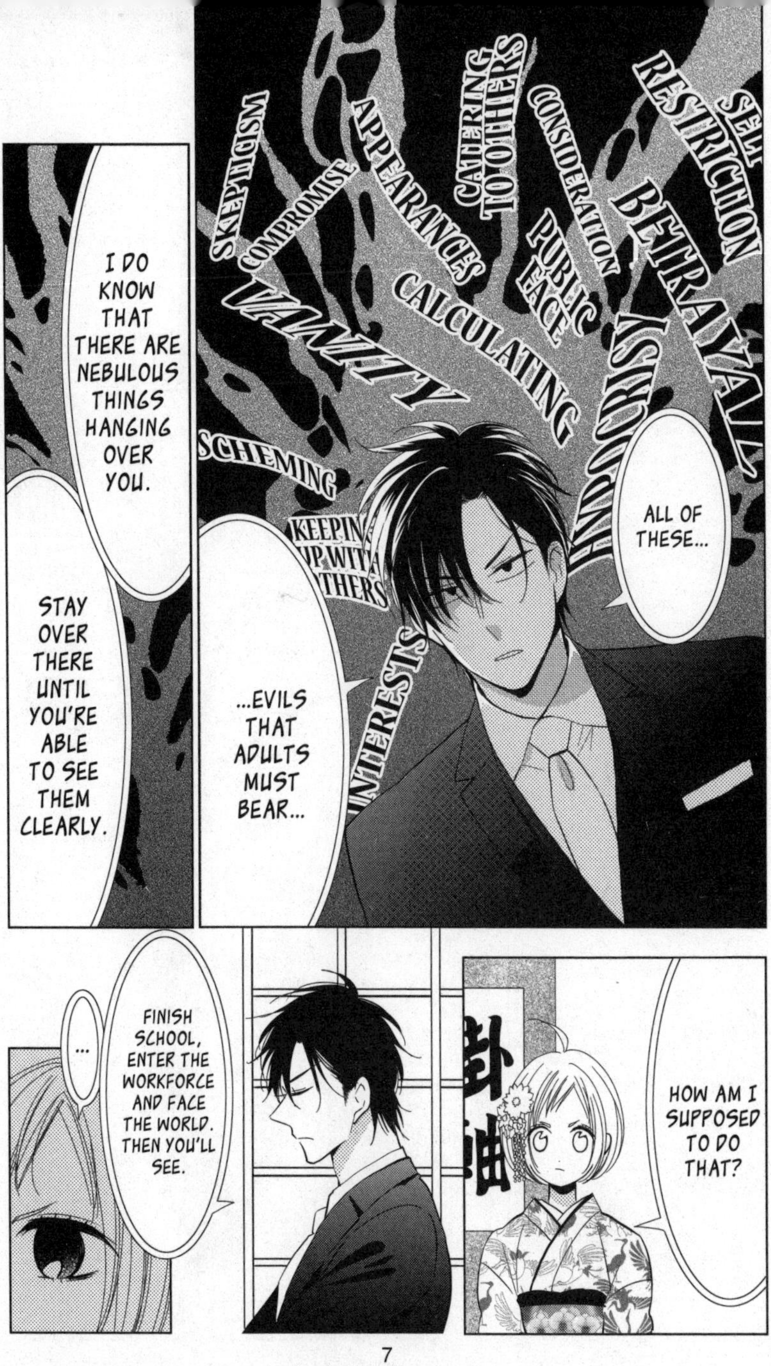
SELF RESTRICTION
BETRAYAL
CONSIDERATION
CATERING TO OTHERS
APPEARANCES
COMPROMISE
SKEPTICISM
PUBLIC FACE
CALCULATING
VANITY
SCHEMING
INTERESTS
ALL OF THESE...
...EVILS THAT ADULTS MUST BEAR...
I DO KNOW THAT THERE ARE NEBULOUS THINGS HANGING OVER YOU.
STAY OVER THERE UNTIL YOU'RE ABLE TO SEE THEM CLEARLY.
HOW AM I SUPPOSED TO DO THAT?
FINISH SCHOOL, ENTER THE WORKFORCE AND FACE THE WORLD. THEN YOU'LL SEE.
...

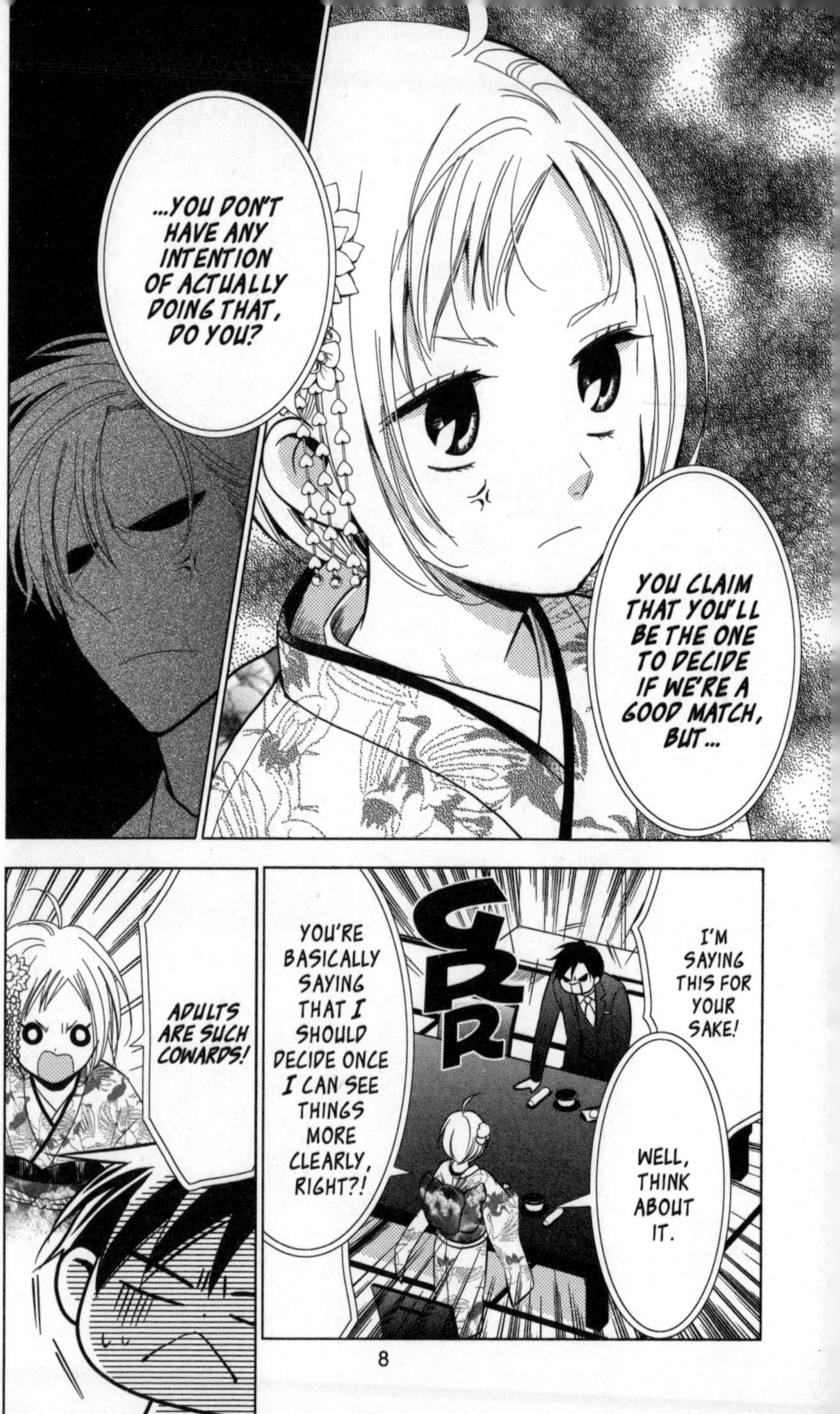
YOU CLAIM THAT YOU'LL BE THE ONE TO DECIDE IF WE'RE A GOOD MATCH, BUT...
...YOU DON'T HAVE ANY INTENTION OF ACTUALLY DOING THAT, DO YOU?
I'M SAYING THIS FOR YOUR SAKE!
WELL, THINK ABOUT IT.
GR
YOU'RE BASICALLY SAYING THAT I SHOULD DECIDE ONCE I CAN SEE THINGS MORE CLEARLY, RIGHT?!
ADULTS ARE SUCH COWARDS!

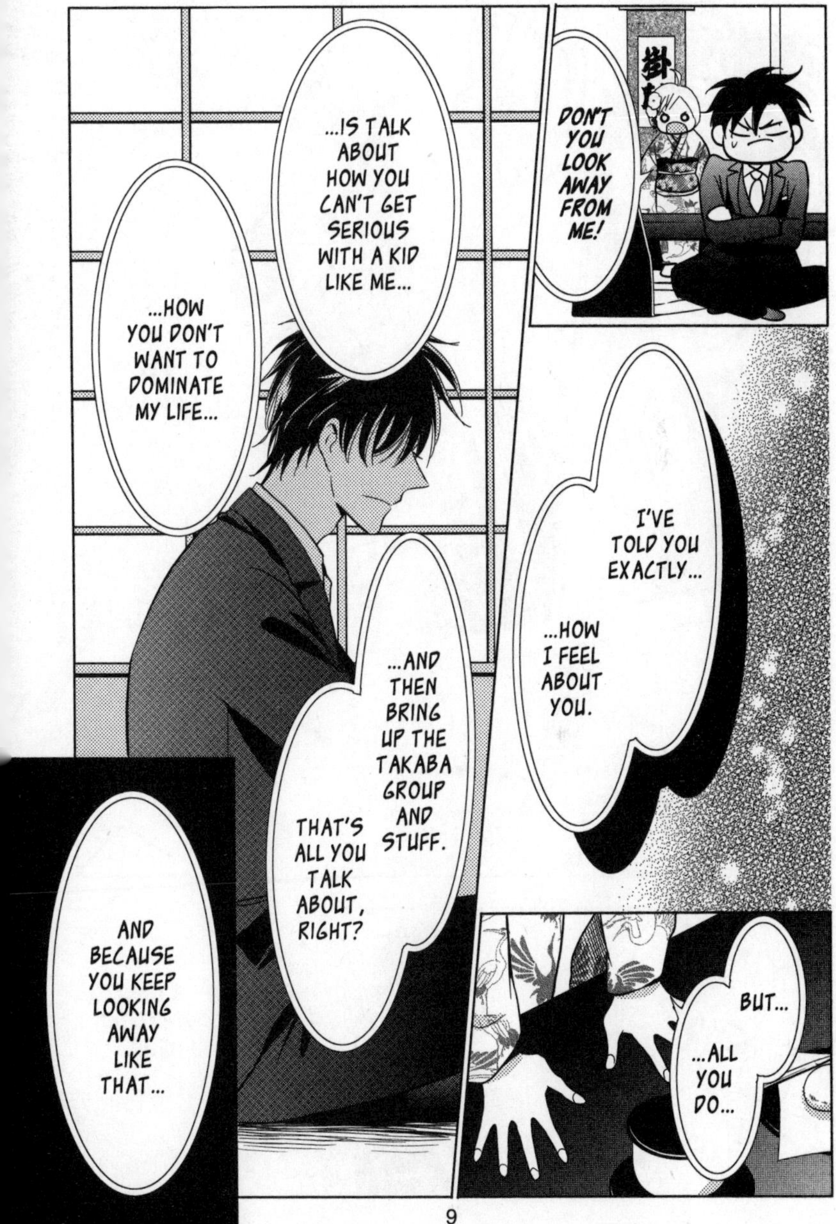
DON'T YOU LOOK AWAY FROM ME!
I'VE TOLD YOU EXACTLY...
...HOW I FEEL ABOUT YOU.
BUT...
...ALL YOU DO...
...IS TALK ABOUT HOW YOU CAN'T GET SERIOUS WITH A KID LIKE ME...
...HOW YOU DON'T WANT TO DOMINATE MY LIFE...
...AND THEN BRING UP THE TAKABA GROUP AND STUFF.
THAT'S ALL YOU TALK ABOUT, RIGHT?
AND BECAUSE YOU KEEP LOOKING AWAY LIKE THAT...

GRAB

!!

...THIS HAPPENED!

PLEASE LOOK AT ME!

MWA HA HA.

AAHH!

...

I....!

...THE TRUTH ABOUT YOUR FEELINGS!

I ONLY WANT TO HEAR...

10

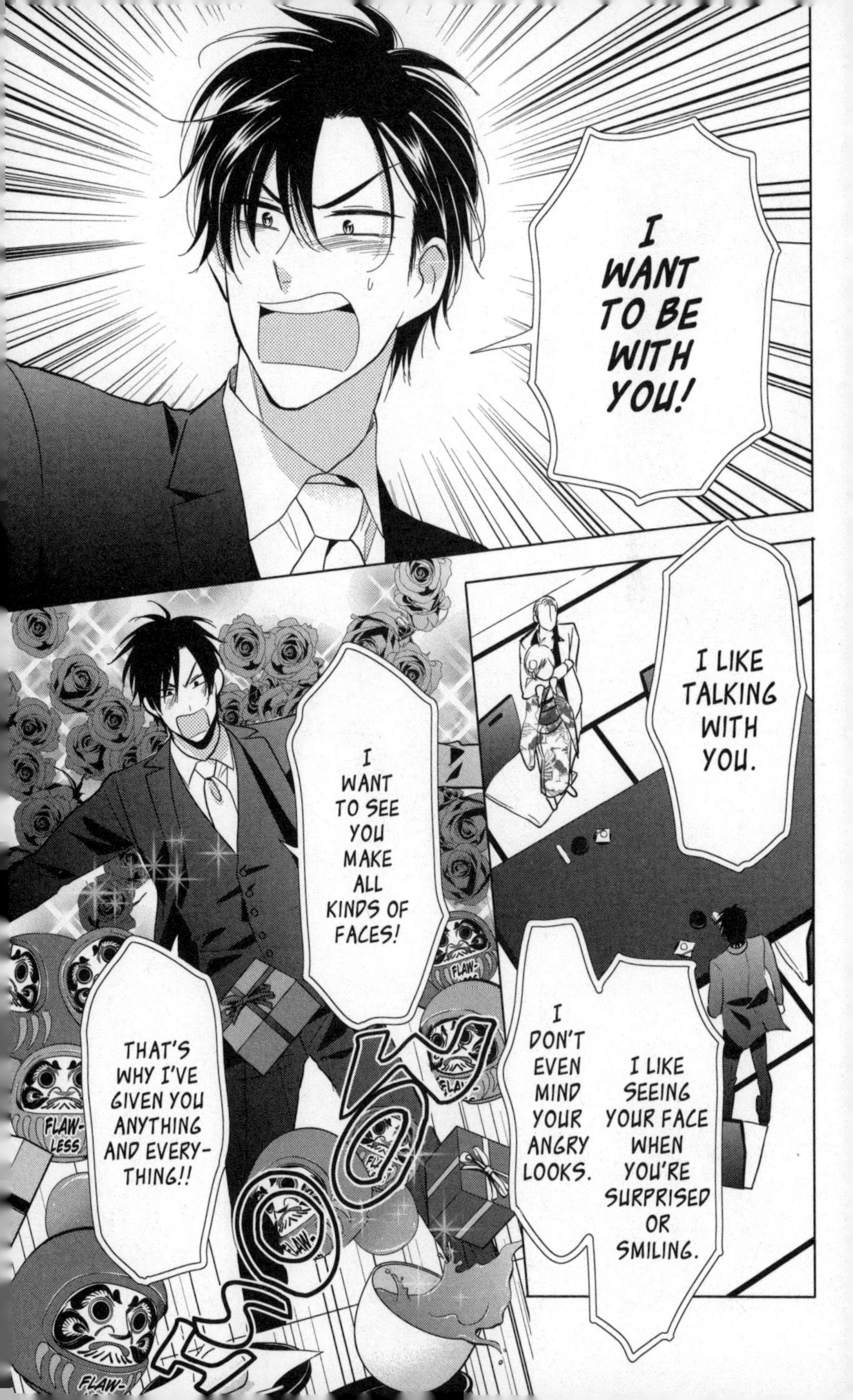
I WANT TO BE WITH YOU!
I LIKE TALKING WITH YOU.
I LIKE SEEING YOUR FACE WHEN YOU'RE SURPRISED OR SMILING.
I DON'T EVEN MIND YOUR ANGRY LOOKS.
I WANT TO SEE YOU MAKE ALL KINDS OF FACES!
THAT'S WHY I'VE GIVEN YOU ANYTHING AND EVERY-THING!!
FLAW-LESS

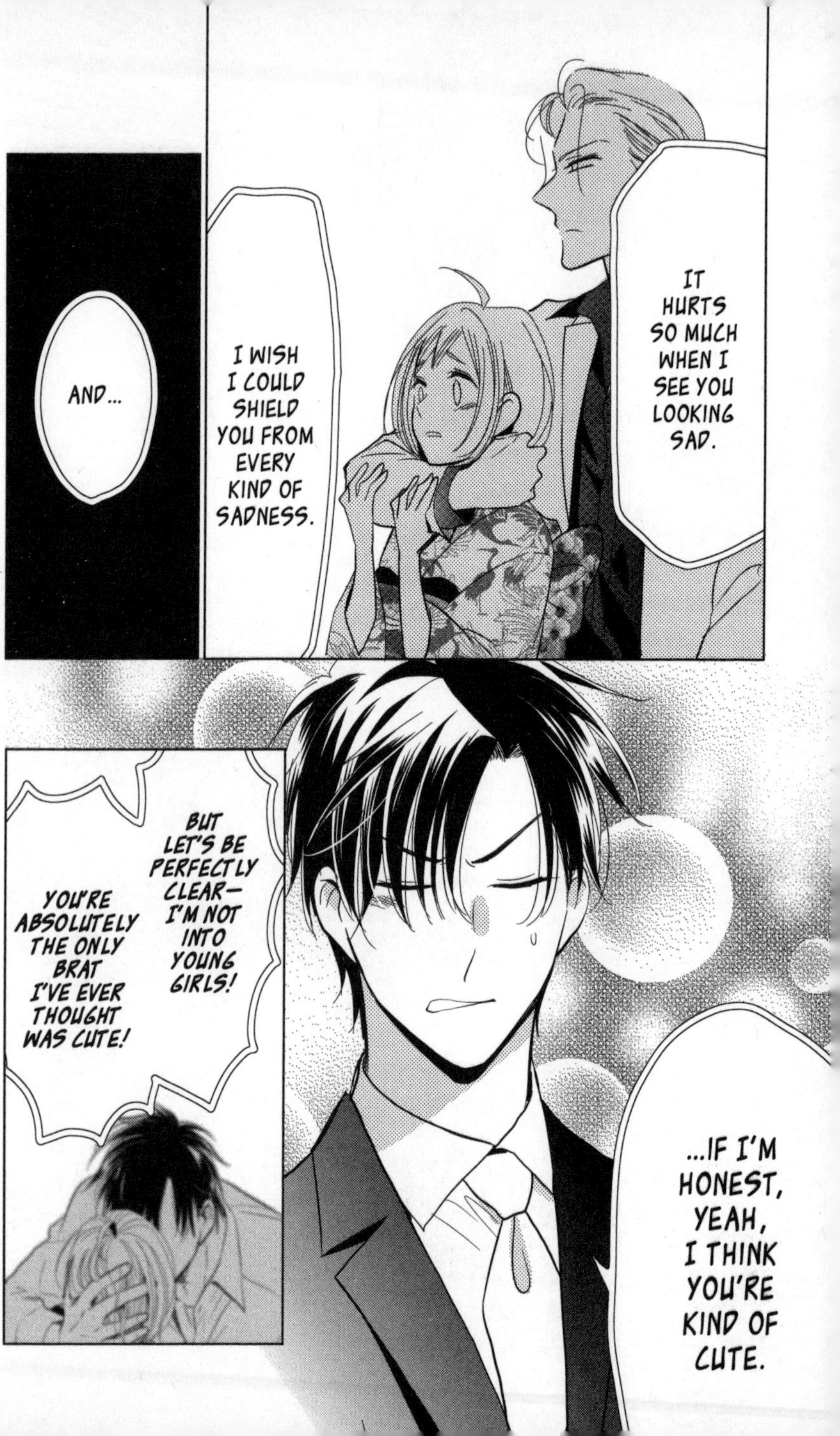
IT HURTS SO MUCH WHEN I SEE YOU LOOKING SAD.
I WISH I COULD SHIELD YOU FROM EVERY KIND OF SADNESS.
AND...
...IF I'M HONEST, YEAH, I THINK YOU'RE KIND OF CUTE.
BUT LET'S BE PERFECTLY CLEAR—I'M NOT INTO YOUNG GIRLS!
YOU'RE ABSOLUTELY THE ONLY BRAT I'VE EVER THOUGHT WAS CUTE!

...WHAT'D BE BEST FOR YOU.

I REALLY...

...COULDN'T FIGURE OUT...

BUT...

WHEN THAT HAPPENED...

...

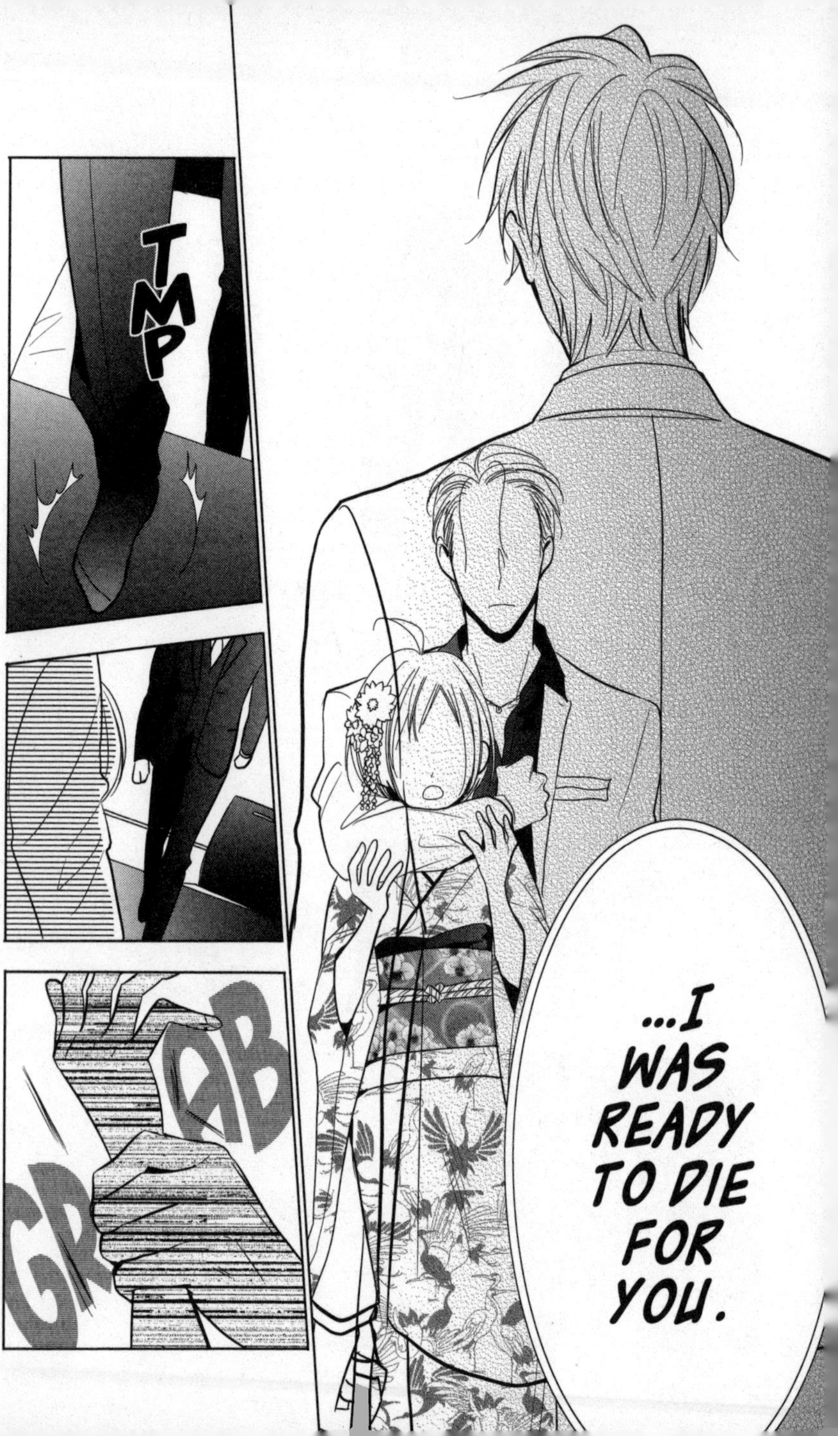
...I WAS READY TO DIE FOR YOU.
TMP
GRAB

THERE'S
...

...NOTHING
MORE TO
SAY.

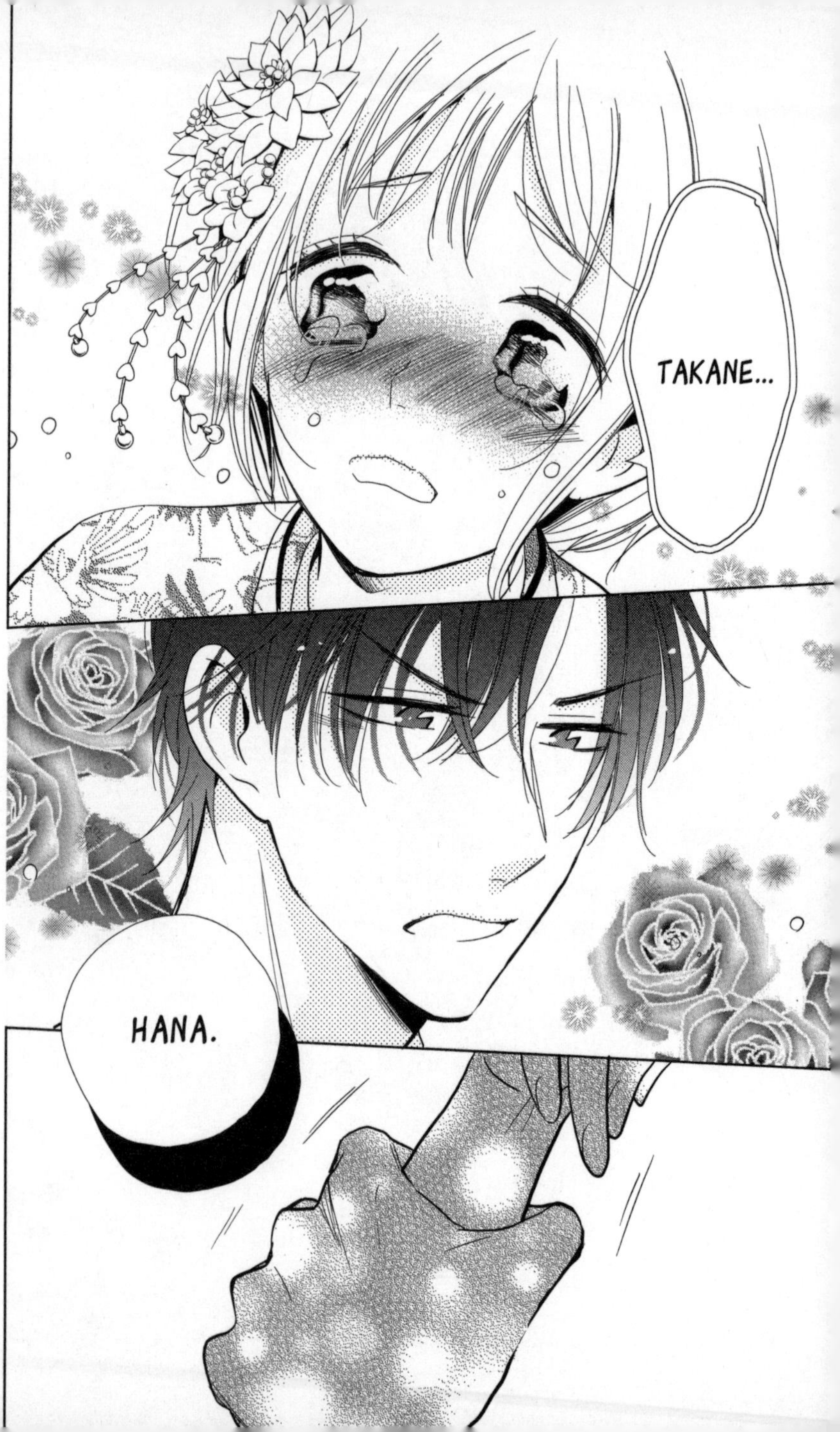
TAKANE...
HANA.

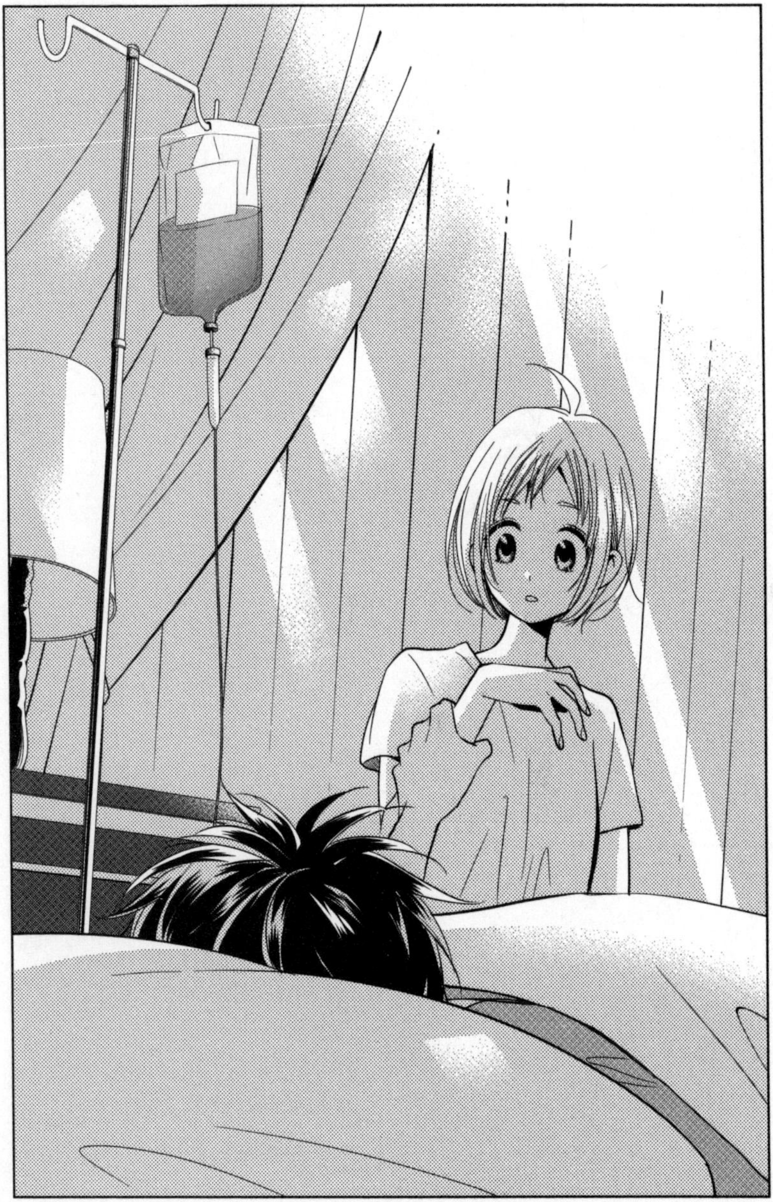

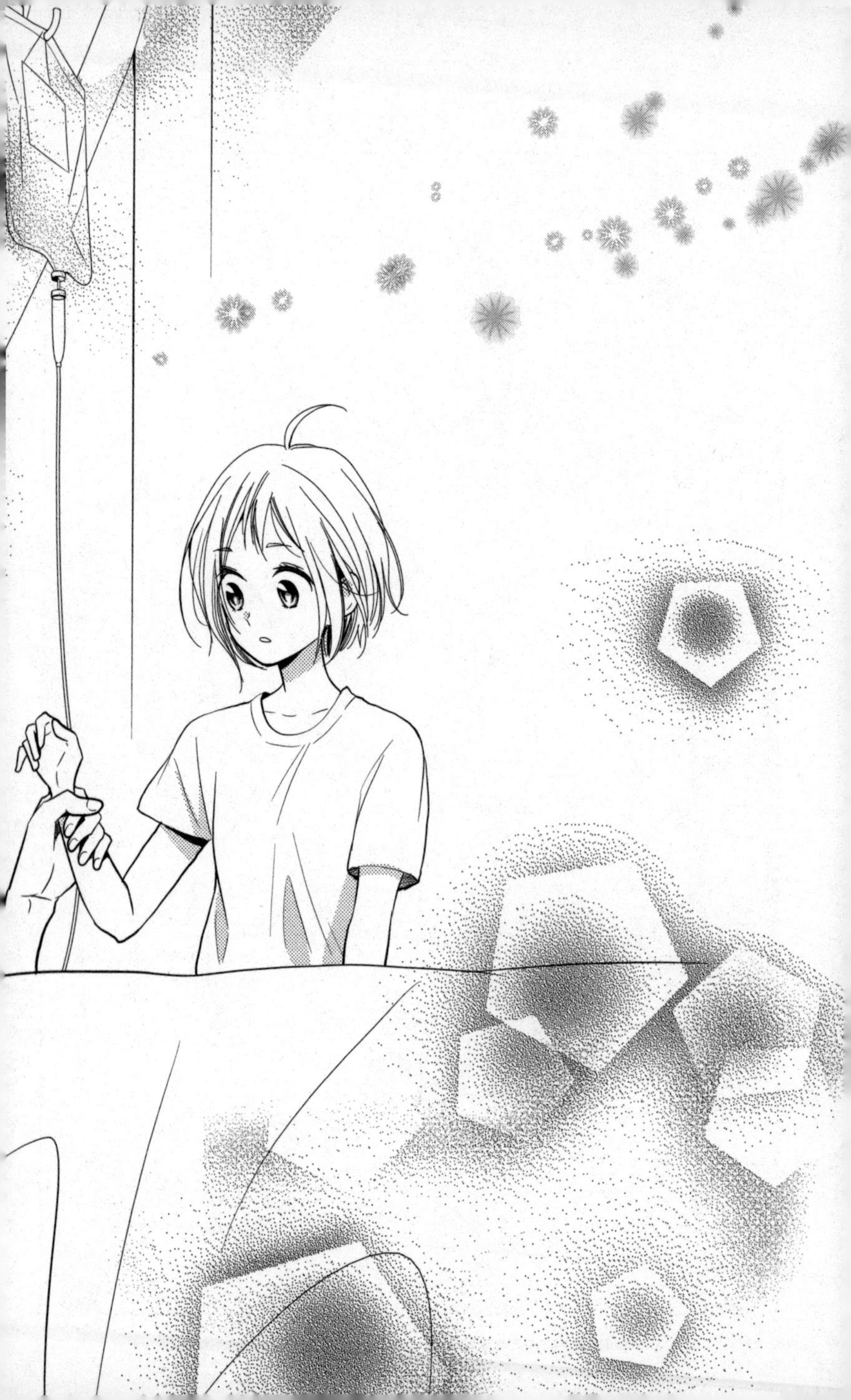

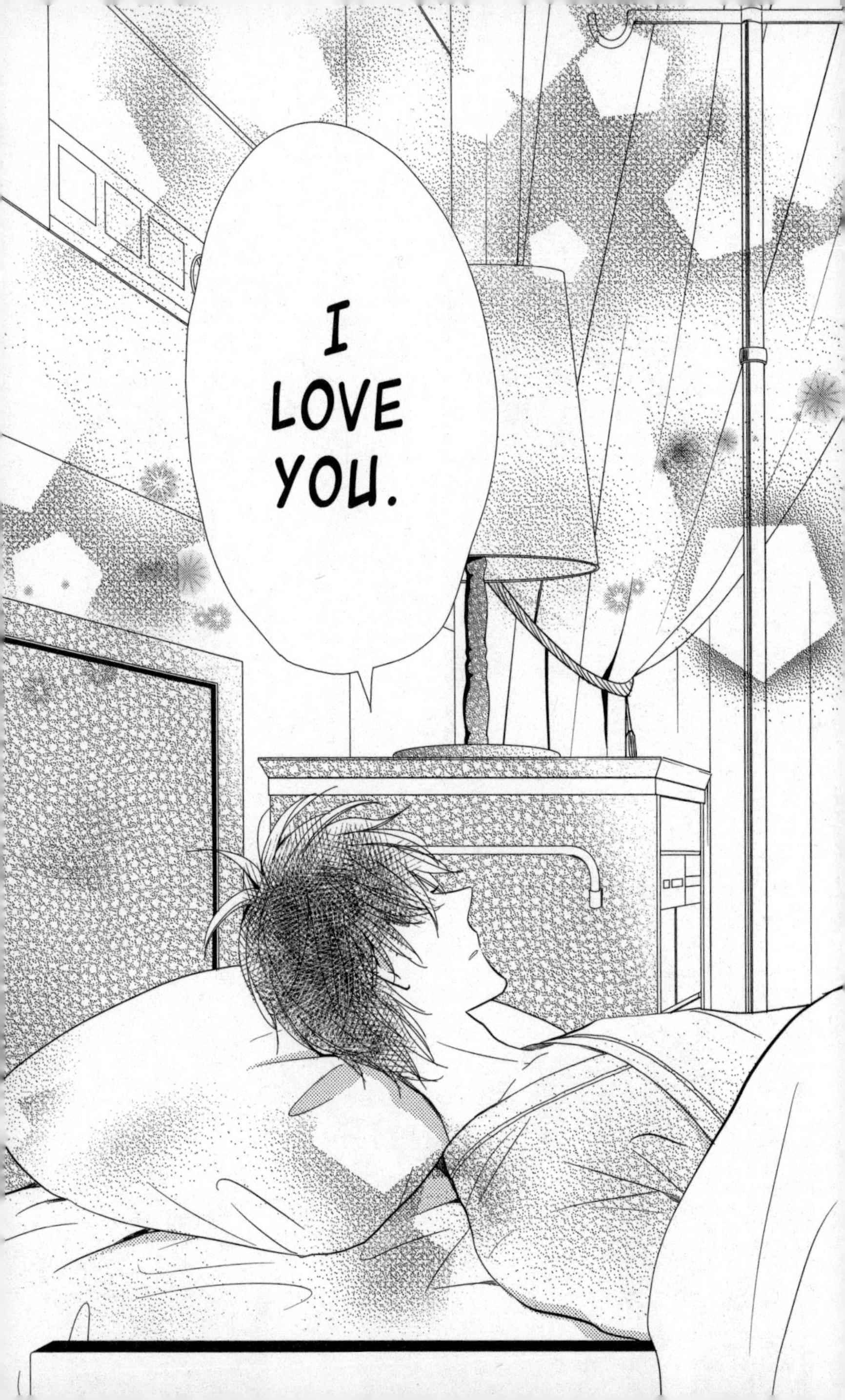
I LOVE YOU.

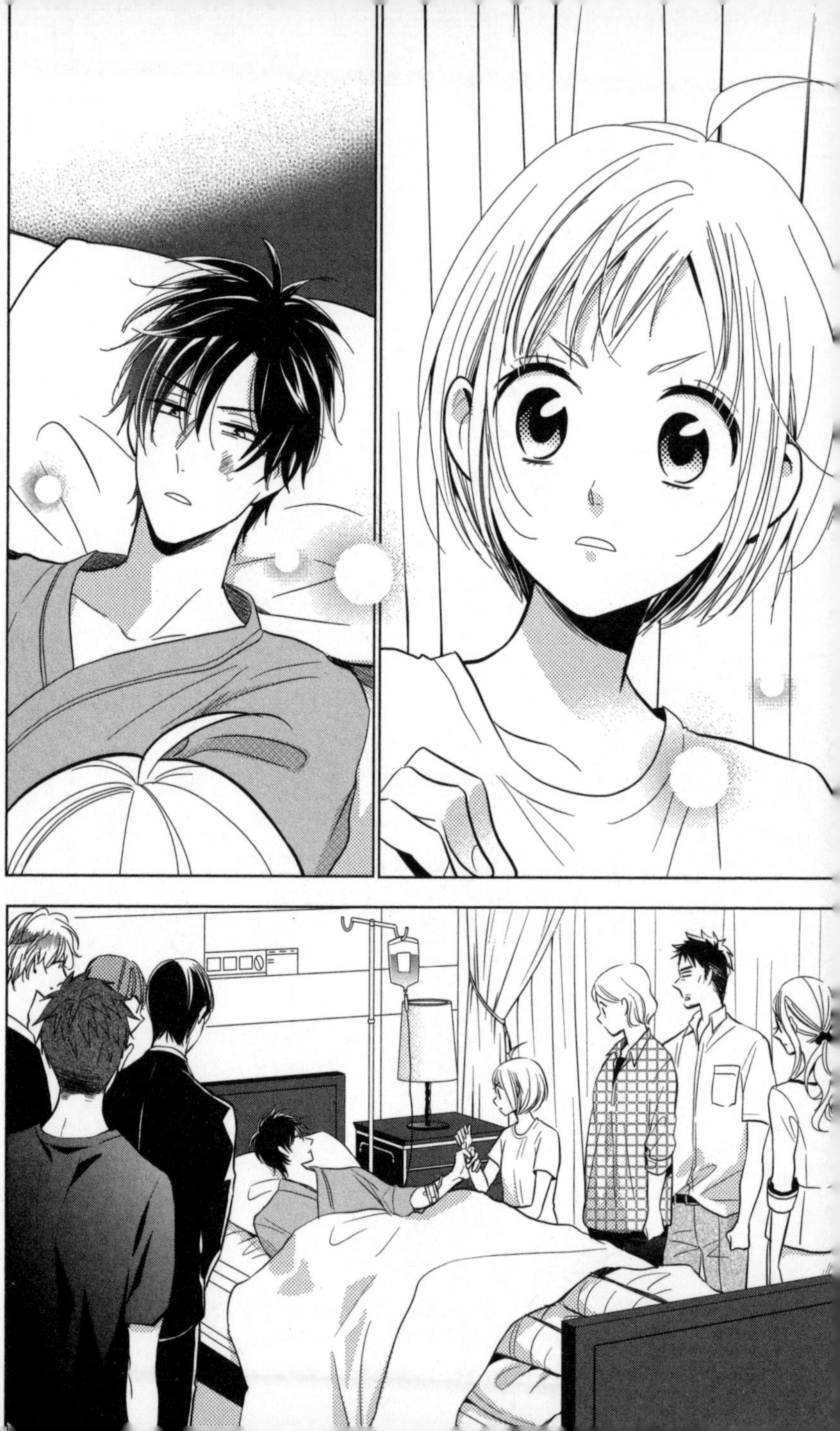

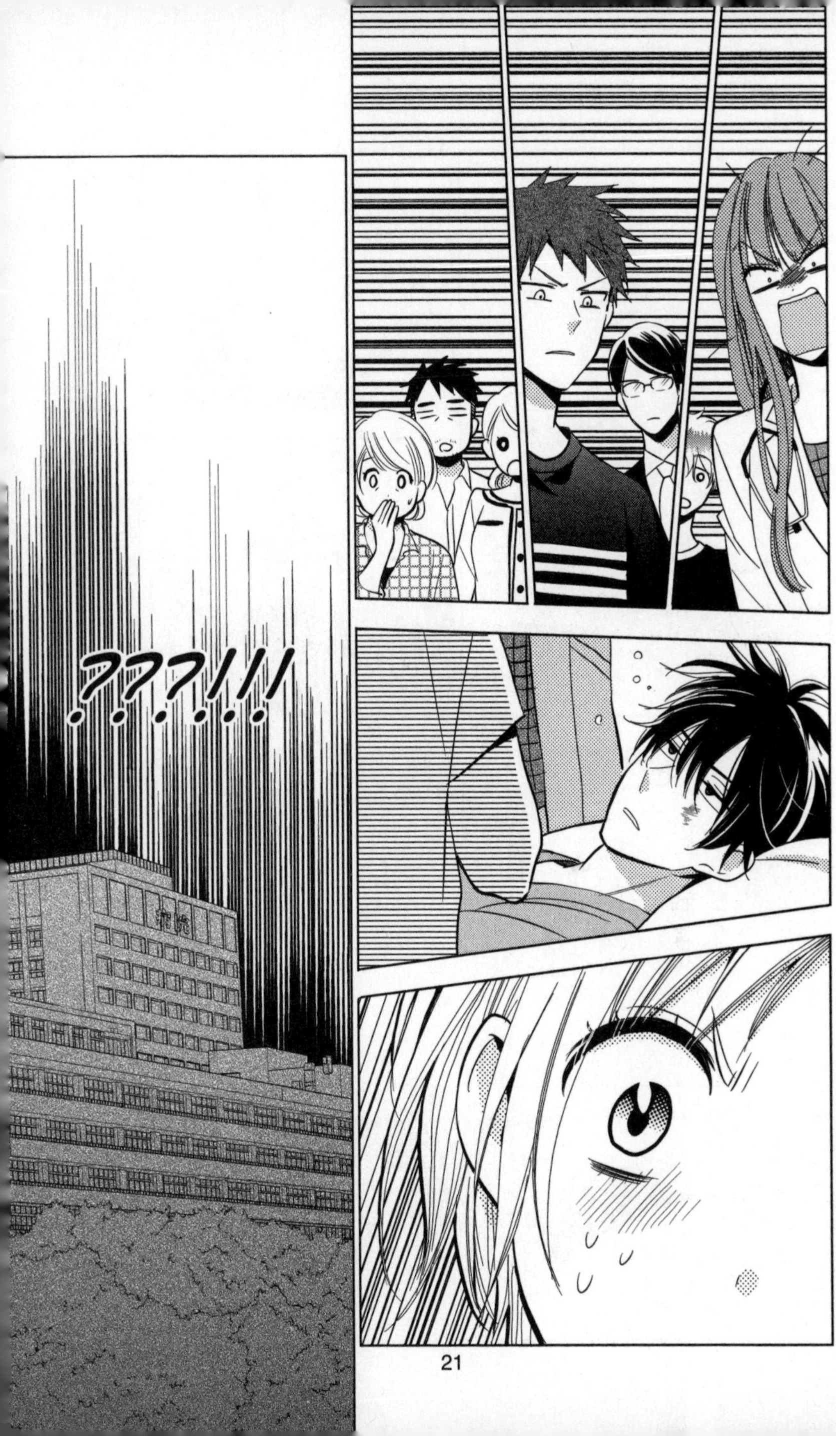
???!!!

WE'LL LEAVE YOU TWO ALONE.

There's nothing you can do about it.

Just for now, okay?

FILING OUT

UM...

THAT'S THE FIRST THING HE SAYS...?

WHEN YOU SAY "LOVE"...

HE SAID "HANA"...

22

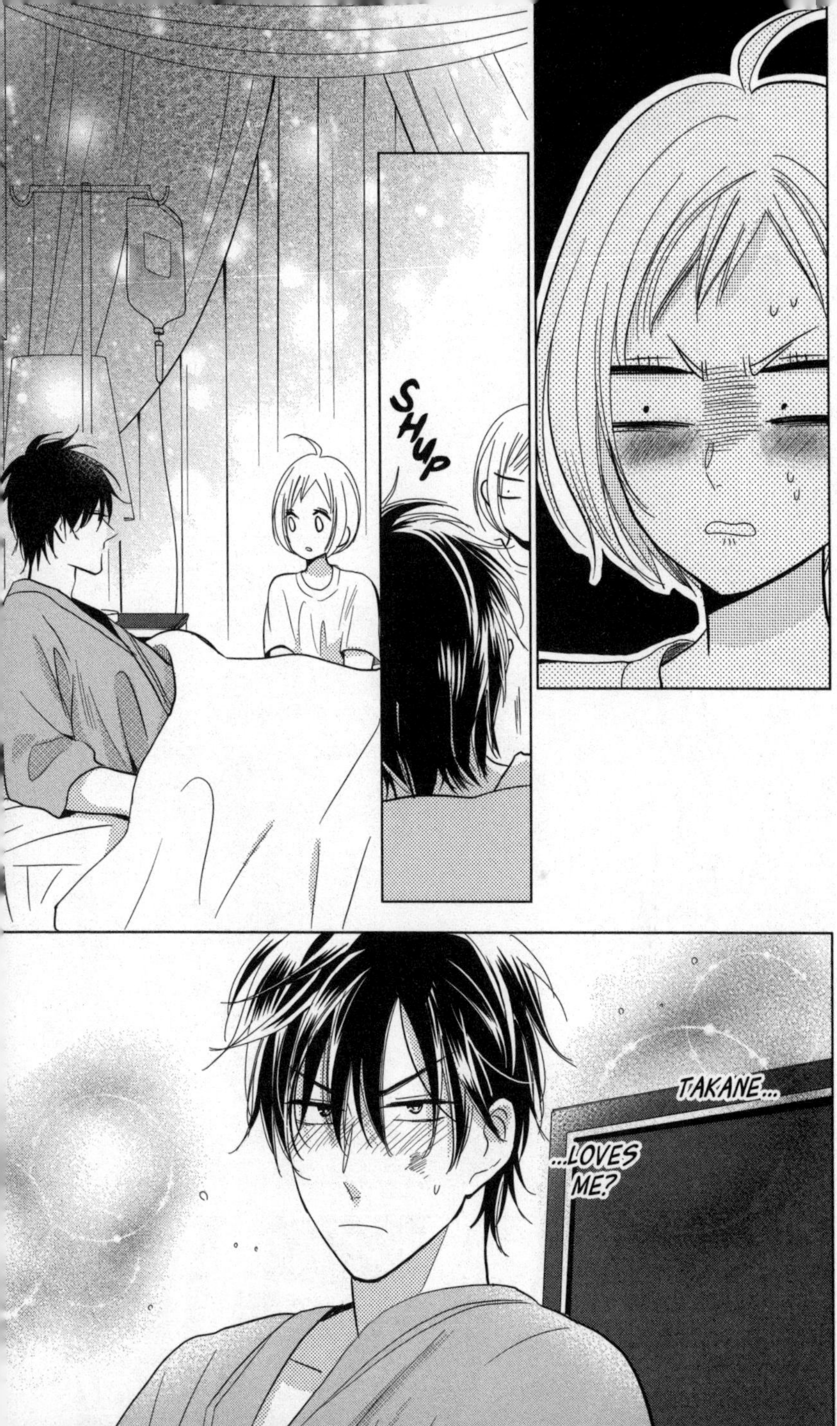
SHUP
TAKANE...
...LOVES ME?

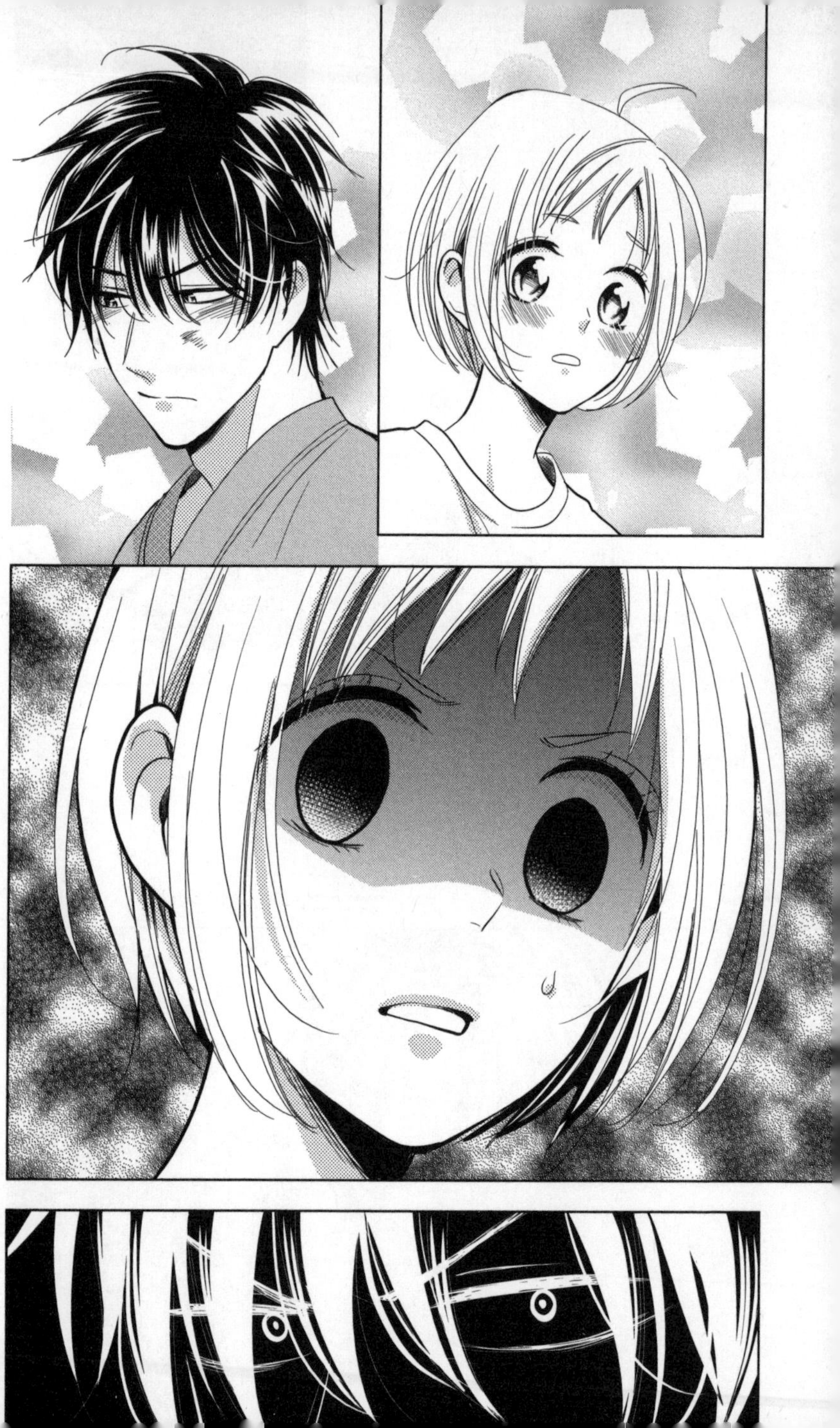

NO WAY.

I GOT KIDNAPPED BY YOUR COUSIN!

YOU ALMOST DIED BECAUSE OF ME.

WHAT...?

HUH?

25

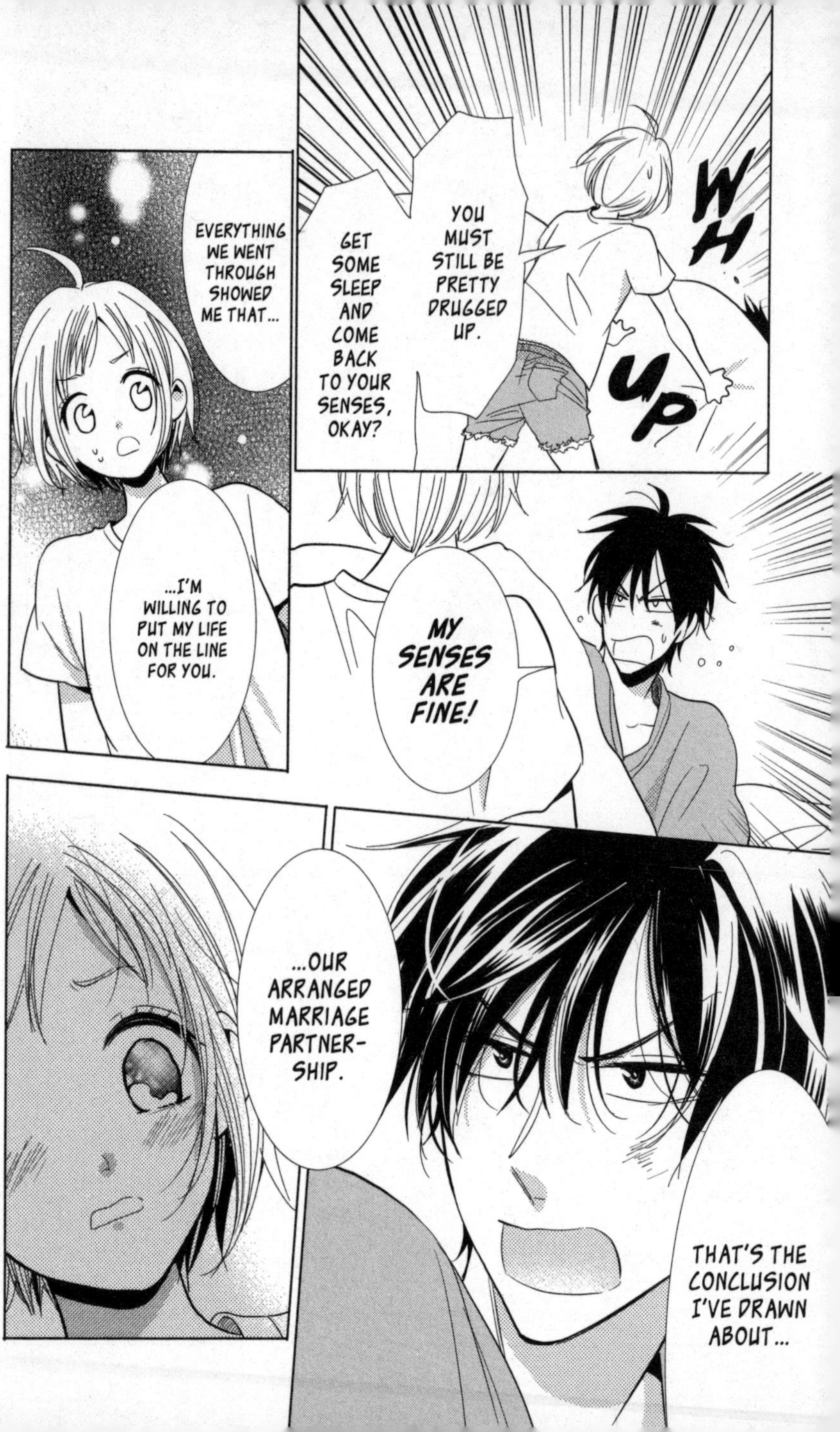
WH UP
YOU MUST STILL BE PRETTY DRUGGED UP.
GET SOME SLEEP AND COME BACK TO YOUR SENSES, OKAY?
MY SENSES ARE FINE!
EVERYTHING WE WENT THROUGH SHOWED ME THAT...
...I'M WILLING TO PUT MY LIFE ON THE LINE FOR YOU.
THAT'S THE CONCLUSION I'VE DRAWN ABOUT...
...OUR ARRANGED MARRIAGE PARTNER-SHIP.

• Bonus Story 1 •

I'm going to give some details about the bonus stories in this volume.

Bonus Story 1 was written at the same time I was writing volume 5, so it was a while ago.

It takes place when Takane lived alone in his high-rise condo, so this was a peek into his private life. The daruma bread you've seen a few times in the main story makes its first appearance here.

• Bonus Story 2 •

A story from when things started settling down after our heroes moved in together. Cockroaches exist even in newly built houses—apparently they sneak in during construction. Incidentally, I've never tried the method Takane uses at the end of the story, so I'm not sure if it works or not.

HE'S SO BLASE!!

...GIVEN EVERYTHING THAT'S HAPPENED, HE'S FEELING AWFULLY EMOTIONAL, AND IT'S GETTING THE BEST OF HIM.

I BET THAT...

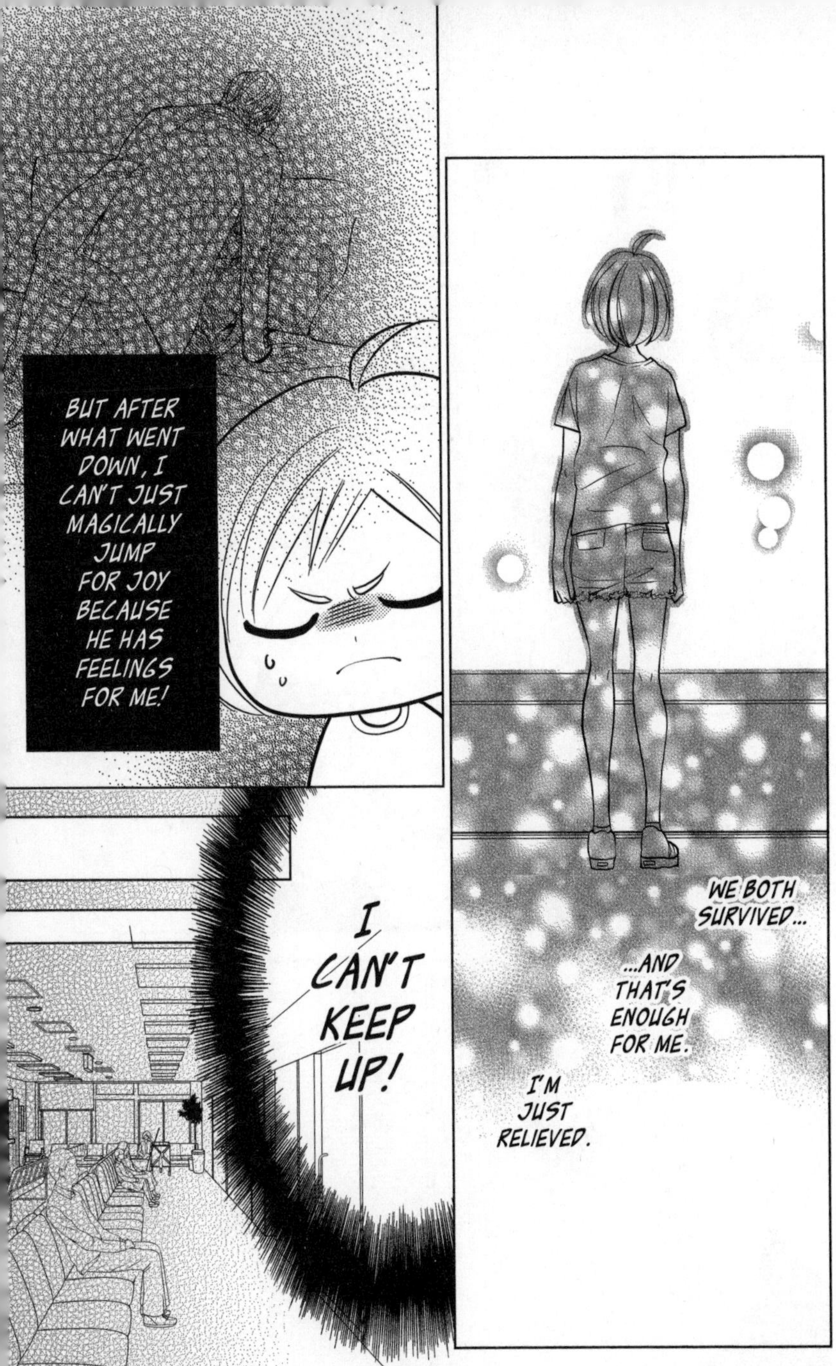
WE BOTH SURVIVED...
...AND THAT'S ENOUGH FOR ME.
I'M JUST RELIEVED.
BUT AFTER WHAT WENT DOWN, I CAN'T JUST MAGICALLY JUMP FOR JOY BECAUSE HE HAS FEELINGS FOR ME!
I CAN'T KEEP UP!

SOB

SOB

I THINK I'LL GO SEE WHAT'S GOING ON IN TAKANE'S ROOM.

UMM...

I NEED TO HAVE SOME WORDS WITH HIM.

I'LL COME TOO.

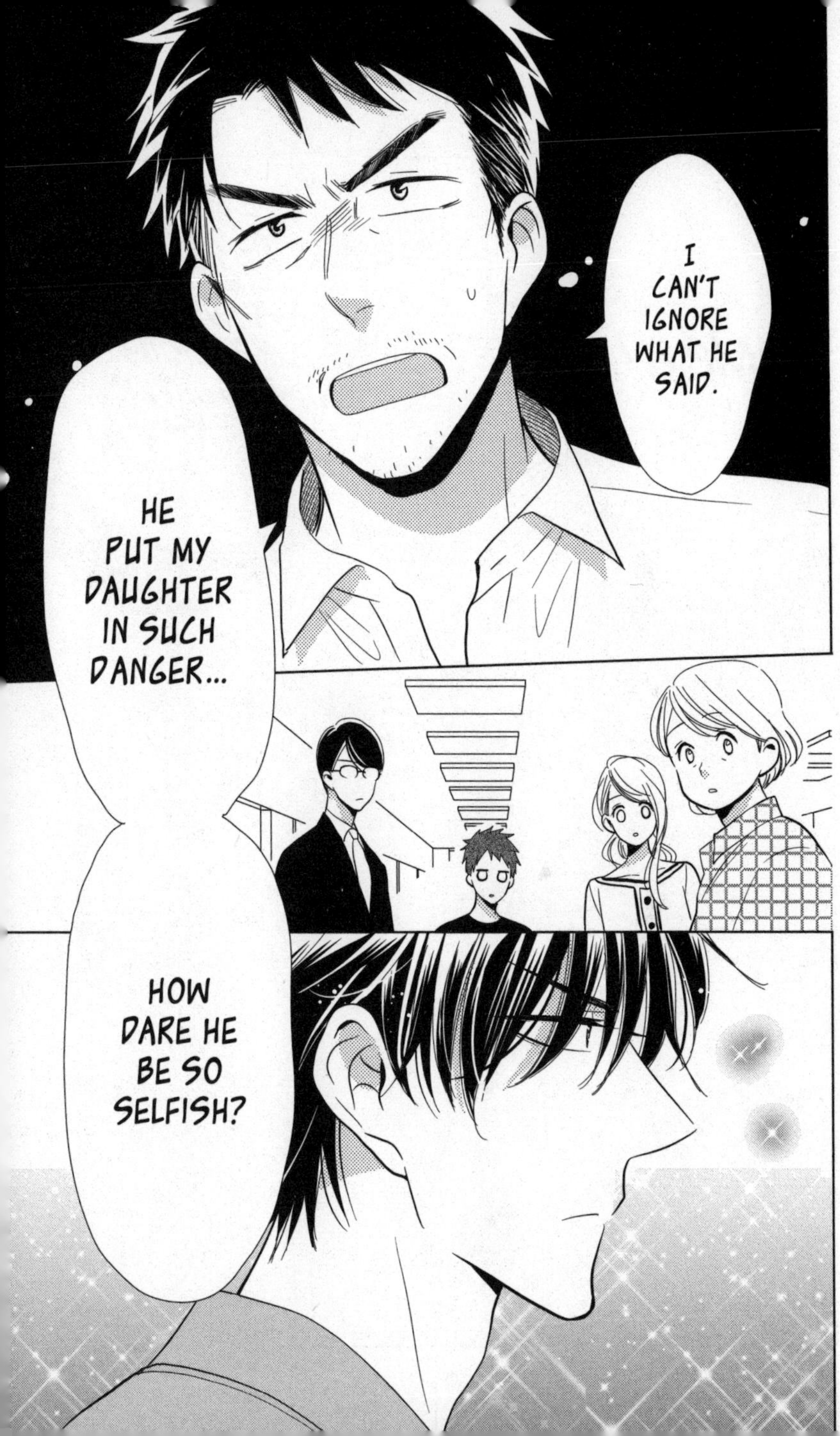
I CAN'T IGNORE WHAT HE SAID.
HE PUT MY DAUGHTER IN SUCH DANGER...
HOW DARE HE BE SO SELFISH?

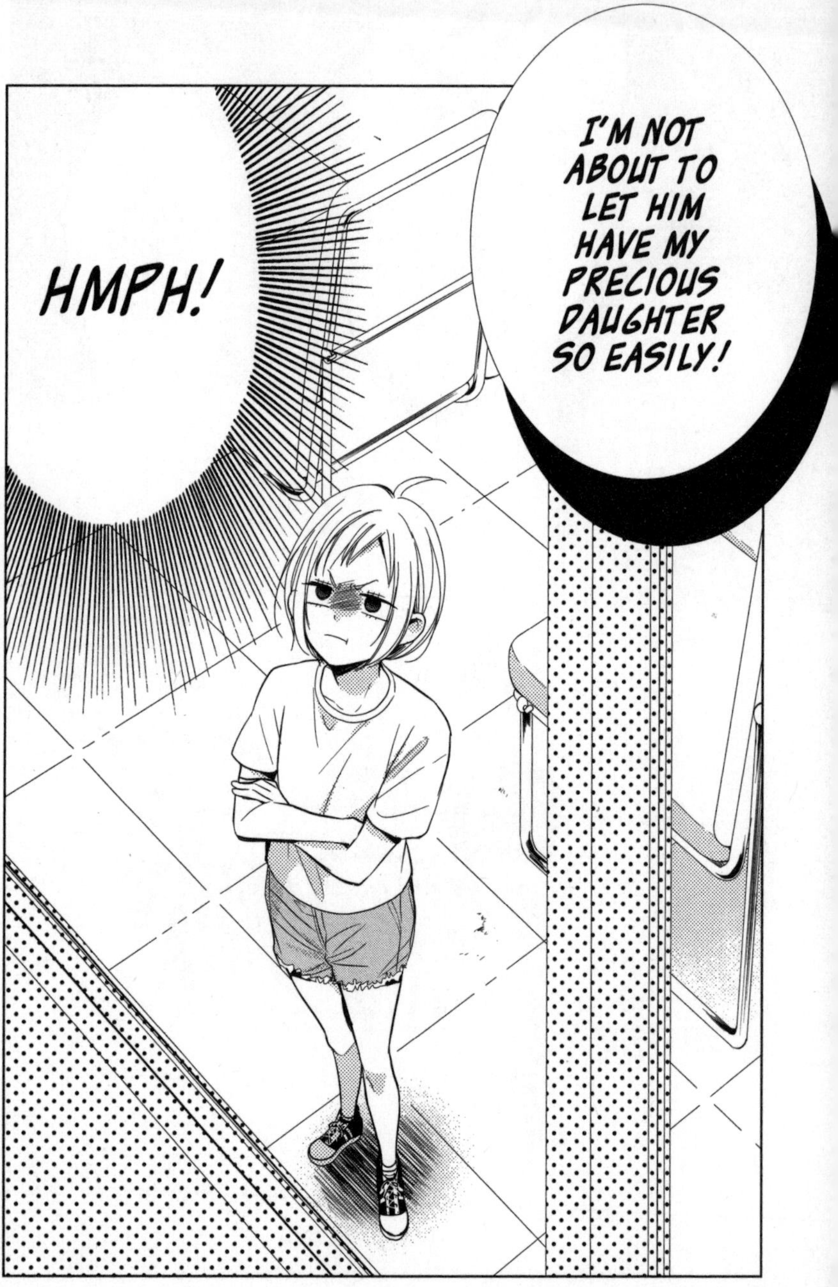
I'M NOT ABOUT TO LET HIM HAVE MY PRECIOUS DAUGHTER SO EASILY!
HMPH!

Chapter 65

Snapping Back to Reality

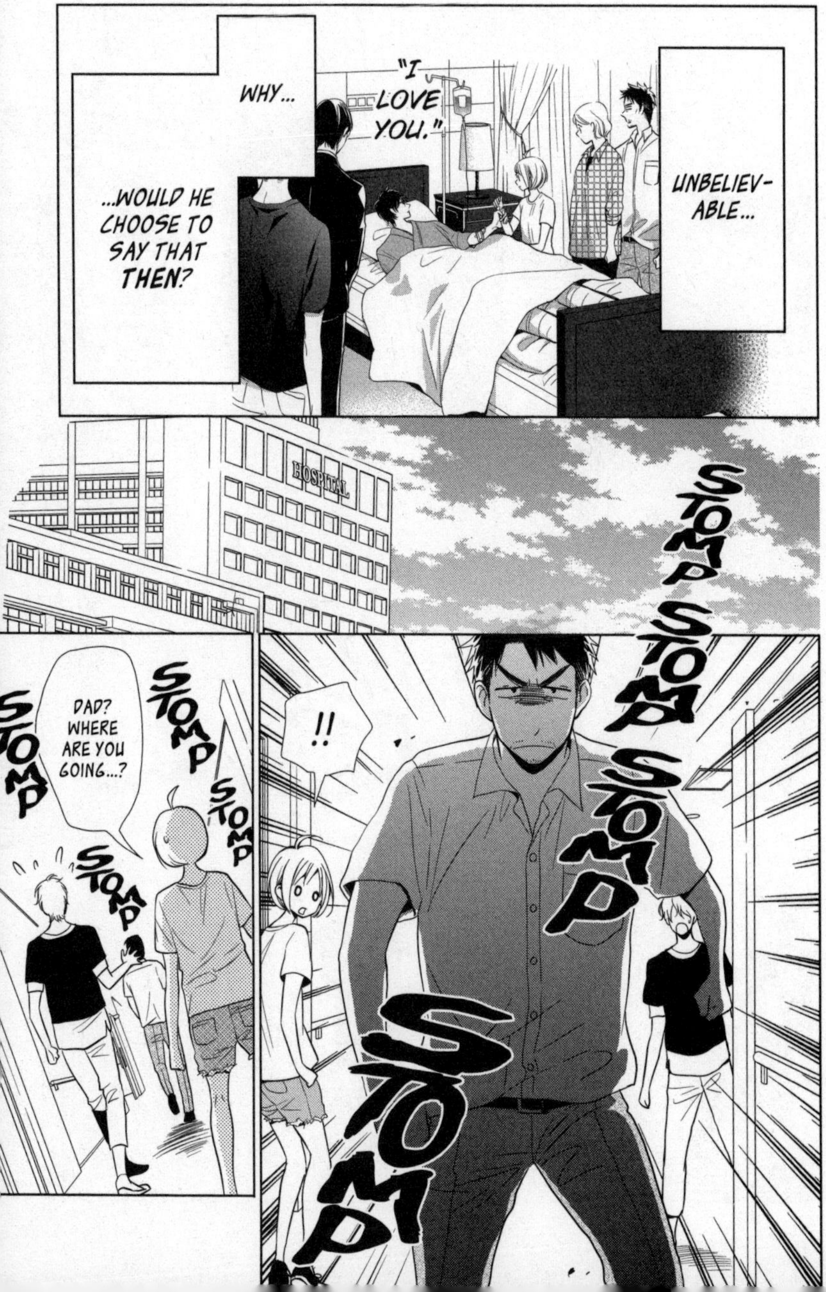

UNBELIEV-ABLE...
"I LOVE YOU."
WHY...
...WOULD HE CHOOSE TO SAY THAT THEN?
HOSPITAL
STOMP STOMP STOMP STOMP
!!
STOMP STOMP STOMP
DAD? WHERE ARE YOU GOING...?
STOMP

ZWAK

...

THAT'S RIGHT...

HEY, HOLD ON—

DID YOU MEAN YOU WANT TO DATE MY DAUGH-TER?

WE NEED TO TALK.

...FATHER.

"FATHER"?!

YOU HAVE NO RIGHT TO CALL ME THAT.

GLARE

WELL, YOU ARE GOING TO BE MY FATHER!

POINT

THAT'S TERRI-FYING!!!

POINTING RIGHT BACK

37

SO... ARE YOU SAYING YOU'RE THINKING OF MARRIAGE DOWN THE ROAD?

?!

...AND CONTINUING THINGS FROM THERE MAKES NO SENSE IF YOU'RE NOT EXPECTING IT TO RUN ITS COURSE.

AGREEING TO AN ARRANGED MARRIAGE MEETING...

I THINK THAT GOES WITHOUT SAYING.

THAT...

THAT'S LIKE BEING *ENGAGED* ALREADY.

DONG

SHOVE

CUT IT OUT.

...YOU HAVE TO REALIZE THAT IF YOU START DATING A HIGH SCHOOL STUDENT, YOUR REPUTATION WILL BE RUINED.

I DON'T KNOW WHAT LED YOU TO THAT DECISION, BUT...

WAIT A MINUTE!!

RINO...

Ahh.

BE QUIET!!

IT'S NOT HER FAULT

...BUT I CAN'T STAND THE THOUGHT OF YOU GOING THROUGH LIFE BRANDED AS A PEDOPHILE.

TAKANE SENPAI...!!

39

RAGH

RAGH

RAGH

RAGH

YOU SHOULD JUST GO OUT WITH ME.

OKAY?!

I HAVEN'T FORGOTTEN THE DAYS WHEN YOU TREATED ME LIKE YOUR GOFER.

TEAM "LET'S SUBDUE TAKANE"

...

I don't want a son like him!

WHY SHOULD I CARE WHAT ANYONE ELSE THINKS OF ME?

I KNOW MY OWN WORTH!

IT'S... NOT MY PLACE TO SAY...

Why would that make him act this way...?

YOU'RE SURE THERE WASN'T ANYTHING ELSE?

I'LL ASK TAKANE FOR MORE INFO LATER.

OKAY.

GASP

HANA.

DID HE REALLY JUST FALL DOWN THE STAIRS?

Calm down, dear.

40

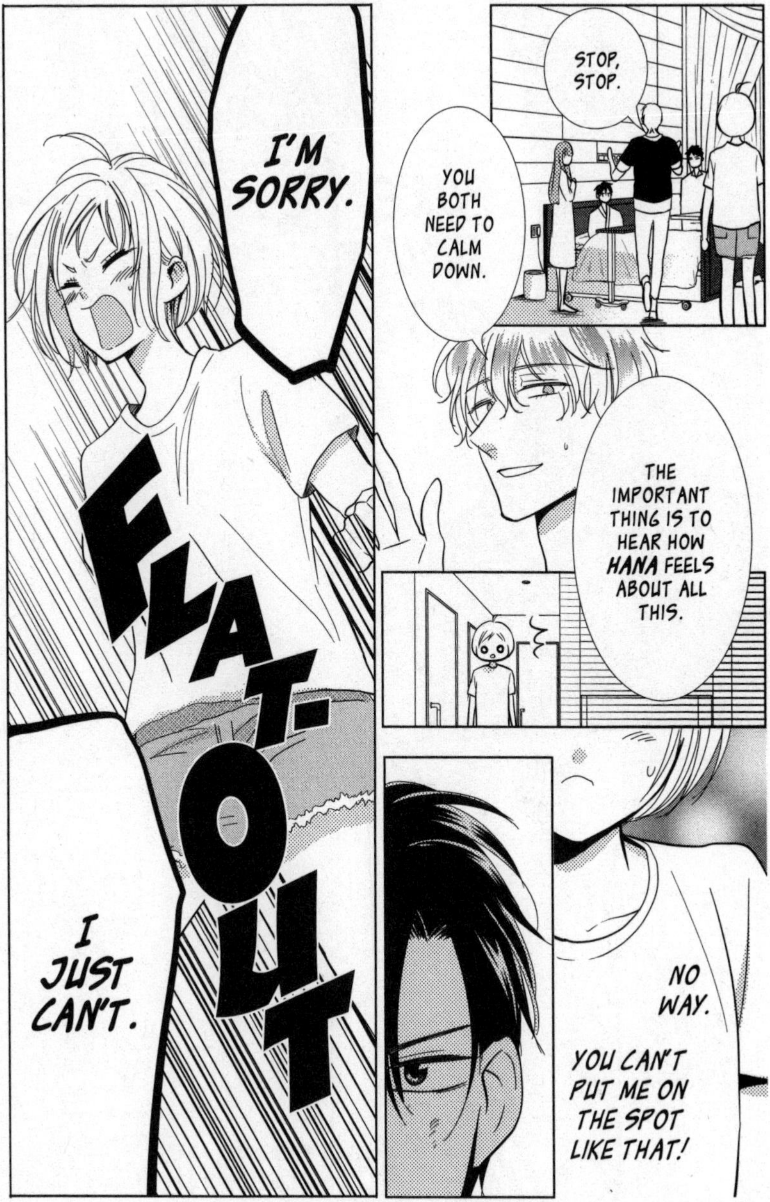
STOP, STOP.
YOU BOTH NEED TO CALM DOWN.
THE IMPORTANT THING IS TO HEAR HOW *HANA* FEELS ABOUT ALL THIS.
NO WAY.
YOU CAN'T PUT ME ON THE SPOT LIKE THAT!
I'M SORRY.
FLAT-OUT
I JUST CAN'T.

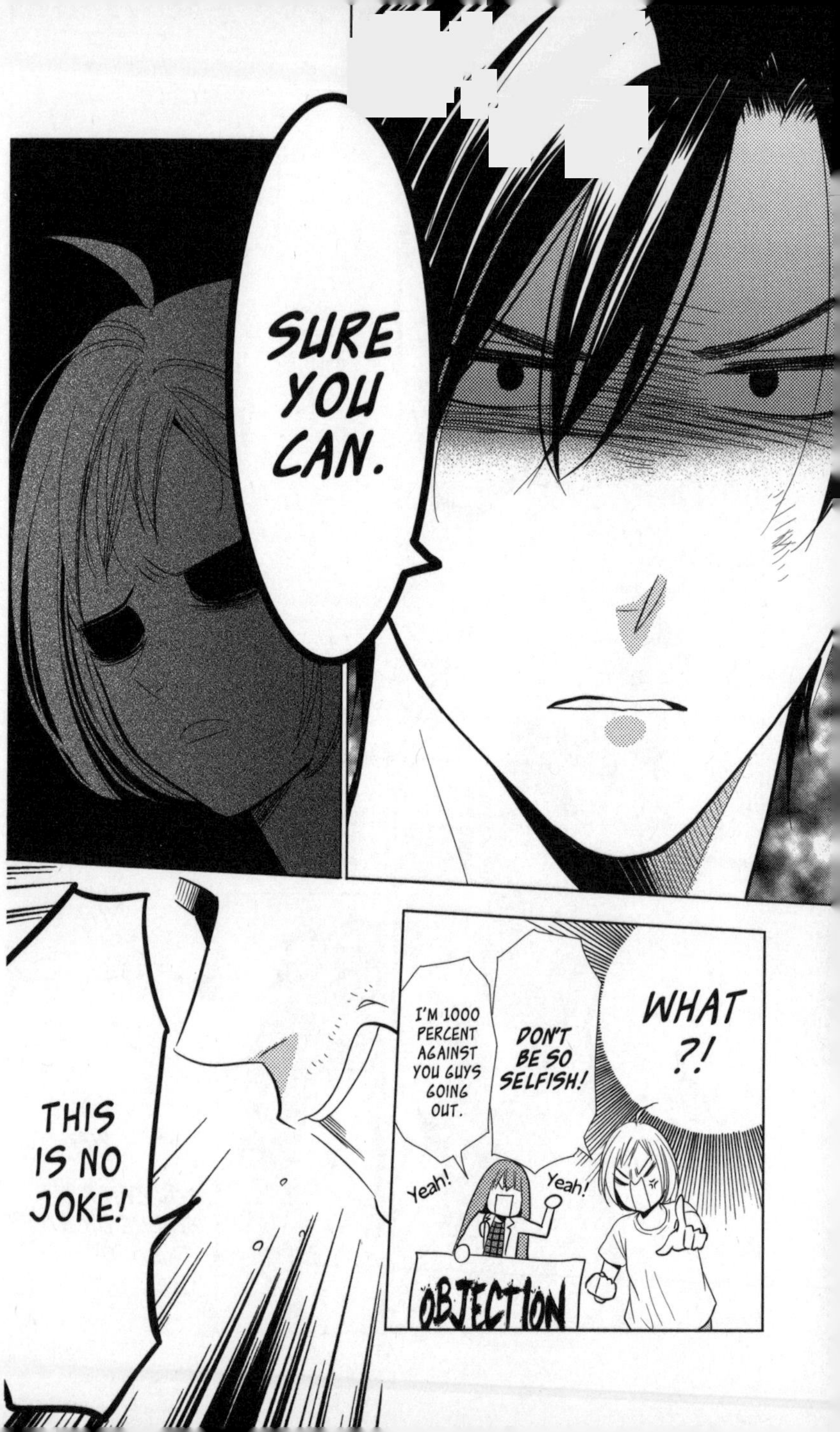
SURE YOU CAN.
WHAT ?!
DON'T BE SO SELFISH!
I'M 1000 PERCENT AGAINST YOU GUYS GOING OUT.
Yeah!
Yeah!
OBJECTION
THIS IS NO JOKE!

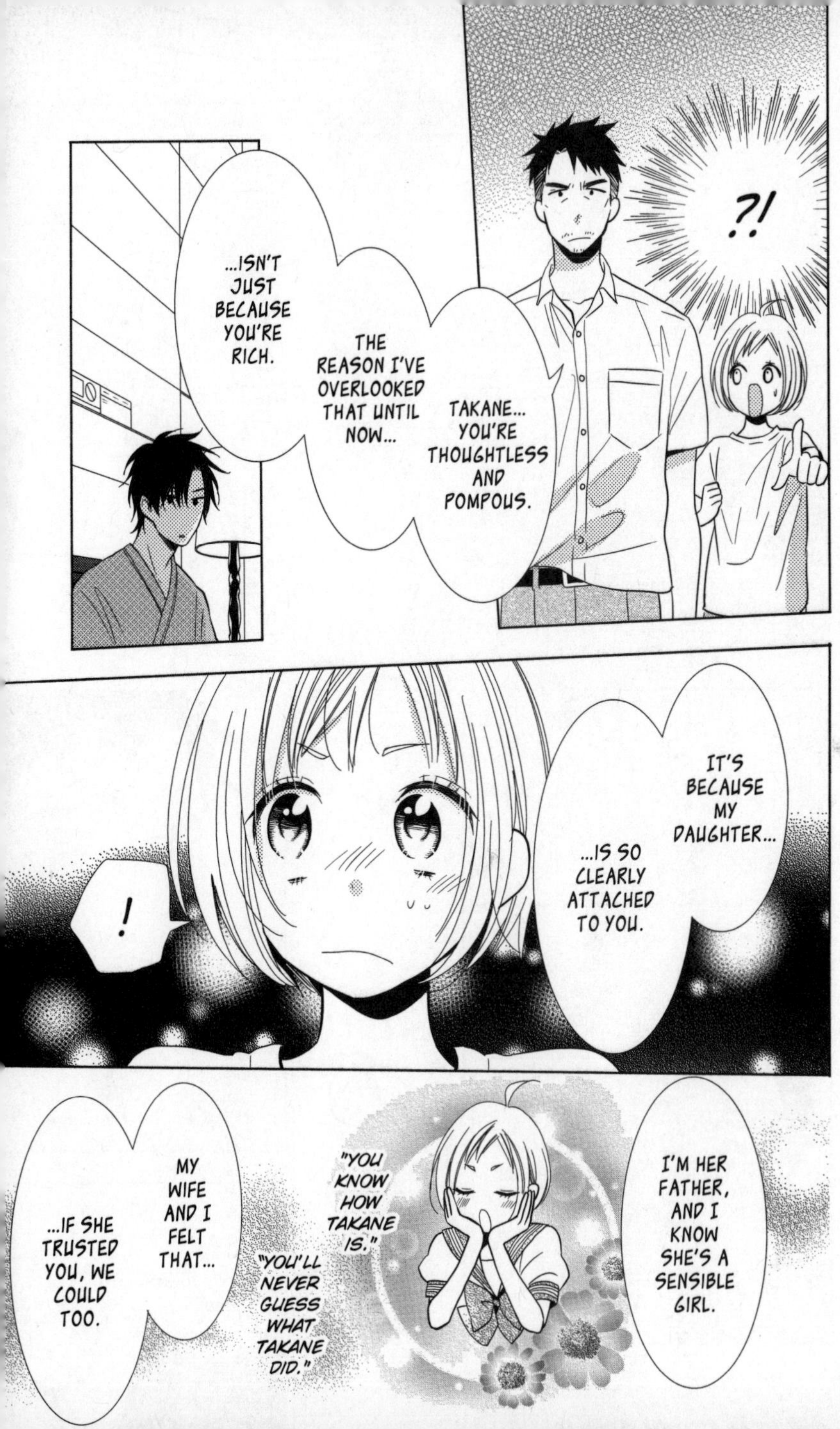
?!
TAKANE... YOU'RE THOUGHTLESS AND POMPOUS.
THE REASON I'VE OVERLOOKED THAT UNTIL NOW...
...ISN'T JUST BECAUSE YOU'RE RICH.
IT'S BECAUSE MY DAUGHTER...
...IS SO CLEARLY ATTACHED TO YOU.
!
I'M HER FATHER, AND I KNOW SHE'S A SENSIBLE GIRL.
"YOU KNOW HOW TAKANE IS."
"YOU'LL NEVER GUESS WHAT TAKANE DID."
MY WIFE AND I FELT THAT...
...IF SHE TRUSTED YOU, WE COULD TOO.

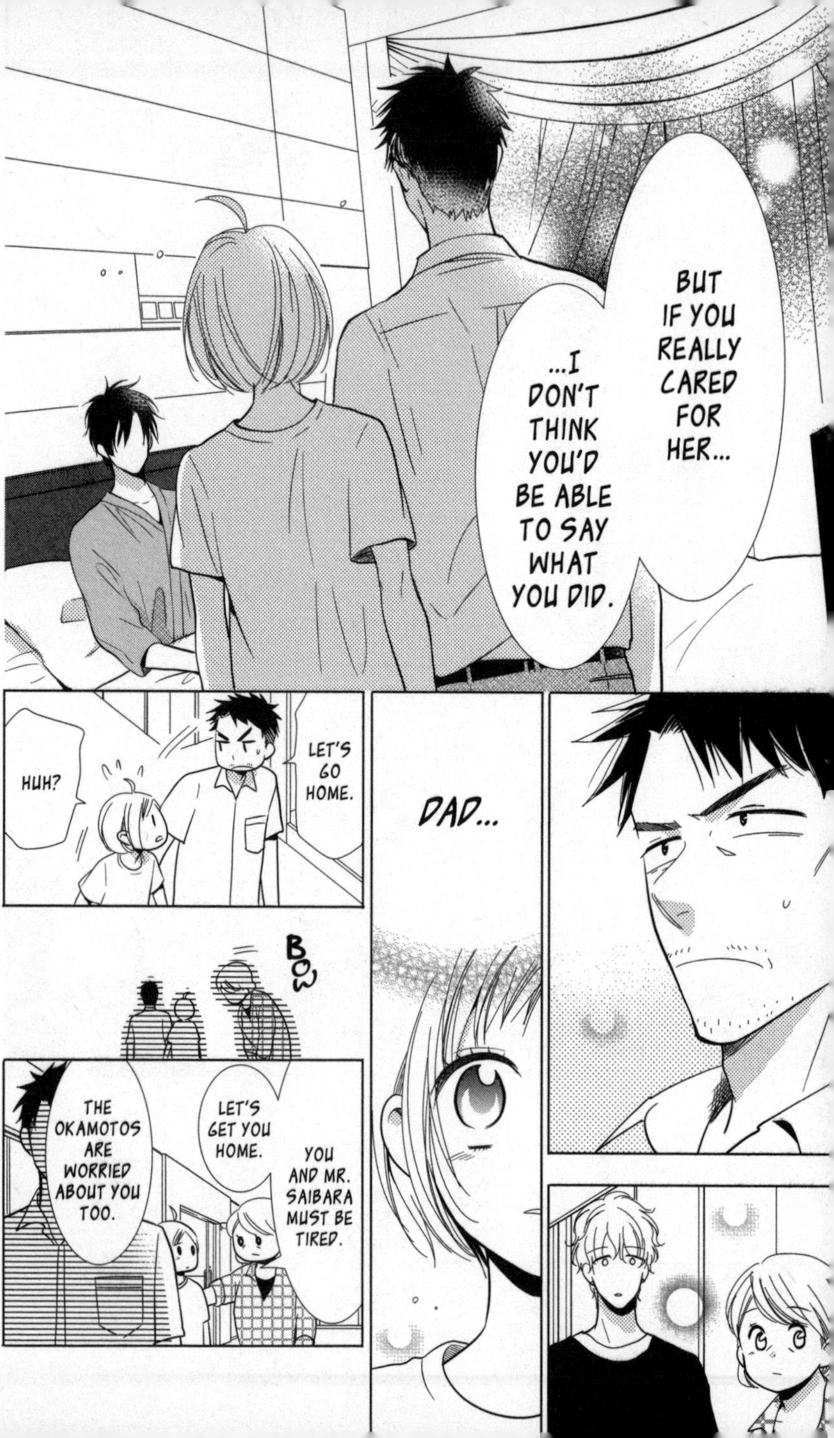
BUT IF YOU REALLY CARED FOR HER...
...I DON'T THINK YOU'D BE ABLE TO SAY WHAT YOU DID.
DAD...
LET'S GO HOME.
HUH?
BOW
LET'S GET YOU HOME.
YOU AND MR. SAIBARA MUST BE TIRED.
THE OKAMOTOS ARE WORRIED ABOUT YOU TOO.

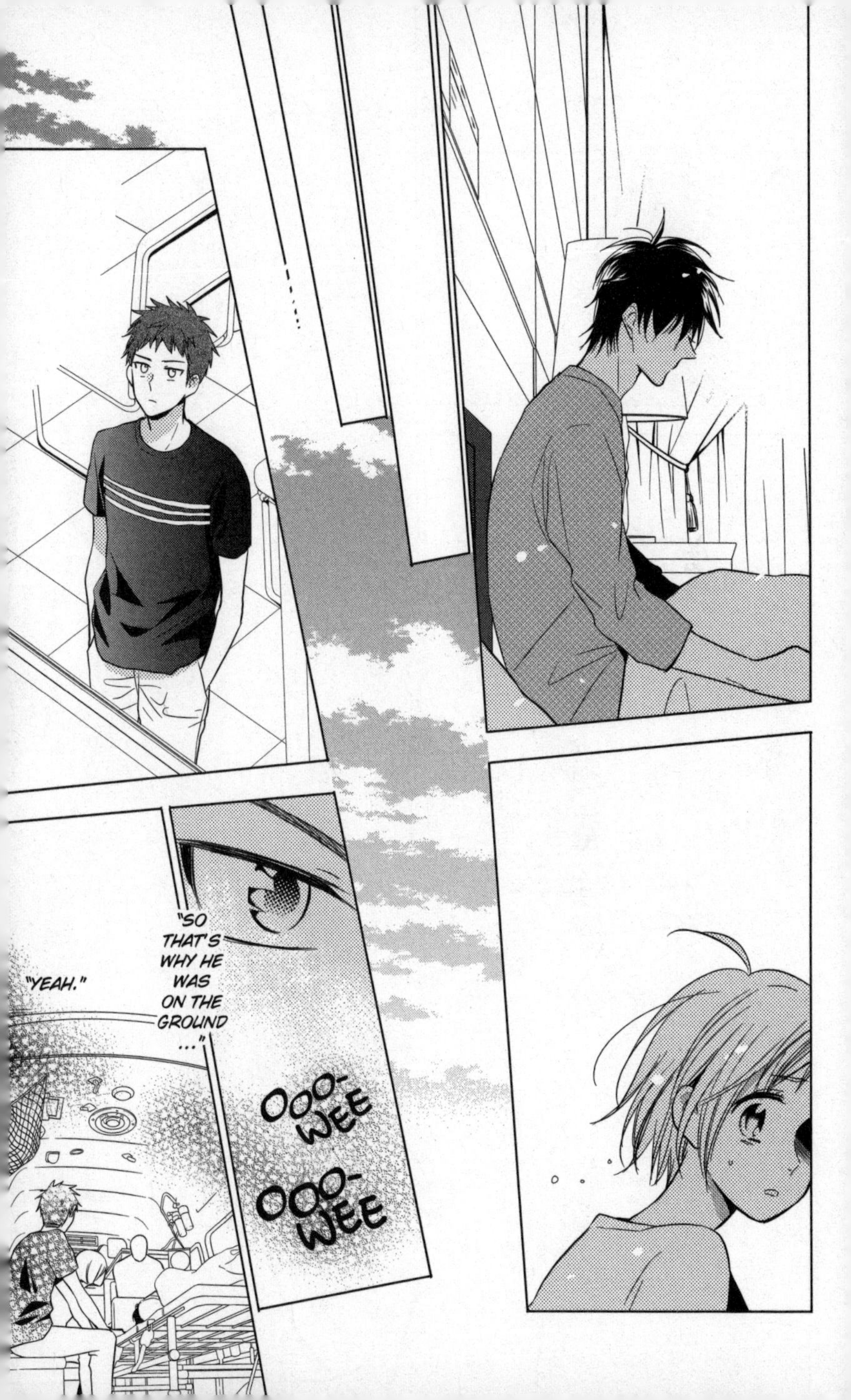
"SO THAT'S WHY HE WAS ON THE GROUND..."
OOO-WEE OOO-WEE
"YEAH."

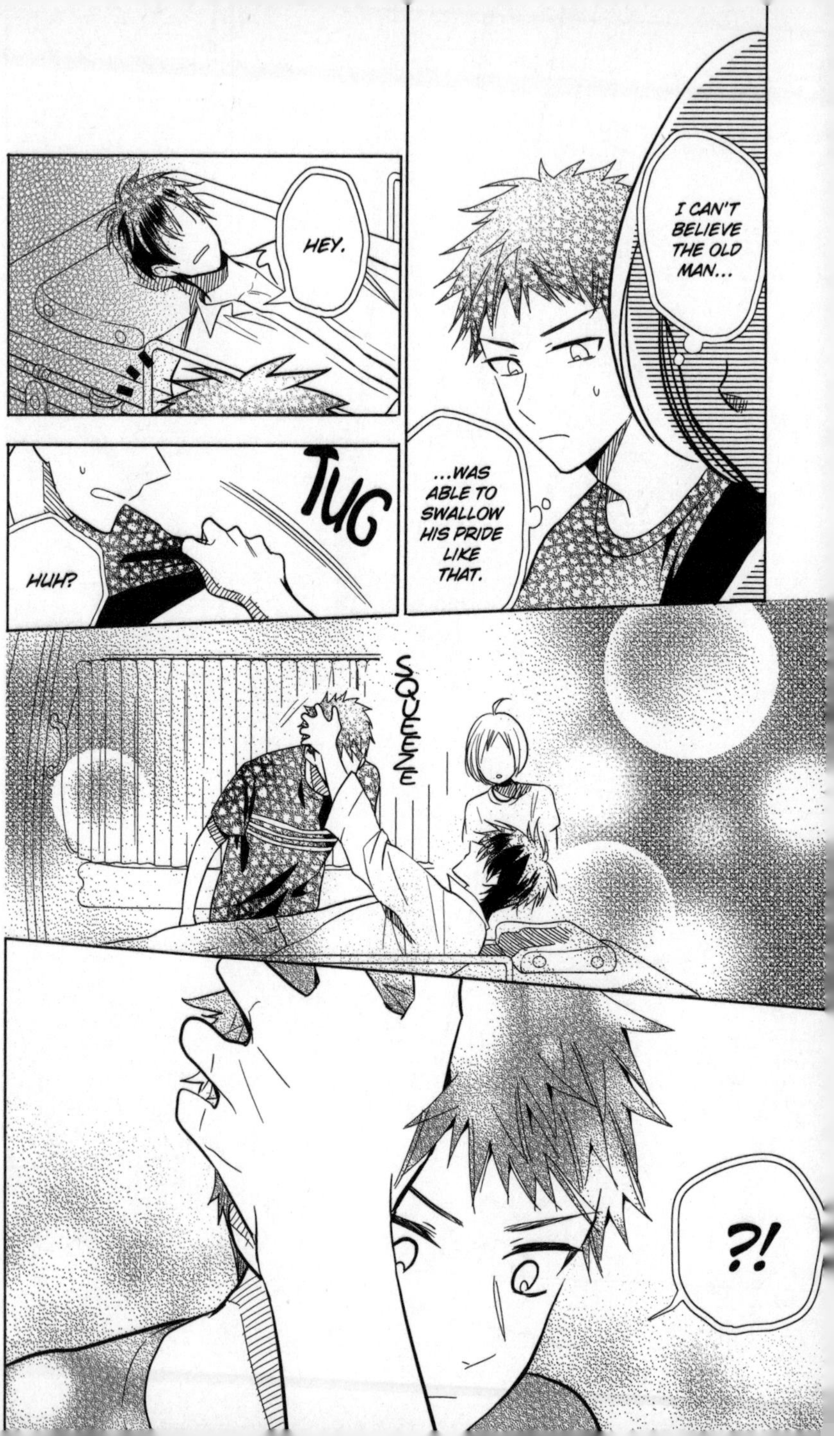
I CAN'T BELIEVE THE OLD MAN...
...WAS ABLE TO SWALLOW HIS PRIDE LIKE THAT.
HEY.
TUG
HUH?
SQUEEEZE
?!

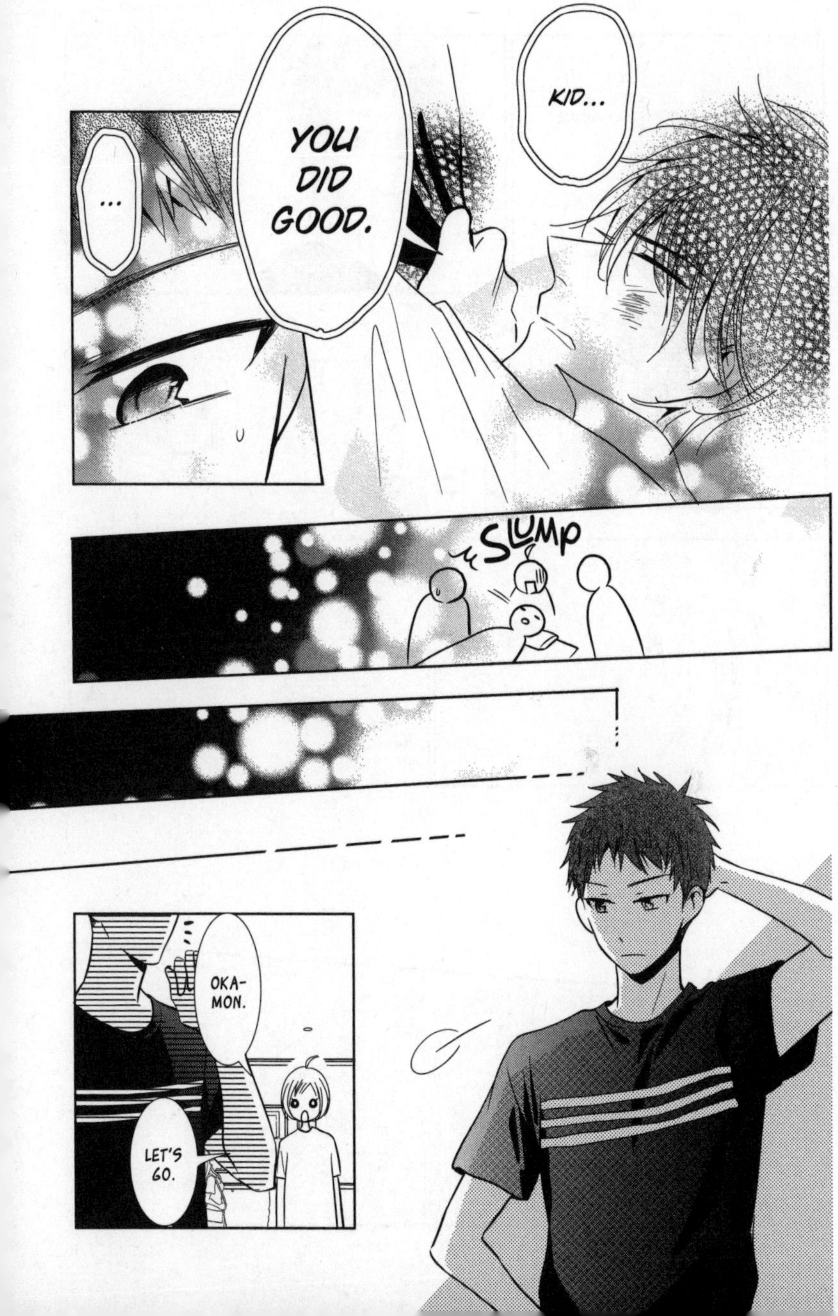
KID...
YOU DID GOOD.
...
SLUMP
OKA-MON.
LET'S GO.

"I LOVE YOU."

I TURNED HIM DOWN.

I CAN'T EVEN THINK ABOUT THAT RIGHT NOW.

OH...

?

YEAH.

...

I SEE.

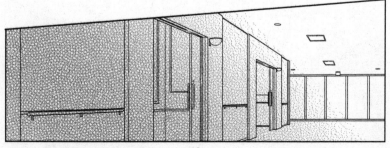

THE OFFICE EQUIPMENT AND DOCUMENTS HAVE ALL ARRIVED AND ARE SET UP NOW.

DIRECTOR.

YOU'RE NOT EVEN MY DOCTOR. STOP HANGING AROUND.

Get back to work.

NOOOO!!

Workers

SOB

SIGH

NOT A CHANCE!

YOU CAN'T MAKE AN INJURED PATIENT WORK!

QUIET. I REQUESTED THEM. REMOVE THIS ANNOYING RESIDENT FROM THE ROOM.

YES, SIR.

HEY!!

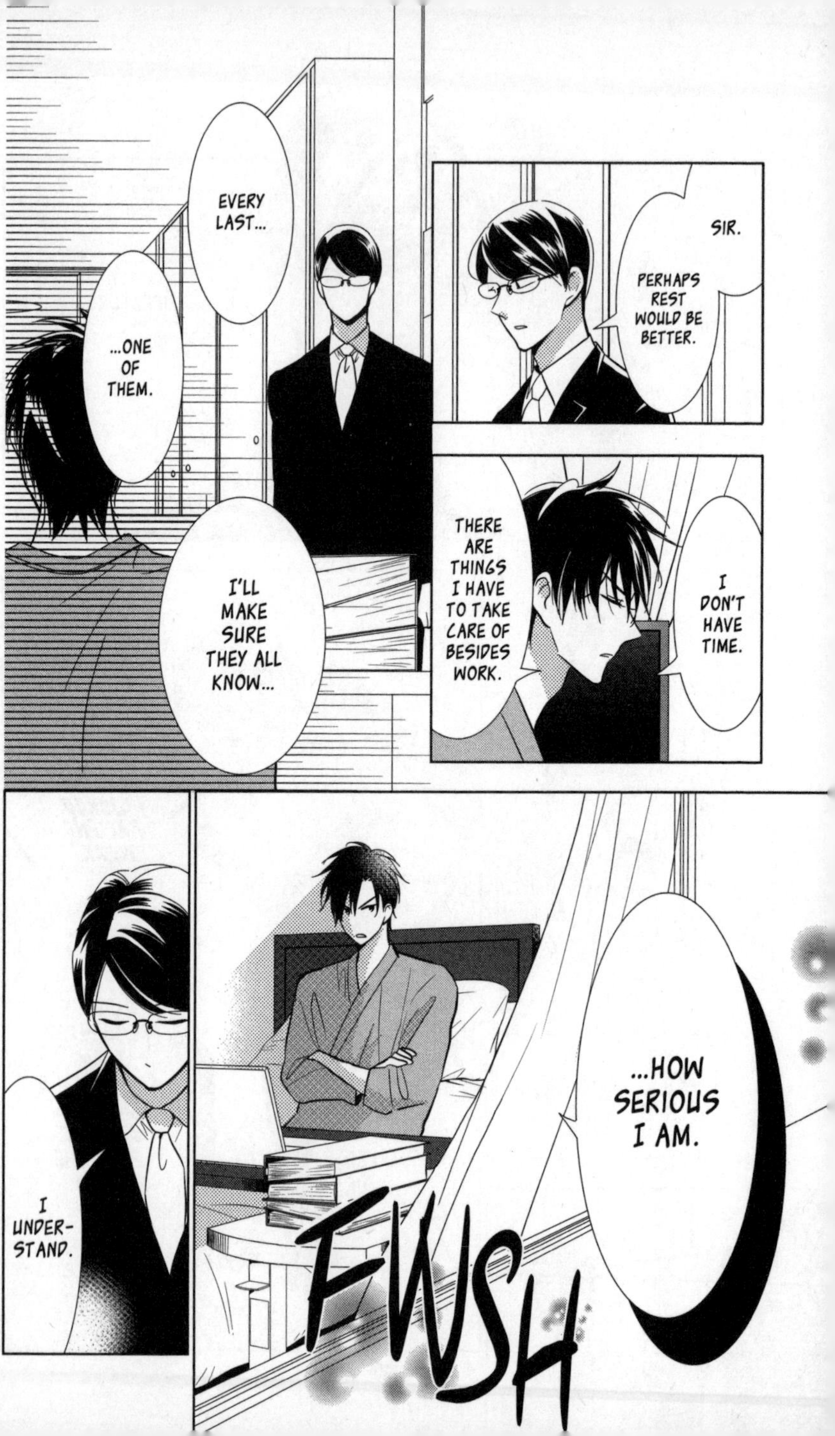
SIR.
PERHAPS REST WOULD BE BETTER.
I DON'T HAVE TIME.
THERE ARE THINGS I HAVE TO TAKE CARE OF BESIDES WORK.
EVERY LAST...
...ONE OF THEM.
I'LL MAKE SURE THEY ALL KNOW...
...HOW SERIOUS I AM.
FWSH
I UNDER-STAND.

• Bonus
Story 3 •

The story of Hana's summer vacation takes place between Takane turning her down and Yakumo kidnapping her.

Hiromi and Hana are five years apart, so technically, their age gap is more "okay" than the one with Takane. (*Ha ha.*)

But at the same time, a five-year gap in your teens seems to be a world of a difference. Isn't that weird?

I've come to realize I really enjoy drawing kids. But for some reason, every single kid is a boy.

• Special
Thanks To... •

Head editor I

Head editor H

Atsu

Emi

S from Naht Co., Ltd.

The person who designed this cover.

Everyone involved in sales and marketing.

And every single person involved with *Takane & Hana*!

Thank you always for your support.

I'VE MADE A LOT OF TROUBLE FOR YOU.

KIRIGASAKI.

I'LL HEAD BACK TO THE OFFICE NOW. IF YOU NEED ANYTHING, YOU CAN REACH ME THERE.

I OWE YOU FOR DECEIVING YOU.

NOT AT ALL.

...

...A SECRET.

SERIOUSLY, THOUGH, HOW DID YOU MANAGE TO ELUDE THEM?

THAT'S...

THAT WAS A REAL SHOCK, DAD.

52

BUT DAD, YOU'RE THE ONE WHO GOT ME INTO ALL THIS TO BEGIN WITH.

WE WERE ALL SO PANICKED WHEN YOU DISAPPEARED, HANA.

IT'S WHAT DADS DO!

W-WELL, OF COURSE I DID!

I NEVER PICTURED YOU SAYING SOMETHING LIKE THAT.

YEAH, WORRIED SICK.

WELL, UH... ER...

PLUS, WE'D NEVER HAVE TO WORRY ABOUT GOING HUNGRY, RIGHT?

A HIGH-CLASS GUY WHO CAN HAVE ANY GIRL HE WANTS PICKS MY DAUGHTER.

...IT'S SOMETHING TO BE PROUD OF!

FROM A PARENT'S PERSPECTIVE...

...

NOW, DEAR.

...

AND WE'D PROBABLY GET CUTE GRANDKIDS SINCE HE'S GOOD-LOOKING...

...SPEAKS UP IF HIS KID'S LIFE IS IN DANGER.

BUT...

...EVEN A FOOLISH DAD LIKE ME...

...

...

...

...YOUR OLD MAN'S A FOOL.

I'M SURE YOU'RE PERFECTLY AWARE THAT...

THAT'S ALL.

I'M REALLY GLAD YOU'RE OKAY.

BUT...

...WHAT ARE WE GONNA DO IF HE SAYS WE HAVE TO MOVE OUT?

PFFT

...WHAT'S IMPORTANT IS THAT YOU'RE RESPONSIBLE WHEN IT MATTERS.

FOOL OR NOT...

I DIDN'T THINK ABOUT THAT!

OH NO, WHAT'LL WE DO?

W-w-what'll we do, honey?

Calm down.

THE THING IS...

55

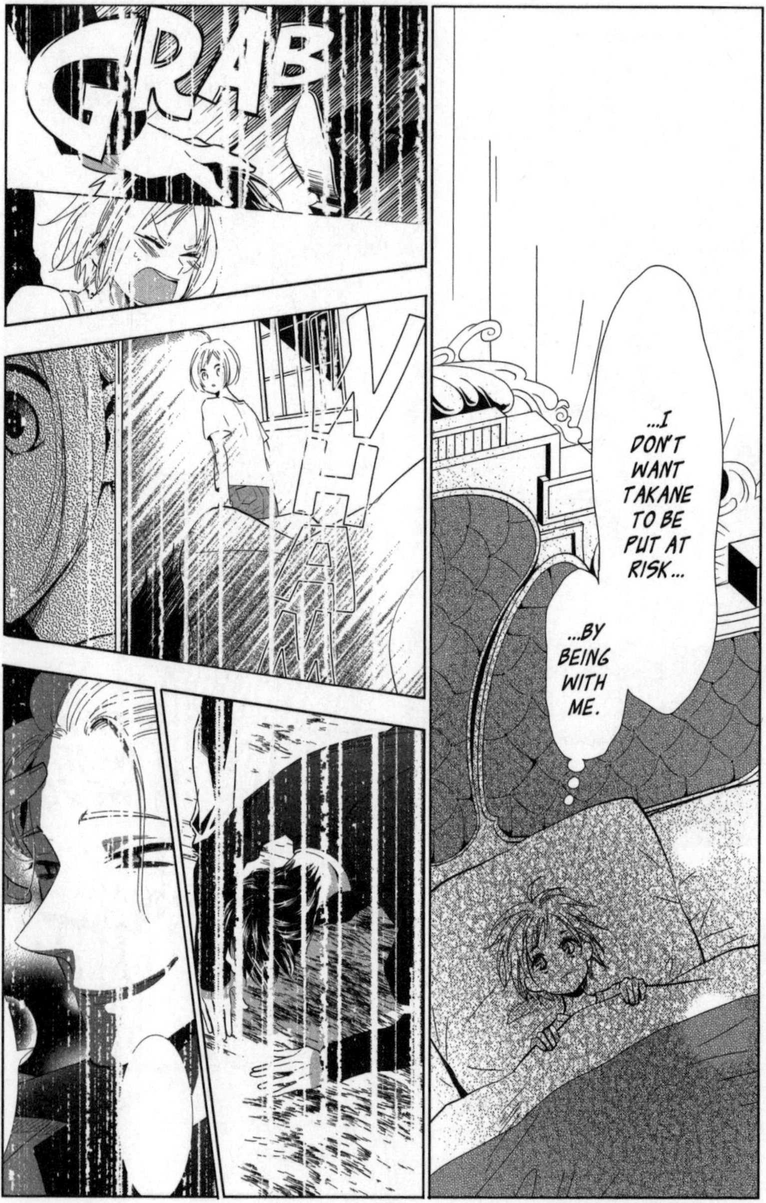
...I DON'T WANT TAKANE TO BE PUT AT RISK...
...BY BEING WITH ME.
GRAB
WHAMM

BLUSH

I'M ECSTATIC THAT HE PROTECTED ME, BUT...

BUT THEN WHEN HE STARTED TO PUT **HIS** FEELINGS FIRST, THAT ALSO MADE ME UNEASY.

...WHEN HE...

...PUT MY FEELINGS FIRST, IT MADE ME FEEL UNEASY.

MAYBE I'M JUST SELFISH TOO...

CHIRP

CHIRP

I'LL TAKE YOU TO SCHOOL LATER, THEN.

I REALLY WANT A GOOD RUN.

YOU'RE STILL GOING? WHY NOT TAKE A BREAK?

CHAK

I HAVE PRACTICE.

MORN-ING. YOU'RE UP EARLY.

DAZE

3-2 NONOMURA

WHAT HAPPENED REALLY WAS A PRETTY BIG DEAL.

SHE'S WORRIED ABOUT ME.

WELL, I GUESS I CAN'T BLAME HER.

I HOPE TAKANE'S ABLE TO CALM DOWN A BIT TOO.

SPLASH SPLASH SPLASH

NOW THAT I'VE HAD TIME TO THINK...

...I CAN SEE HOW MANY PEOPLE WERE AFFECTED.

?!

AAH!

CHAK

MOM ?!

WHAT'S WRONG?

-2 MURA

59

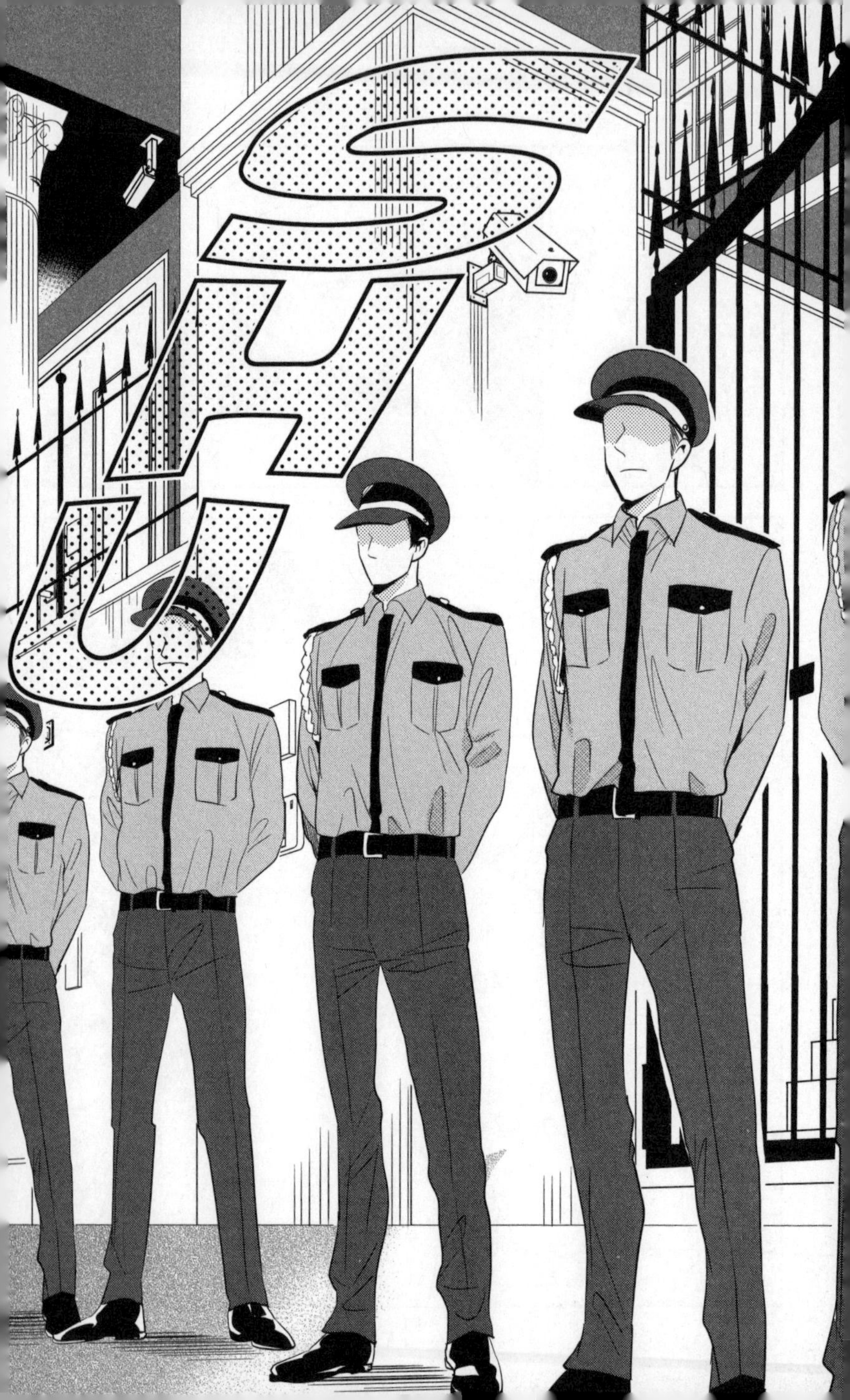
SHU

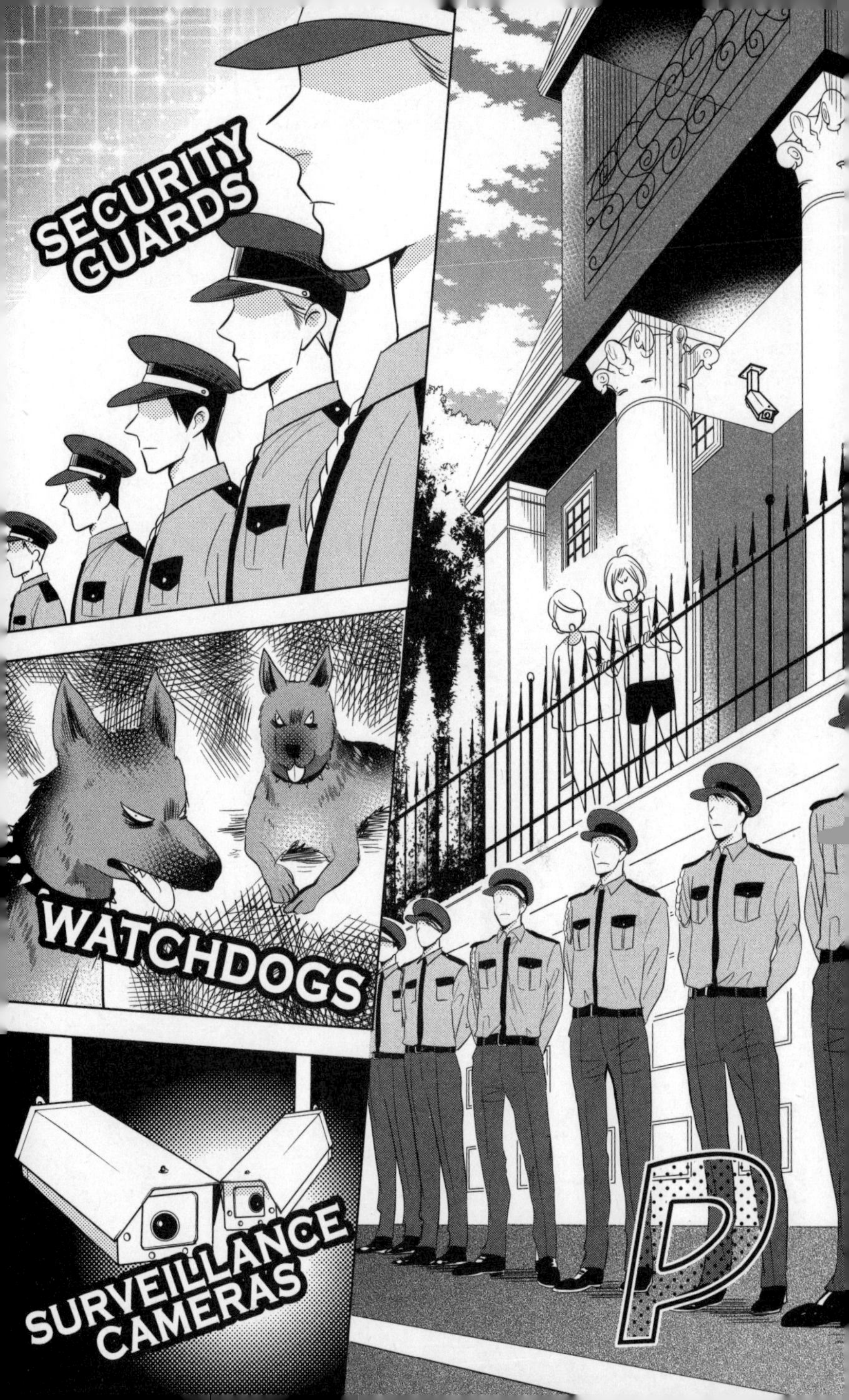
SECURITY GUARDS
WATCHDOGS
SURVEILLANCE CAMERAS
P

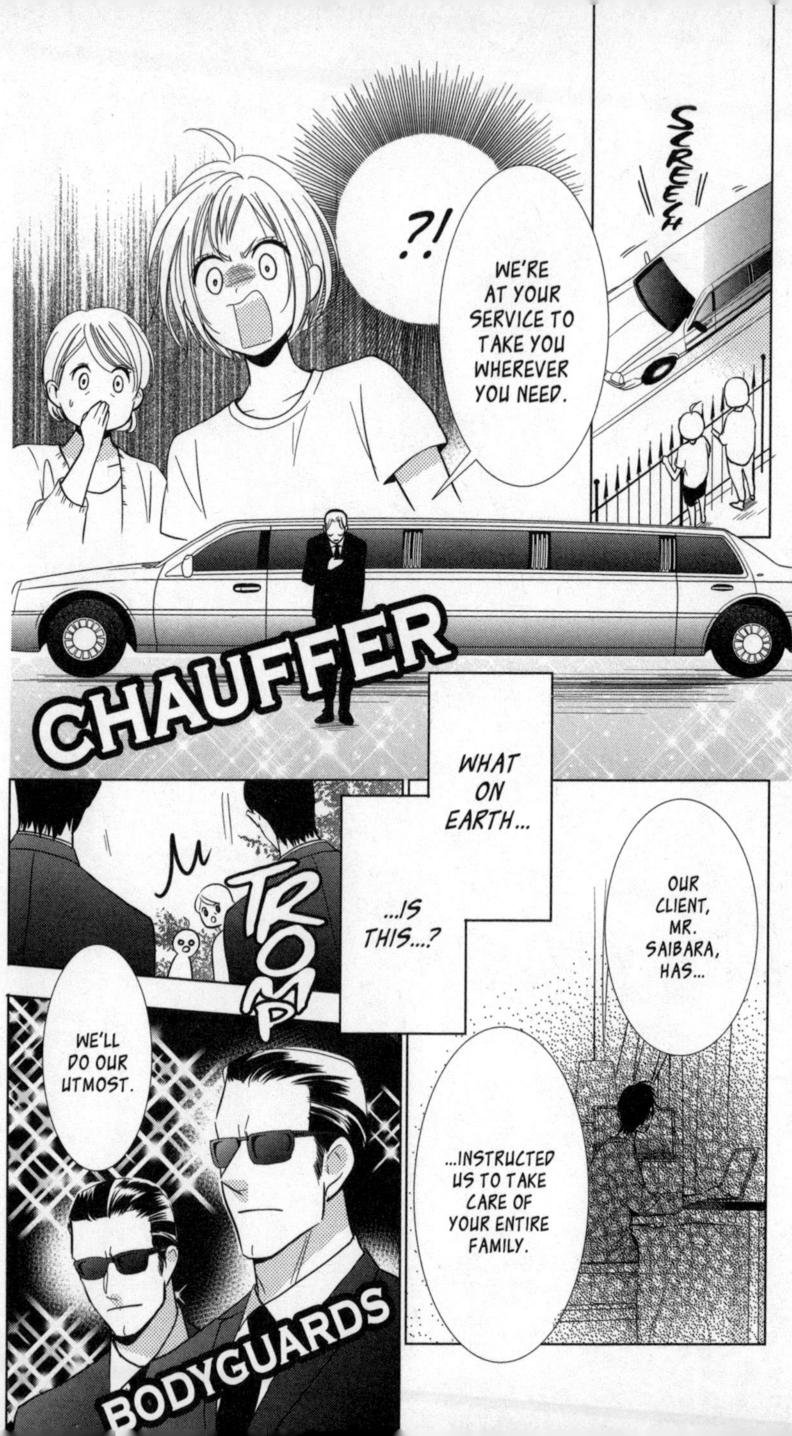
SCREECH
?!
WE'RE AT YOUR SERVICE TO TAKE YOU WHEREVER YOU NEED.
CHAUFFER
WHAT ON EARTH...
...IS THIS...?
OUR CLIENT, MR. SAIBARA, HAS...
...INSTRUCTED US TO TAKE CARE OF YOUR ENTIRE FAMILY.
TROMP
WE'LL DO OUR UTMOST.
BODYGUARDS

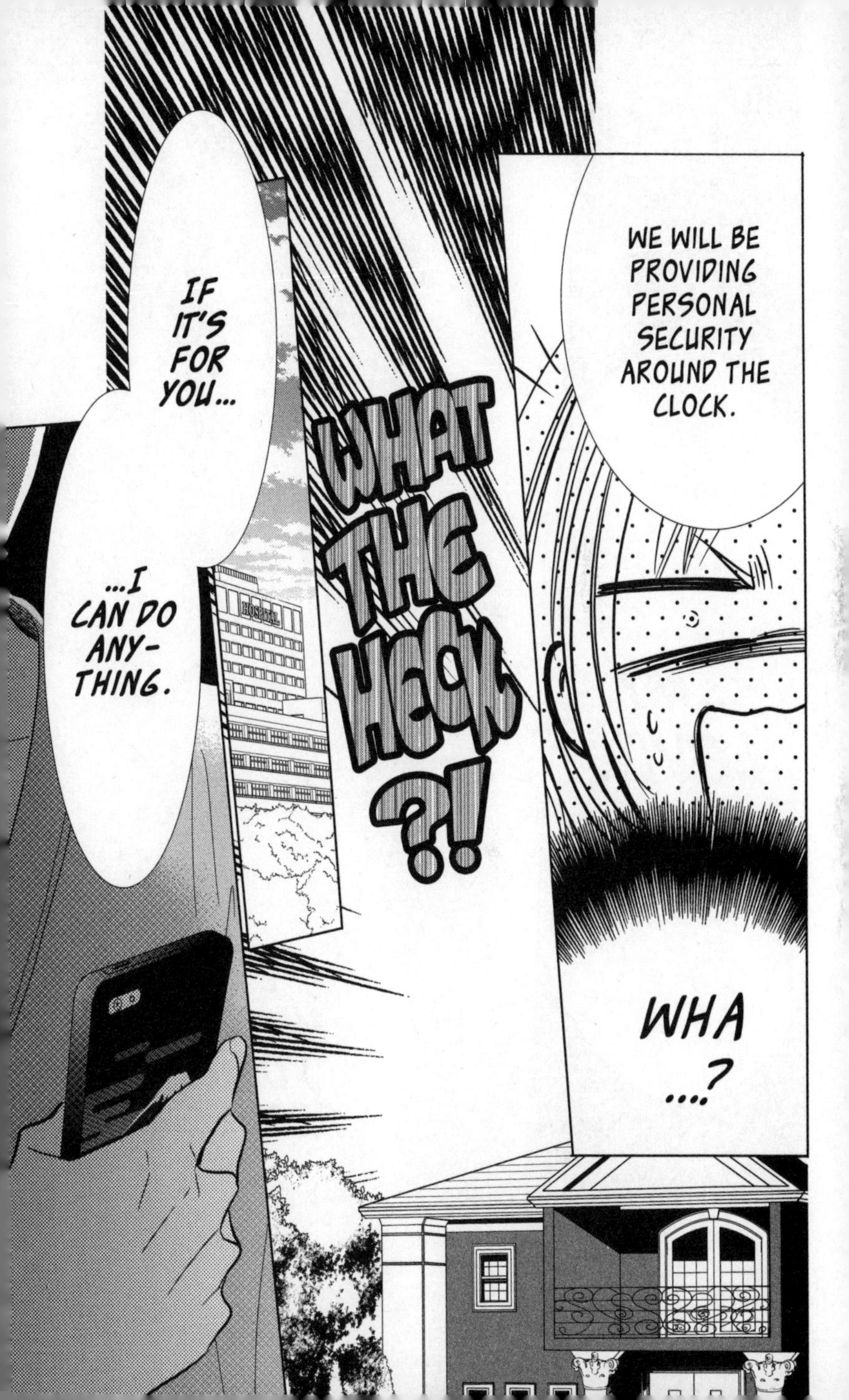
WE WILL BE PROVIDING PERSONAL SECURITY AROUND THE CLOCK.
WHA ...?
WHAT THE HECK?!
HOSPITAL
IF IT'S FOR YOU...
...I CAN DO ANY-THING.

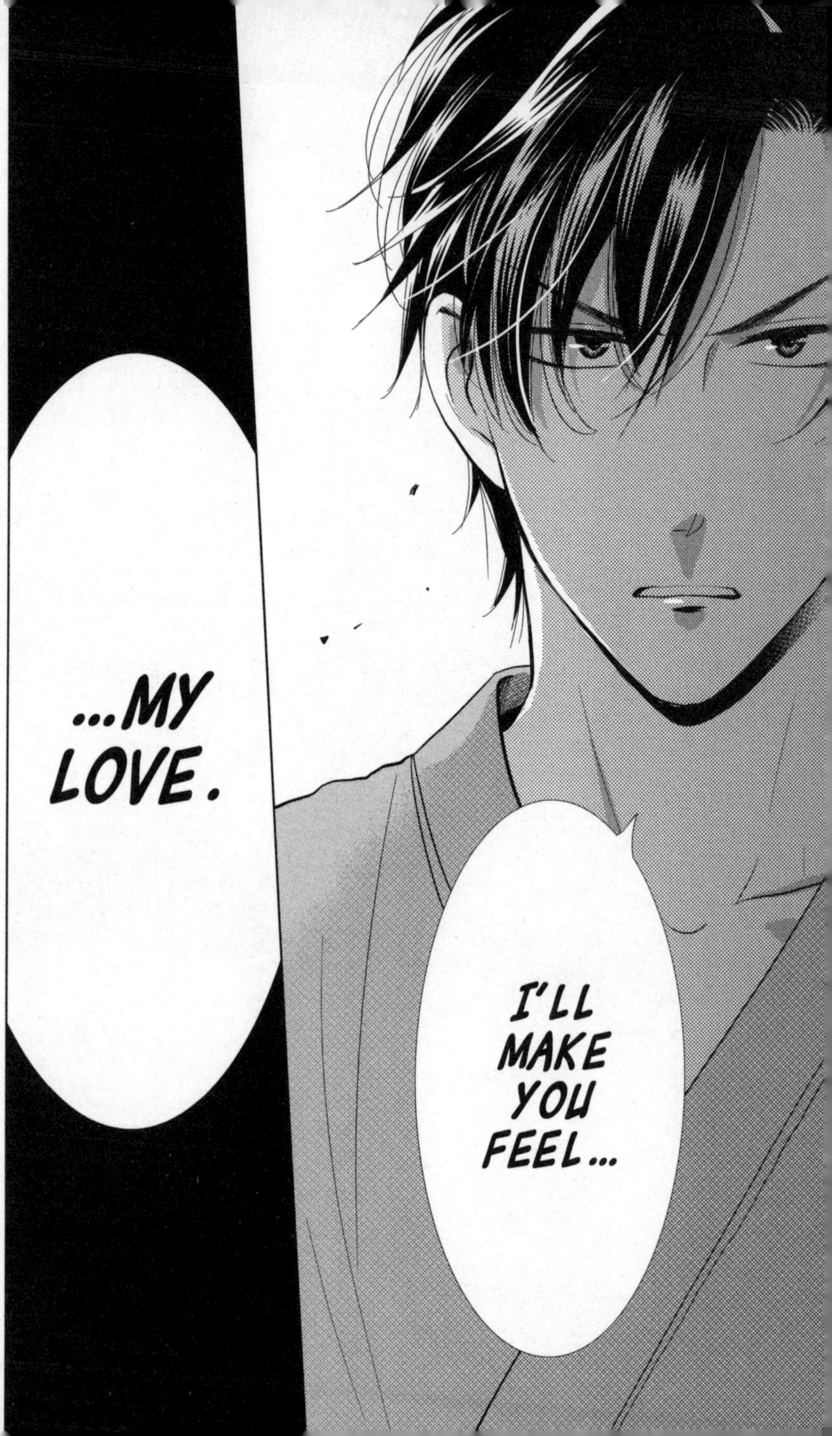
I'LL MAKE YOU FEEL...
...MY LOVE.

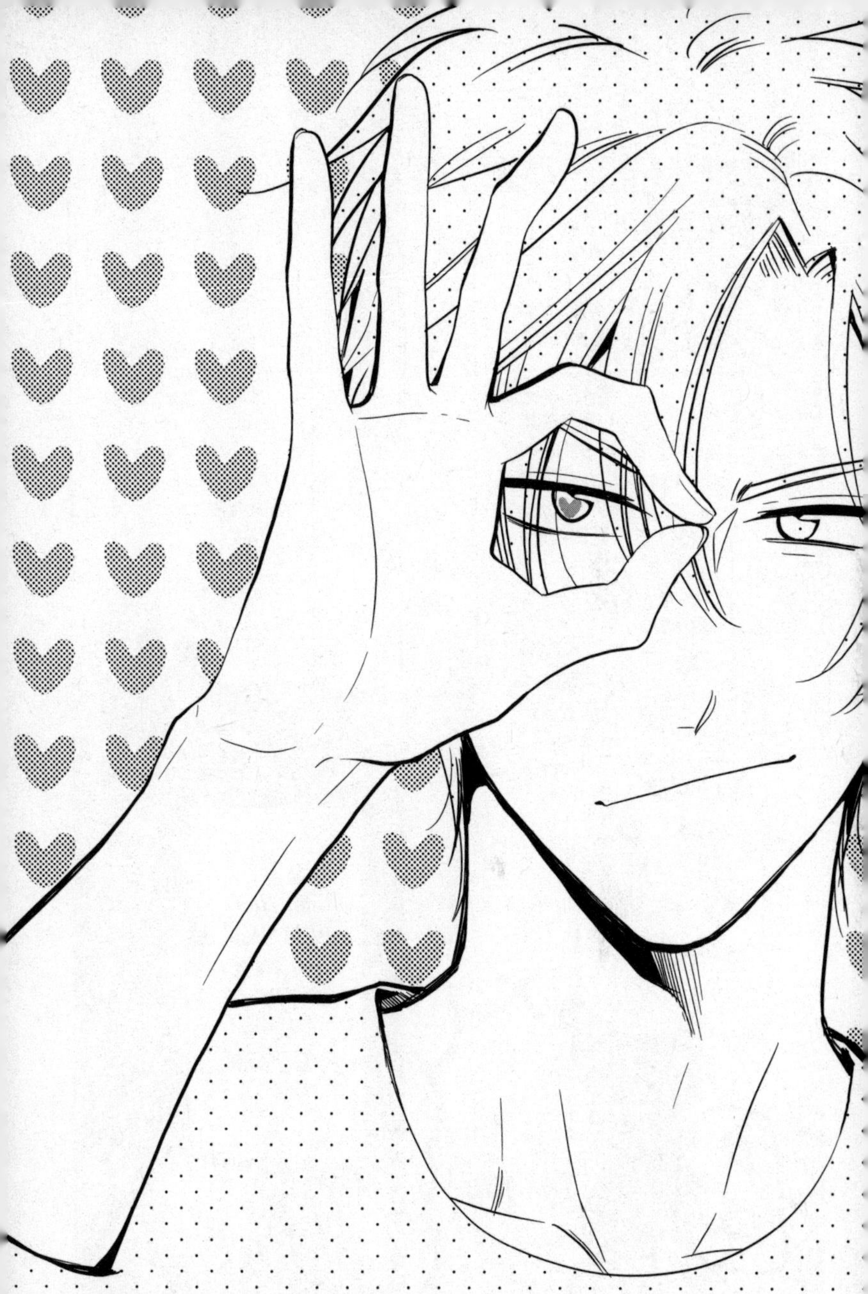

Chapter 66

VROOM

HAVING A BRUSH WITH DEATH HAS FLIPPED SOME WEIRD SWITCH IN TAKANE.

I HAVE TO TRY TO CALM HIM DOWN.

EVEN THOUGH OBON* IS OVER...

...SUMMER'S STILL GOING STRONG.

THE HOT WEATHER STOKES THE FIRE IN EVERYONE.

MIIN

MIIN

MIIN

BAM

TAKANE!

*An annual Buddhist event in August for commemorating one's ancestors

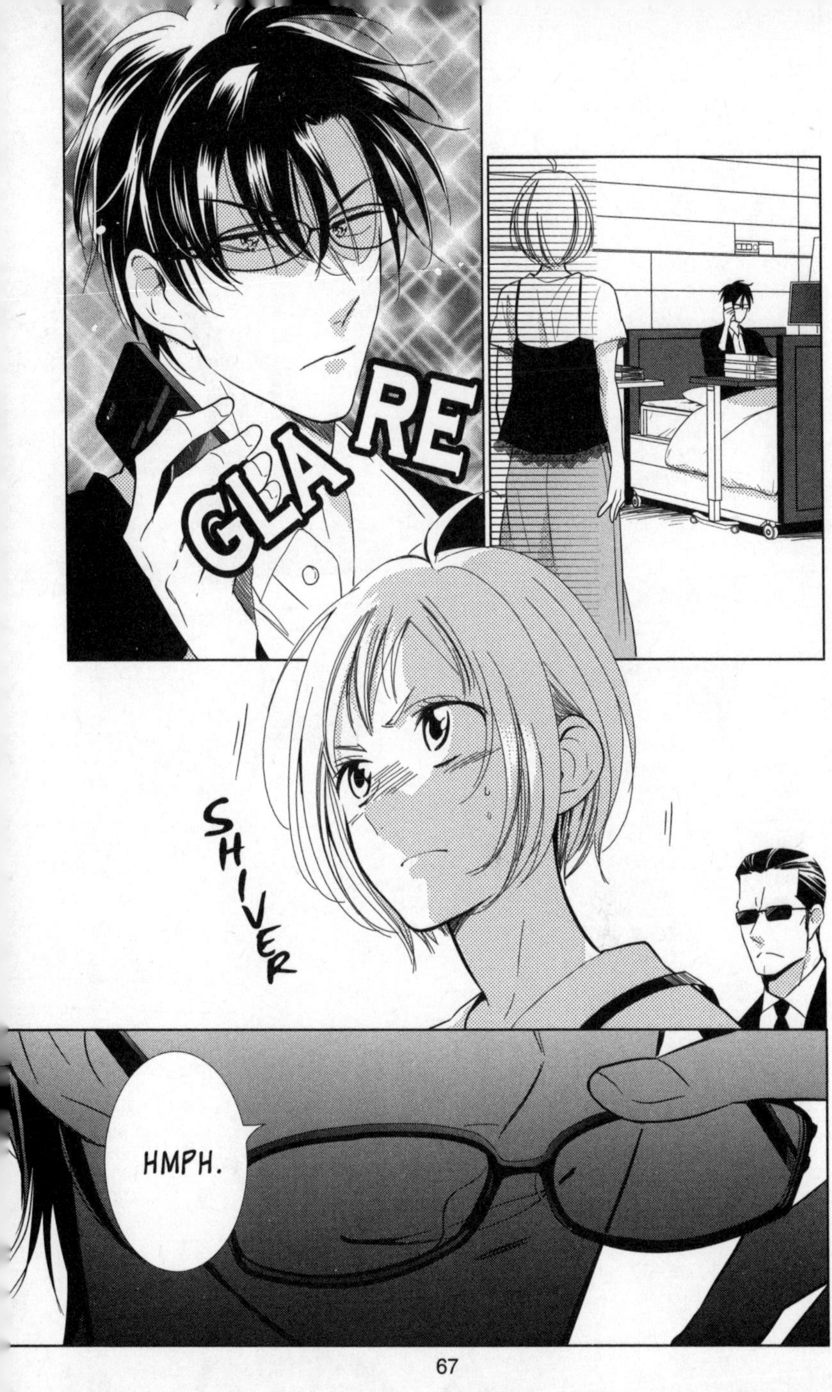
GLARE
SHIVER
HMPH.

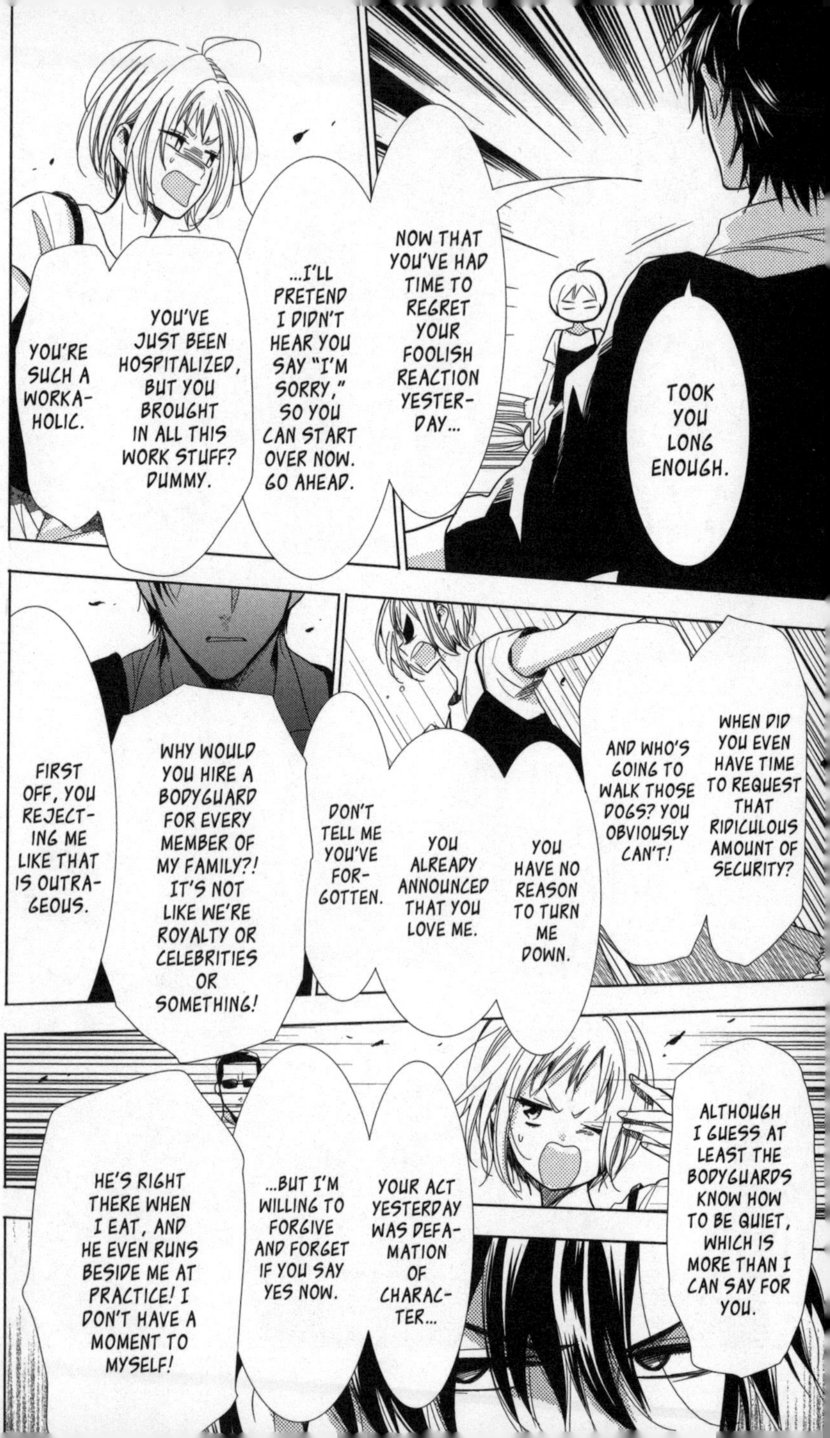
TOOK YOU LONG ENOUGH.
NOW THAT YOU'VE HAD TIME TO REGRET YOUR FOOLISH REACTION YESTERDAY...
...I'LL PRETEND I DIDN'T HEAR YOU SAY "I'M SORRY," SO YOU CAN START OVER NOW. GO AHEAD.
YOU'VE JUST BEEN HOSPITALIZED, BUT YOU BROUGHT IN ALL THIS WORK STUFF? DUMMY.
YOU'RE SUCH A WORKAHOLIC.
WHEN DID YOU EVEN HAVE TIME TO REQUEST THAT RIDICULOUS AMOUNT OF SECURITY?
AND WHO'S GOING TO WALK THOSE DOGS? YOU OBVIOUSLY CAN'T!
YOU HAVE NO REASON TO TURN ME DOWN.
YOU ALREADY ANNOUNCED THAT YOU LOVE ME.
DON'T TELL ME YOU'VE FORGOTTEN.
WHY WOULD YOU HIRE A BODYGUARD FOR EVERY MEMBER OF MY FAMILY?! IT'S NOT LIKE WE'RE ROYALTY OR CELEBRITIES OR SOMETHING!
FIRST OFF, YOU REJECTING ME LIKE THAT IS OUTRAGEOUS.
ALTHOUGH I GUESS AT LEAST THE BODYGUARDS KNOW HOW TO BE QUIET, WHICH IS MORE THAN I CAN SAY FOR YOU.
YOUR ACT YESTERDAY WAS DEFAMATION OF CHARACTER...
...BUT I'M WILLING TO FORGIVE AND FORGET IF YOU SAY YES NOW.
HE'S RIGHT THERE WHEN I EAT, AND HE EVEN RUNS BESIDE ME AT PRACTICE! I DON'T HAVE A MOMENT TO MYSELF!

SHUT UP AND LISTEN TO ME!

...

AH!

Calm down, now. Remember, this is a hospital.

CLINK

SAY WHAT YOU WANT, BUT THE BOTTOM LINE IS YOU'RE HERE BECAUSE YOU'RE WORRIED ABOUT ME.

I'M GENTLE WITH INJURED PEOPLE WHO REST LIKE THEY'RE SUPPOSED TO.

I'M INJURED. TAKE IT DOWN A NOTCH.

HONESTLY... YOU WERE IN A HUFF FROM THE MINUTE YOU WALKED IN...

...MS. HUFF 'N' PUFF.

69

HMPH.

YOU SHOULD BE ASHAMED TO ADMIT THAT. EVEN LITTLE KIDS KNOW THAT WORD.

"LIMIT" ISN'T PART OF MY VOCABU-LARY.

THERE'S A LIMIT TO THIS STUFF!

YOU'RE THE ONE WHO'S WORRIED. THIS IS TOO MUCH!

Okay, but look!

LINED UP!

I SEE.

I MEAN, IT'S GREAT THAT HE'S BETTER, BUT...

HOW'RE YOUR LEGS?

ALREADY GOOD AS NEW.

HE'S IN BETTER SPIRITS THAN BEFORE HE WAS HOSPITAL-IZED.

PRE-CISELY.

BECAUSE YOU'RE AN ELITE?

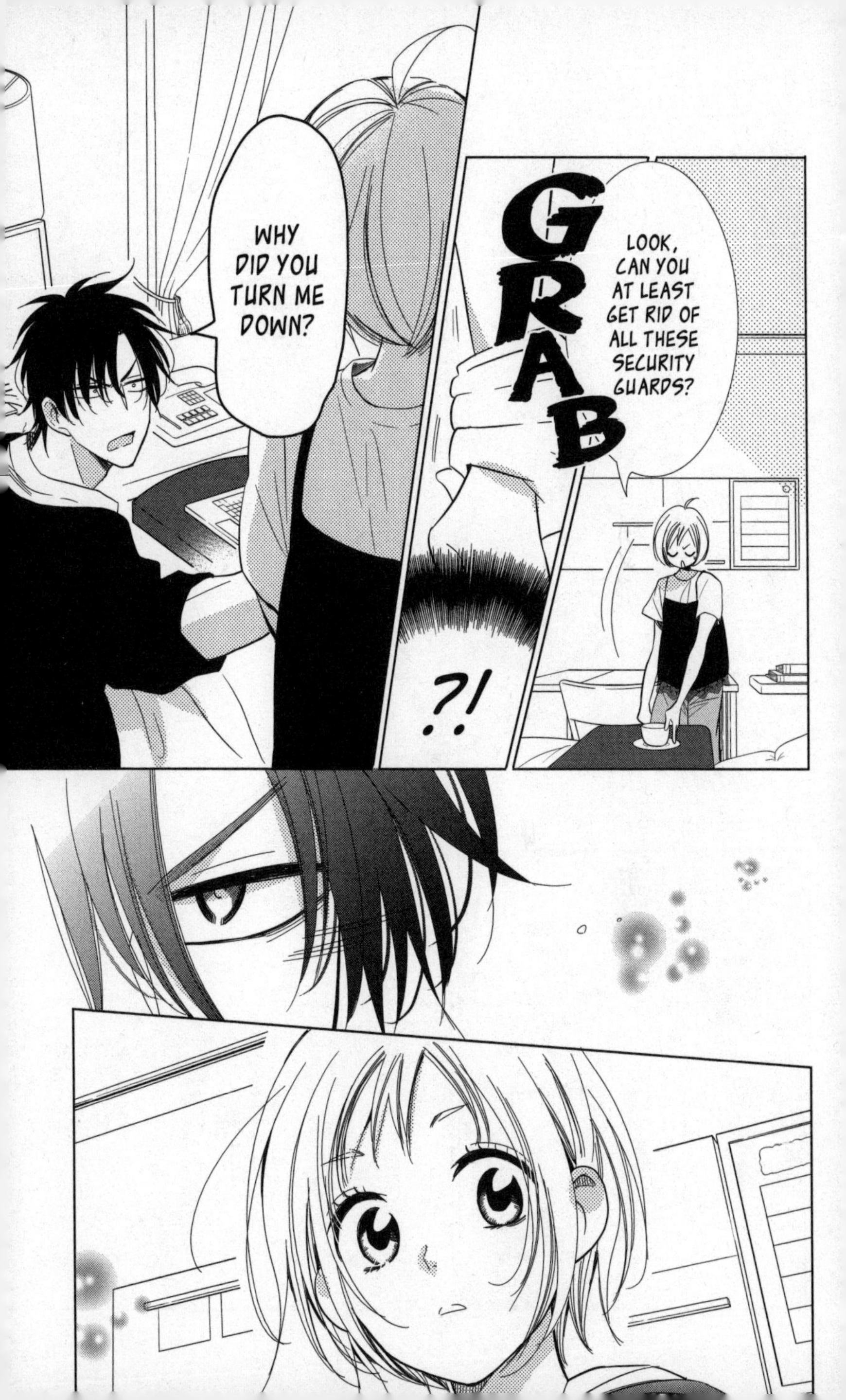
LOOK, CAN YOU AT LEAST GET RID OF ALL THESE SECURITY GUARDS?
GRAB
?!
WHY DID YOU TURN ME DOWN?

WHEN I SAID THAT, I...I JUST LOST MY HEAD FOR A SEC.

YEAH, RIGHT! THE VOICE RECORDER IN MY HEART PRESERVED EVERYTHING ABOUT THAT MOMENT, RIGHT DOWN TO THE WAY YOU WERE BREATHING.

WELL, SAME HERE. I REMEMBER EXACTLY WHAT YOU SAID IN RESPONSE.

SO CAN YOU PLEASE STOP TEASING ME NOW?

DON'T YOU HAVE...

...THOSE FEELINGS FOR ME ANY-MORE?

!

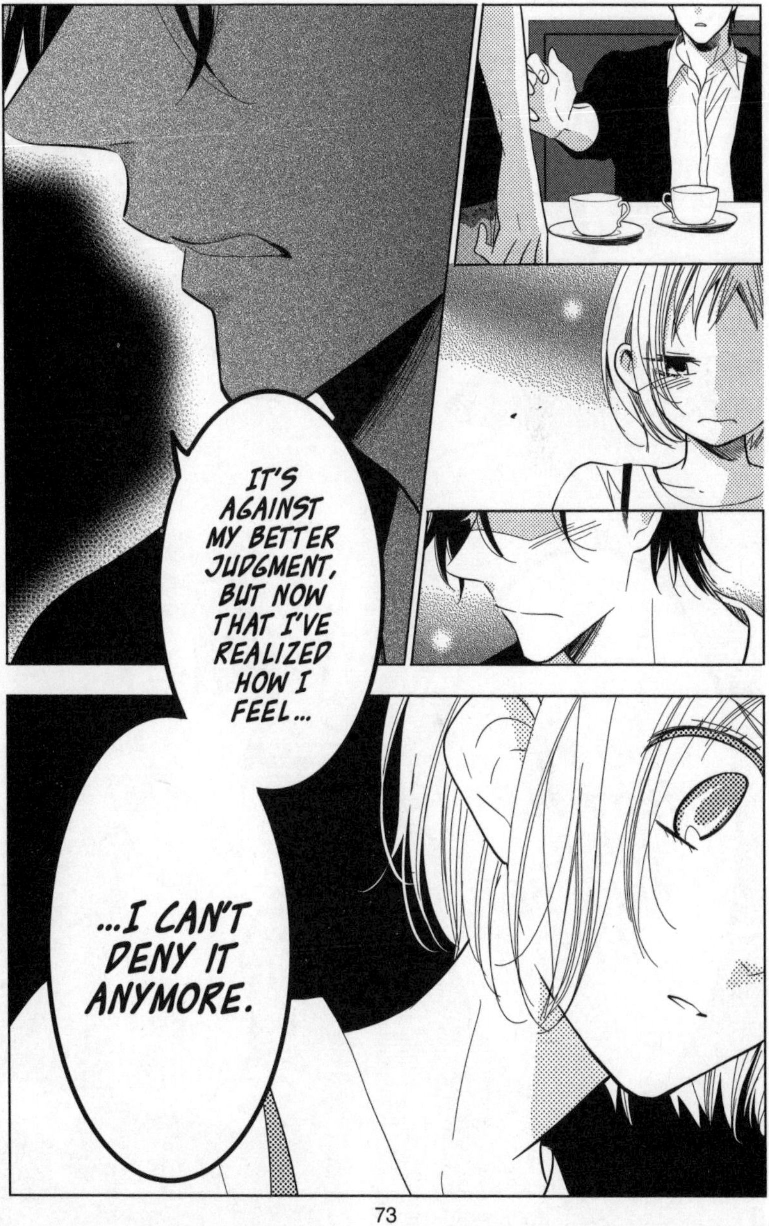
IT'S AGAINST MY BETTER JUDGMENT, BUT NOW THAT I'VE REALIZED HOW I FEEL...
...I CAN'T DENY IT ANYMORE.

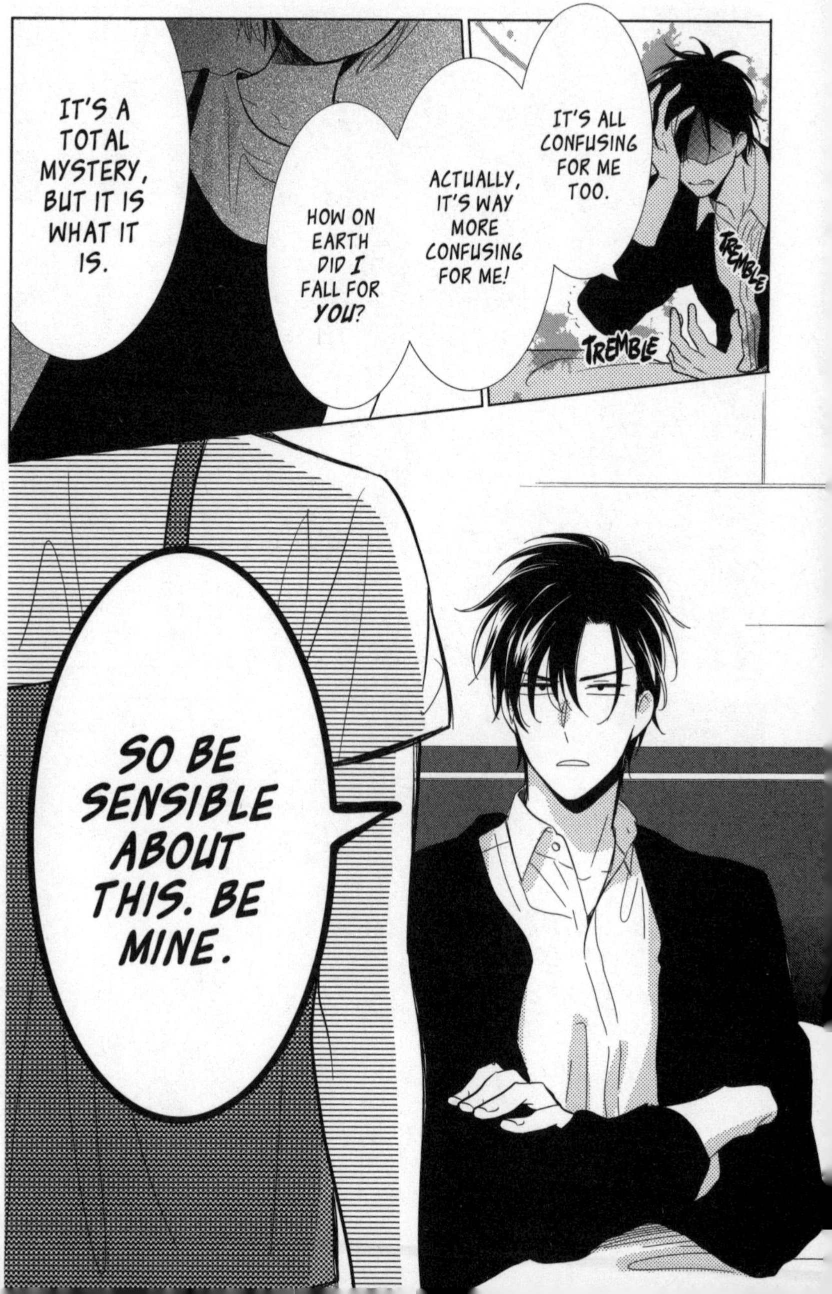
IT'S ALL CONFUSING FOR ME TOO.
TREMBLE
TREMBLE
ACTUALLY, IT'S WAY MORE CONFUSING FOR ME!
HOW ON EARTH DID I FALL FOR YOU?
IT'S A TOTAL MYSTERY, BUT IT IS WHAT IT IS.
SO BE SENSIBLE ABOUT THIS. BE MINE.

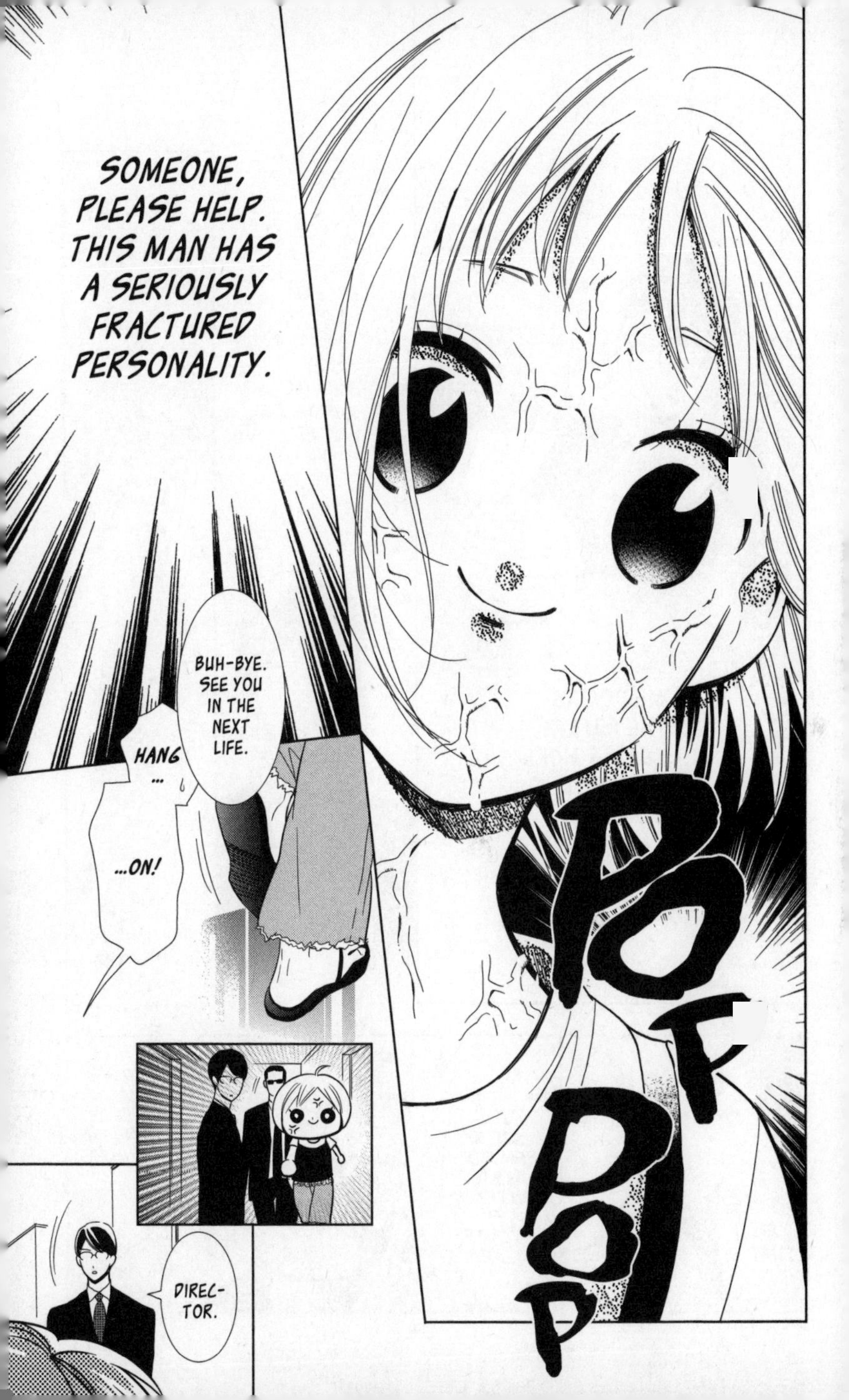

SOMEONE, PLEASE HELP. THIS MAN HAS A SERIOUSLY FRACTURED PERSONALITY.
POP
BUH-BYE. SEE YOU IN THE NEXT LIFE.
HANG...
...ON!
DIREC-TOR.

I PROBABLY NEED TO COME CLEAN ABOUT MY ARRANGED MARRIAGE PARTNERSHIP.

WHAT'S YOUR NEXT STEP?

I'M LOOKING TO THE FUTURE. IT'LL BRING MORE PROBLEMS, BUT IT'S SAFER TO HAVE THE OLD MAN'S APPROVAL.

!

...

BUT...

...BEFORE ALL THAT...

I'LL GET MY NEW BUSINESSES ON TRACK BY YEAR'S END.

OPENING OVERSEAS OFFICES AND MARKET EXPANSION.

TO DO THAT, I NEED TO SHOW HIM RESULTS.

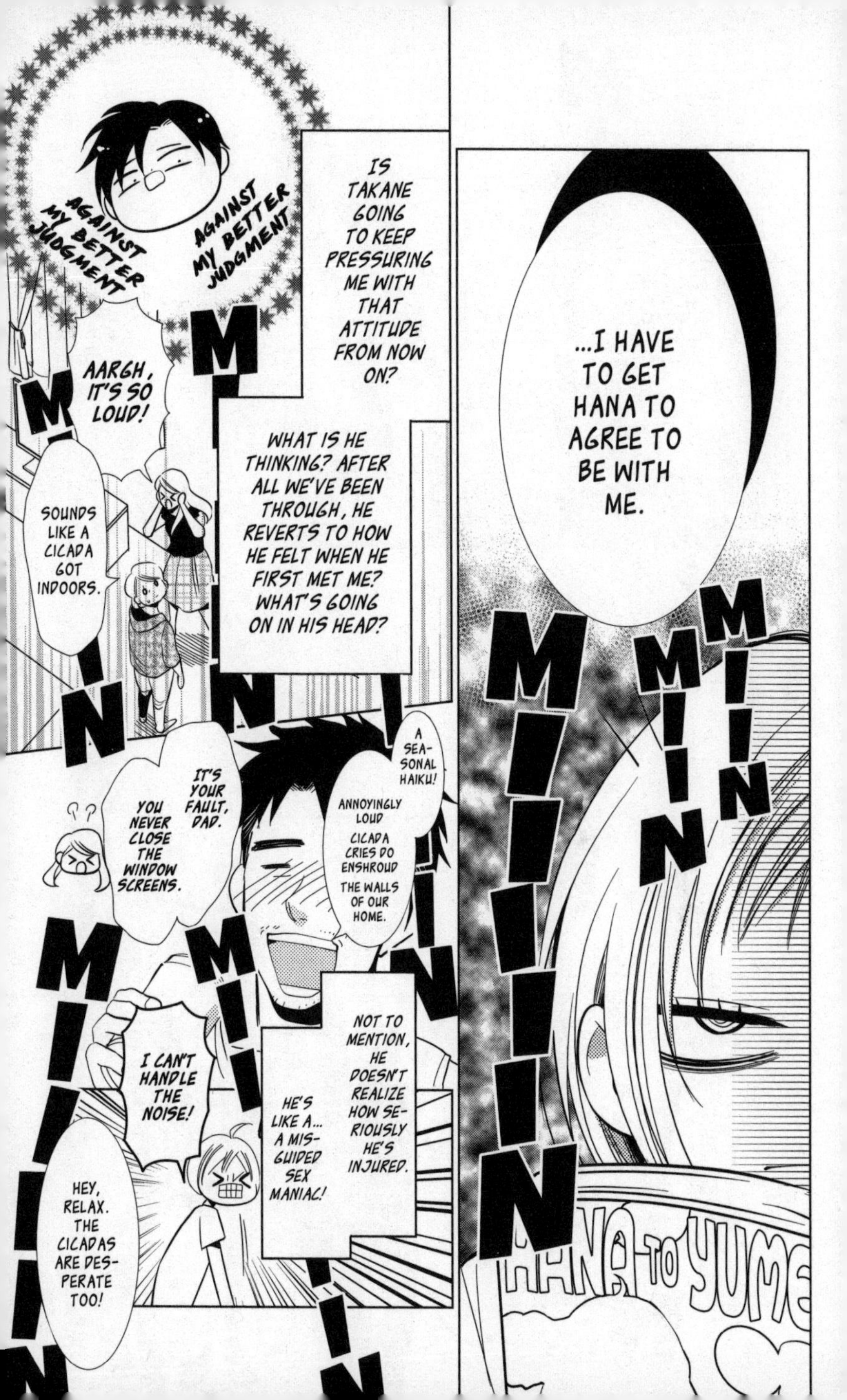

...I HAVE TO GET HANA TO AGREE TO BE WITH ME.
MIIIIN
MIN MIN
HANA TO YUME
IS TAKANE GOING TO KEEP PRESSURING ME WITH THAT ATTITUDE FROM NOW ON?
AGAINST MY BETTER JUDGMENT
AGAINST MY BETTER JUDGMENT
WHAT IS HE THINKING? AFTER ALL WE'VE BEEN THROUGH, HE REVERTS TO HOW HE FELT WHEN HE FIRST MET ME? WHAT'S GOING ON IN HIS HEAD?
AARGH, IT'S SO LOUD!
SOUNDS LIKE A CICADA GOT INDOORS.
MIN MIN
A SEA-SONAL HAIKU!
ANNOYINGLY LOUD CICADA CRIES DO ENSHROUD THE WALLS OF OUR HOME.
IT'S YOUR FAULT, DAD.
YOU NEVER CLOSE THE WINDOW SCREENS.
NOT TO MENTION, HE DOESN'T REALIZE HOW SE-RIOUSLY HE'S INJURED.
HE'S LIKE A... A MIS-GUIDED SEX MANIAC!
I CAN'T HANDLE THE NOISE!
HEY, RELAX. THE CICADAS ARE DES-PERATE TOO!
MIIIIN

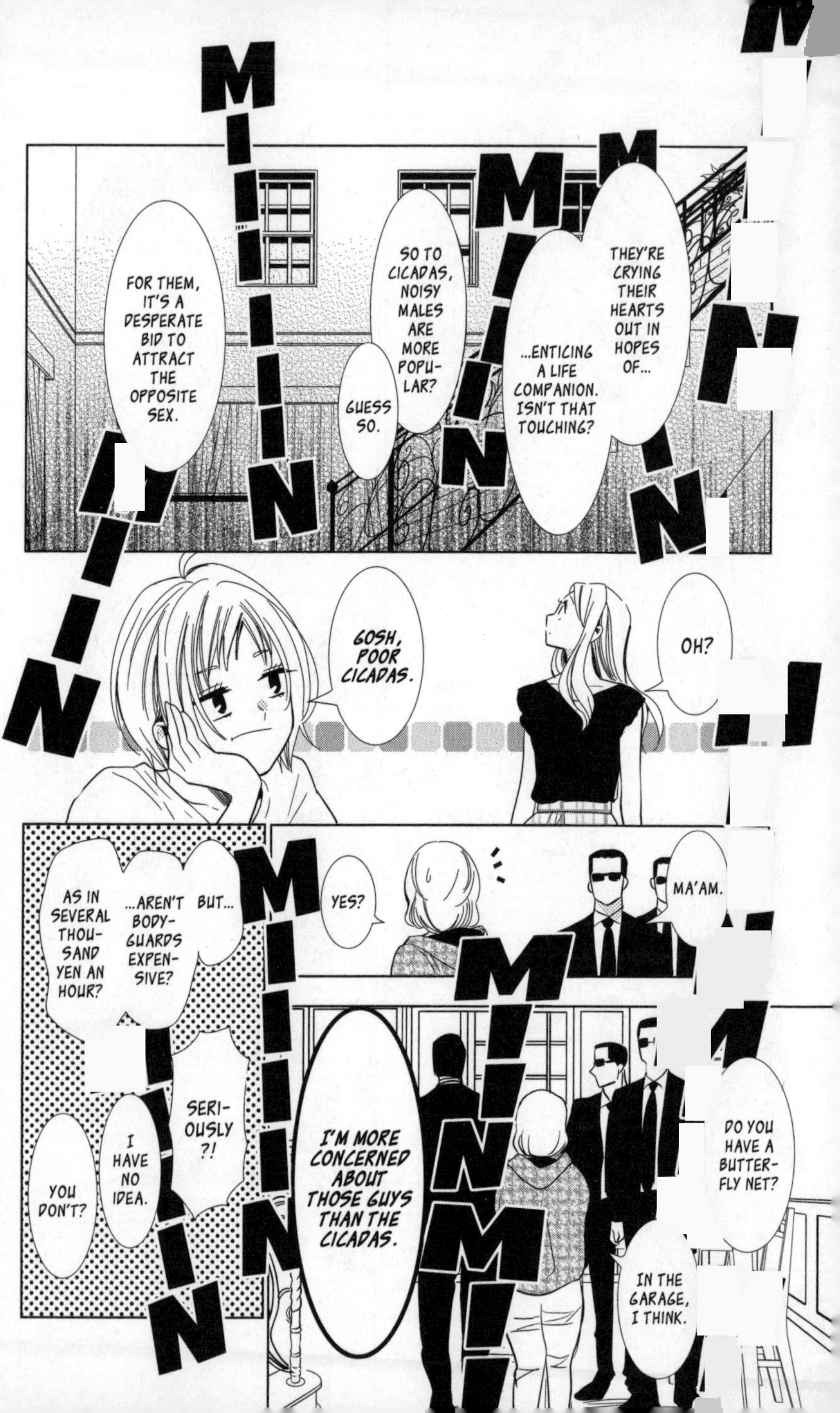
THEY'RE CRYING THEIR HEARTS OUT IN HOPES OF...
...ENTICING A LIFE COMPANION. ISN'T THAT TOUCHING?
SO TO CICADAS, NOISY MALES ARE MORE POPU-LAR?
GUESS SO.
FOR THEM, IT'S A DESPERATE BID TO ATTRACT THE OPPOSITE SEX.
MIIIN
OH?
GOSH, POOR CICADAS.
MA'AM.
YES?
BUT...
...AREN'T BODY-GUARDS EXPEN-SIVE?
AS IN SEVERAL THOU-SAND YEN AN HOUR?
DO YOU HAVE A BUTTER-FLY NET?
IN THE GARAGE, I THINK.
I'M MORE CONCERNED ABOUT THOSE GUYS THAN THE CICADAS.
SERI-OUSLY ?!
I HAVE NO IDEA.
YOU DON'T?

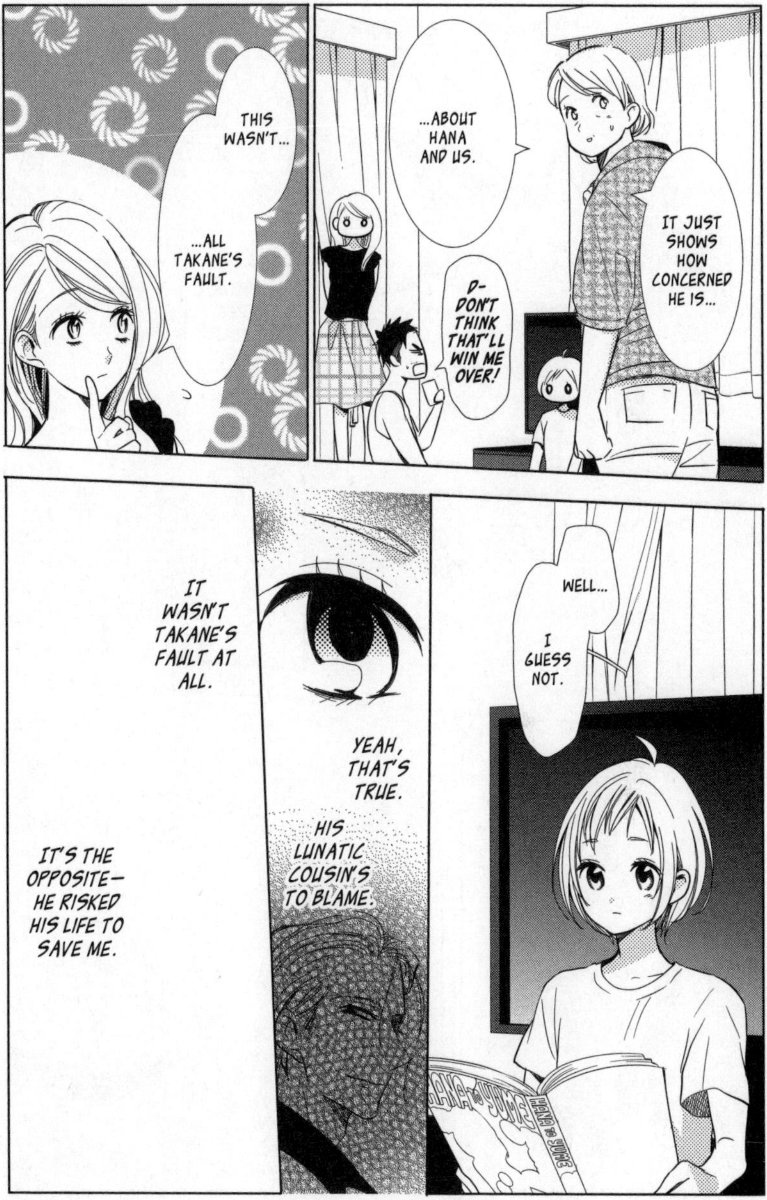
IT JUST SHOWS HOW CONCERNED HE IS...
...ABOUT HANA AND US.
D-DON'T THINK THAT'LL WIN ME OVER!
THIS WASN'T...
...ALL TAKANE'S FAULT.
WELL...
I GUESS NOT.
YEAH, THAT'S TRUE.
HIS LUNATIC COUSIN'S TO BLAME.
IT WASN'T TAKANE'S FAULT AT ALL.
IT'S THE OPPOSITE—HE RISKED HIS LIFE TO SAVE ME.
HANA TO YUME

ACTUALLY, I GUESS...

...I HAVEN'T EVEN THANKED HIM.

"I LOVE YOU."

MIINN MIINN

He feels ...the same.

GOSH...

NOW THAT I'VE HAD A CHANCE TO CATCH MY BREATH, IT'S REALLY HITTING ME.

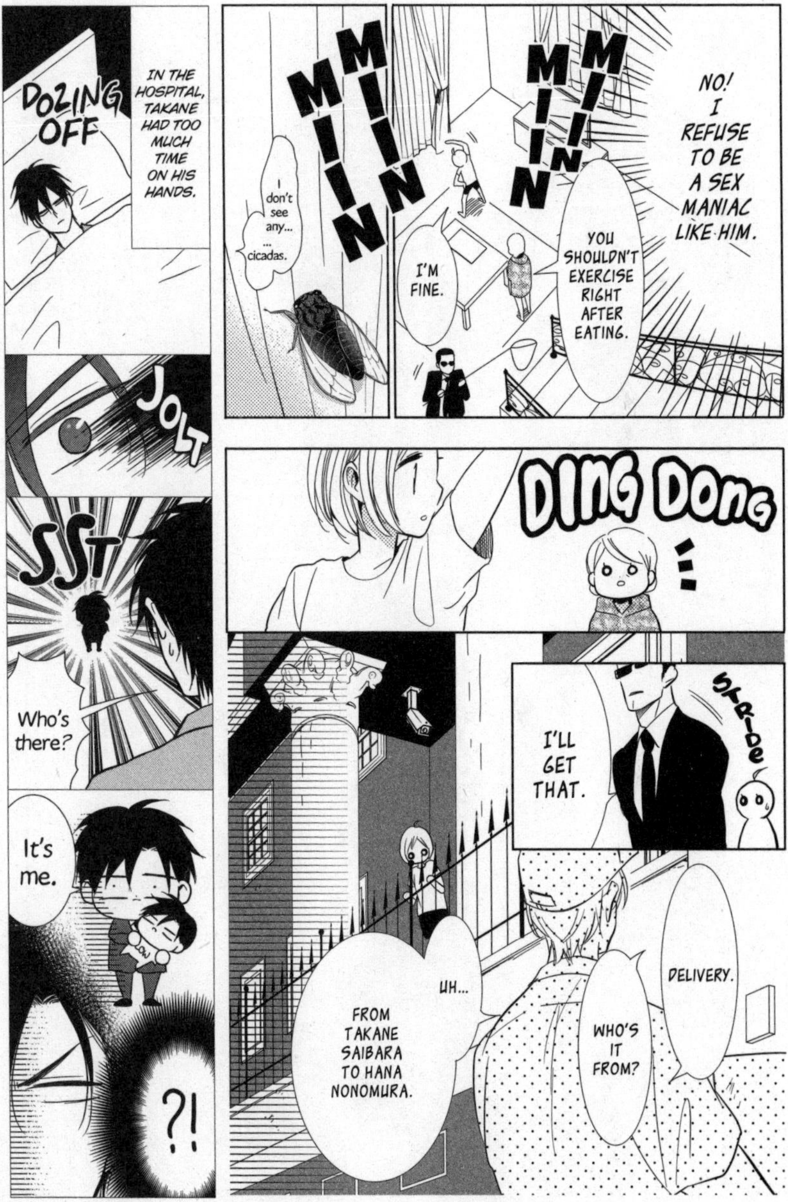

MIIIN
MIIIN
NO! I REFUSE TO BE A SEX MANIAC LIKE HIM.
YOU SHOULDN'T EXERCISE RIGHT AFTER EATING.
I'M FINE.
MIIIN
MIIIN
I don't see any... ...cicadas.
DING DONG
STRIDE
I'LL GET THAT.
DELIVERY.
WHO'S IT FROM?
UH...
FROM TAKANE SAIBARA TO HANA NONOMURA.
DOZING OFF
IN THE HOSPITAL, TAKANE HAD TOO MUCH TIME ON HIS HANDS.
JOLT
SST
Who's there?
It's me.
?!

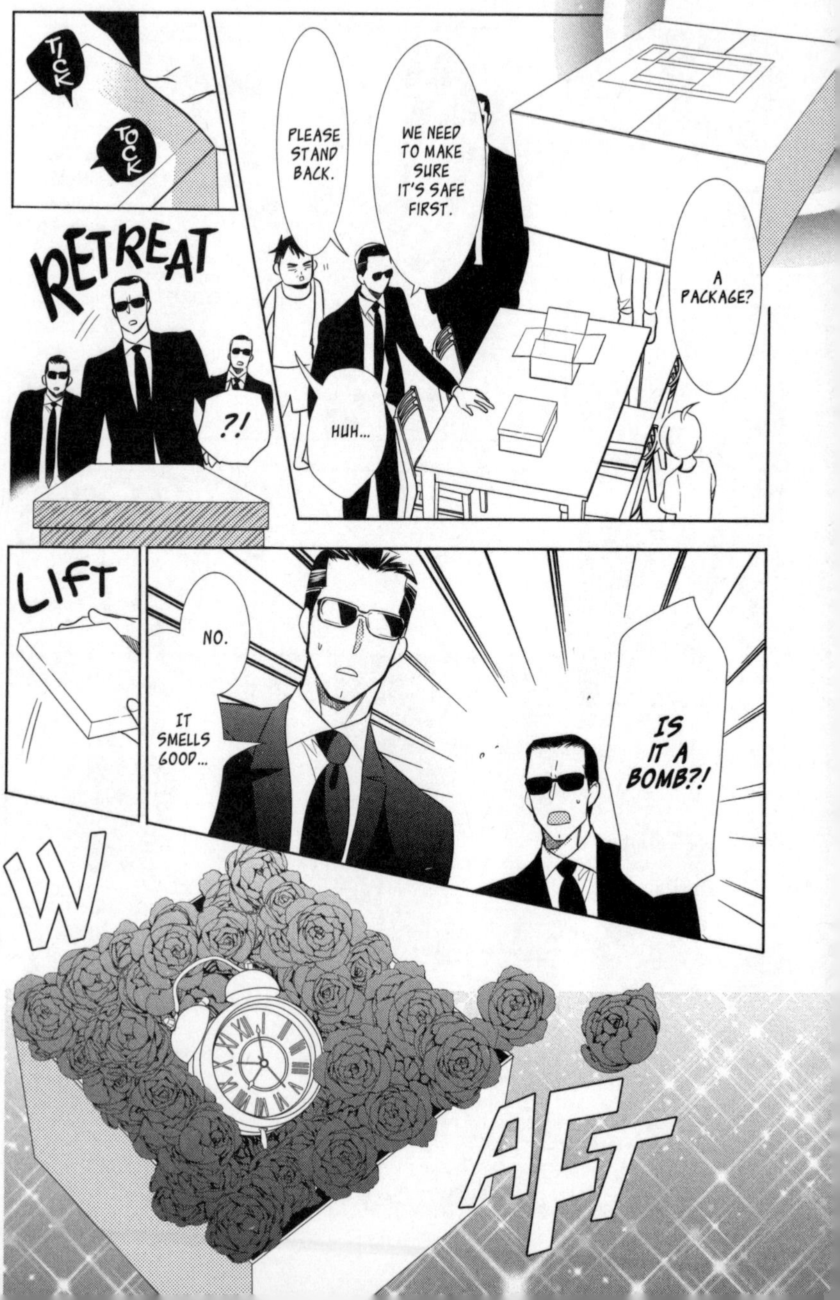
A PACKAGE?
WE NEED TO MAKE SURE IT'S SAFE FIRST.
PLEASE STAND BACK.
HUH...
TICK
TOCK
RETREAT
?!
IS IT A BOMB?!
NO.
IT SMELLS GOOD...
LIFT
W
AFT

A GIRL WHO GOES BACK TO SLEEP WON'T MAKE THE CUT AS MY WOMAN!

WAKE UP! IT'S MORNING!

AN ALARM CLOCK?

And roses...

?

CLICK

THINK OF TIME AS YOUR GREATEST PARTNER! IT'LL MOTIVATE AND DRIVE YOU!

MY WOMAN SHOULDN'T SQUANDER HER TIME IN IDLENESS.

TEN MINUTES A DAY ADDS UP TO 60 HOURS A YEAR.

SIXTY HOURS!

I BET YOU'RE THINKING, "IT'S ONLY TEN MINUTES! WHAT'S THE BIG DEAL?"

I KNOW YOU'RE TRYING TO STAY IN BED FOR "JUST TEN MORE MINUTES," SLUGGARD.

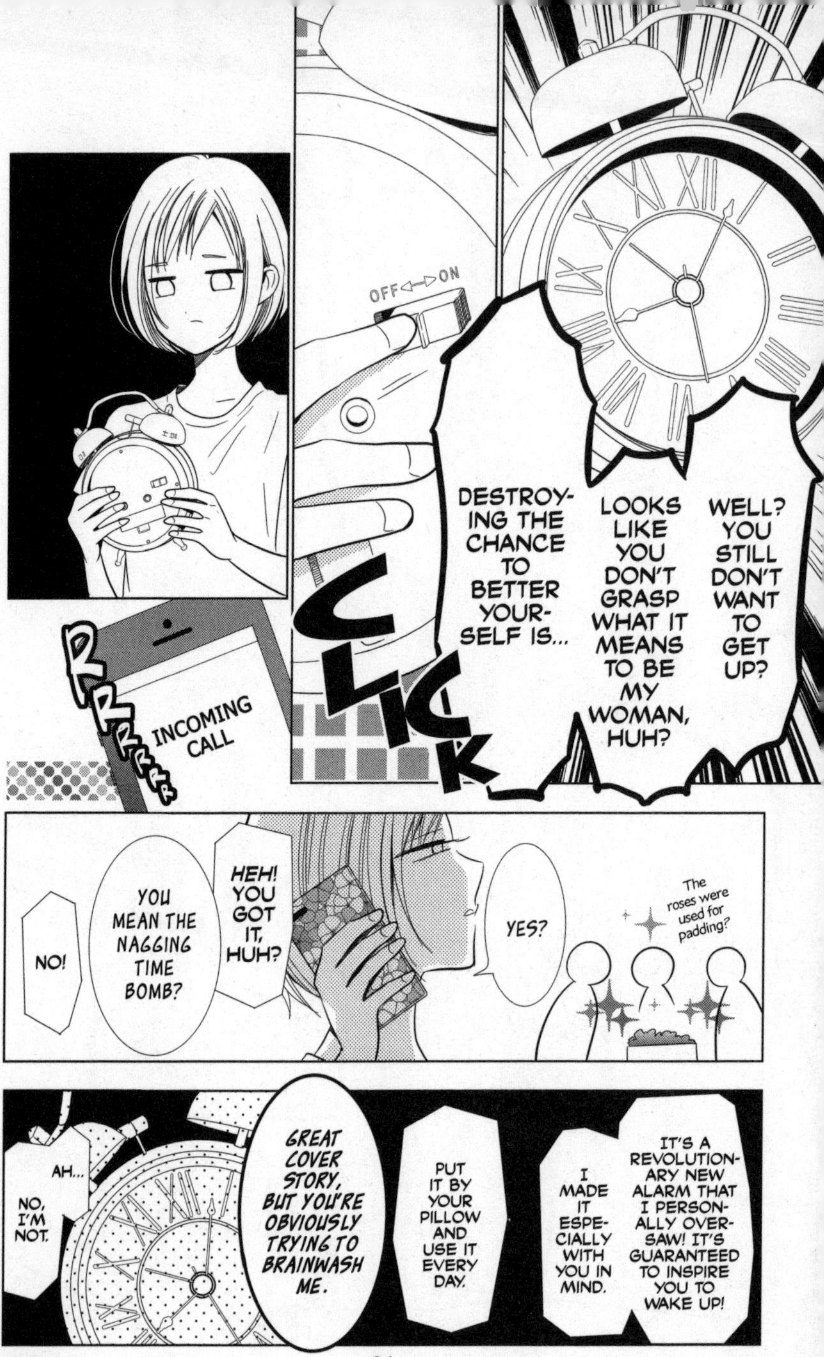
WELL? YOU STILL DON'T WANT TO GET UP?
LOOKS LIKE YOU DON'T GRASP WHAT IT MEANS TO BE MY WOMAN, HUH?
DESTROYING THE CHANCE TO BETTER YOURSELF IS...
OFF ON
CLICK
RRRRRRR
INCOMING CALL
The roses were used for padding?
YES?
HEH! YOU GOT IT, HUH?
YOU MEAN THE NAGGING TIME BOMB?
NO!
IT'S A REVOLUTIONARY NEW ALARM THAT I PERSONALLY OVERSAW! IT'S GUARANTEED TO INSPIRE YOU TO WAKE UP!
I MADE IT ESPECIALLY WITH YOU IN MIND.
PUT IT BY YOUR PILLOW AND USE IT EVERY DAY.
GREAT COVER STORY, BUT YOU'RE OBVIOUSLY TRYING TO BRAINWASH ME.
AH...
NO, I'M NOT.

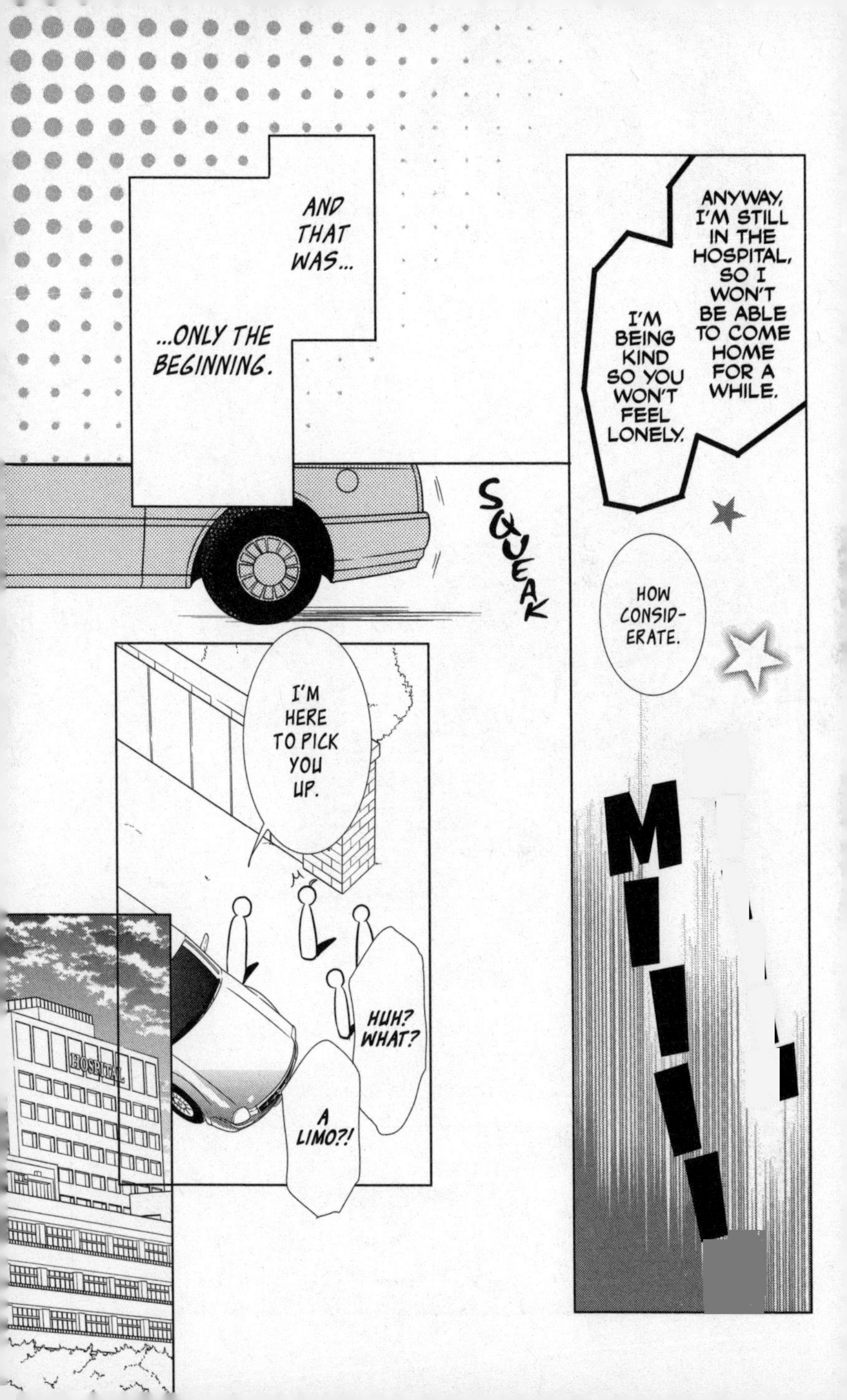
ANYWAY, I'M STILL IN THE HOSPITAL, SO I WON'T BE ABLE TO COME HOME FOR A WHILE.
I'M BEING KIND SO YOU WON'T FEEL LONELY.
HOW CONSID-ERATE.
AND THAT WAS...
...ONLY THE BEGINNING.
SQUEAK
I'M HERE TO PICK YOU UP.
HUH? WHAT?
A LIMO?!

It's hard to walk in this.

NO MATTER WHAT IT TAKES...

GLEAM GLEAM

...HE WANTS ME...

...TO SAY YES.

My head's so heavy...

86

DON'T CALL IT THAT.

WHAT, THE DACHSHUND CAR?

I GOT YOU THE FINEST CAR, SO STOP COMPLAINING.

BECAUSE...

...YOU'RE SUFFERING FROM "I CAN'T BE TRUE TO MY FEELINGS" SYNDROME, SO I'M GOING TO COUNSEL YOU.

I THINK YOU'LL MAKE IT WORSE.

A RIDE IS FINE, BUT WHY'D HE DROP ME OFF AT THE HOSPITAL, NOT HOME?

Fine, fine.

SIT.

PLUS, THE VIEW'S DECENT... WAIT, THAT'S NOT WHY YOU'RE HERE.

THERE'S ALSO A MEETING ROOM AND AN OFFICE FOR MY SECRETARY, SO I GUESS IT'S A LITTLE BETTER THAN NORMAL.

YES, TRUE.

IT'S NORMAL.

IT SO ISN'T.

WHY DO YOU HAVE A DINING ROOM IN YOUR HOSPITAL SUITE?

YOU'RE HILARIOUS.

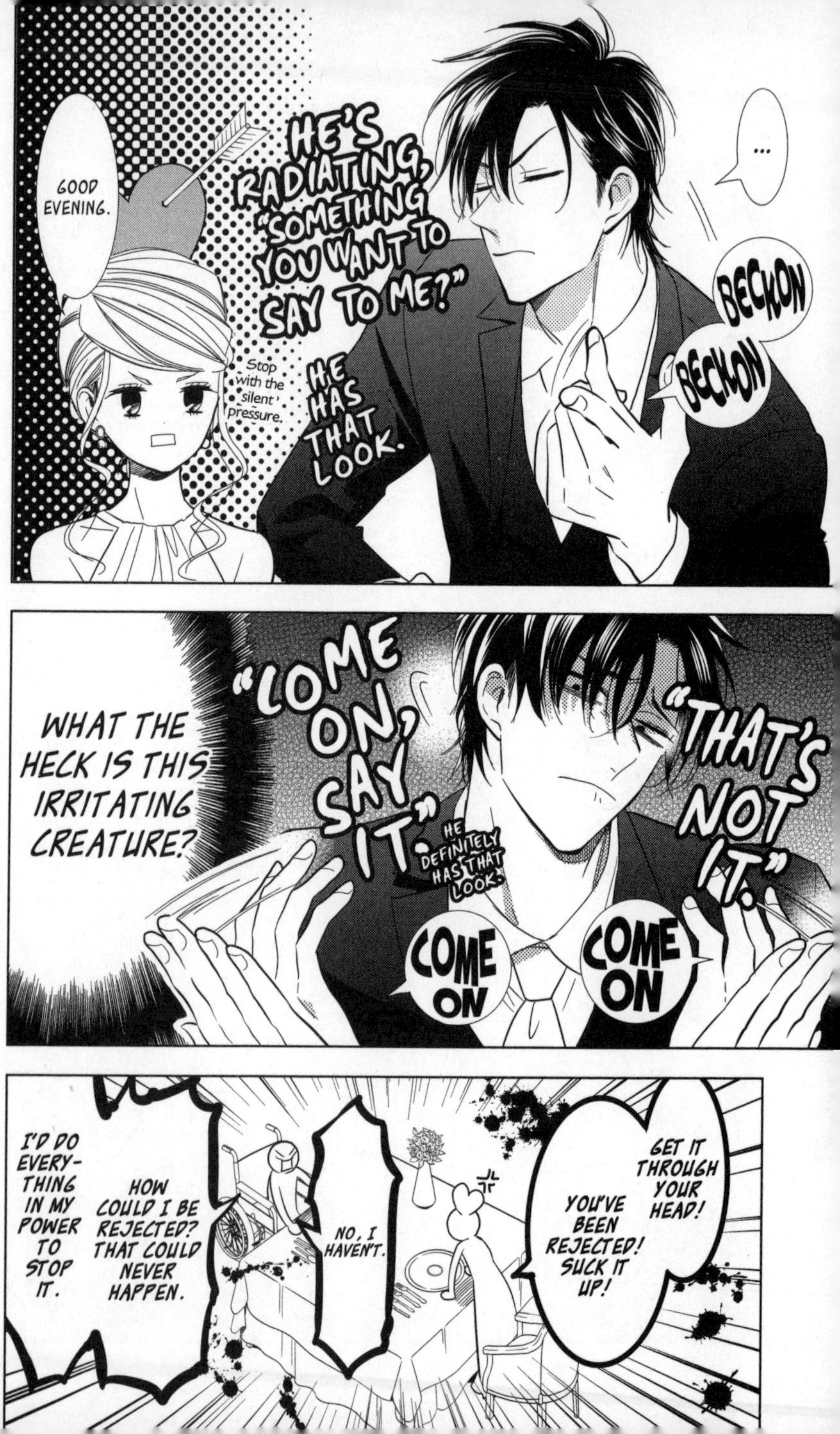
...
BECKON
BECKON
HE'S RADIATING, "SOMETHING YOU WANT TO SAY TO ME?"
HE HAS THAT LOOK.
Stop with the silent pressure.
GOOD EVENING.
"THAT'S NOT IT."
COME ON
COME ON
HE DEFINITELY HAS THAT LOOK.
"COME ON, SAY IT."
WHAT THE HECK IS THIS IRRITATING CREATURE?
GET IT THROUGH YOUR HEAD!
YOU'VE BEEN REJECTED! SUCK IT UP!
NO, I HAVEN'T.
HOW COULD I BE REJECTED? THAT COULD NEVER HAPPEN.
I'D DO EVERY-THING IN MY POWER TO STOP IT.

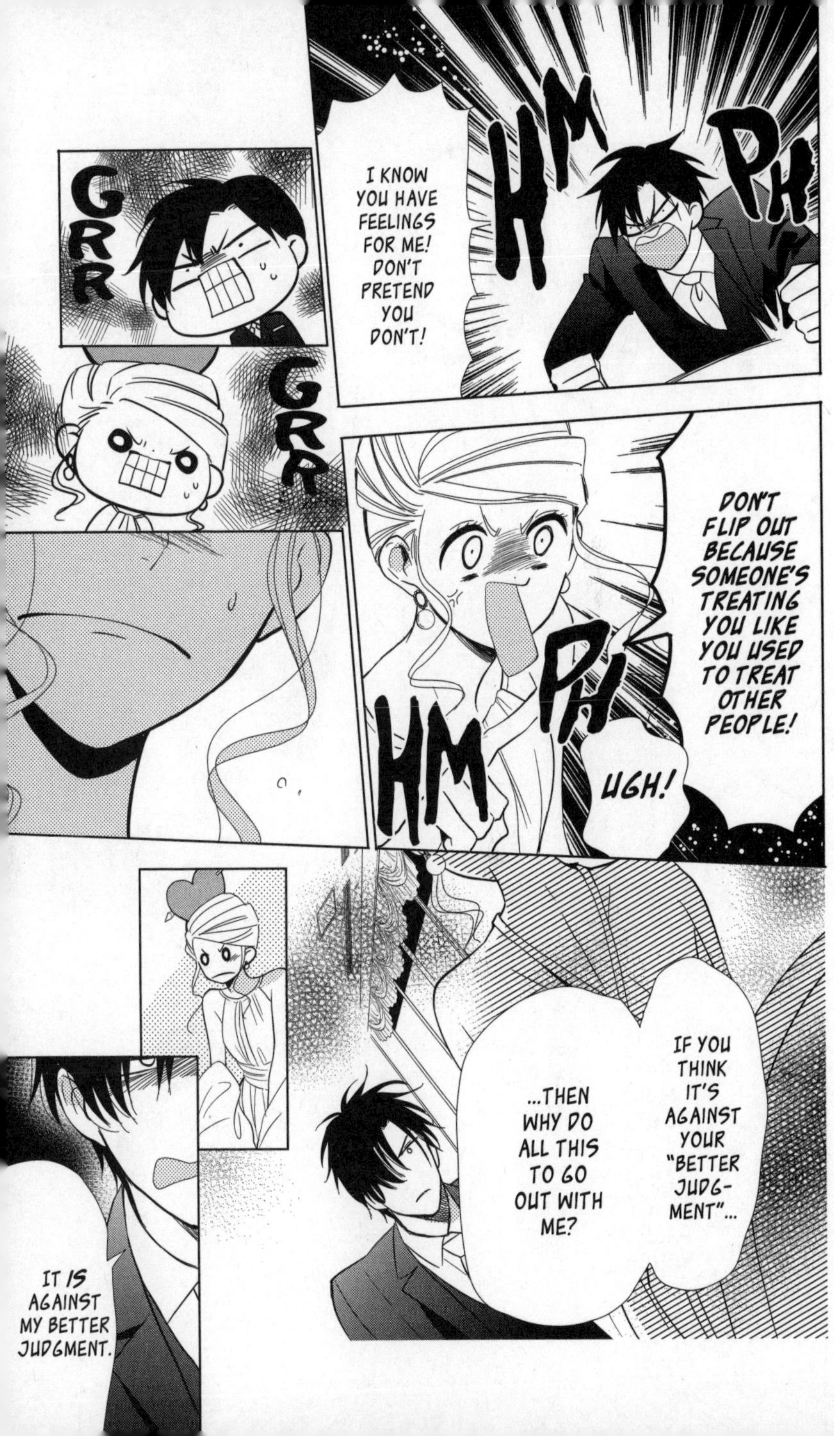
HMPH
I KNOW YOU HAVE FEELINGS FOR ME! DON'T PRETEND YOU DON'T!
GRR
DON'T FLIP OUT BECAUSE SOMEONE'S TREATING YOU LIKE YOU USED TO TREAT OTHER PEOPLE!
HMPH
UGH!
GRR
IF YOU THINK IT'S AGAINST YOUR "BETTER JUDG-MENT"...
...THEN WHY DO ALL THIS TO GO OUT WITH ME?
IT *IS* AGAINST MY BETTER JUDGMENT.

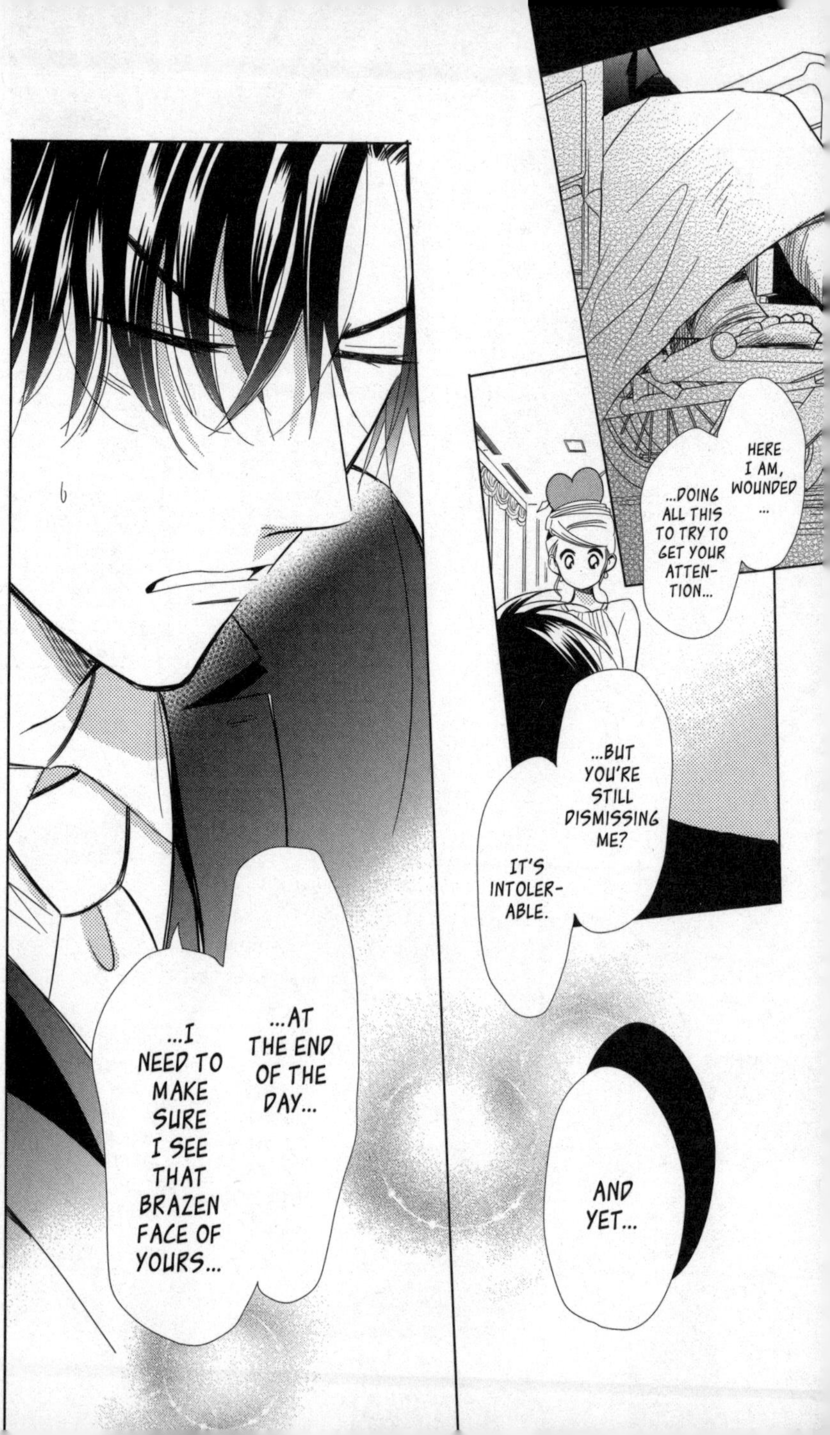
HERE I AM, WOUNDED...
...DOING ALL THIS TO TRY TO GET YOUR ATTENTION...
...BUT YOU'RE STILL DISMISSING ME?
IT'S INTOLERABLE.
AND YET...
...AT THE END OF THE DAY...
...I NEED TO MAKE SURE I SEE THAT BRAZEN FACE OF YOURS...

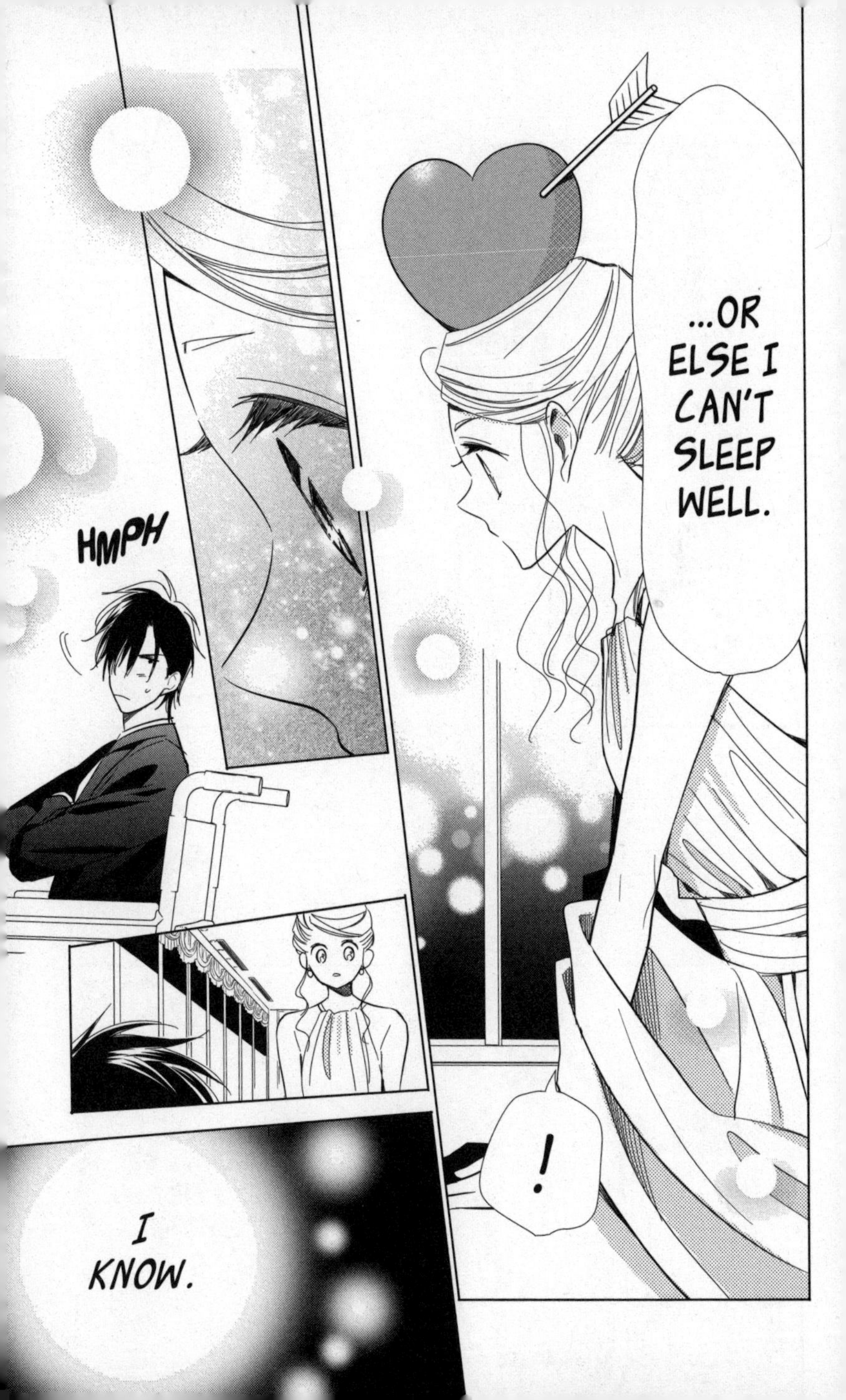
...OR ELSE I CAN'T SLEEP WELL.
HMPH
!
I KNOW.

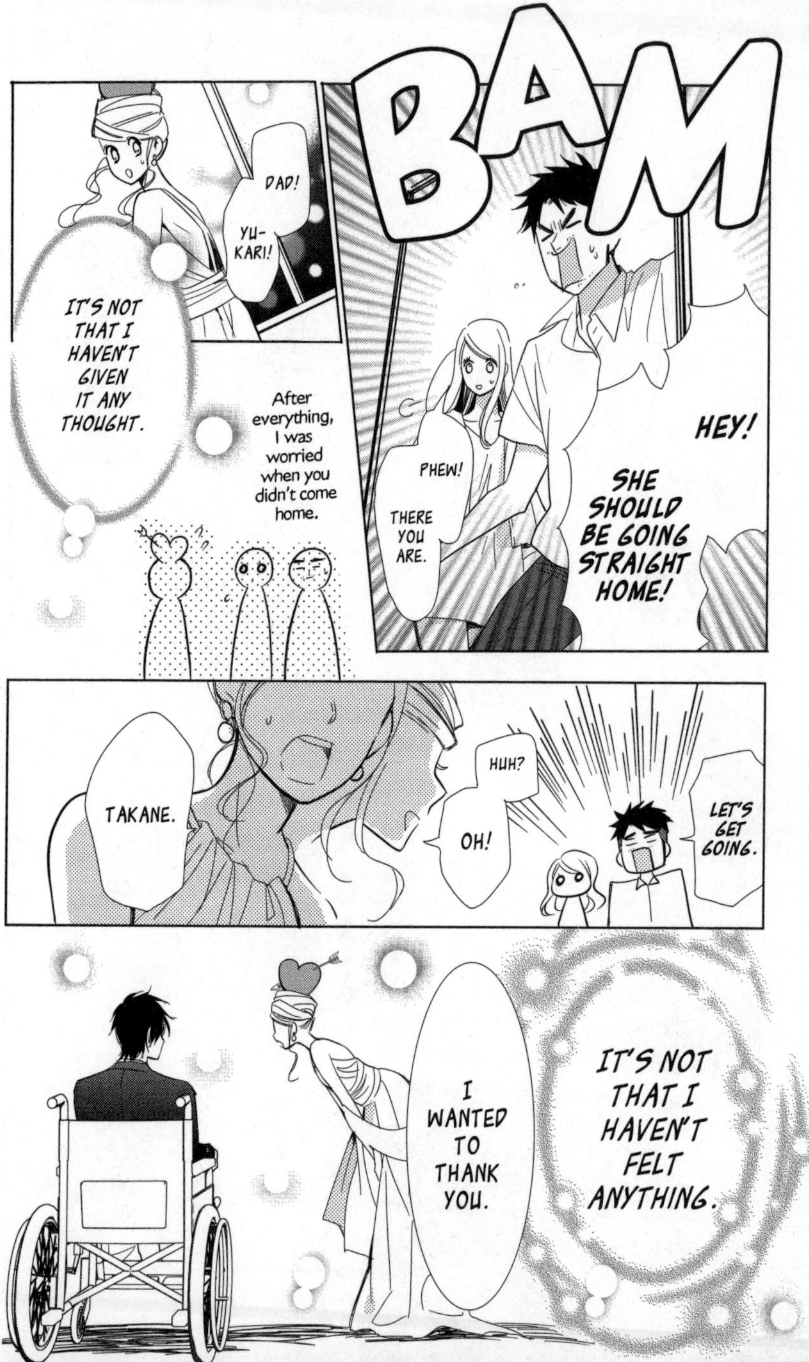
BAM
HEY!
SHE SHOULD BE GOING STRAIGHT HOME!
PHEW!
THERE YOU ARE.
DAD!
YU-KARI!
IT'S NOT THAT I HAVEN'T GIVEN IT ANY THOUGHT.
After everything, I was worried when you didn't come home.
LET'S GET GOING.
HUH?
OH!
TAKANE.
IT'S NOT THAT I HAVEN'T FELT ANYTHING.
I WANTED TO THANK YOU.

WE
FEEL
THE
SAME
WAY.

BUT...

IF YOU HADN'T COME TO SAVE ME...

...I WOULDN'T BE HERE RIGHT NOW, OR ABLE TO COMPLAIN TO YOU.

...I'M FINE NOW, OKAY?

GOT THAT?

SO PLEASE REDUCE THE NUMBER OF GUARDS.

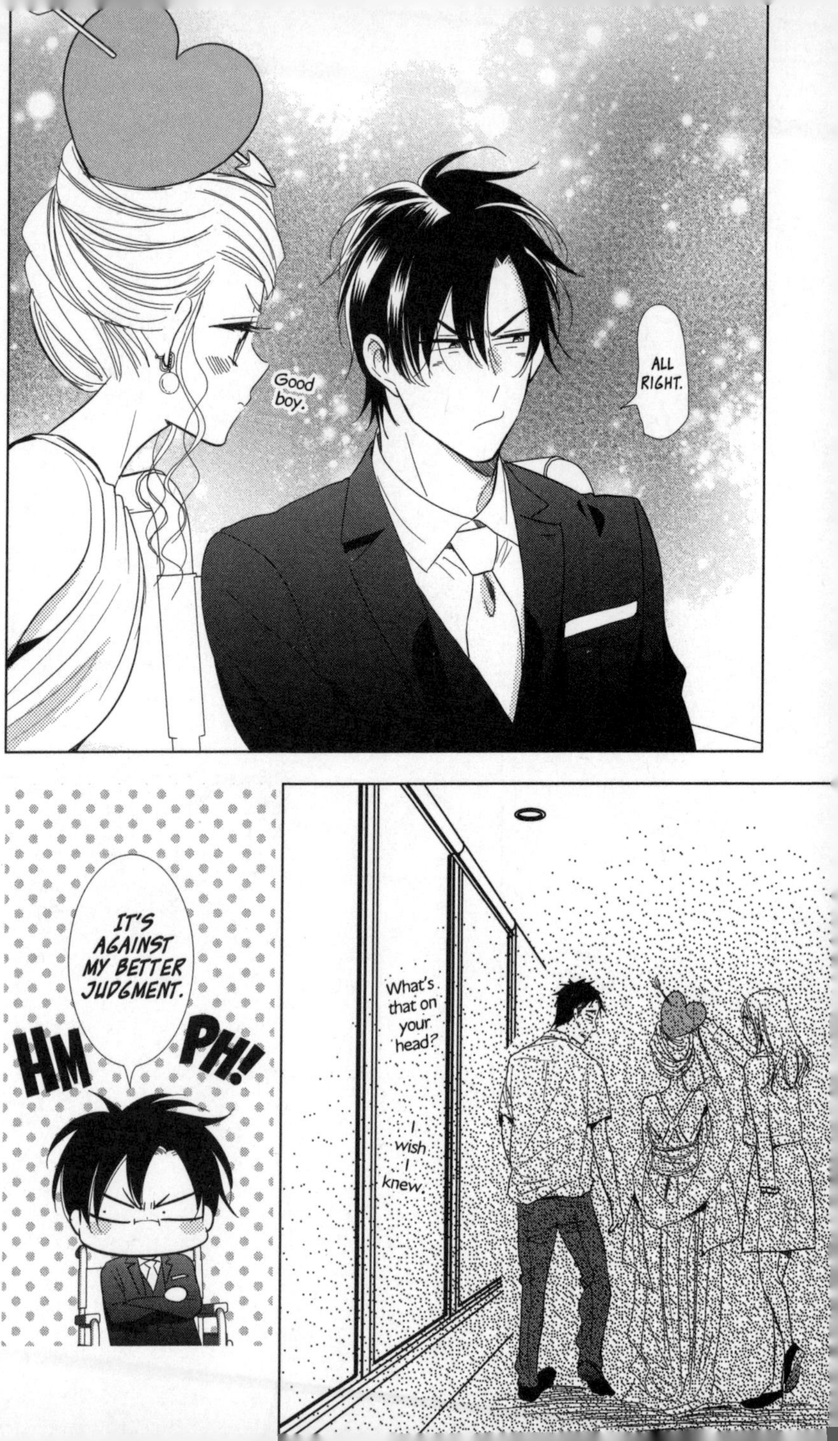
ALL RIGHT.
Good boy.
What's that on your head?
I wish I knew.
IT'S AGAINST MY BETTER JUDGMENT.
HMPH!

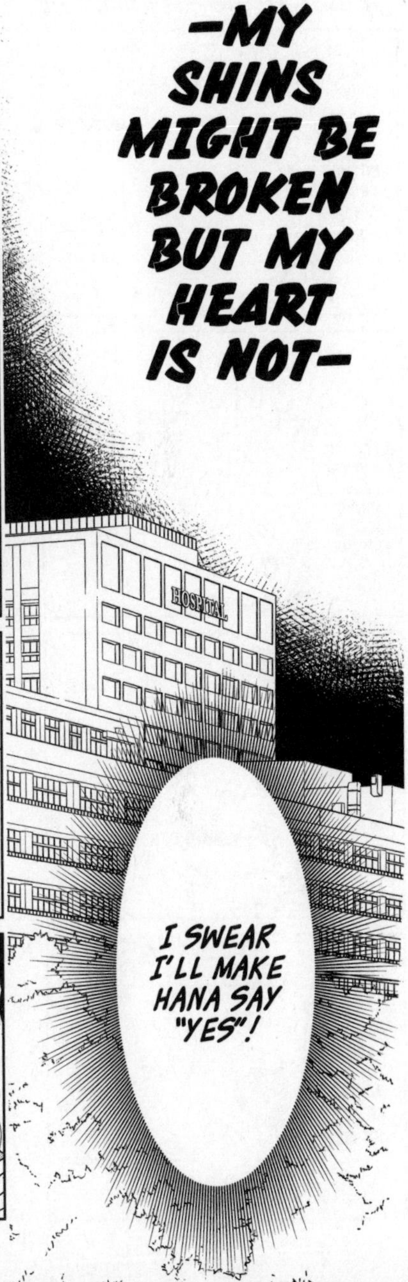

—MY SHINS MIGHT BE BROKEN BUT MY HEART IS NOT—
HOSPITAL
I SWEAR I'LL MAKE HANA SAY "YES"!

Takane in the Hospital

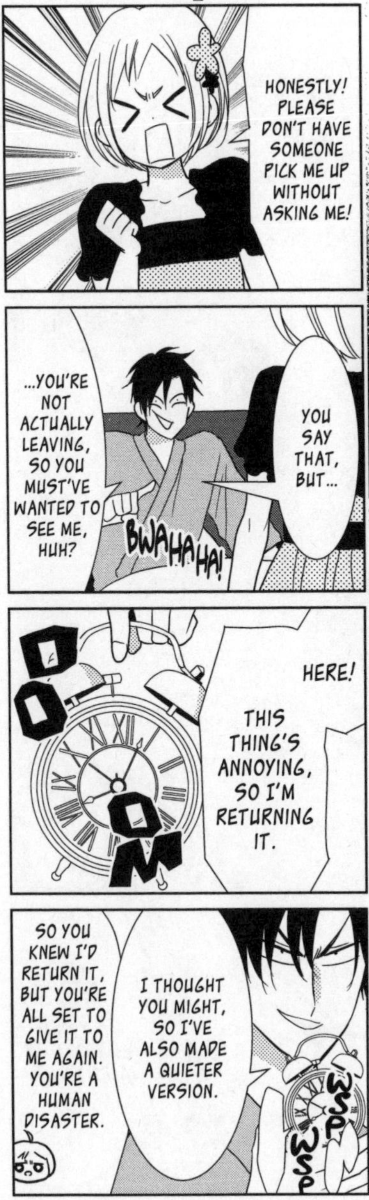

HONESTLY! PLEASE DON'T HAVE SOMEONE PICK ME UP WITHOUT ASKING ME!
YOU SAY THAT, BUT...
...YOU'RE NOT ACTUALLY LEAVING, SO YOU MUST'VE WANTED TO SEE ME, HUH?
BWAHAHAHA!
HERE!
THIS THING'S ANNOYING, SO I'M RETURNING IT.
DOOM
I THOUGHT YOU MIGHT, SO I'VE ALSO MADE A QUIETER VERSION.
SO YOU KNEW I'D RETURN IT, BUT YOU'RE ALL SET TO GIVE IT TO ME AGAIN. YOU'RE A HUMAN DISASTER.
WSP WSP

Present

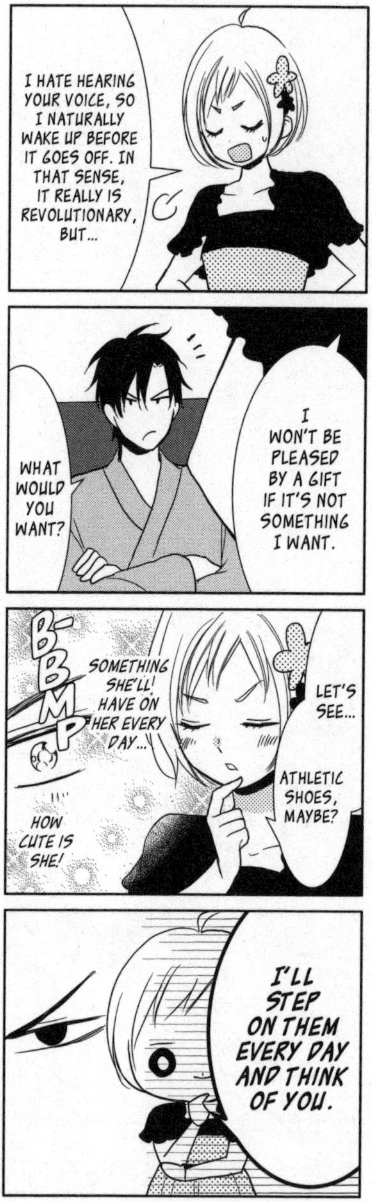
I HATE HEARING YOUR VOICE, SO I NATURALLY WAKE UP BEFORE IT GOES OFF. IN THAT SENSE, IT REALLY IS REVOLUTIONARY, BUT...
I WON'T BE PLEASED BY A GIFT IF IT'S NOT SOMETHING I WANT.
WHAT WOULD YOU WANT?
LET'S SEE...
ATHLETIC SHOES, MAYBE?
SOMETHING SHE'LL HAVE ON HER EVERY DAY...
B-BBMP
HOW CUTE IS SHE!
I'LL STEP ON THEM EVERY DAY AND THINK OF YOU.

A Boy to Be Stepped On

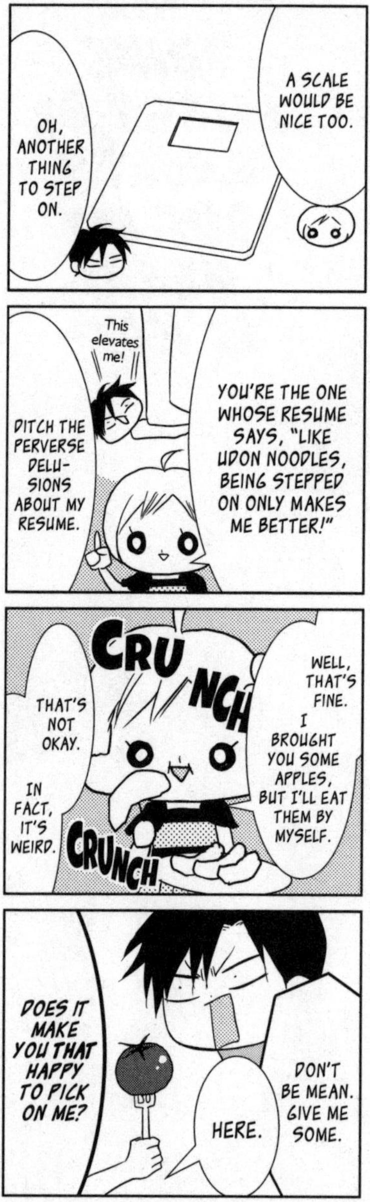
A SCALE WOULD BE NICE TOO.
OH, ANOTHER THING TO STEP ON.
YOU'RE THE ONE WHOSE RESUME SAYS, "LIKE UDON NOODLES, BEING STEPPED ON ONLY MAKES ME BETTER!"
This elevates me!
DITCH THE PERVERSE DELU-SIONS ABOUT MY RESUME.
WELL, THAT'S FINE. I BROUGHT YOU SOME APPLES, BUT I'LL EAT THEM BY MYSELF.
CRUNCH
THAT'S NOT OKAY.
IN FACT, IT'S WEIRD.
CRUNCH
DON'T BE MEAN. GIVE ME SOME.
HERE.
DOES IT MAKE YOU THAT HAPPY TO PICK ON ME?

Love Letter

WHAT A SELFISH GIRL. IF SHE DOESN'T WANT ANYTHING, I'LL WRITE HER A LETTER.

TAP
TAP
TAP TAP

HAVE YOU EVER WRITTEN A LOVE LETTER?

OF COURSE NOT. BUT IT SHOULD BE A PIECE OF CAKE GIVEN MY WRITING TALENT.

THE POINT IS... ...TO SELL YOURSELF TO THE OTHER PERSON, RIGHT?

THIS IS... ...A BUSINESS PROPOSAL, NOT A LETTER.

> Takane Saibara, Hana Nonomura
> Proposal to enter into a partnership
> ~Benefits associated with dating~

The Ten-Times Game

A game Hana taught him →

HEY. LET'S PLAY THE TEN-TIMES GAME.

ARGH!

WHATEVER IT TAKES, I JUST WANT HER TO SAY "YES."

OKAY. PLEASE SAY "PAD KID POURED CURD PULLED COD" TEN TIMES.

I DON'T REMEMBER IT BEING SUCH AN EVIL GAME.

HEE HEE

SAY "YES" TEN TIMES.

YES, YES.
YES.
YES.
YES.
YES.

BE MY GIRL—

DEATH.

97

Present

Video Letter

HANA WAS GIVEN A MYSTERIOUS DVD.

IT SEEMS COWARDLY.

HMM... I'M NOT SURE ABOUT COMMUNICATING SOMETHING THAT IMPORTANT IN A LETTER.

SO YOU'RE COMPLETELY DISMISSING LOVE LETTERS.

SO?

I BET YOU'RE STARTING TO THINK ABOUT SAYING "YES," HUH?

THERE ARE SUBTLE NUANCES YOU CAN'T CONVEY IN WRITING.

THANKS FOR THE REFLECTIVE DISC. IT'LL MAKE A GREAT BIRD DETERRENT.

OH!

THEN HOW ABOUT MAKING A VIDEO INSTEAD?

BIRDS STAYED AWAY, AND IT EVEN WORKED ON HANA.

THAT...

...LOOKS LIKE A SOFTCORE PORN DVD.

TAKANE SAIBARA BY YOUR SIDE

My Shins Might Be Broken but My Heart Is Not / The End

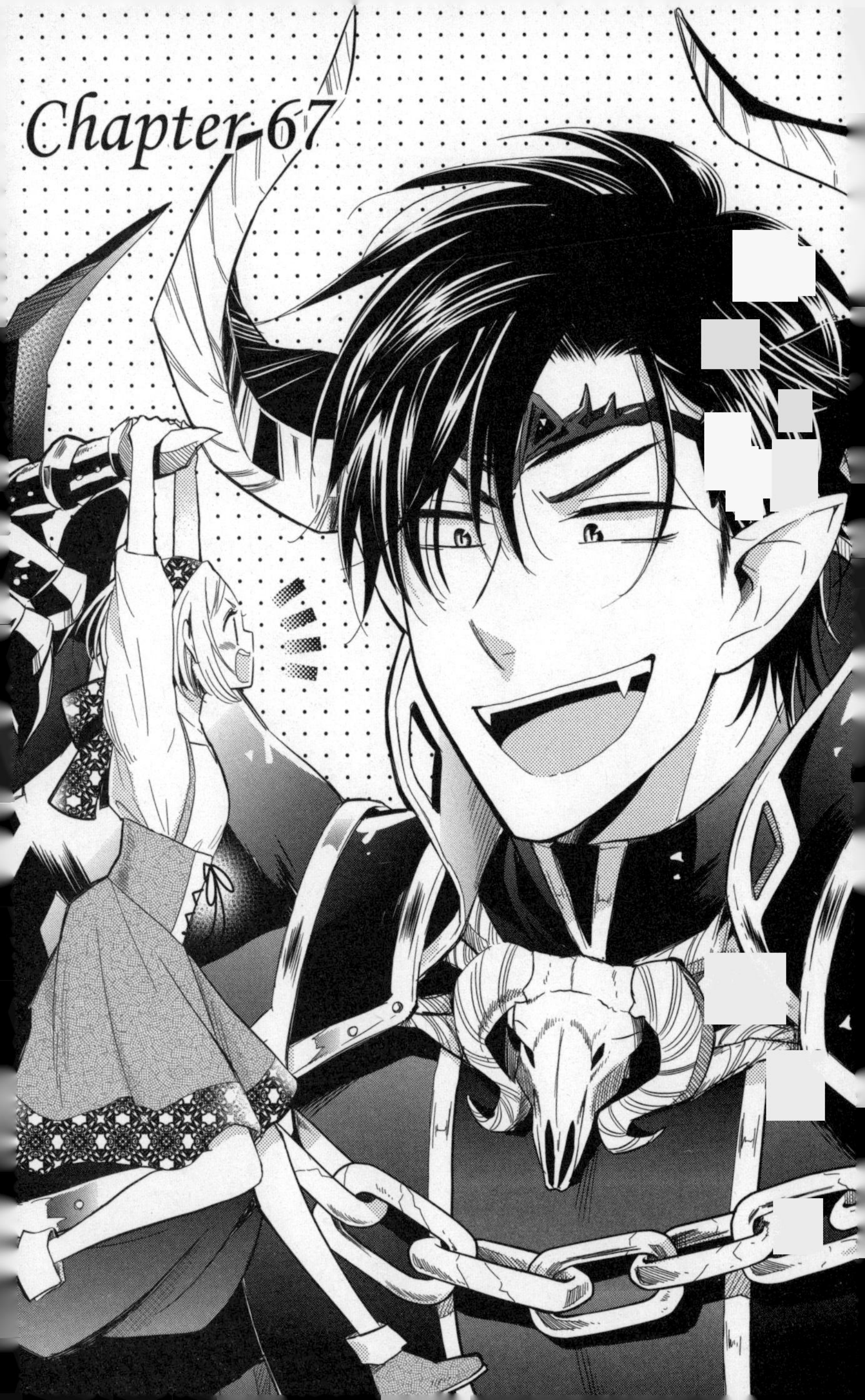
Chapter 67

ONCE UPON A TIME, THERE WAS A VILLAGE CALLED NONOMURA.
IT WAS AN ORDINARY, PEACEFUL VILLAGE.
BUT THEN ONE DAY, THE EVIL KING CAME AND TOOK AWAY THE VILLAGE CHIEF'S DAUGHTER.
WHAT?! WHY MY DAUGHTER ...?
FWOOO
YOUNG GIRL.
I'VE BROUGHT YOU HERE TO BE MY BRIDE. DON'T REFUSE ME.
INCH
DO AS I SAY AND I'LL ENSURE YOU DON'T REGRET IT.
INCH

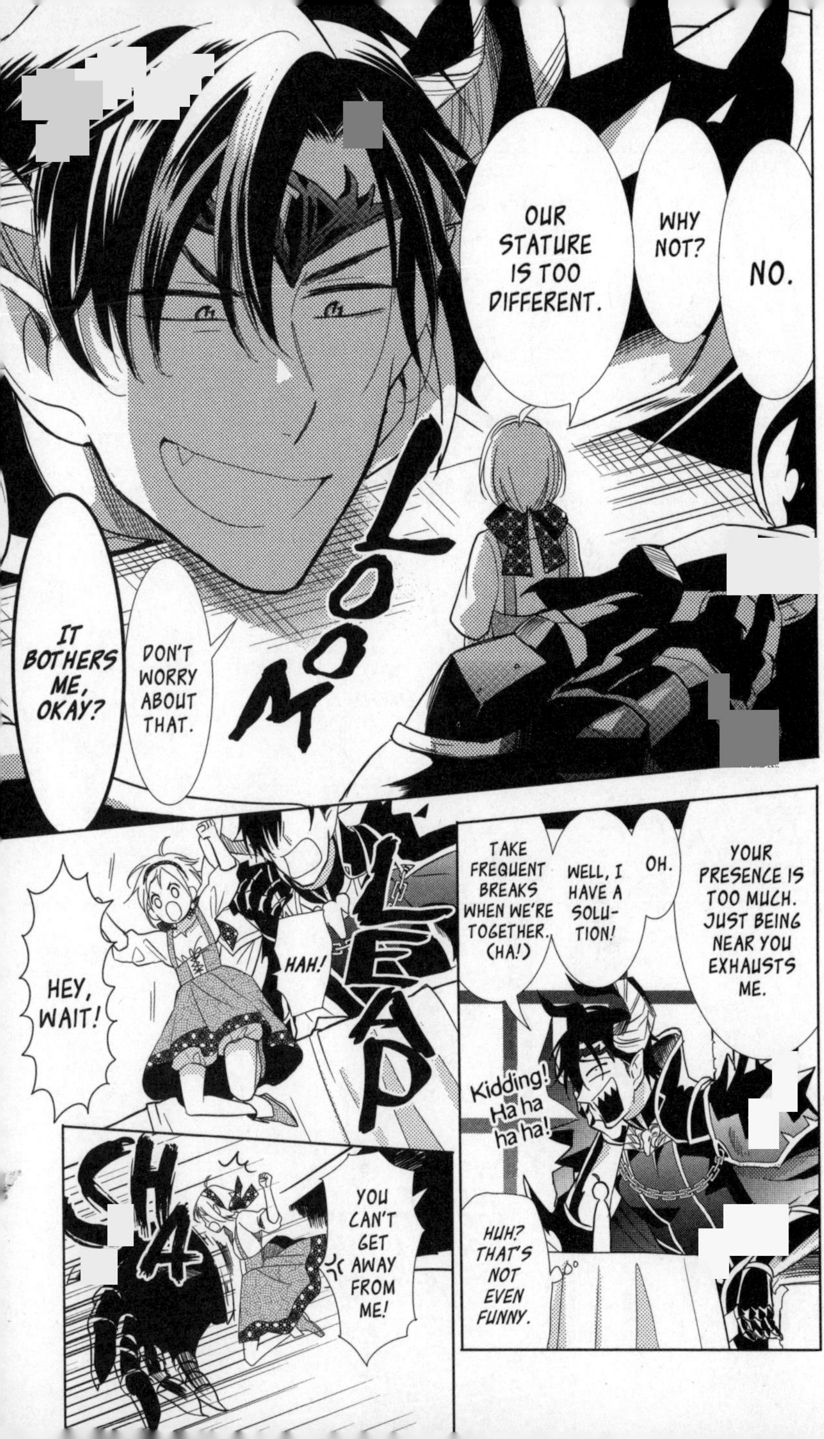
NO.
WHY NOT?
OUR STATURE IS TOO DIFFERENT.
LOOM
DON'T WORRY ABOUT THAT.
IT BOTHERS ME, OKAY?
YOUR PRESENCE IS TOO MUCH. JUST BEING NEAR YOU EXHAUSTS ME.
OH.
WELL, I HAVE A SOLUTION!
TAKE FREQUENT BREAKS WHEN WE'RE TOGETHER. (HA!)
Kidding! Ha ha ha ha!
HUH? THAT'S NOT EVEN FUNNY.
LEAP
HAH!
HEY, WAIT!
CHA
YOU CAN'T GET AWAY FROM ME!

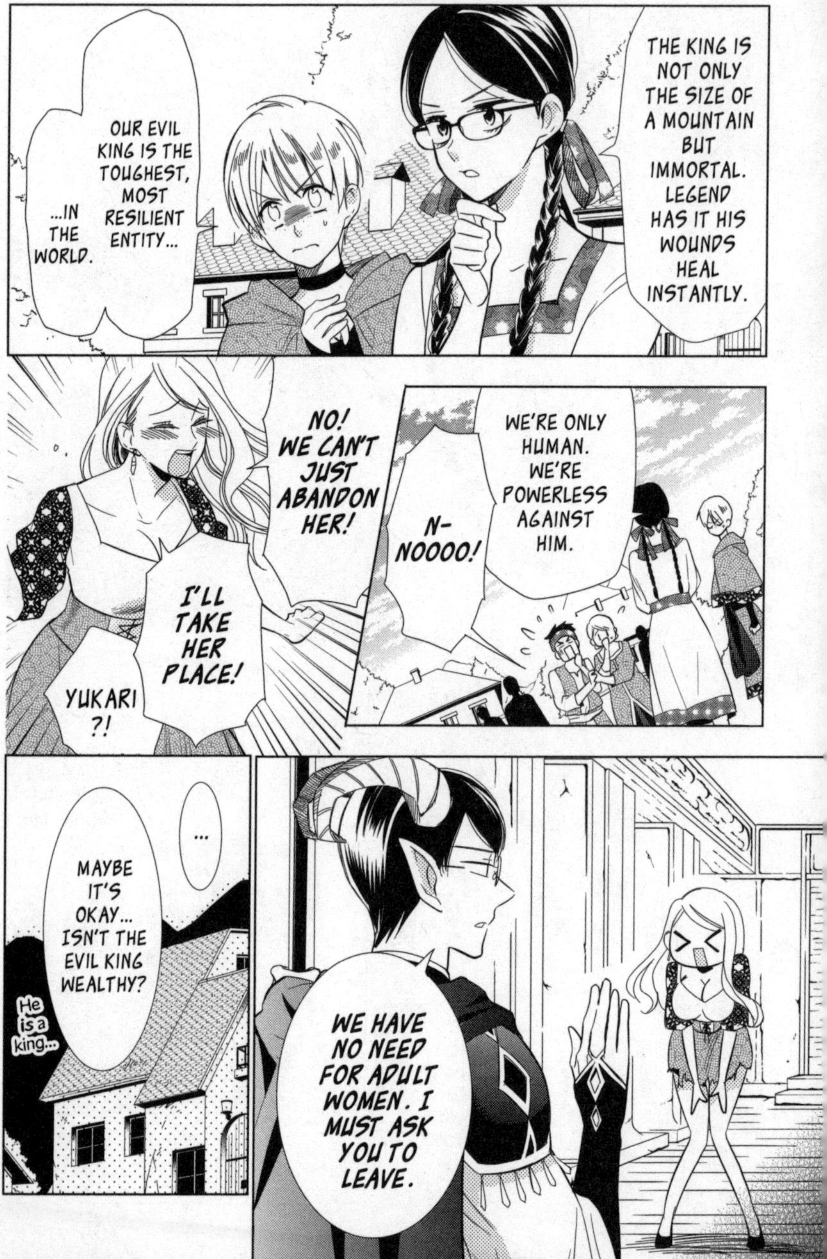
THE KING IS NOT ONLY THE SIZE OF A MOUNTAIN BUT IMMORTAL. LEGEND HAS IT HIS WOUNDS HEAL INSTANTLY.
OUR EVIL KING IS THE TOUGHEST, MOST RESILIENT ENTITY...
...IN THE WORLD.
WE'RE ONLY HUMAN. WE'RE POWERLESS AGAINST HIM.
N-NOOOO!
NO! WE CAN'T JUST ABANDON HER!
I'LL TAKE HER PLACE!
YUKARI ?!
...
MAYBE IT'S OKAY... ISN'T THE EVIL KING WEALTHY?
He is a king...
WE HAVE NO NEED FOR ADULT WOMEN. I MUST ASK YOU TO LEAVE.

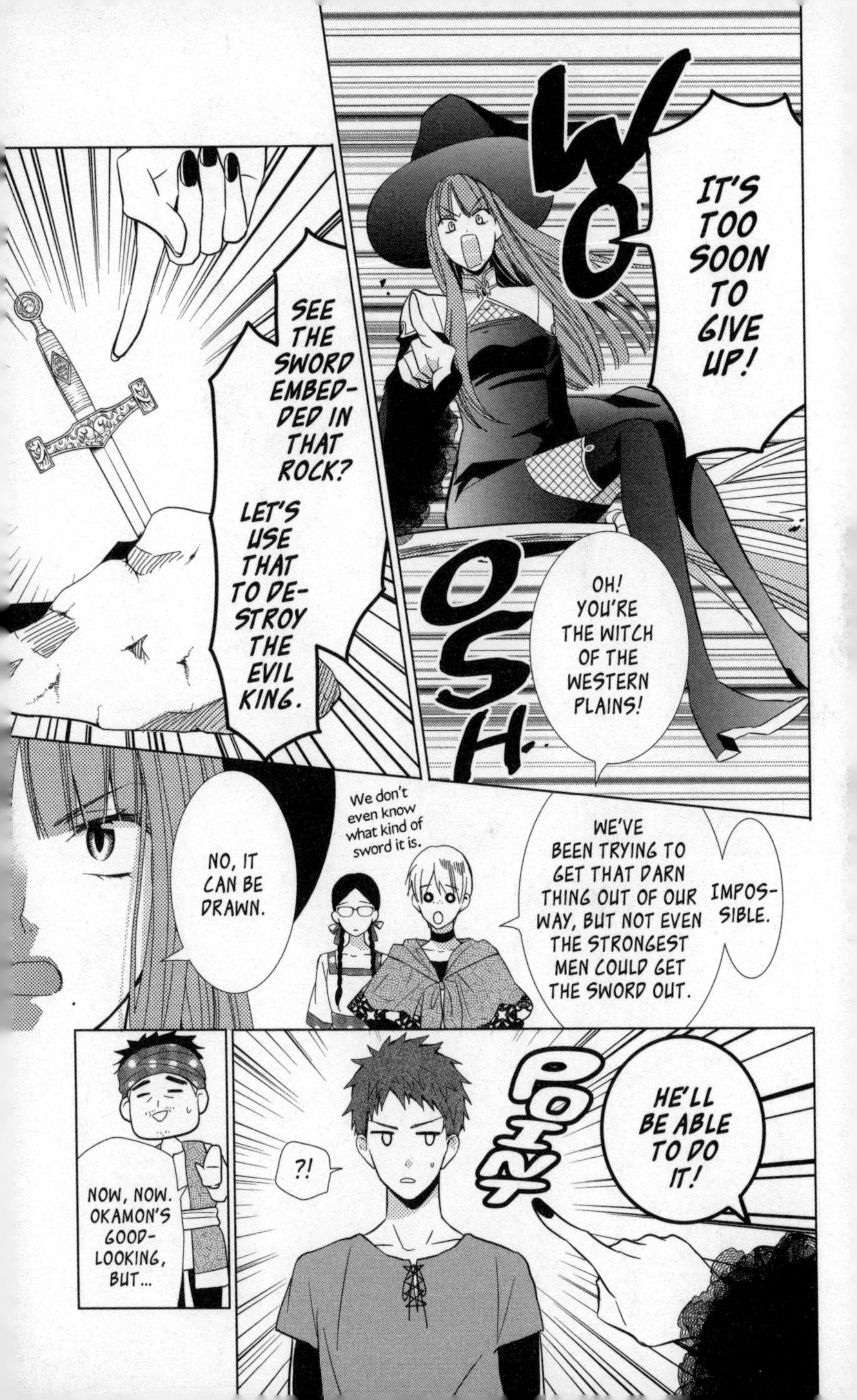
IT'S TOO SOON TO GIVE UP!
WOOSH
OH! YOU'RE THE WITCH OF THE WESTERN PLAINS!
SEE THE SWORD EMBEDDED IN THAT ROCK?
LET'S USE THAT TO DESTROY THE EVIL KING.
IMPOSSIBLE.
WE'VE BEEN TRYING TO GET THAT DARN THING OUT OF OUR WAY, BUT NOT EVEN THE STRONGEST MEN COULD GET THE SWORD OUT.
We don't even know what kind of sword it is.
NO, IT CAN BE DRAWN.
HE'LL BE ABLE TO DO IT!
POINT
?!
NOW, NOW. OKAMON'S GOOD-LOOKING, BUT...

IGNORE HIM AND GIVE IT A TRY.

BESIDES, THE EVIL KING IS VERY STRONG-WILLED.

...UNTIL HE'S A BIT OLDER AND LESS INNOCENT, IT'LL BE TOO TOUGH FOR HIM.

WHY ...?

IT CAME OUT!

WAIT, IS THAT...?

THE HOLY SWORD, "RESERVED FOR CHILDHOOD FRIENDS"!

To be wielded exclusively by childhood friends

OKAMON, THERE'S SOMETHING WRITTEN ON THE BACK!

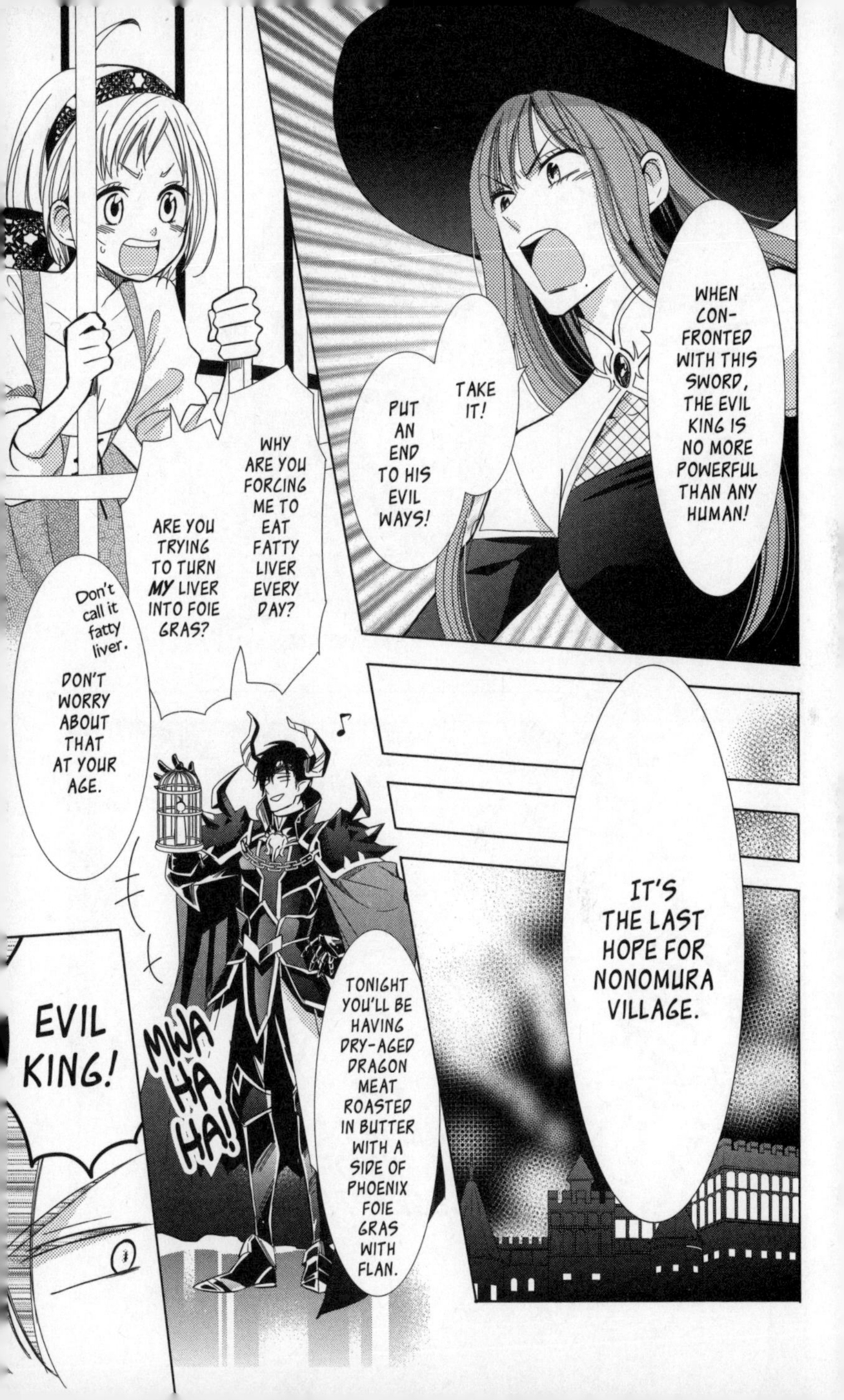
WHEN CON-FRONTED WITH THIS SWORD, THE EVIL KING IS NO MORE POWERFUL THAN ANY HUMAN!
TAKE IT!
PUT AN END TO HIS EVIL WAYS!
WHY ARE YOU FORCING ME TO EAT FATTY LIVER EVERY DAY?
ARE YOU TRYING TO TURN *MY* LIVER INTO FOIE GRAS?
Don't call it fatty liver.
DON'T WORRY ABOUT THAT AT YOUR AGE.
IT'S THE LAST HOPE FOR NONOMURA VILLAGE.
TONIGHT YOU'LL BE HAVING DRY-AGED DRAGON MEAT ROASTED IN BUTTER WITH A SIDE OF PHOENIX FOIE GRAS WITH FLAN.
MWA HA HA HA!
EVIL KING!

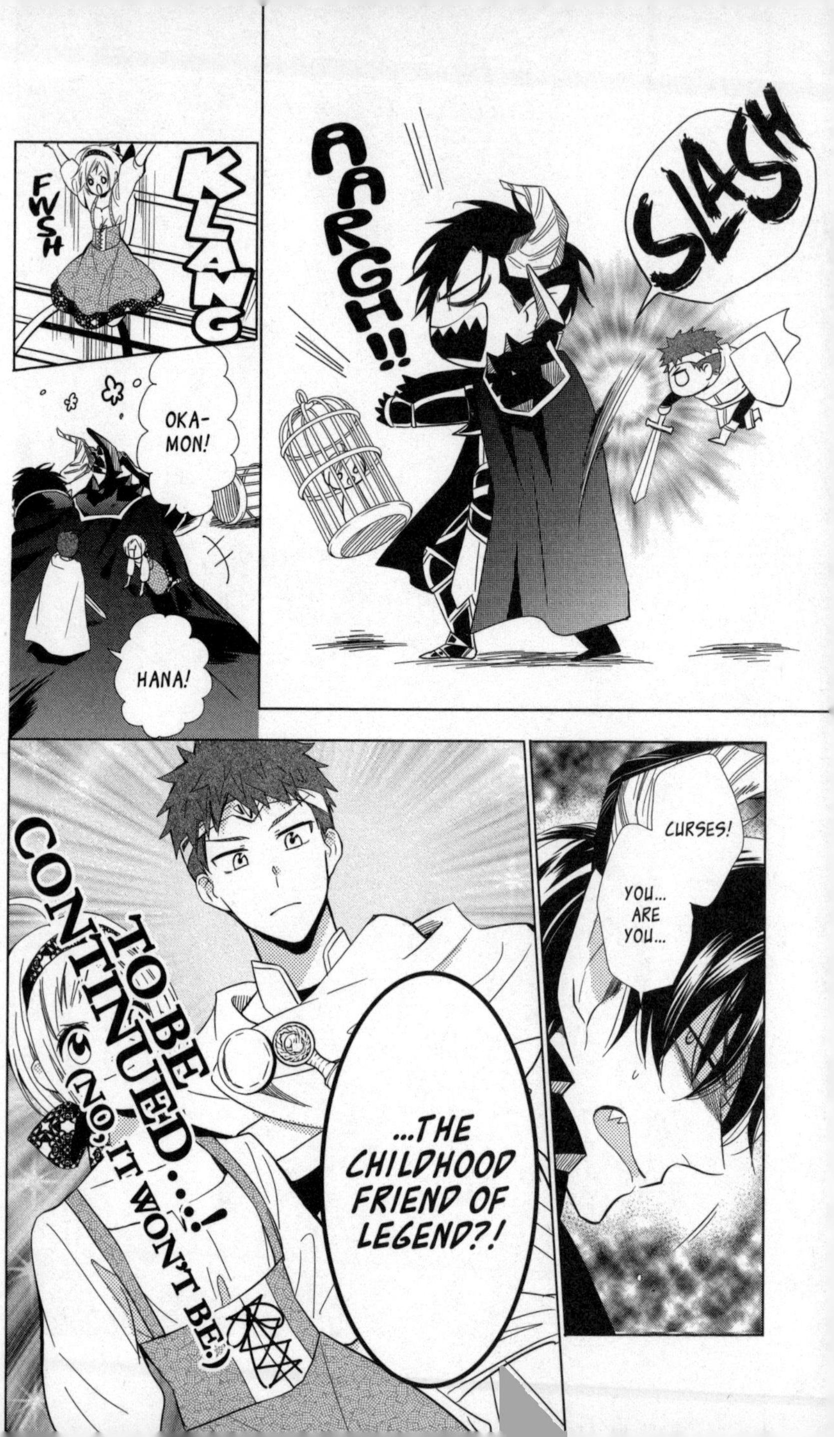
SLASH
AARGH!!
KLANG
FWSH
OKA-MON!
HANA!
CURSES!
YOU... ARE YOU...
...THE CHILDHOOD FRIEND OF LEGEND?!
TO BE CONTINUED...!
(NO, IT WON'T BE.)

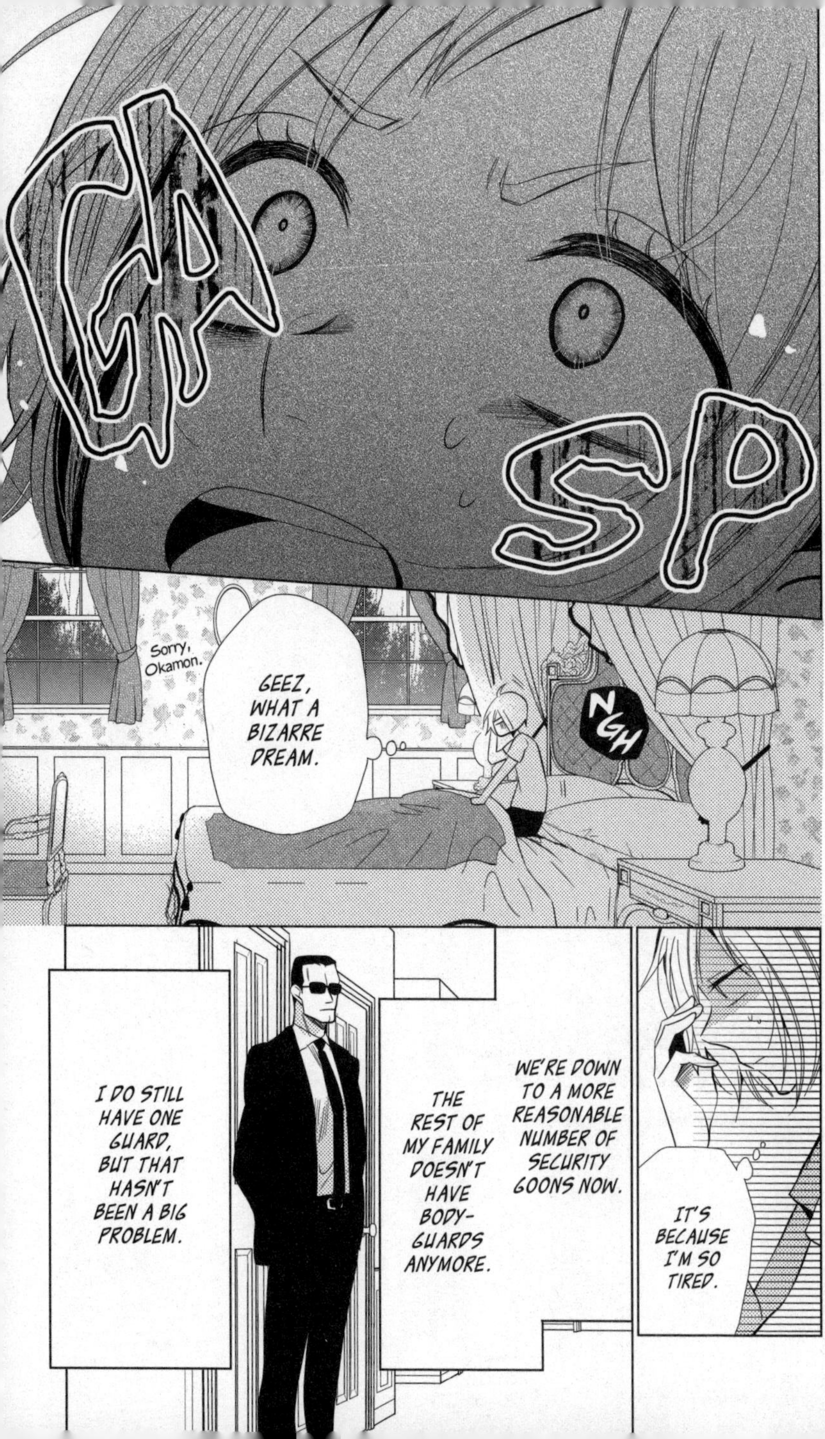
GA
SP
NGH
GEEZ, WHAT A BIZARRE DREAM.
Sorry, Okamon.
IT'S BECAUSE I'M SO TIRED.
WE'RE DOWN TO A MORE REASONABLE NUMBER OF SECURITY GOONS NOW.
THE REST OF MY FAMILY DOESN'T HAVE BODY-GUARDS ANYMORE.
I DO STILL HAVE ONE GUARD, BUT THAT HASN'T BEEN A BIG PROBLEM.

AND HAVE SOME FOIE GRAS WHILE YOU'RE AT IT, OKAY?

IN HIS HOSPITAL ROOM, JUST THE TWO OF US...

CRUNK

JUST BE HONEST ABOUT IT AND YOU'LL FEEL WAY BETTER.

I'VE COLLECTED EVIDENCE TO PROVE IT.

LOOK, WE BOTH KNOW HOW YOU FEEL ALREADY.

THE NONSTOP PARADE OF GIFTS THAT SCREAM, "LOOK AT ME, I'M HERE!"...

BUT... THAT'S THE FIFTH SERVING...

...HE GRILLED ME LIKE A DETECTIVE TRYING TO FORCE A CRIMINAL TO CONFESS.

EVERY SINGLE DAY...

I SPEND ALL MY TIME TAKING CARE OF ROSES.

MY STOMACH FEELS LIKE LEAD.

IT'S MENTALLY EXHAUSTING.

NOT REMOTE-LY.

ARE YOU OKAY?

HANA?

I'M SERIOUSLY REACHING MY LIMIT HERE.

ZOD

THE OLD MAN?

Second semester starts now!

DONNG

DONG

DONG

DONG

NOT EXACTLY.

TIRED FROM TOO MANY DATES?

WELL... HE'S BEEN PURSUING ME NONSTOP LATELY.

HUH? WHAT'S GOING ON?

HE DIDN'T WANT ANYONE FEELING SORRY FOR HIM, SO HE SAID NOT TO TELL ANYBODY.

YOU DIDN'T TELL US!

HE'S BEEN IN THE HOSPITAL.

DUN DUN DA DA DUN DA DA DUN DADA

O-OF COURSE! THIS MUST ALL BE FROM FRUSTRATION!

That's gotta be it!

MAYBE HE'S DEPRESSED 'CAUSE HIS ACTIVITIES ARE RESTRICTED.

DID YOU KNOW, OKAMON?

HE'S NOT GIVING ME A CHOICE!

THAT'S HOW YOU FEEL, BUT YOU'RE STILL HANGING OUT WITH HIM.

GOSH...

YEAH.

What's with this guy?

!!!

SHE ASSIGNED DARTH VADER AS HIS RINGTONE...?!

TAKANE?

OH, IT'S TAKANE.

RUMMAGE

*Naka means "medium."

Shame on me. I had too much time on my hands and fell back to sleep.

Who are you?

I'm **Naka**ne.*

The rational one who knows my own flaws.

This is Hikune. He's the delicate one who's overwhelmed by his own weakness. He's napping.

You're Takane.

The most stupid one.

Huh? You mean most **invincible**.

HE'S COMING HOME TODAY.

YEAH?

I got a call.

I hadn't heard.

8 : 26   64%

TAKANE   CONTACTS

I'm being discharged today.

IN ANY CASE... IT'S GREAT THAT HE'S HAD A SMOOTH RECOVERY.

MRMR

NONE OF US ARE STRONG ENOUGH TO CARRY A BIG GUY LIKE HIM.

WE'LL HAVE TO CARRY HIM UP THE FRONT STEPS IN HIS WHEELCHAIR.

I'd throw my back out.

MRMR

Now that you mention it...

OH...

...HE MUST STILL BE USING A WHEELCHAIR, RIGHT?

HE SAID HE DIDN'T NEED ANYTHING, BUT...

WORSTCASE SCENARIO, HE MAY HAVE TO SLEEP IN THE GARAGE.

YEAH, BUT WE WON'T ALWAYS ALL BE HOME.

IF THE FOUR OF US WORK TOGETHER, WE SHOULD BE ABLE TO MANAGE.

I GUESS WE HAVE TO.

MR MR

We have extra rooms.

IF HE CAN'T GO UP THE STAIRS, WHY DON'T WE LET HIM USE A SPARE ROOM DOWN HERE?

THERE HE IS!

WELCOME HOME...

Bodyguard

GASP

CHAK

I KNOW! WHY DON'T WE GET THE SECURITY GUARD AND MR. MORIO TO HELP US...?

112

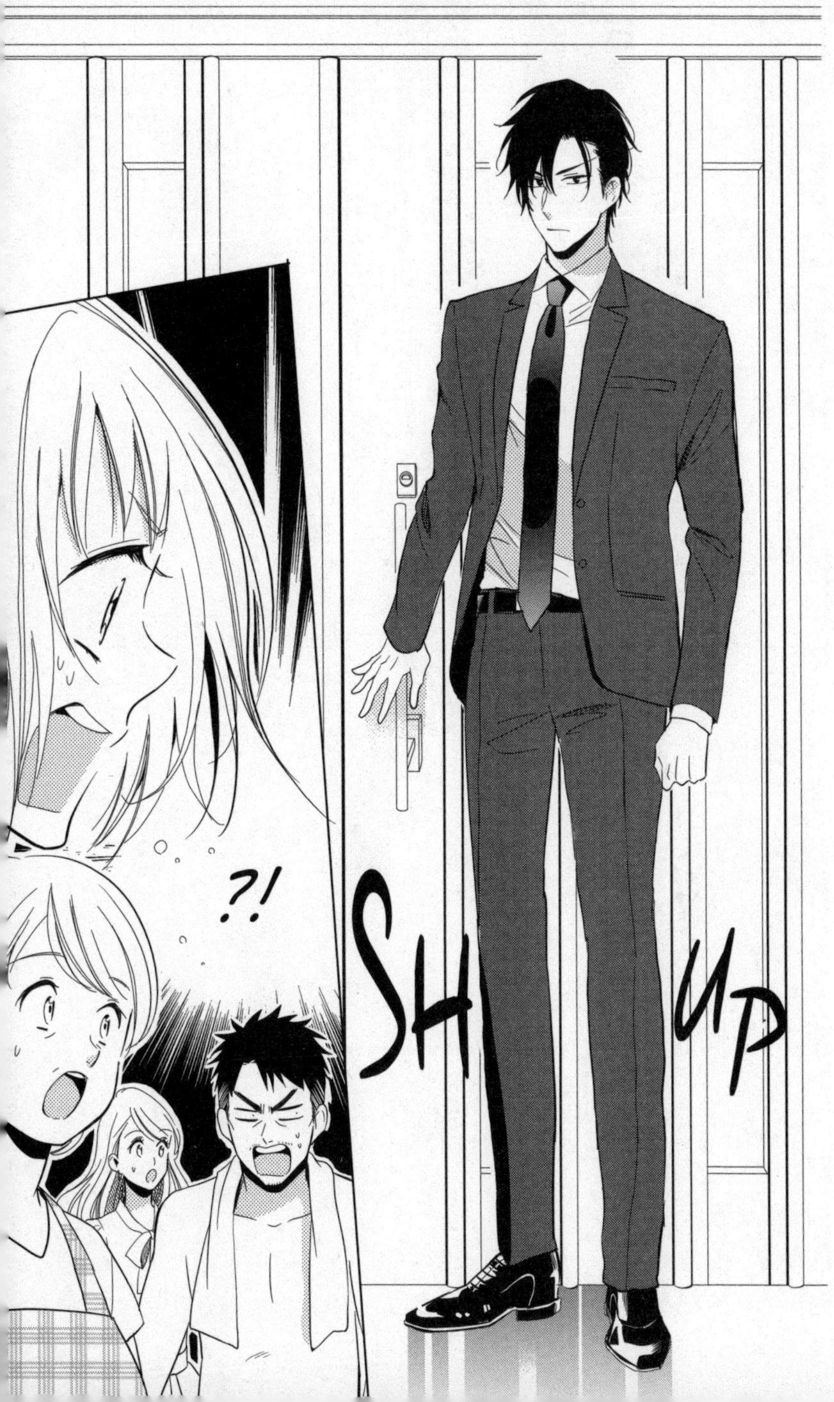
SHUP
?!

HEALED?

THAT'S WHAT HE SAID.

I'M FULLY HEALED.

BUT YOUR LEGS... WHERE ARE YOUR CASTS?

IT'S NICE TO BE BACK.

I SEE.

YOU'RE HEALED!

Y-YES...

HELLO!

Unknown workers

CHAK

?!

WELL, I'M EXTRA-ORDI-NARY.

THAT'S AMAZ-ING.

They're so fancy!

yay!

ONE BOX EACH?!

Goodbye!

SOME FRUIT TO THANK YOU FOR YOUR KINDNESS WHILE I WAS IN THE HOSPITAL.

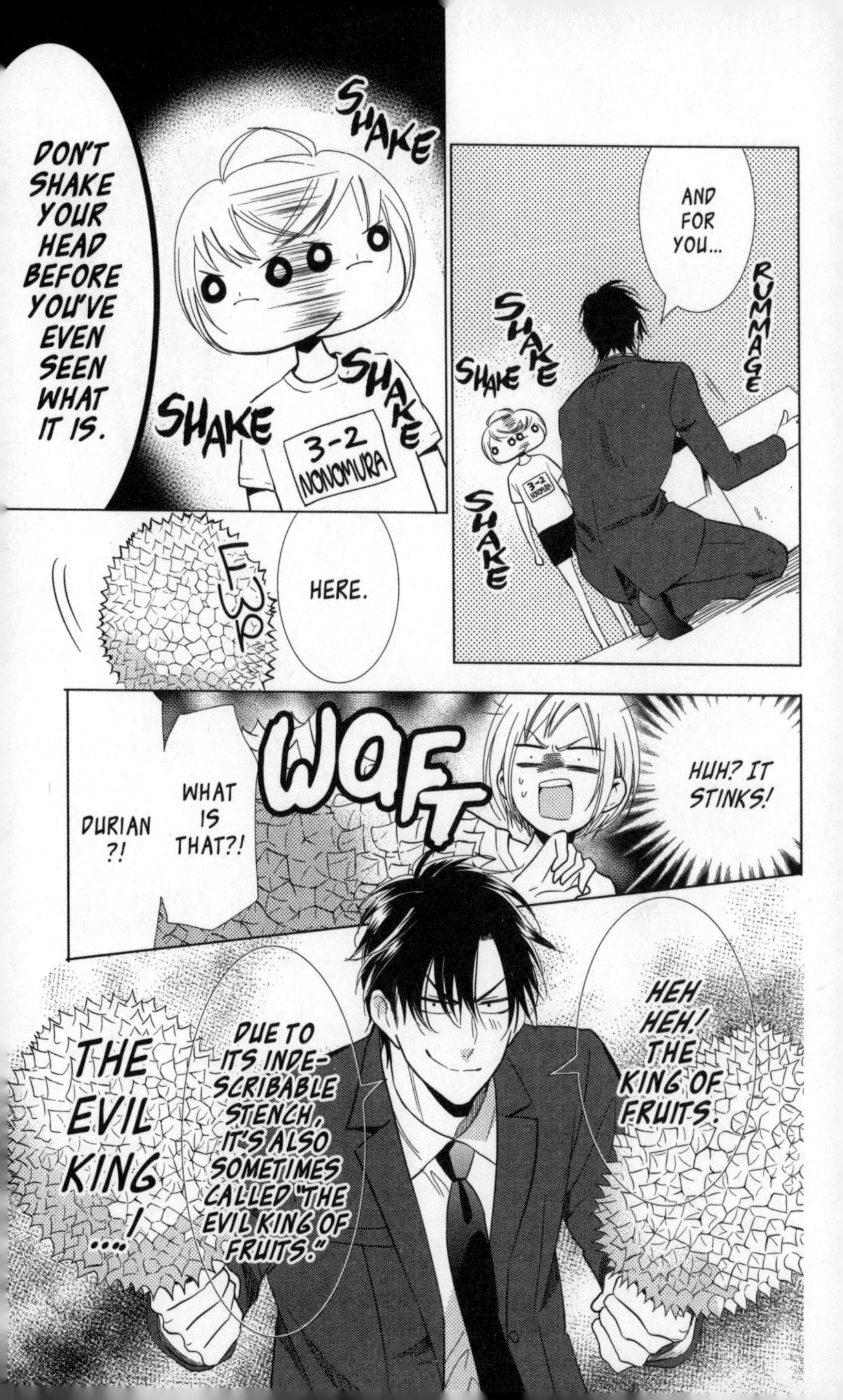
AND FOR YOU...
RUMMAGE
SHAKE
SHAKE
SHAKE
SHAKE
SHAKE
SHAKE
DON'T SHAKE YOUR HEAD BEFORE YOU'VE EVEN SEEN WHAT IT IS.
3-2 NONOMURA
HERE.
FWP
HUH? IT STINKS!
WAFT
WHAT IS THAT?!
DURIAN?!
HEH HEH! THE KING OF FRUITS.
DUE TO ITS INDE-SCRIBABLE STENCH, IT'S ALSO SOMETIMES CALLED "THE EVIL KING OF FRUITS."
THE EVIL KING ...!

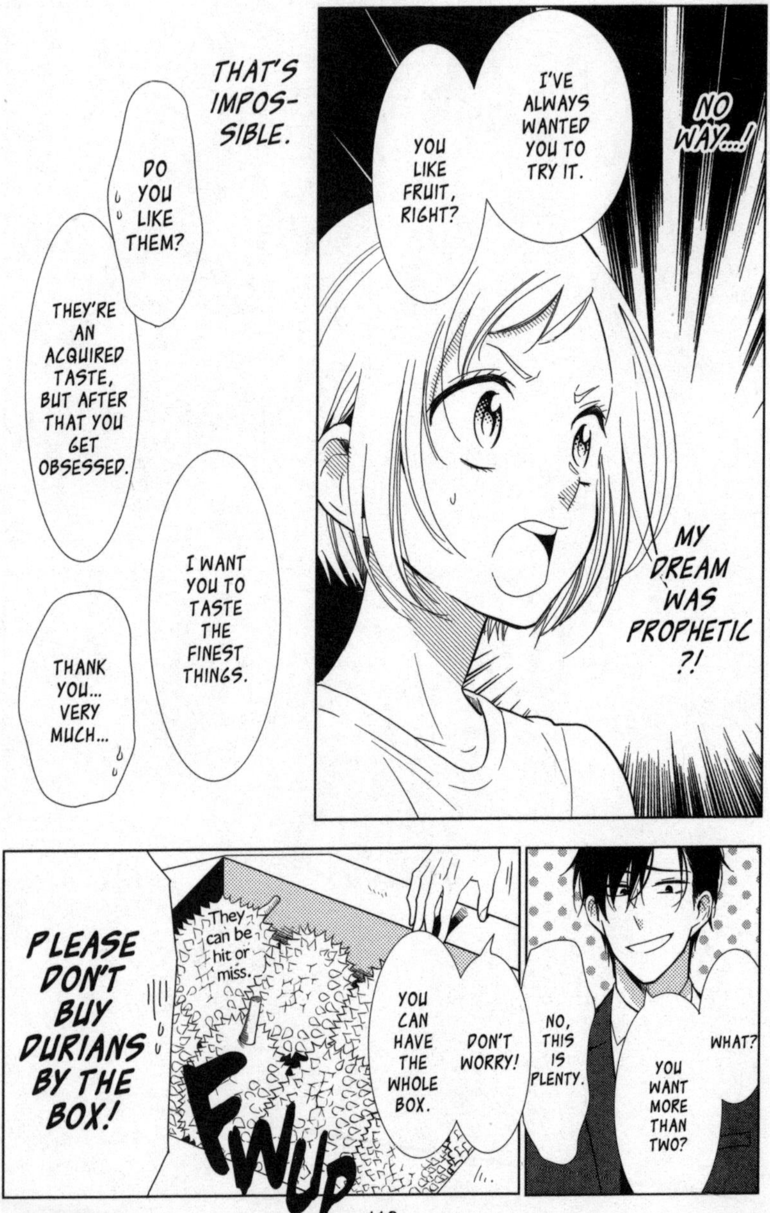
NO WAY...!
I'VE ALWAYS WANTED YOU TO TRY IT.
YOU LIKE FRUIT, RIGHT?
MY DREAM WAS PROPHETIC?!
THAT'S IMPOSSIBLE.
DO YOU LIKE THEM?
THEY'RE AN ACQUIRED TASTE, BUT AFTER THAT YOU GET OBSESSED.
I WANT YOU TO TASTE THE FINEST THINGS.
THANK YOU... VERY MUCH...
WHAT?
YOU WANT MORE THAN TWO?
NO, THIS IS PLENTY.
DON'T WORRY!
YOU CAN HAVE THE WHOLE BOX.
They can be hit or miss.
FWUP
PLEASE DON'T BUY DURIANS BY THE BOX!

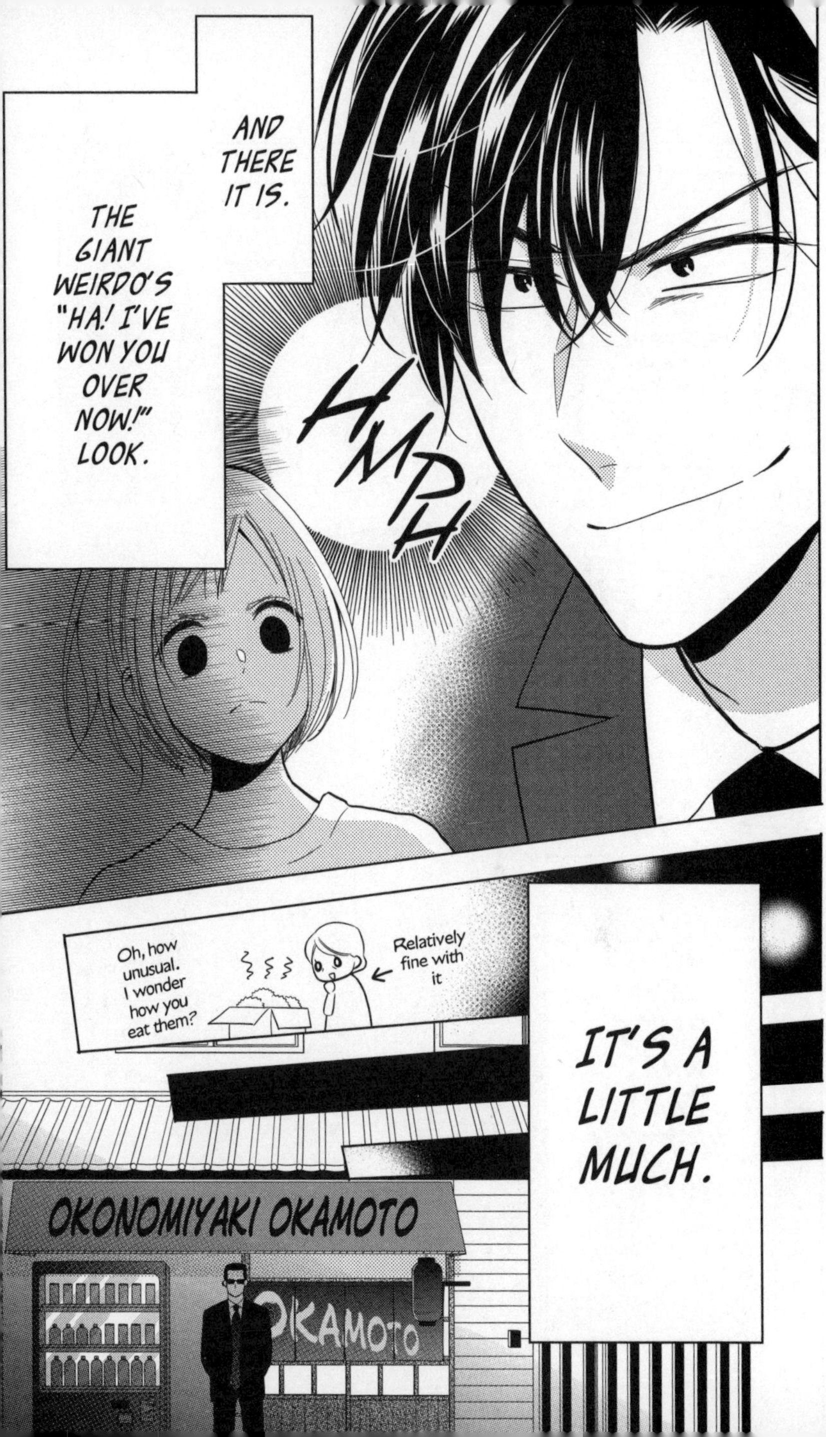
AND THERE IT IS.
THE GIANT WEIRDO'S "HA! I'VE WON YOU OVER NOW!" LOOK.
HMPH
IT'S A LITTLE MUCH.
Relatively fine with it
Oh, how unusual. I wonder how you eat them?
OKONOMIYAKI OKAMOTO
OKAMOTO

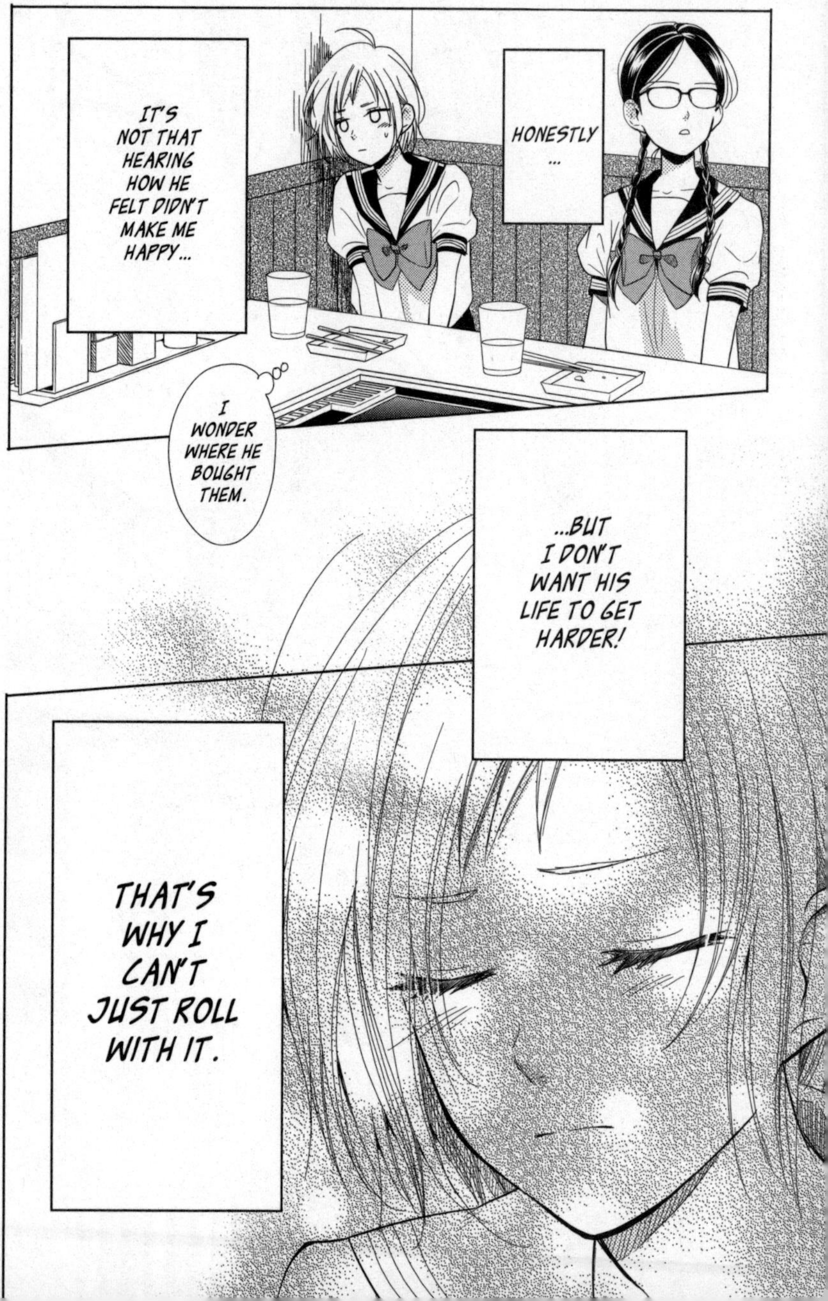
HONESTLY ...
IT'S NOT THAT HEARING HOW HE FELT DIDN'T MAKE ME HAPPY...
I WONDER WHERE HE BOUGHT THEM.
...BUT I DON'T WANT HIS LIFE TO GET HARDER!
THAT'S WHY I CAN'T JUST ROLL WITH IT.

SLAM

WE'RE OFF. COMING, HANA?

I'M STAYING AS LONG AS I CAN. MY LIVING ROOM REEKS.

REEKS?

IF WE TAKE THAT NEXT STEP AND THE WORLD EATS HIM ALIVE, THERE'LL BE NO GOING BACK.

DON'T SAY IT LIKE THAT!

RINO...

I'LL GO HOME TO HIM IF YOU WON'T!

...AND THEN YOU HAVE THE NERVE TO SAY YOU DON'T WANT TO GO HOME?

NOT ONLY ARE YOU LIVING WITH HIM, BUT YOU MADE HIM ADMIT HE LOVES YOU...

WELL, AREN'T YOU THE LUCKY ONE.

YOU'VE HAD ENOUGH.

ANOTHER ONE!

DESPONDENT

I THINK WE CAN ASSUME HANA HAS GOOD REASONS FOR HOW SHE FEELS.

LOOK HOW EXHAUSTED SHE IS.

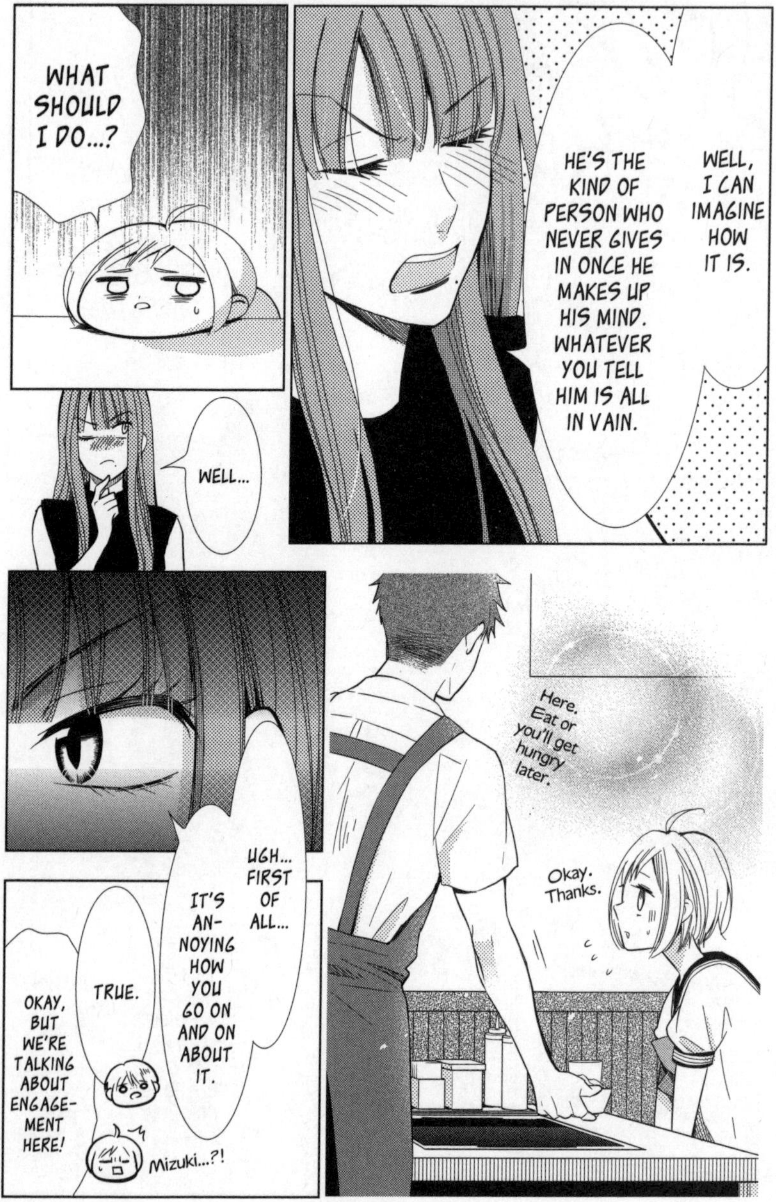
WELL, I CAN IMAGINE HOW IT IS.
HE'S THE KIND OF PERSON WHO NEVER GIVES IN ONCE HE MAKES UP HIS MIND. WHATEVER YOU TELL HIM IS ALL IN VAIN.
WHAT SHOULD I DO...?
WELL...
Here. Eat or you'll get hungry later.
Okay. Thanks.
UGH... FIRST OF ALL...
IT'S ANNOYING HOW YOU GO ON AND ON ABOUT IT.
TRUE.
OKAY, BUT WE'RE TALKING ABOUT ENGAGEMENT HERE!
Mizuki...?!

I'LL GLADLY BE ON YOUR SIDE.

HEY, I'LL HELP YOU IF YOU'RE LOOKING FOR A WAY TO **NOT** GO OUT WITH HIM!

Are you saying you can't handle having something so smelly near you?

Huh? Leave it upstairs?

What are you talking about?

THAT STUFF...

...MAKES ME THINK TWICE.

YES.

SOMETHING VALUABLE.

SINCE HE'S BASICALLY A DECENT PERSON, HE WON'T TRY TO GET HIS WAY AT THE COST OF DESTROYING SOMETHING YOU HAVE.

IS THERE A WAY TO REIN HIM IN AT THIS POINT?

YEAH, EVEN HANA CAN'T STOP HIM.

THAT'S TRUE.

SOMETHING HANA HAS?

WELL...

HERE'S MY THEORY.

FOR EXAMPLE...

SILENCE

...A BOY-FRIEND.

THE "SORRY, BUT I HAVE A BOYFRIEND" SCENARIO?

OH!

IT'S A WAY OF SAYING "IT'S NOT ABOUT YOU."

JUST PRETEND YOU DO!

SILLY.

BUT I DON'T HAVE A BOYFRIEND.

YOU TWO GO WAY BACK, RIGHT?

HOW ABOUT IT?

HEY, SOUMA!

HOW ABOUT PRETENDING TO BE HER BOYFRIEND?

HANG ON!

I CAN'T ASK HIM TO DO THAT!!!

MIZUKI!

IT COULD TOTALLY WORK.

Ha ha ha!

SOUNDS GREAT!

Has a bit of a clue

Clueless

I FEEL LIKE...

EVEN IF IT IS TO TRICK TAKANE... RIGHT?!

RIGHT ?!

DON'T TAKE IT TOO SERIOUSLY. YOU JUST HAVE TO PRETEND.

Rino, the booze is making you say weird stuff.

It's mean, right?

Hana

I'M NOT SO SURE...

YOU'D BE DOING HER A FAVOR.

HIC

ZWAK

123

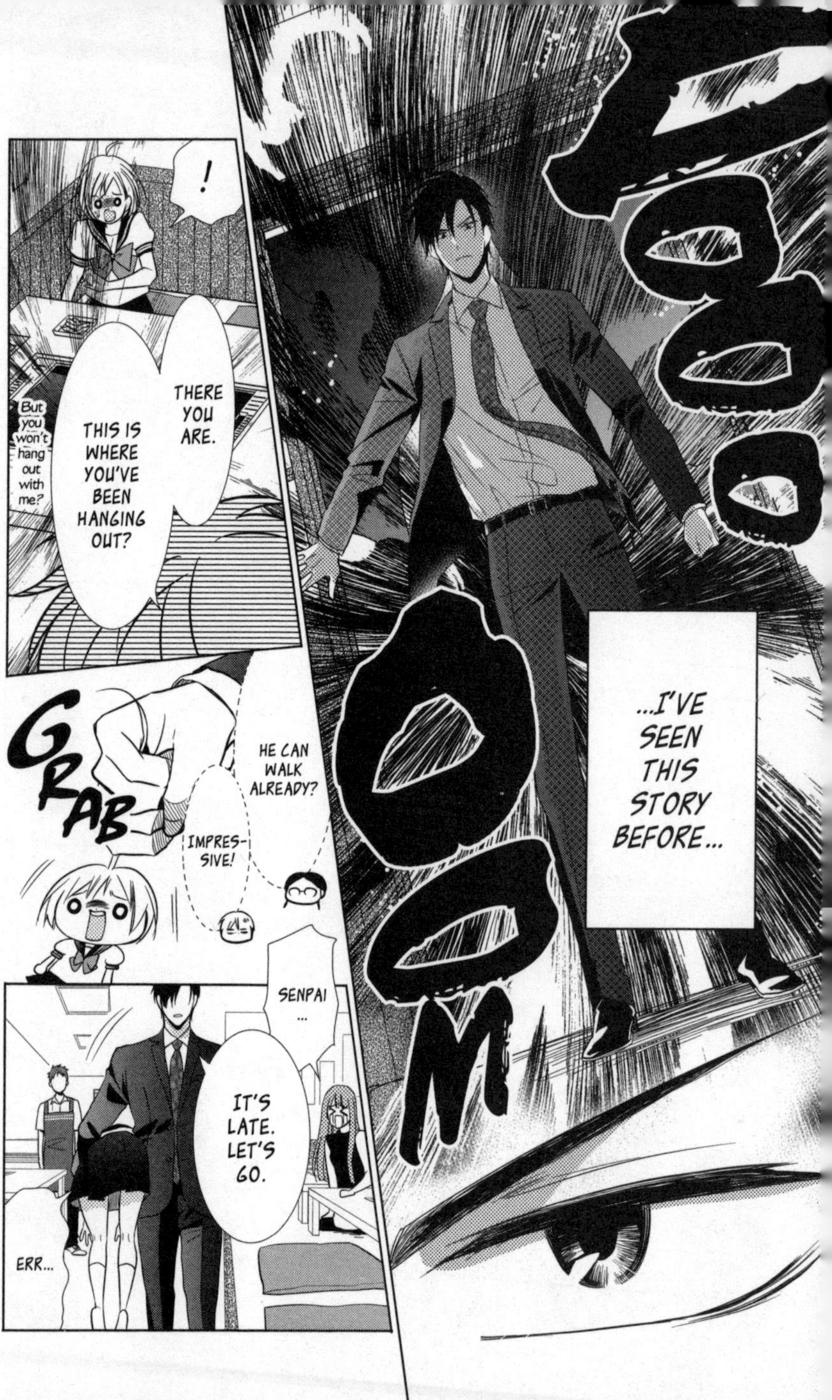

...I'VE SEEN THIS STORY BEFORE...
!
THERE YOU ARE.
THIS IS WHERE YOU'VE BEEN HANGING OUT?
But you won't hang out with me?
GRAB
HE CAN WALK ALREADY?
IMPRES-SIVE!
SENPAI...
IT'S LATE. LET'S GO.
ERR...

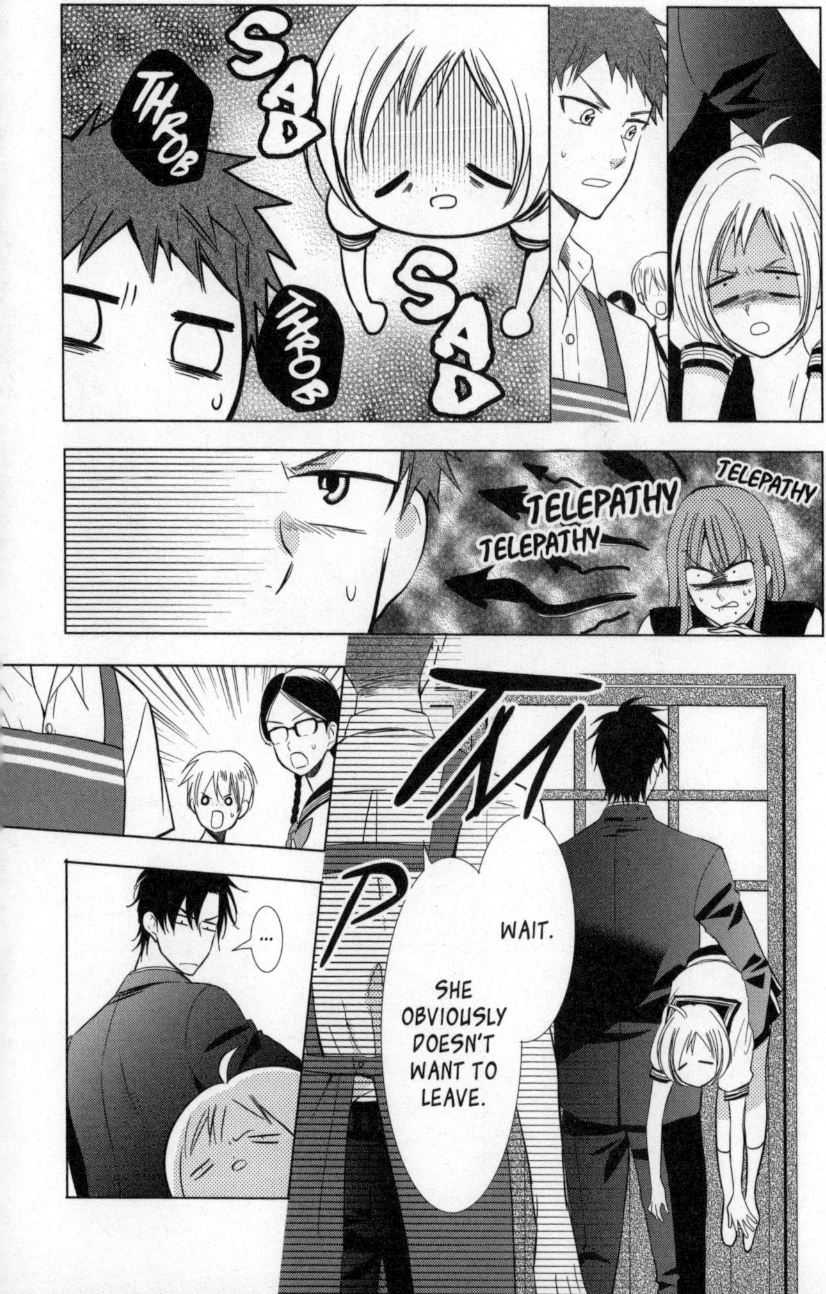
SAD
SAD
THROB
THROB
TELEPATHY
TELEPATHY
TELEPATHY
TMP
WAIT.
SHE OBVIOUSLY DOESN'T WANT TO LEAVE.
...

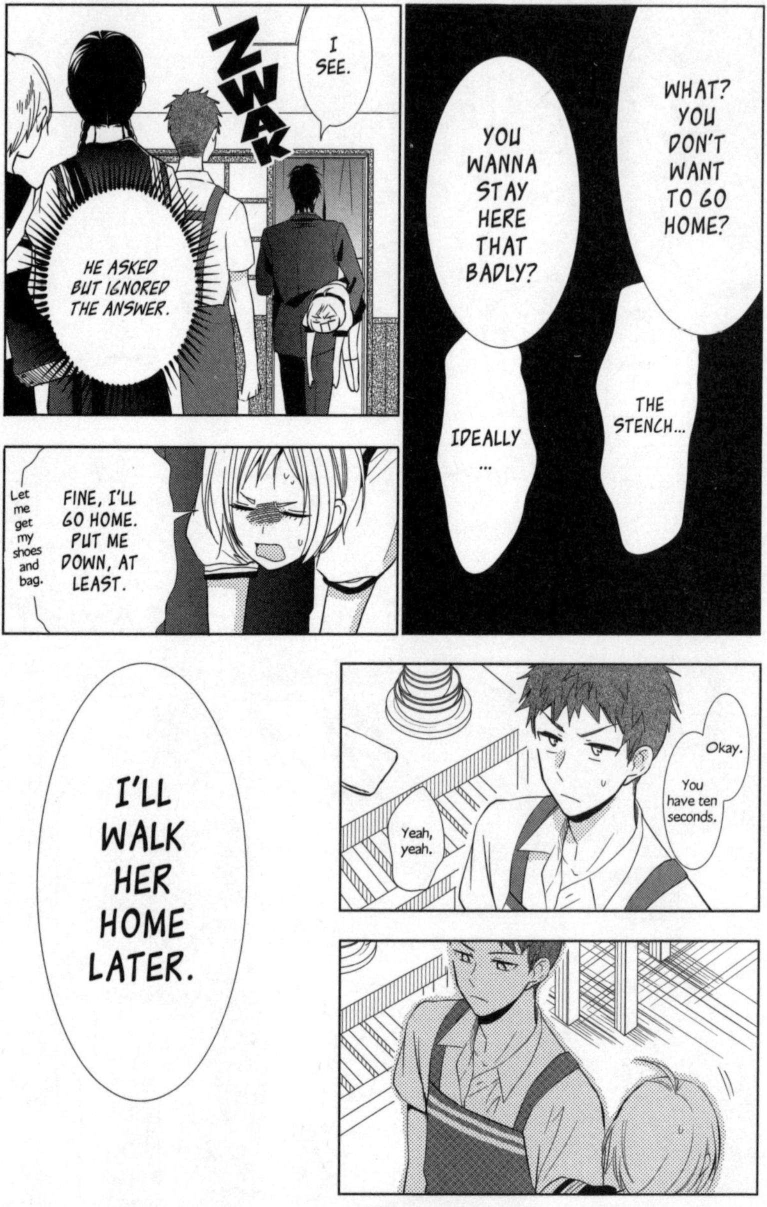
WHAT? YOU DON'T WANT TO GO HOME?
YOU WANNA STAY HERE THAT BADLY?
THE STENCH...
IDEALLY ...
I SEE.
ZWAK
HE ASKED BUT IGNORED THE ANSWER.
FINE, I'LL GO HOME. PUT ME DOWN, AT LEAST.
Let me get my shoes and bag.
Okay.
You have ten seconds.
Yeah, yeah.
I'LL WALK HER HOME LATER.

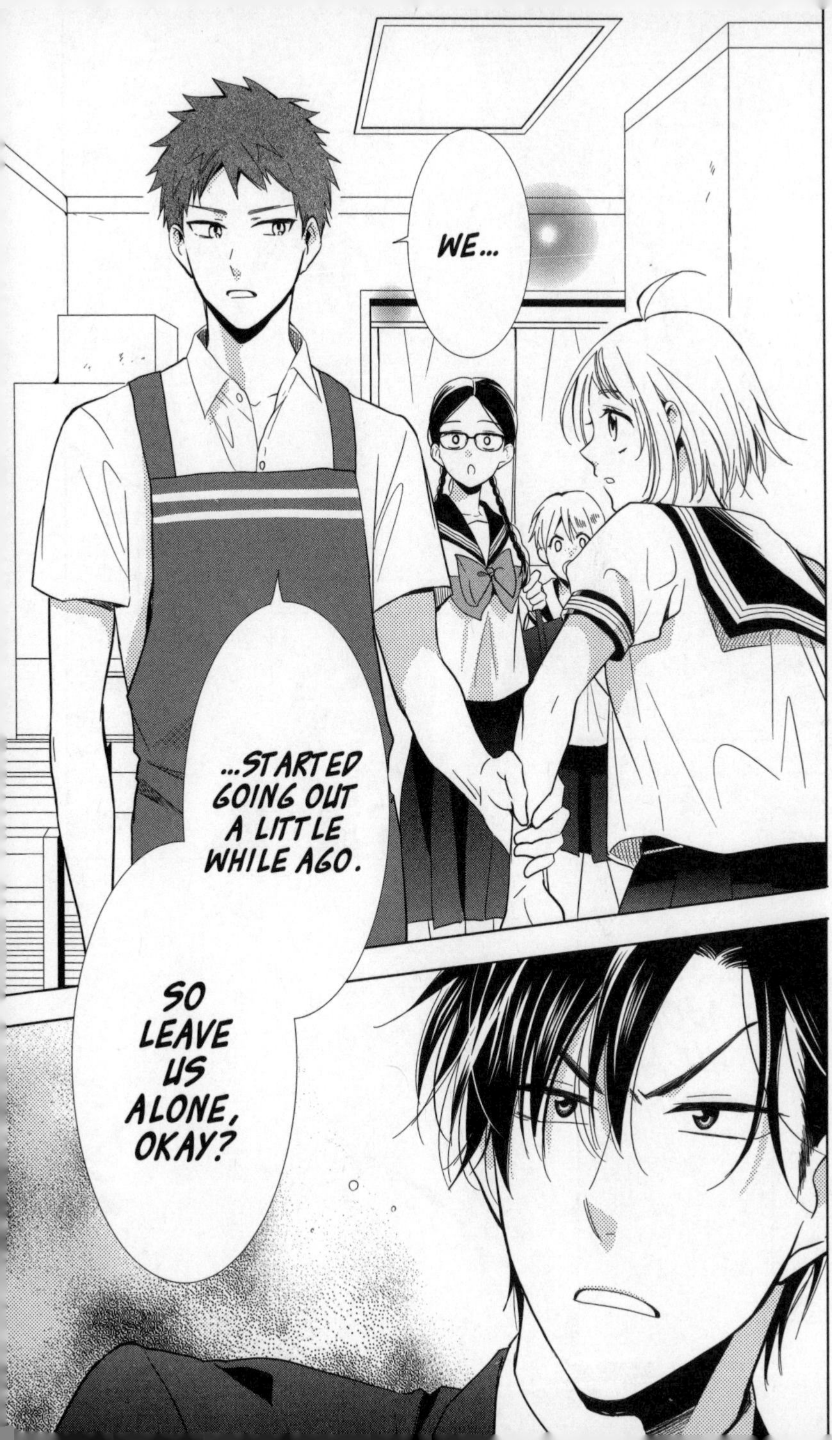
WE...
...STARTED GOING OUT A LITTLE WHILE AGO.
SO LEAVE US ALONE, OKAY?

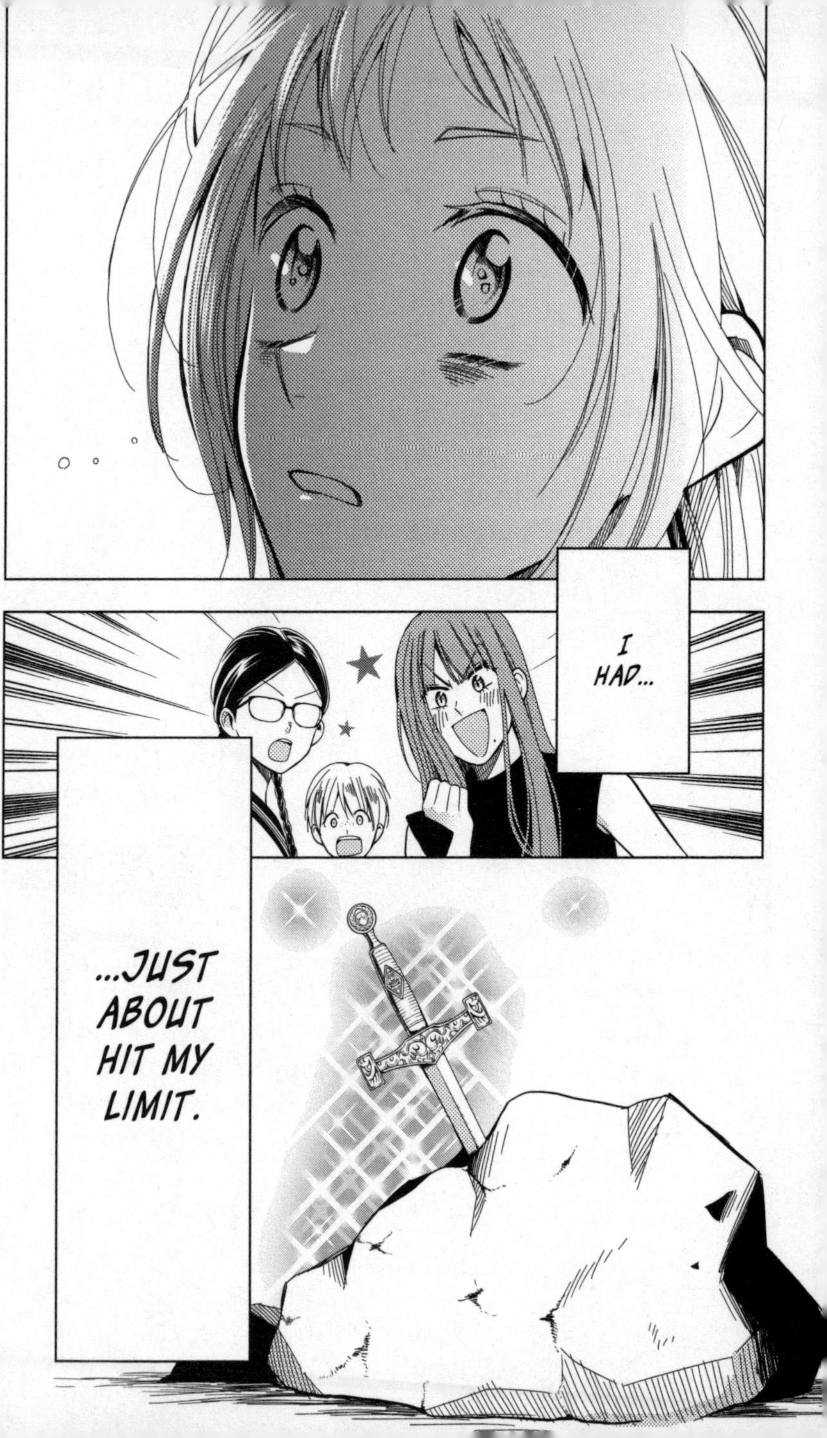
I HAD...
...JUST ABOUT HIT MY LIMIT.

Chapter 68

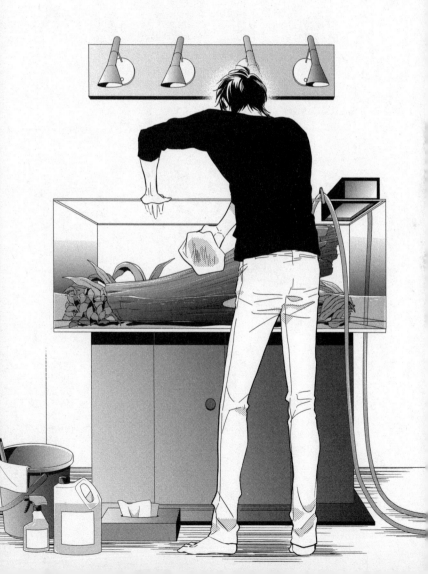

HOW ABOUT YOU AND I ENJOY SOME NICE QUIET TIME ALONE INSTEAD?

NOW, IT'S NOT COOL TO TRY AND BREAK UP THESE TWO YOUNG PEOPLE.

GRAB

SEN-PAI!

HUH?

SHALL WE HEAD OUT TOO?

I'LL WALK YOU TO HIM.

I'M OKAY. I HAVE MR. MORIO.

I'LL WALK YOU.

YEAH.

IT'S LATE, SO YOU REALLY SHOULD GO HOME.

HEY—!

EXCUSE ME! ONE SPECIAL MIX AND TWO WHISKEY AND SODAS, PLEASE.

BUT...

Even though it's stinky.

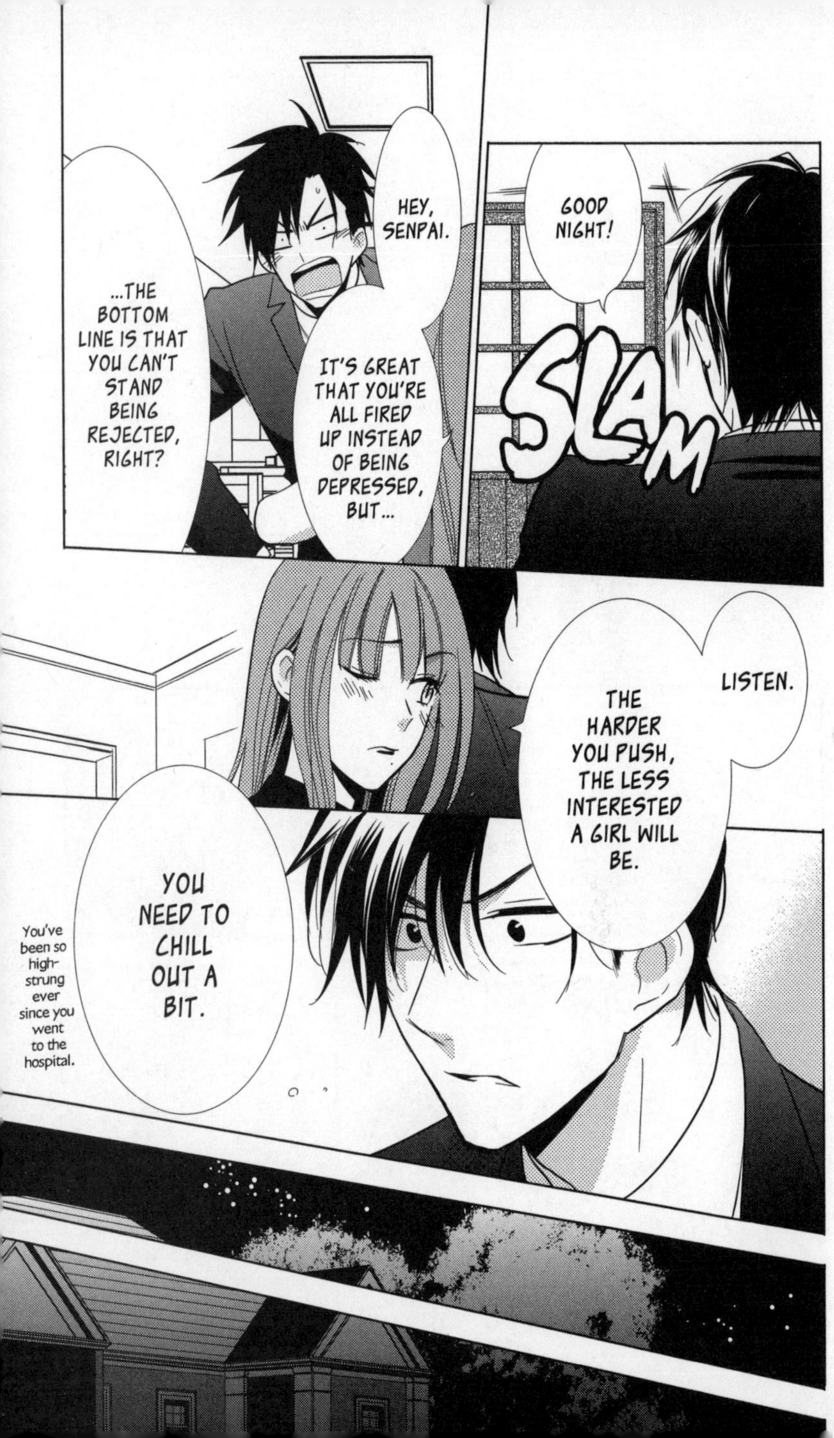
GOOD NIGHT!
SLAM
HEY, SENPAI.
IT'S GREAT THAT YOU'RE ALL FIRED UP INSTEAD OF BEING DEPRESSED, BUT...
...THE BOTTOM LINE IS THAT YOU CAN'T STAND BEING REJECTED, RIGHT?
LISTEN.
THE HARDER YOU PUSH, THE LESS INTERESTED A GIRL WILL BE.
YOU NEED TO CHILL OUT A BIT.
You've been so high-strung ever since you went to the hospital.

KEEP OUT

...

CONFRONTING HER NOW MIGHT NOT BE THE BEST IDEA...

...IS SHE THINKING...?

WHAT ON EARTH...

ALL WHILE I WAS HOSPI-TALIZED?

THANKS FOR SAVING ME. ♥

A likely scenario

...

AH

STARE

MAYBE I DO NEED TO CHILL OUT LIKE RINO SAID.

Morning.

I'M OFF.

HAVE A NICE DAY.

ADDING INSULT TO INJURY....

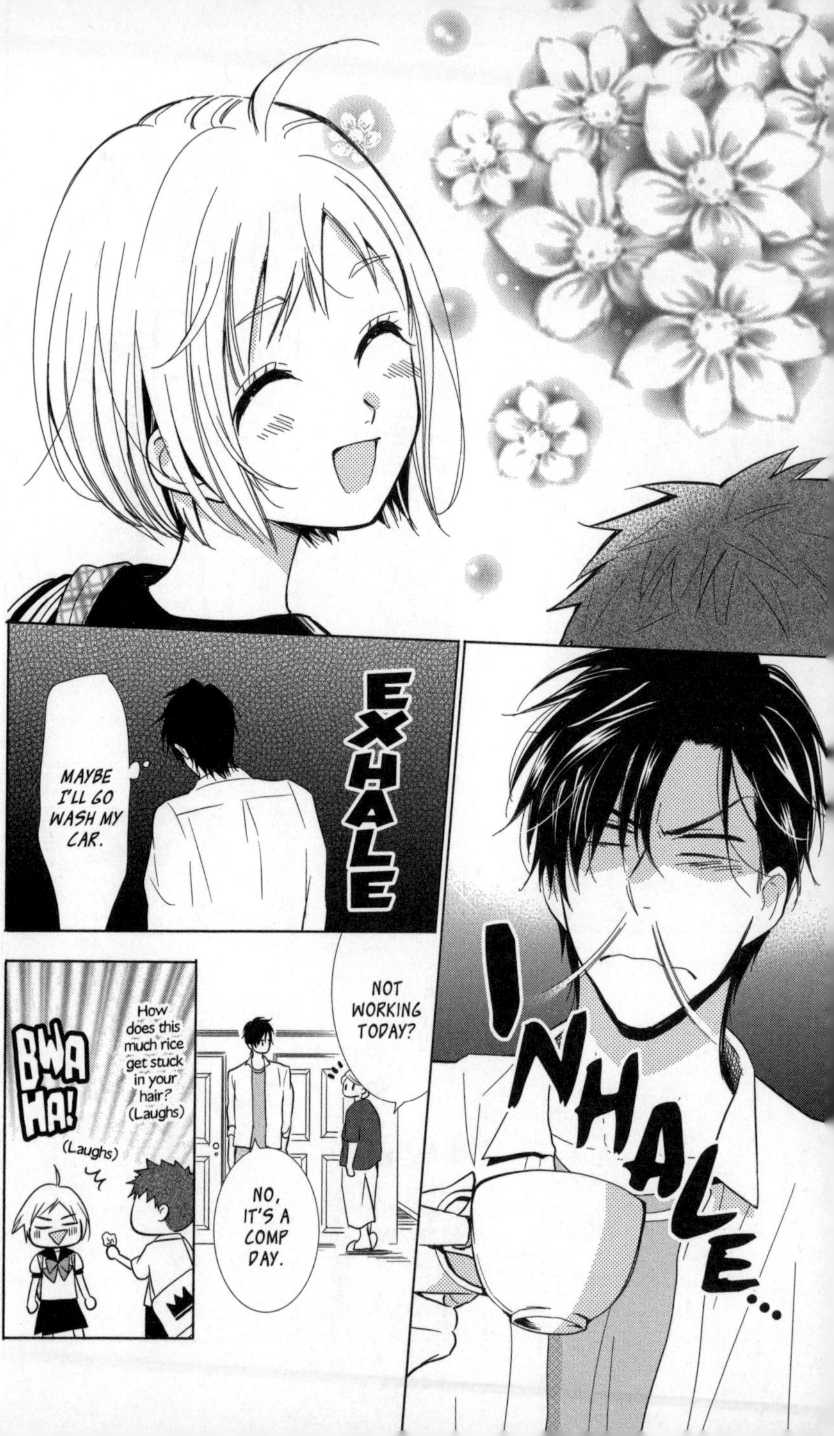
INHALE...
EXHALE
MAYBE I'LL GO WASH MY CAR.
NOT WORKING TODAY?
NO, IT'S A COMP DAY.
BWA HA!
How does this much rice get stuck in your hair? (Laughs)
(Laughs)

TECHNICALLY SPEAKING...

...IT DOESN'T MATTER WHO SHE GOES OUT WITH AS LONG AS I WIN HER IN THE END.

I'M NOT MAD AT ALL.

I'M NOT FRUS-TRATED AT ALL.

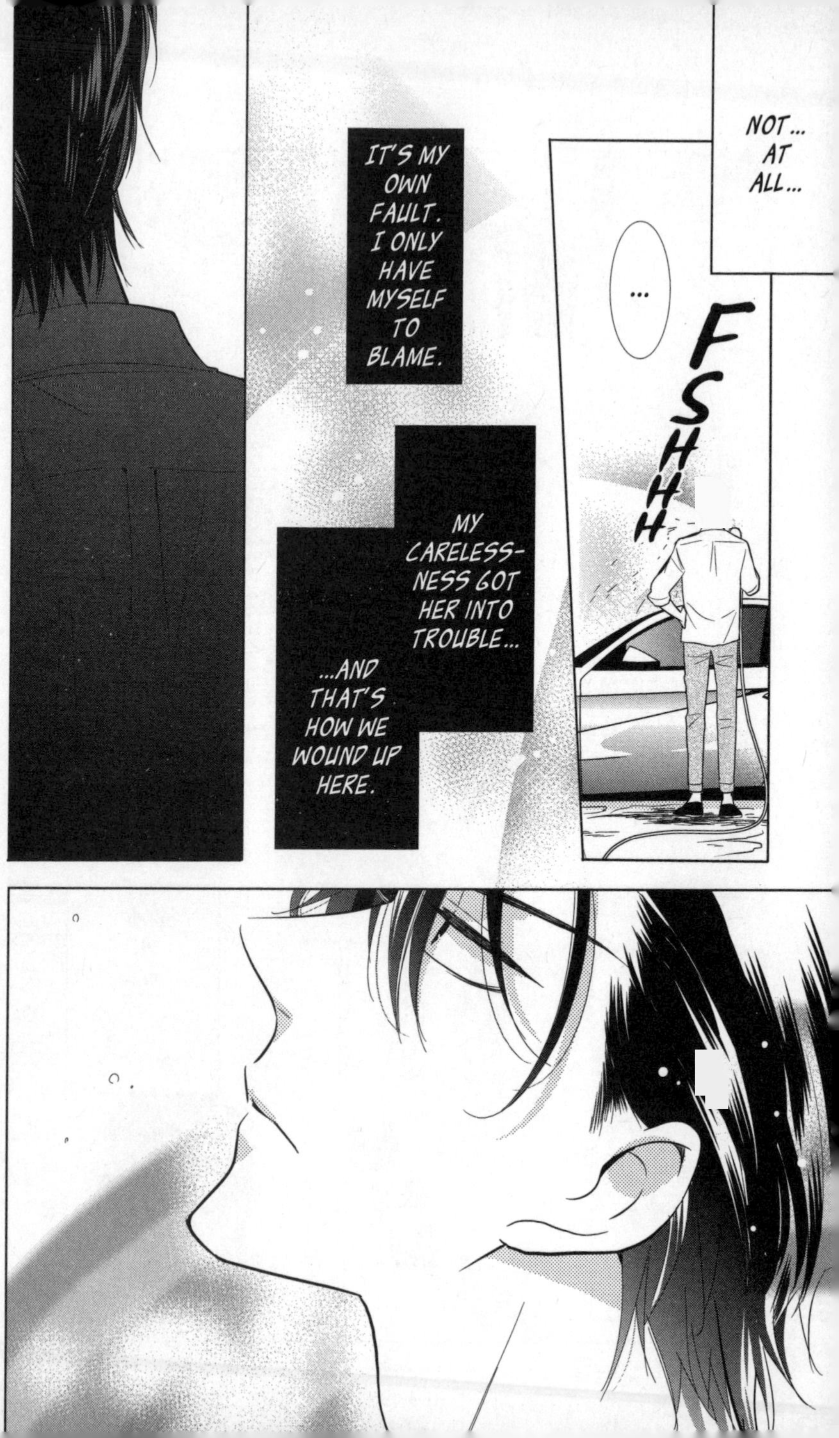
NOT... AT ALL...
...
FSHHHH
IT'S MY OWN FAULT. I ONLY HAVE MYSELF TO BLAME.
MY CARELESS-NESS GOT HER INTO TROUBLE...
...AND THAT'S HOW WE WOUND UP HERE.

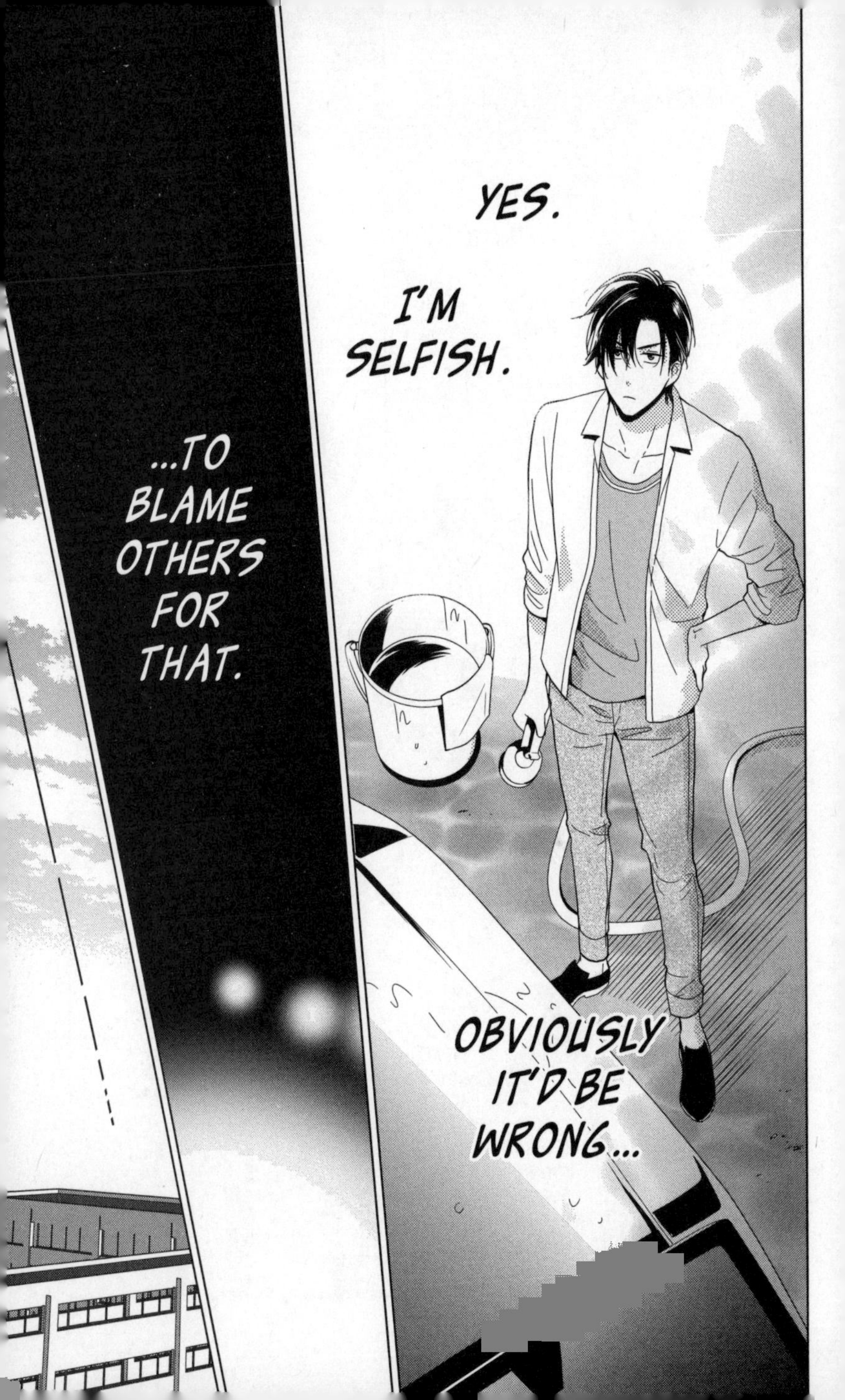
YES.
I'M SELFISH.
OBVIOUSLY IT'D BE WRONG...
...TO BLAME OTHERS FOR THAT.

ACTUALLY...

...HE'S BACK TO HIS NORMAL SELF, AMAZINGLY.

REALLY?

WOW, SO IT TOTALLY WORKED.

SO?

HOW'S HE BEEN ACTING?

BUT...

...LIKE I SAID BEFORE...

...AND SUDDENLY YOU'RE SLAMMING THE BRAKES?

I mean, huh?

YOU WERE GOING AFTER TAKANE FOR ALL YOU WERE WORTH...

MNCH MNCH

SAME HERE!

YOU KNOW, I WOULDN'T HAVE EXPECTED YOU TO BE THIS HESITANT ABOUT IT ALL.

138

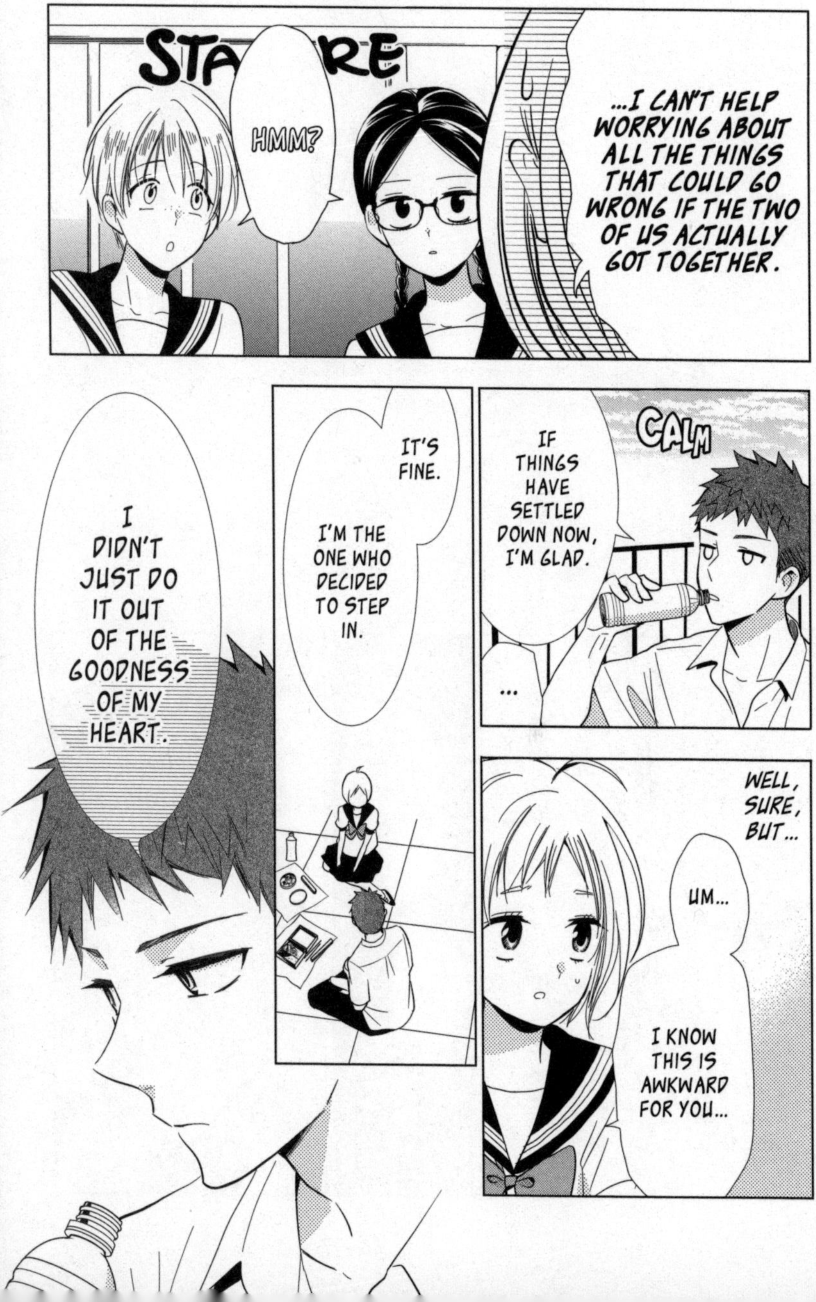

...I CAN'T HELP WORRYING ABOUT ALL THE THINGS THAT COULD GO WRONG IF THE TWO OF US ACTUALLY GOT TOGETHER.
HMM?
CALM
IF THINGS HAVE SETTLED DOWN NOW, I'M GLAD.
...
IT'S FINE.
I'M THE ONE WHO DECIDED TO STEP IN.
WELL, SURE, BUT...
UM...
I KNOW THIS IS AWKWARD FOR YOU...
I DIDN'T JUST DO IT OUT OF THE GOODNESS OF MY HEART.

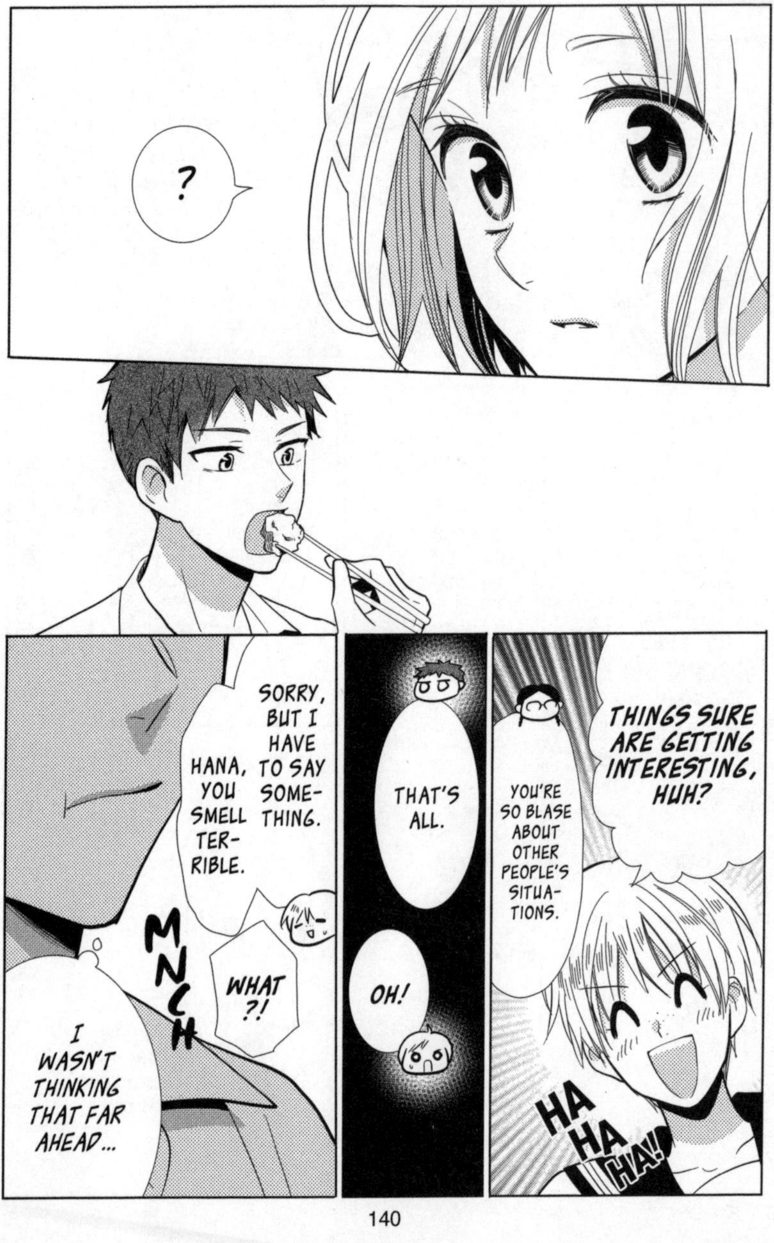
?
SORRY, BUT I HAVE TO SAY SOMETHING.
HANA, YOU SMELL TERRIBLE.
WHAT?!
MNCH
I WASN'T THINKING THAT FAR AHEAD...
THAT'S ALL.
OH!
THINGS SURE ARE GETTING INTERESTING, HUH?
YOU'RE SO BLASE ABOUT OTHER PEOPLE'S SITUATIONS.
HA HA HA!

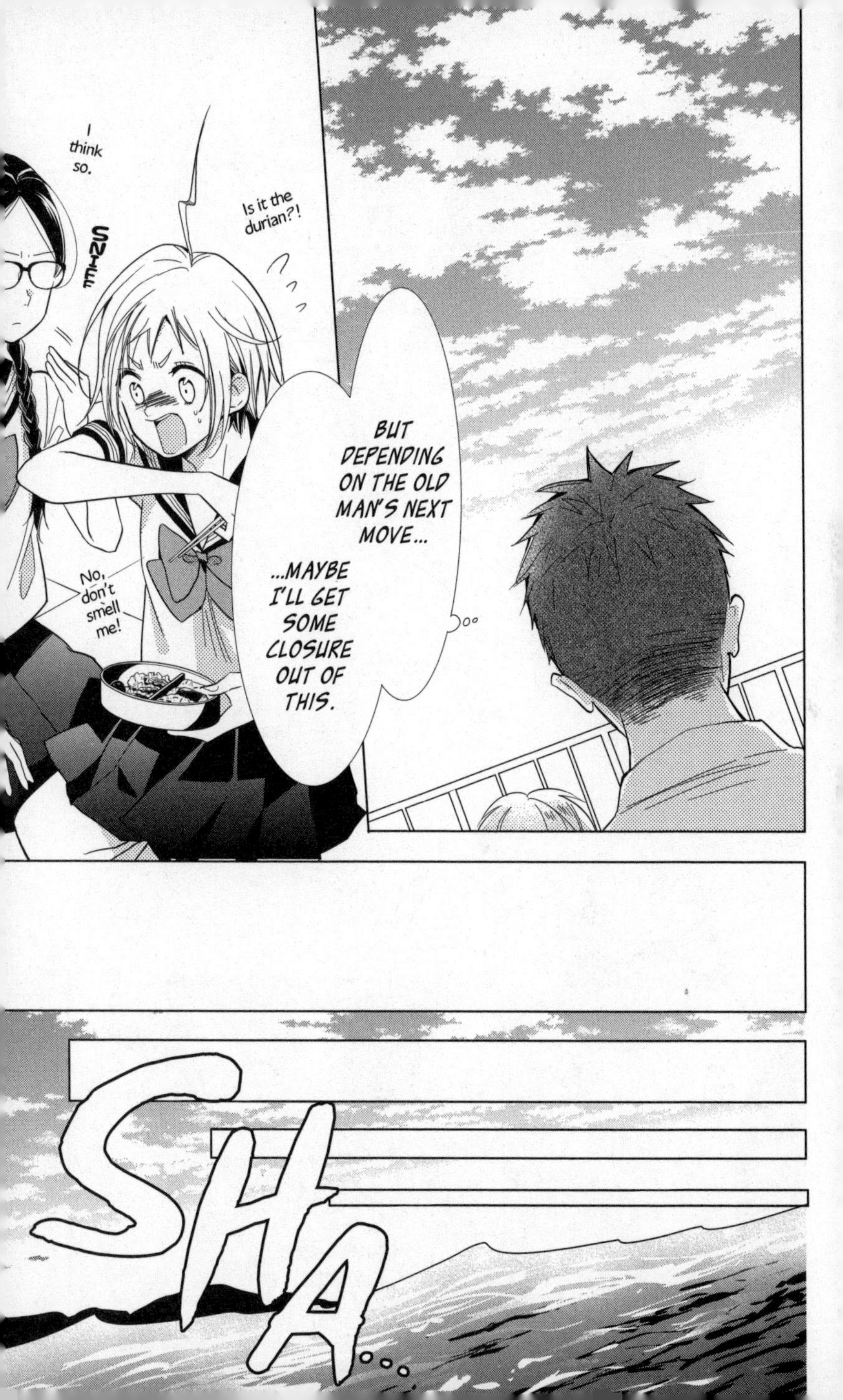
BUT DEPENDING ON THE OLD MAN'S NEXT MOVE...
...MAYBE I'LL GET SOME CLOSURE OUT OF THIS.
Is it the durian?!
I think so.
SNIFF
No, don't smell me!
SHA...

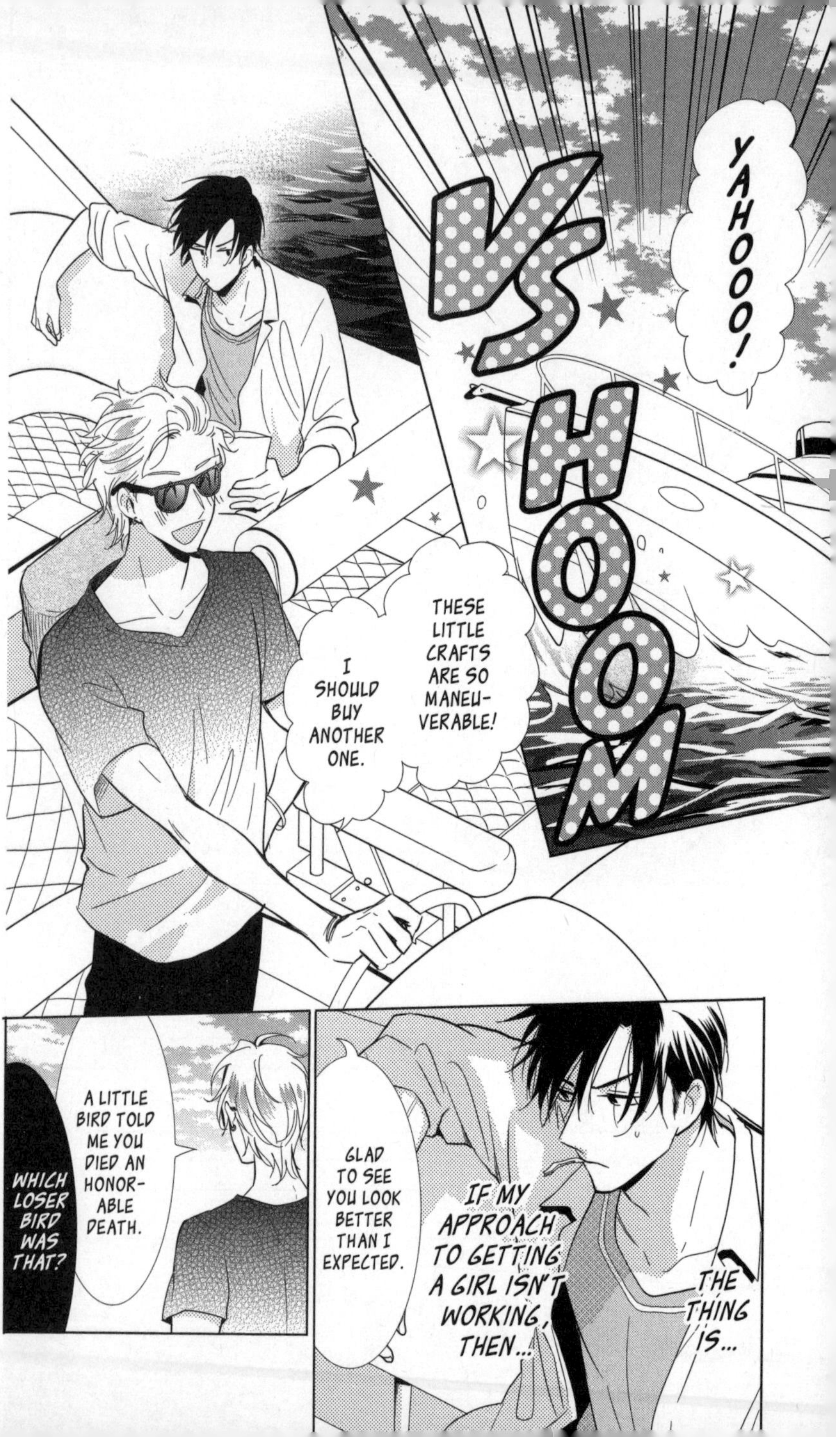
YAHOOOO!
VSHOOOM
THESE LITTLE CRAFTS ARE SO MANEU-VERABLE!
I SHOULD BUY ANOTHER ONE.
GLAD TO SEE YOU LOOK BETTER THAN I EXPECTED.
A LITTLE BIRD TOLD ME YOU DIED AN HONOR-ABLE DEATH.
WHICH LOSER BIRD WAS THAT?
THE THING IS...
IF MY APPROACH TO GETTING A GIRL ISN'T WORKING, THEN...

RUSTLE
RUSTLE
RUSTLE

It's a new taco flavor!

OH!

THAT SNACK'S TASTY, HUH?

IT'S ALL RIGHT. (YUM.)

HMM...

HMPH.

I WAS IN THE MOOD FOR SOME WHITE NOISE.

I INVITED YOU OUT HERE SO YOU COULD HAVE A CHANGE OF PACE.

HMPH

WHAT'S GOOD IS GOOD.

WHY CAN'T YOU EVER JUST SAY THAT? IT'S SO SIMPLE.

THAT'S WHY... OH, NEVER MIND.

YOU WANNA SWIM HOME?

YOU SURE LIKE TO STICK YOUR NOSE INTO EVERYTHING, DON'T YOU? IT'S NONE OF YOUR BUSINESS.

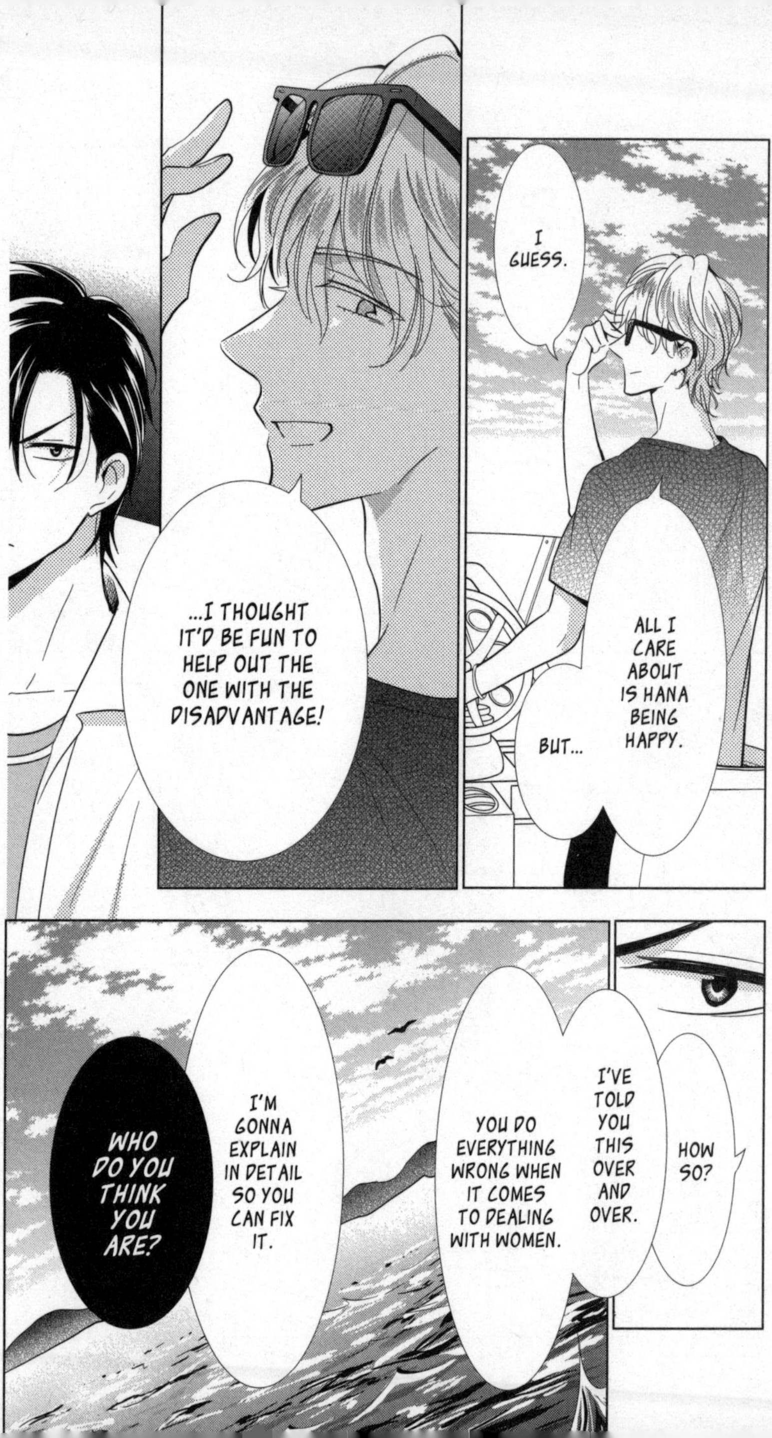
I GUESS.
ALL I CARE ABOUT IS HANA BEING HAPPY.
BUT...
...I THOUGHT IT'D BE FUN TO HELP OUT THE ONE WITH THE DISADVANTAGE!
HOW SO?
I'VE TOLD YOU THIS OVER AND OVER.
YOU DO EVERYTHING WRONG WHEN IT COMES TO DEALING WITH WOMEN.
I'M GONNA EXPLAIN IN DETAIL SO YOU CAN FIX IT.
WHO DO YOU THINK YOU ARE?

After chapter 66

SOUNDS LIKE YOU'RE DYING TO BE FISHING BAIT.

BUT...

...YOU'VE WATCHED THE WAY I APPROACH GIRLS. YOU PUT A TWIST ON IT AND MADE IT YOUR OWN.

C'MON, I'M KID-DING!

I BET USING TALKING BAIT IS FUN!

GRR

...RIGHT?

WHEN ALL IS SAID AND DONE, YOU DO ADMIT THAT...

The staff enjoyed the meal.

Staff

Staff

FWMP

SO...

LET'S PRACTICE. PRETEND THAT'S HANA.

...

AS LONG AS YOU CAN DO THAT, YOU'LL COME OUT A WINNER.

THREE AND FOUR, KEEP QUIET. AND FIVE, MAKE HER FALL FOR YOU.

ONE, COMPLIMENT HER. TWO, COMPLIMENT HER.

ALSO, WHY SHOULD I TRUST YOU WHEN YOU GIVE OFF THAT VIBE?

WHAT DOES IT CONVEY? I DON'T SEE WHAT IT ACCOMPLISHES.

STOP INTERROGATING ME AND LISTEN!

I UNDERSTAND THE PART ABOUT MAKING SURE TO COMPLIMENT HER...

...BUT IF IN PRACTICE IT'S A POINTLESS LIST OF WORDS, WHY DO IT?

146

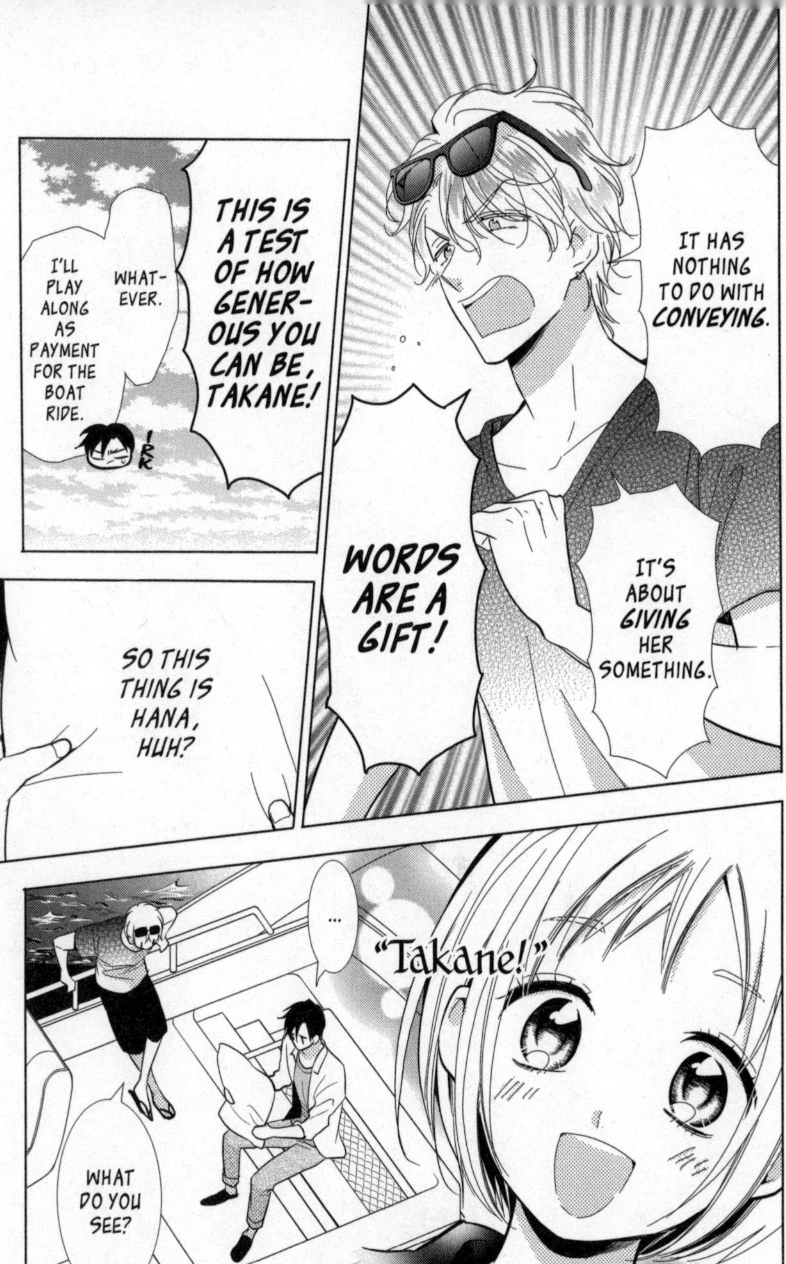
IT HAS NOTHING TO DO WITH CONVEYING.
IT'S ABOUT GIVING HER SOMETHING.
WORDS ARE A GIFT!
THIS IS A TEST OF HOW GENEROUS YOU CAN BE, TAKANE!
WHATEVER.
I'LL PLAY ALONG AS PAYMENT FOR THE BOAT RIDE.
IRK
SO THIS THING IS HANA, HUH?
...
"Takane!"
WHAT DO YOU SEE?

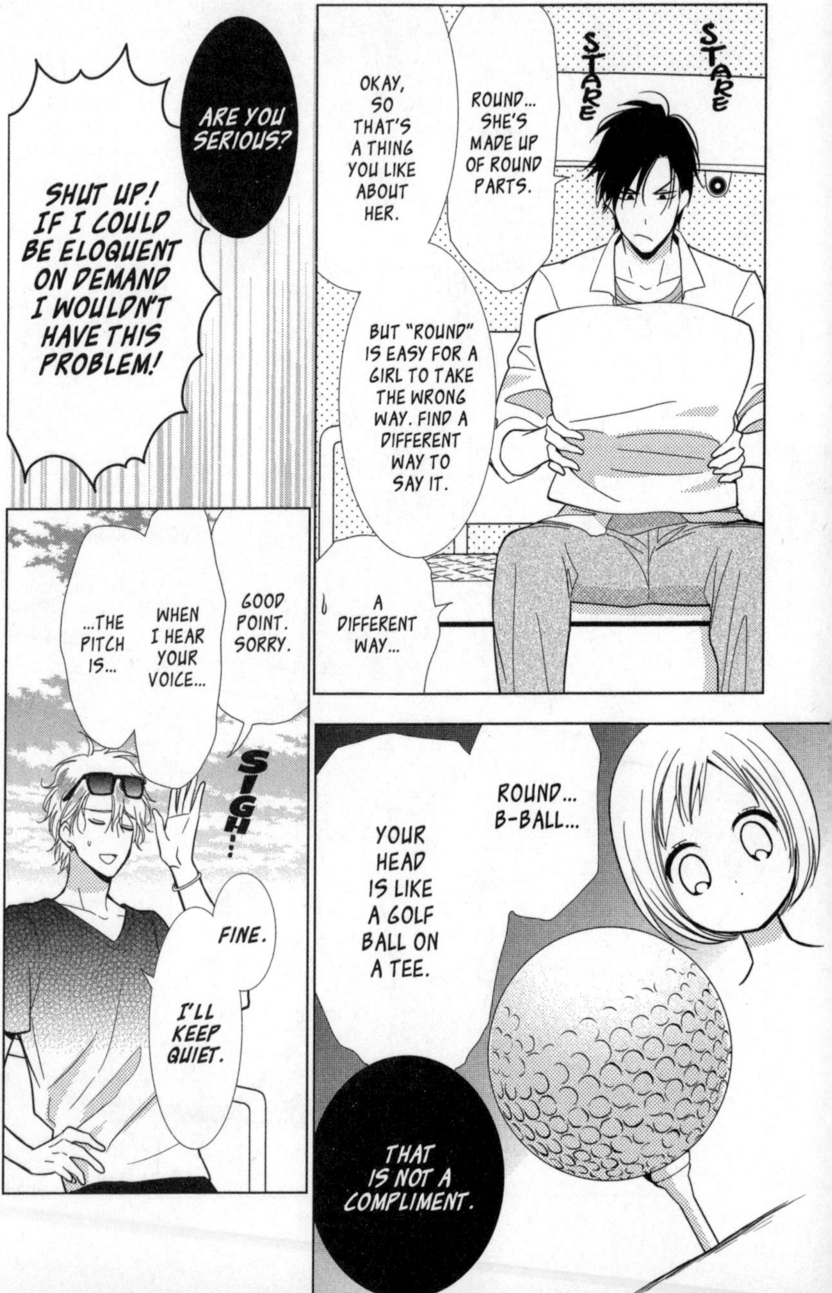
STARE
STARE
ROUND... SHE'S MADE UP OF ROUND PARTS.
OKAY, SO THAT'S A THING YOU LIKE ABOUT HER.
BUT "ROUND" IS EASY FOR A GIRL TO TAKE THE WRONG WAY. FIND A DIFFERENT WAY TO SAY IT.
A DIFFERENT WAY...
ROUND... B-BALL...
YOUR HEAD IS LIKE A GOLF BALL ON A TEE.
THAT IS NOT A COMPLIMENT.
ARE YOU SERIOUS?
SHUT UP! IF I COULD BE ELOQUENT ON DEMAND I WOULDN'T HAVE THIS PROBLEM!
GOOD POINT. SORRY.
WHEN I HEAR YOUR VOICE...
...THE PITCH IS...
SIGH
FINE.
I'LL KEEP QUIET.

...

ALL RIGHT, ALL RIGHT! STOP.

DON'T GLOWER. GAZE LOVINGLY.

STARE

DON'T THINK OF ANYTHING ELSE. SAY "YOU'RE CUTE." DO IT.

YOU'RE...

THE HARDER YOU TRY, THE WORSE IT IS.

JUST PROGRAM YOURSELF TO SAY "YOU'RE CUTE" OVER AND OVER.

HUH?

YOU'RE CU...

149

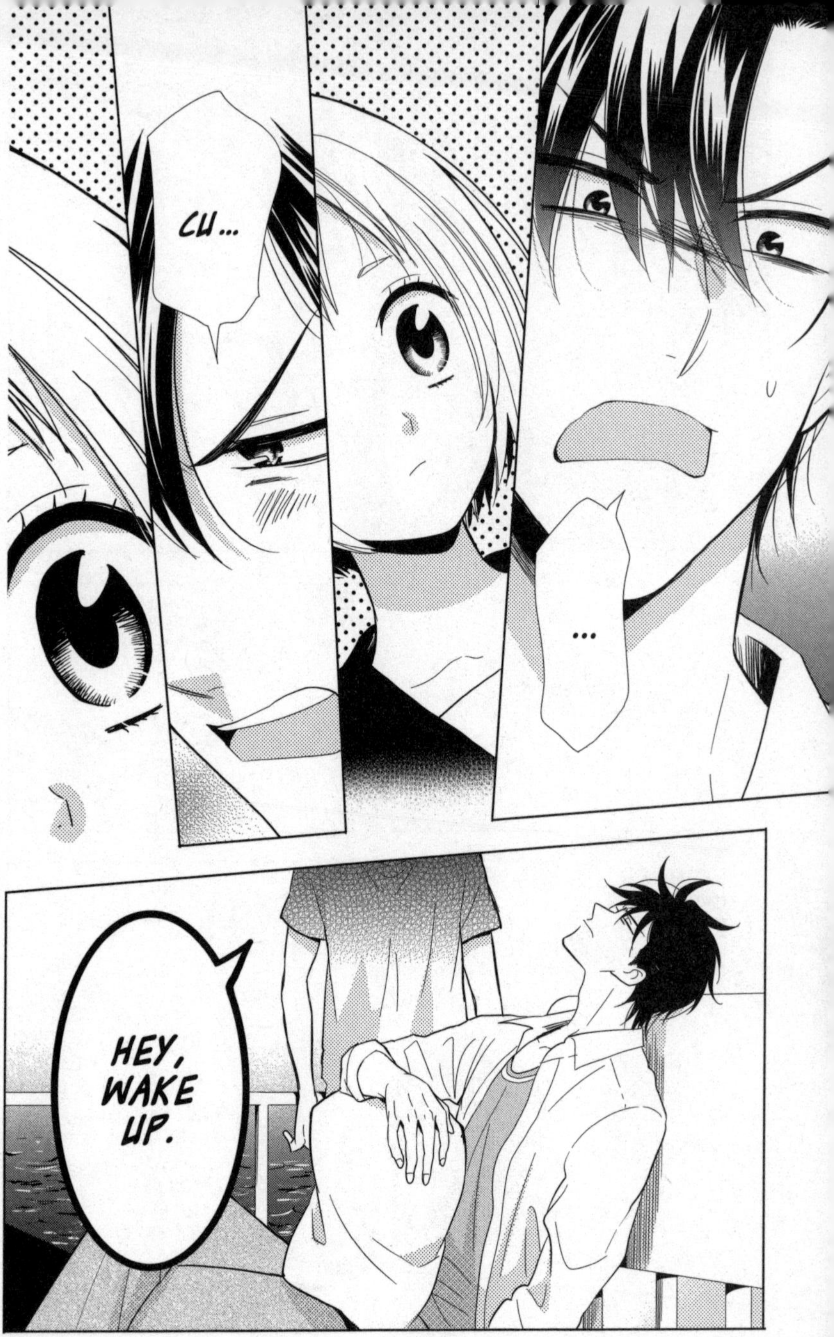
CU...
...
HEY, WAKE UP.

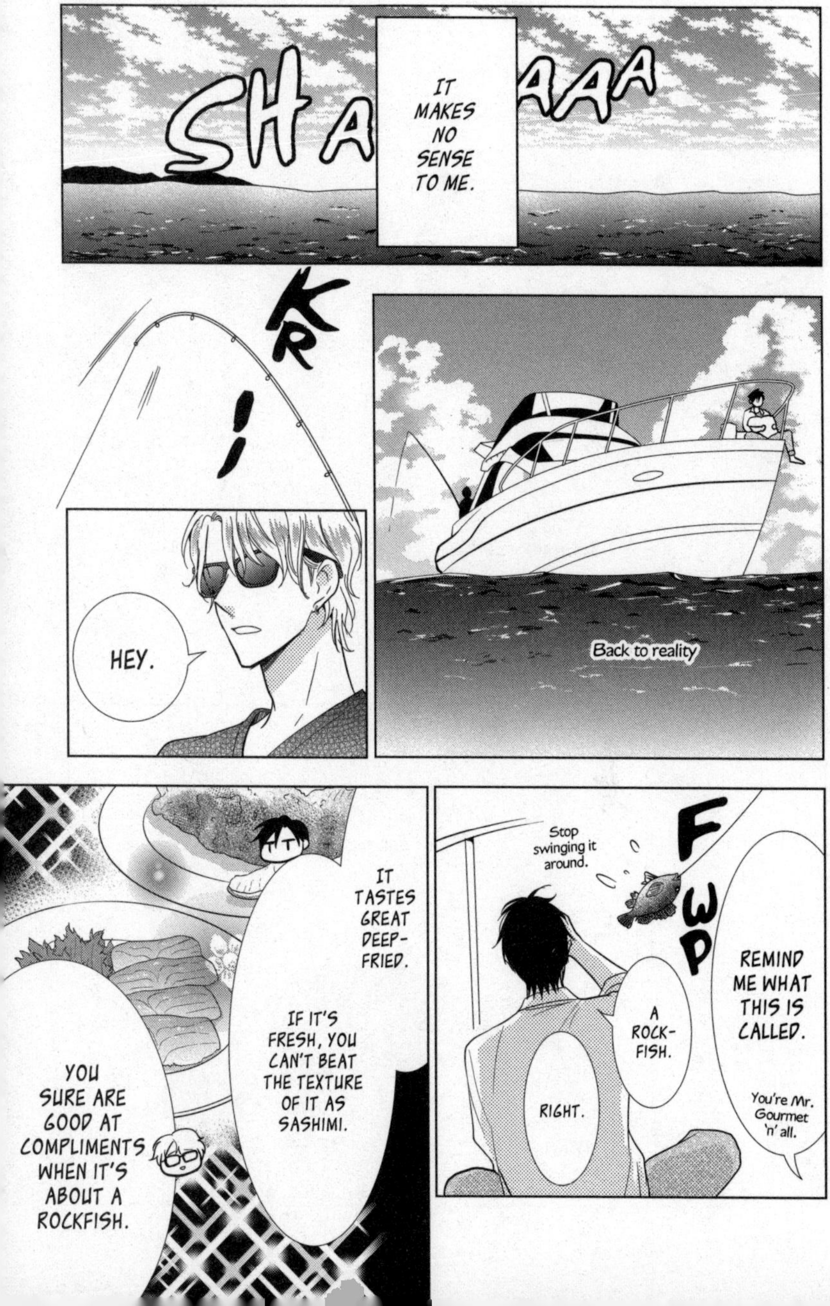
SHAAAAA
IT MAKES NO SENSE TO ME.
Back to reality
KRI
HEY.
FWP
REMIND ME WHAT THIS IS CALLED.
You're Mr. Gourmet 'n' all.
A ROCKFISH.
RIGHT.
Stop swinging it around.
IT TASTES GREAT DEEP-FRIED.
IF IT'S FRESH, YOU CAN'T BEAT THE TEXTURE OF IT AS SASHIMI.
YOU SURE ARE GOOD AT COMPLIMENTS WHEN IT'S ABOUT A ROCKFISH.

FORGET WHAT I SAID. I GOT CARRIED AWAY.

I DO KNOW HOW TO SAY SO.

WHAT'S GOOD IS GOOD.

FLOP FLOP

WORDS SPOKEN FROM YOUR HEART ARE STRAIGHT-FORWARD AND ENGAGING.

I MEAN, THERE'S NO POINT IF I FORCE YOU TO SAY IT.

...CONVEYING HOW YOU REALLY FEEL INSIDE...

...WILL PROBABLY BE THE BEST PRESENT FOR HER.

IN YOUR CASE...

HOW
I...

...REALLY
FEEL
INSIDE...

AT THAT MOMENT...

...THE ONLY THING I SAID WAS...

..."I LOVE YOU."

YEAH?

LUCIANO.

RIGHT?

YOU WERE HELPFUL AFTER ALL.

WAIT, HOW SO?

PLOP

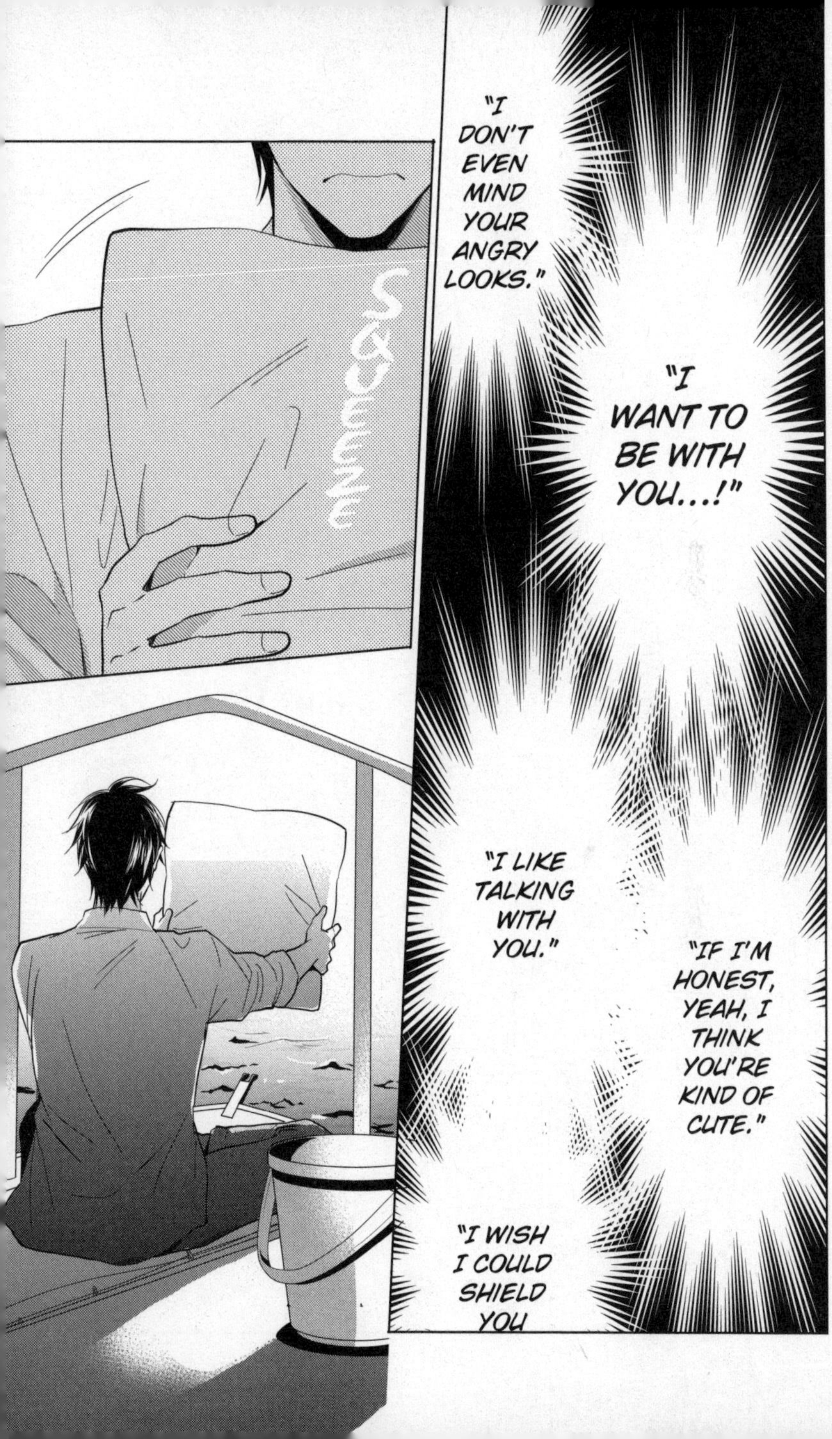
"I DON'T EVEN MIND YOUR ANGRY LOOKS."
"I WANT TO BE WITH YOU...!"
"I LIKE TALKING WITH YOU."
"IF I'M HONEST, YEAH, I THINK YOU'RE KIND OF CUTE."
"I WISH I COULD SHIELD YOU
SQUEEZE

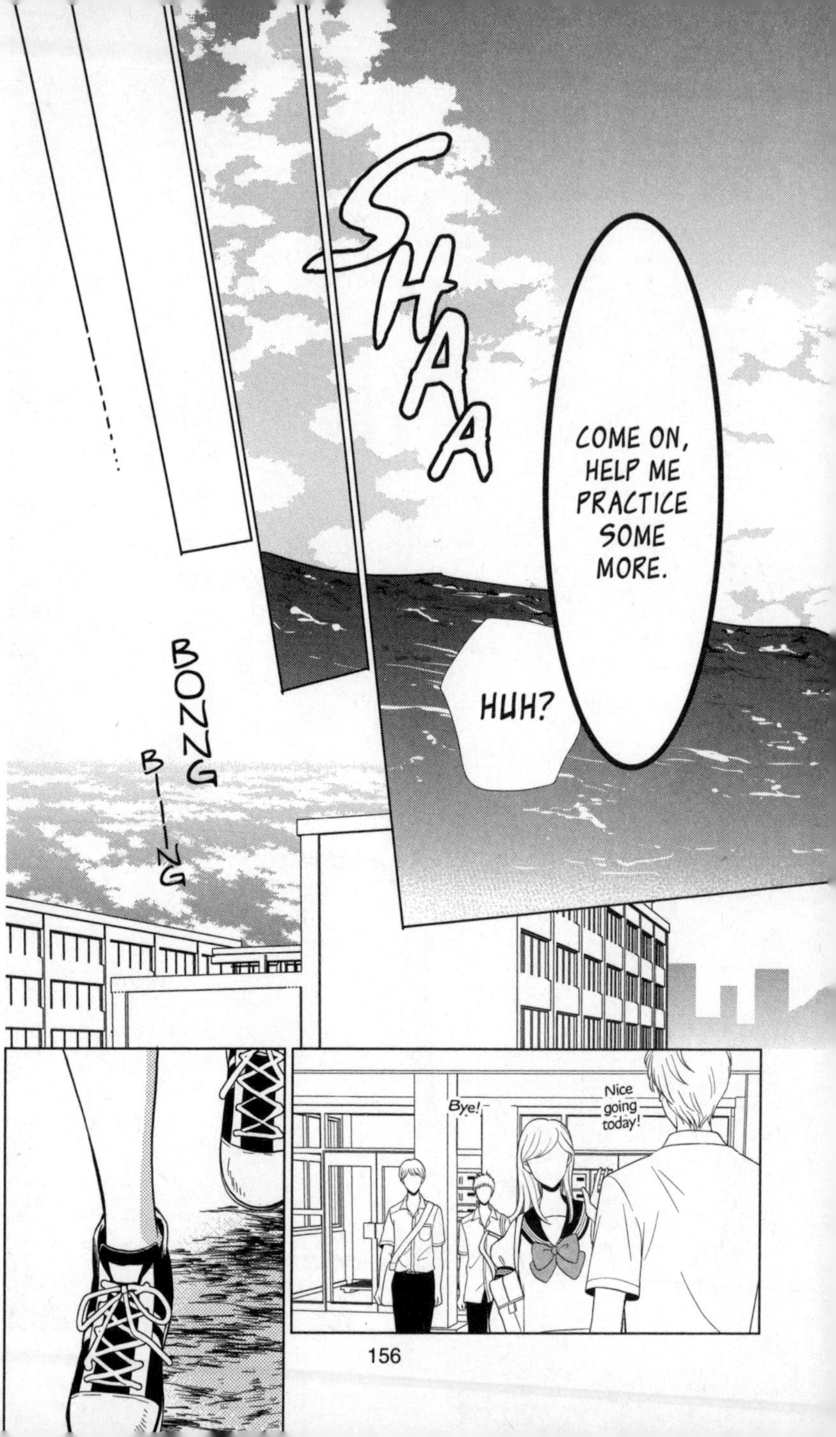
SHAA
COME ON, HELP ME PRACTICE SOME MORE.
HUH?
BONNG
BIING
Nice going today!
Bye!

THANKS TO OKAMON, I'VE GOT A BREAK FROM TAKANE'S WEIRDNESS, BUT...

...WHAT AM I GOING TO DO...

...FROM NOW ON?

TMP

TMP

HEY THERE, SASSY GIRL.

I CAN'T BLAME OTHER PEOPLE FOR BEING CONFUSED.

I DON'T EVEN KNOW WHAT I WANT TO DO.

"HUH?"

RINO ?!

COME WITH ME. I NEED TO TALK TO YOU.

Takane & Hana 12 / The End

ALL IS STILL AS THE RED GLOW OF MORNING SHINES DOWN ON THE CITY LIGHTS.

LIGHT-ROAST DRIP COFFEE.

DRIP

A COMPETENT MAN'S MORNING OF EXCELLENCE...

...STARTS THIS WAY.

Bonus Story 1

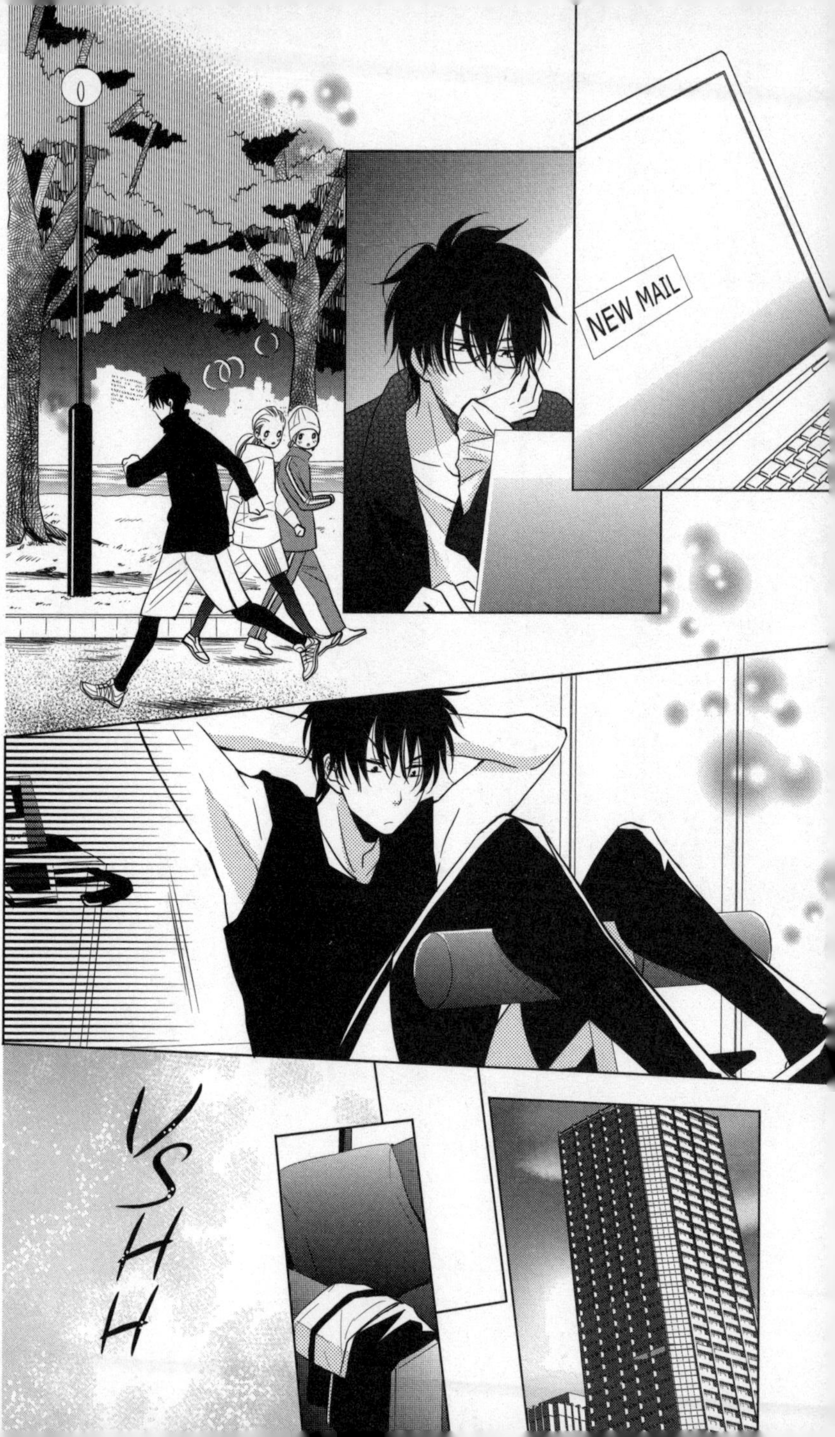
NEW MAIL
SHHH

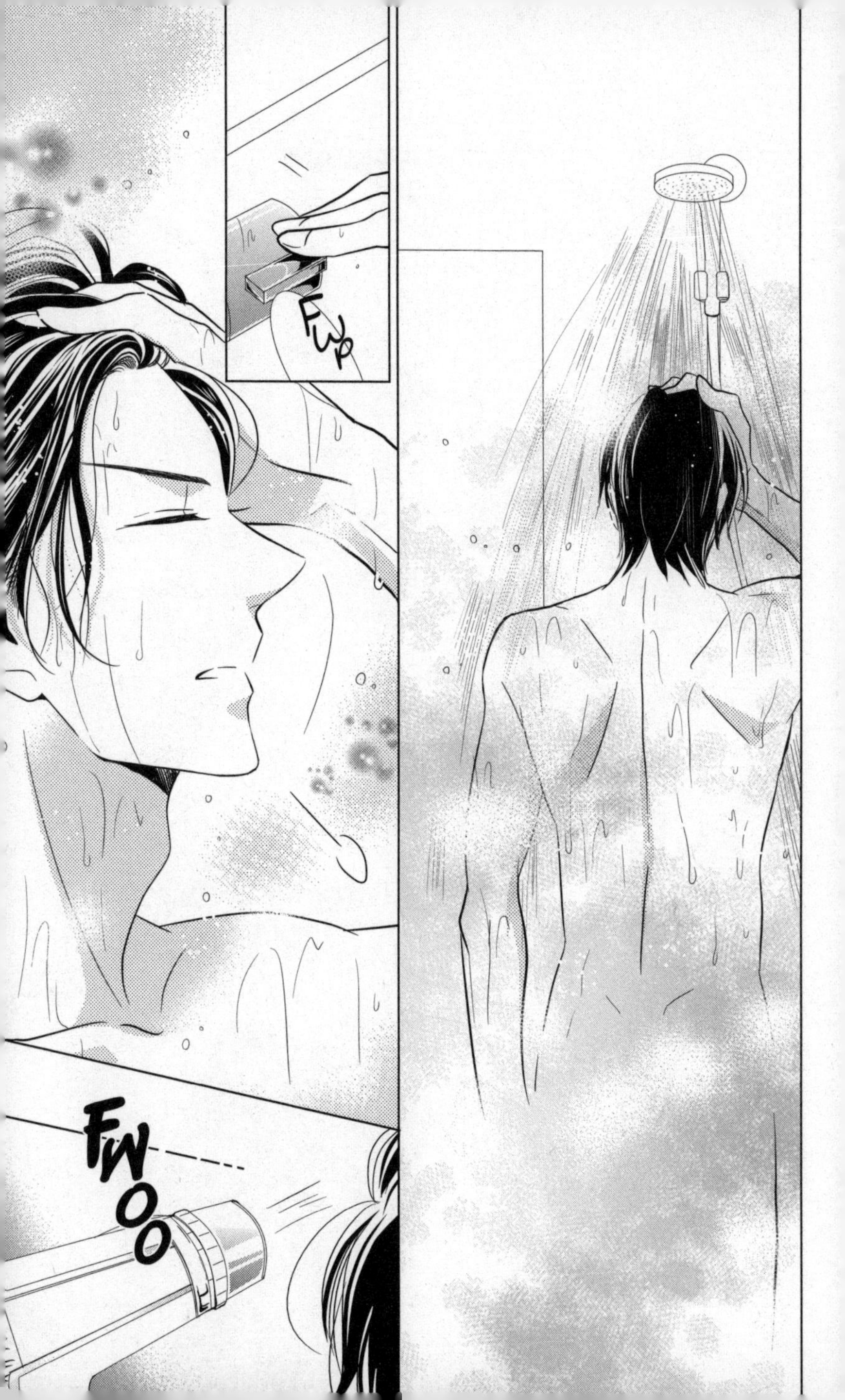
FUP
FWOO

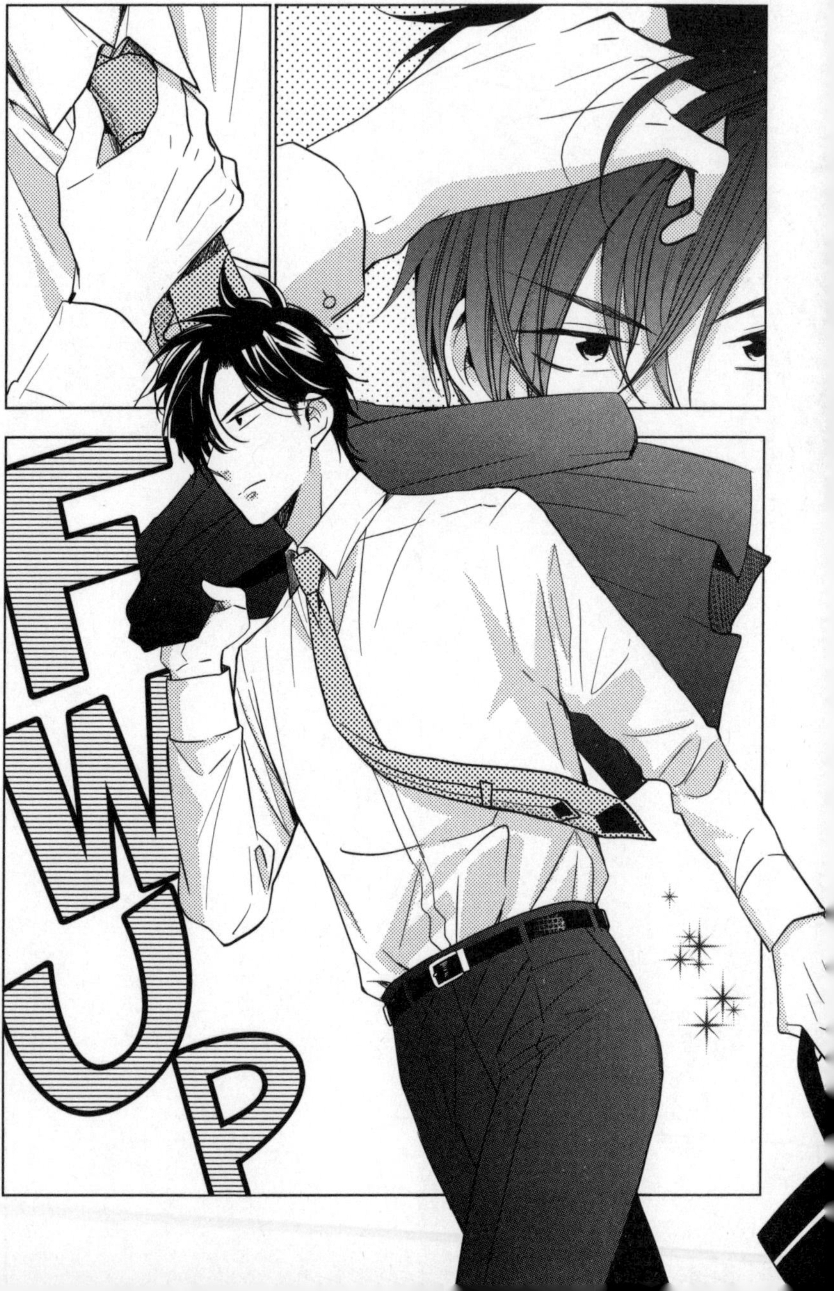

FWUP

WIN THE MORNING, WIN THE DAY.

Have a nice day, Mr. Saibara.

Sky Lounge ←

NIKKEI NEWSPAPER

TO THE WORLD'S ELITE...

...THIS IS COMMON SENSE.

FRANTIC MORNINGS ARE NOT IN MY VOCABULARY.

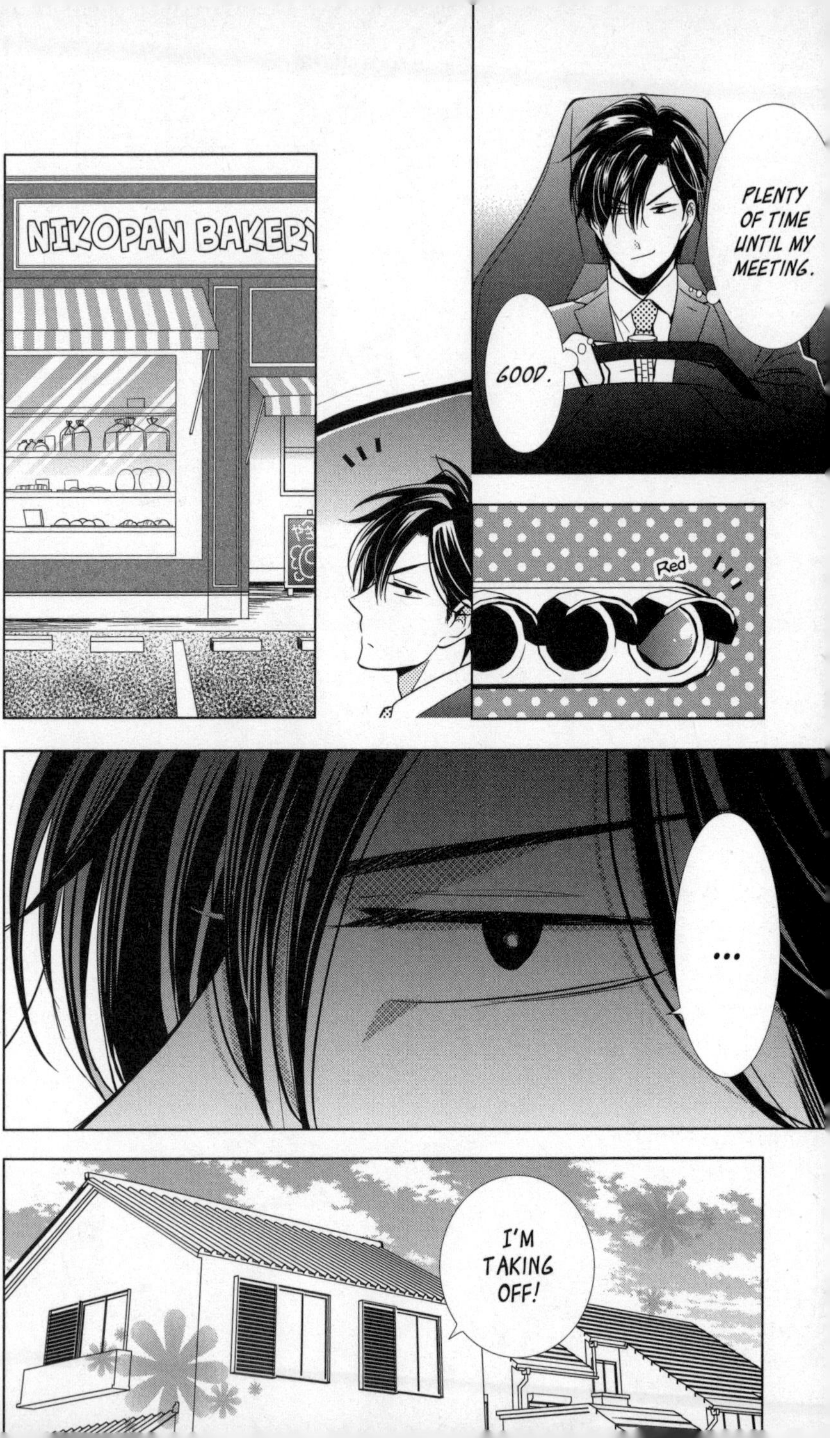
PLENTY OF TIME UNTIL MY MEETING.
GOOD.
Red
NIKOPAN BAKER
...
I'M TAKING OFF!

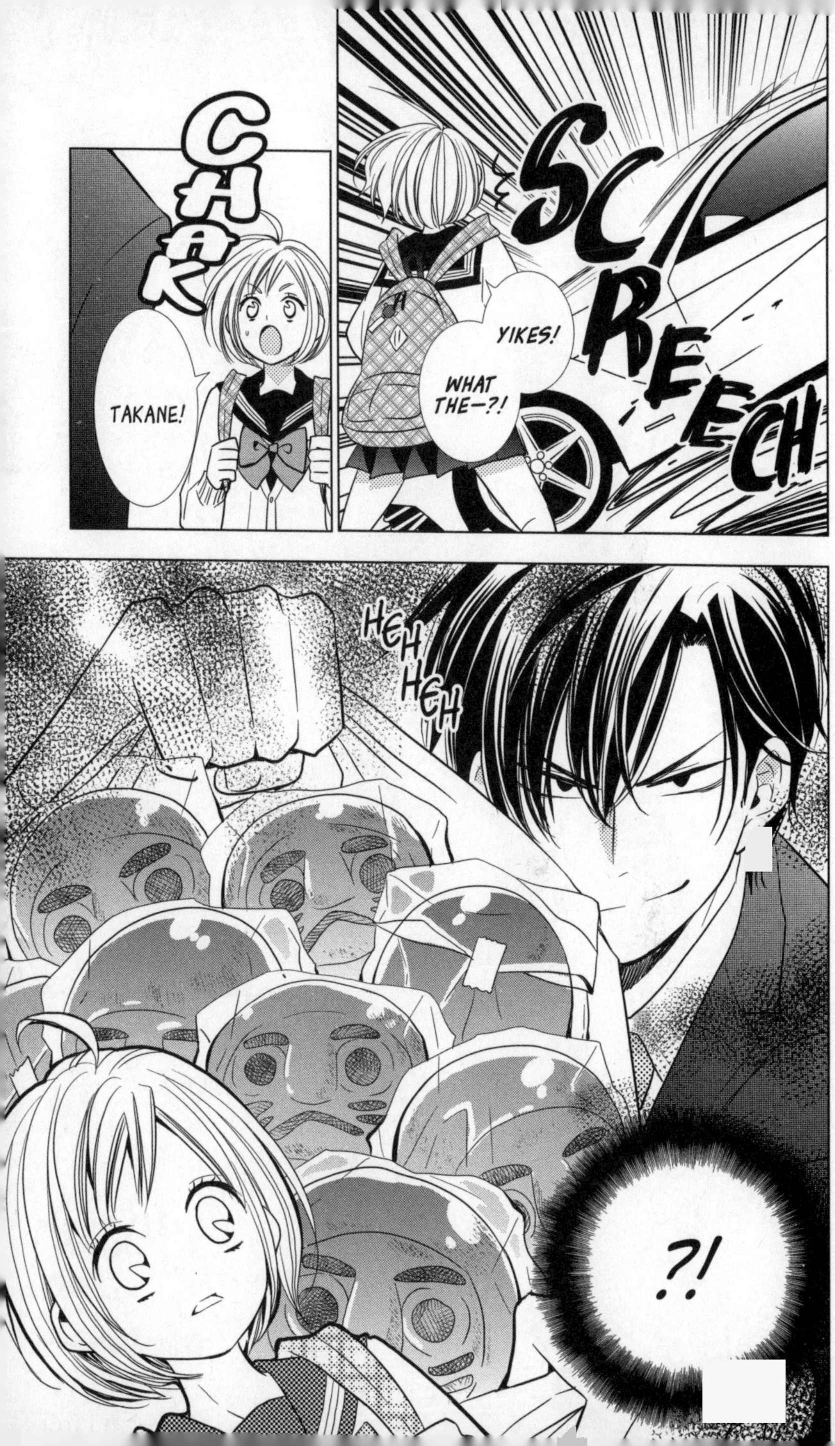
SCREECH
YIKES!
WHAT THE—?!
CHAK
TAKANE!
HEH HEH
?!

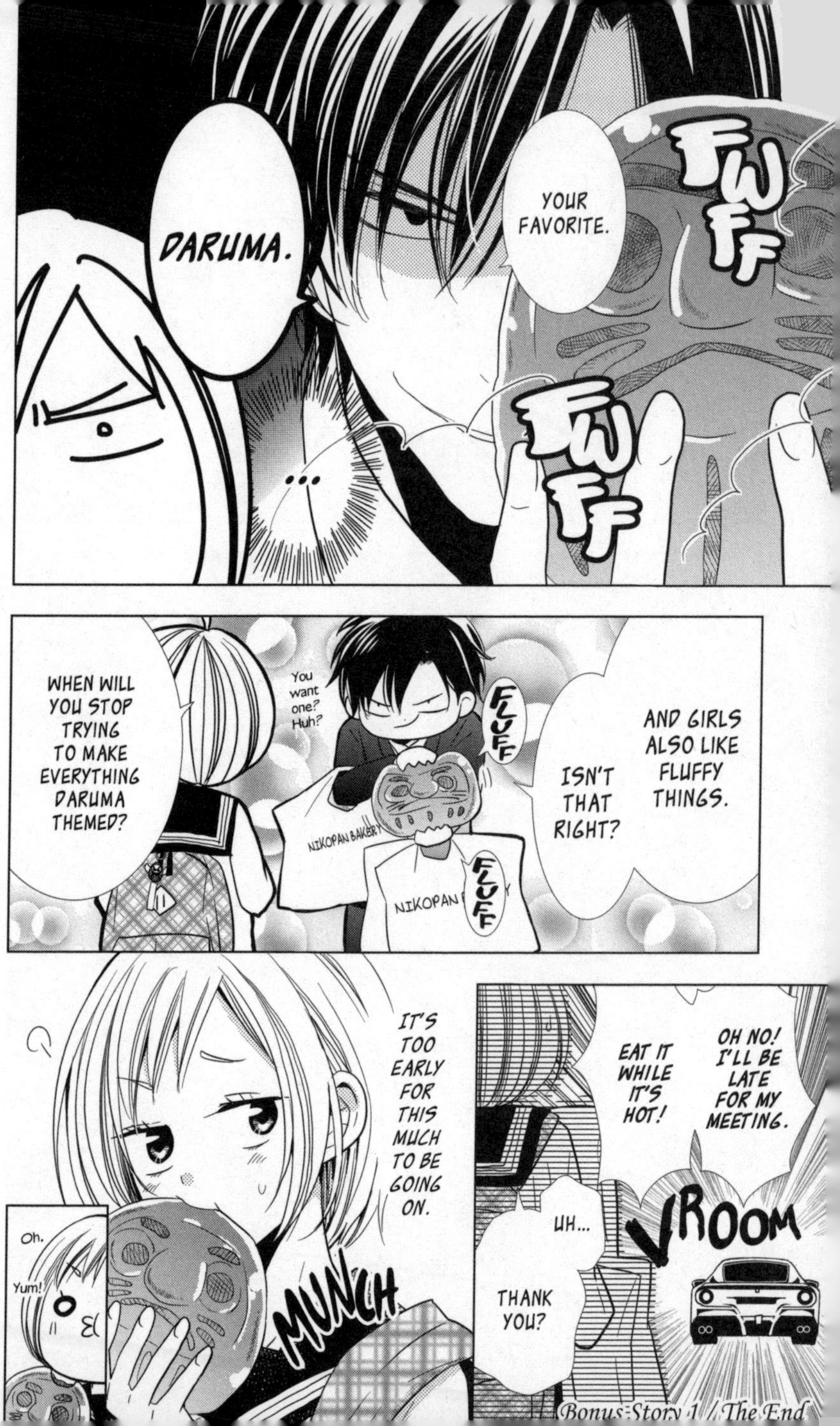
FWFF
YOUR FAVORITE.
DARUMA.
FWFF
...
AND GIRLS ALSO LIKE FLUFFY THINGS.
ISN'T THAT RIGHT?
FLUFF
You want one? Huh?
FLUFF
NIKOPAN BAKERY
NIKOPAN
WHEN WILL YOU STOP TRYING TO MAKE EVERYTHING DARUMA THEMED?
OH NO! I'LL BE LATE FOR MY MEETING.
EAT IT WHILE IT'S HOT!
VROOM
UH...
THANK YOU?
IT'S TOO EARLY FOR THIS MUCH TO BE GOING ON.
MUNCH
Oh.
Yum!
Bonus Story 1 / The End

Bonus
Story 2

A FEW DAYS AFTER...

...TAKANE AGREED TO LIVE WITH US...

R R R R R

COME UPSTAIRS.

WHAT DO YOU WANT? IT'S MIDNIGHT.

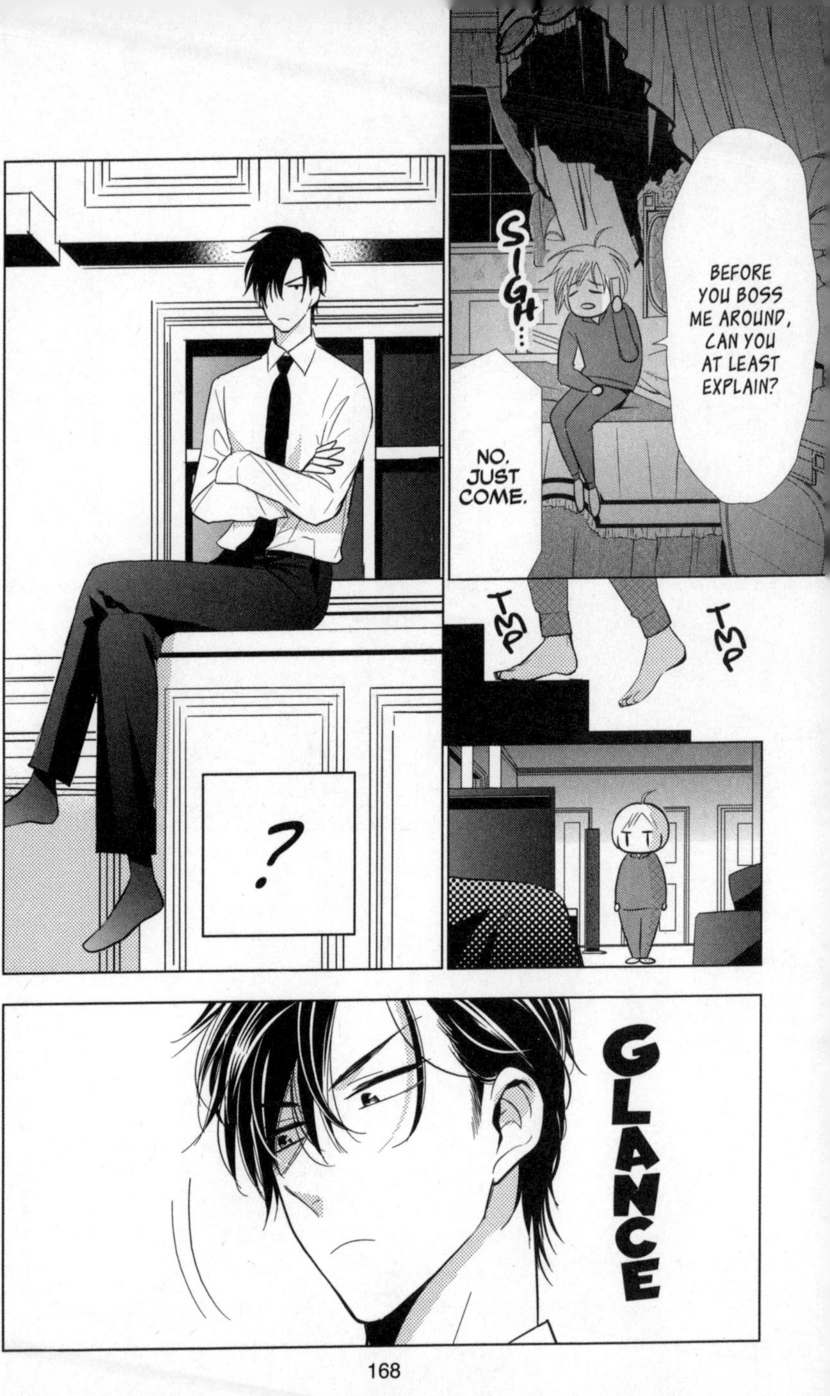
BEFORE YOU BOSS ME AROUND, CAN YOU AT LEAST EXPLAIN?
SIGH...
NO. JUST COME.
TMP
TMP
?
GLANCE

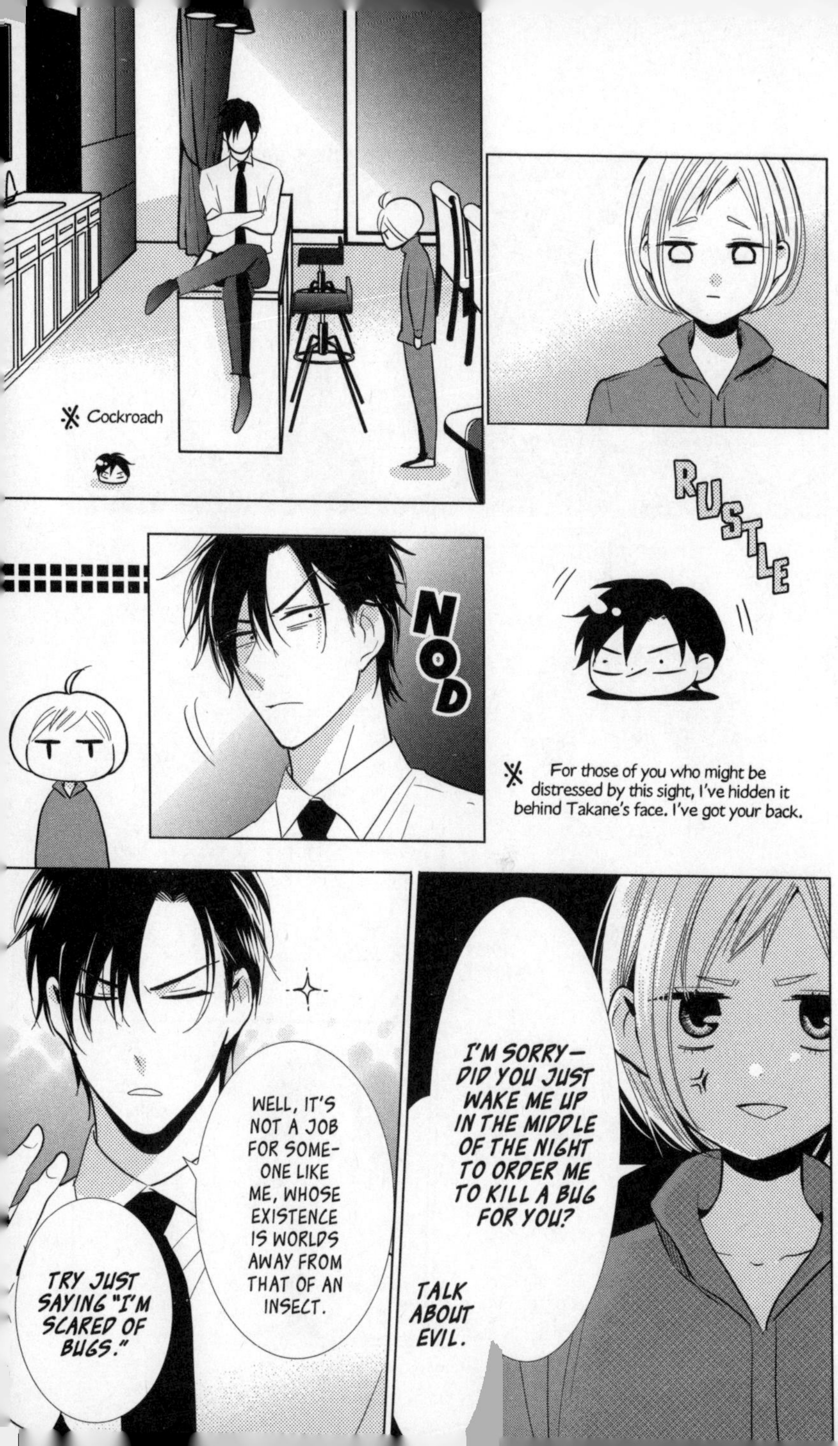
※ Cockroach
RUSTLE
※ For those of you who might be distressed by this sight, I've hidden it behind Takane's face. I've got your back.
NOD
I'M SORRY—DID YOU JUST WAKE ME UP IN THE MIDDLE OF THE NIGHT TO ORDER ME TO KILL A BUG FOR YOU?
TALK ABOUT EVIL.
WELL, IT'S NOT A JOB FOR SOME-ONE LIKE ME, WHOSE EXISTENCE IS WORLDS AWAY FROM THAT OF AN INSECT.
TRY JUST SAYING "I'M SCARED OF BUGS."

WAIT.

TELL ME WHAT TO DO.

GOOD NIGHT.

NO.

I'M OKAY WITH THEM, BUT I'M STILL NOT INTO SMUSHING THEM. DO IT YOURSELF.

STOP COMPLAIN-ING AND DO YOUR JOB.

YOU'RE OKAY WITH THEM, RIGHT? I'M MERELY MATCHING YOUR SKILLS TO THE RIGHT TASK.

RUSTLE

RUSTLE

LIKE THIS.

GRAB IT QUICKLY AND SQUEEZE HARD.

SHA

BE SERIOUS!

CLENCH

IT'S REVOLTING.

DON'T WORRY.

IT MAY SEEM BIG AND CREEPY, BUT IT WON'T BITE.

SOUNDS LIKE SOMEONE I KNOW.

NOD

NOD

Here.

YOU CAN USE OUR BUG SPRAY.

170

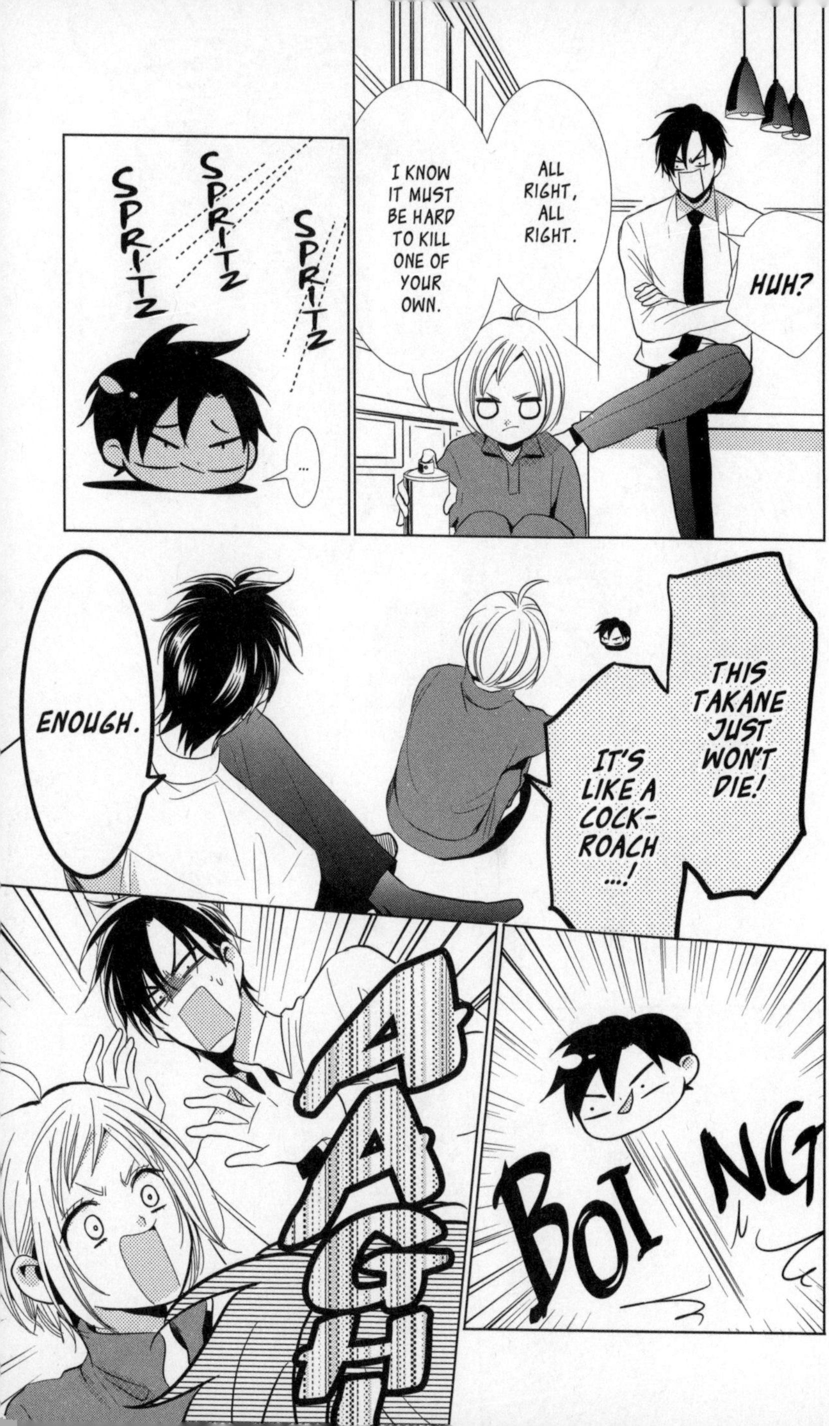

HUH?
ALL RIGHT, ALL RIGHT.
I KNOW IT MUST BE HARD TO KILL ONE OF YOUR OWN.
SPRITZ
SPRITZ
SPRITZ
...
THIS TAKANE JUST WON'T DIE!
IT'S LIKE A COCKROACH...!
ENOUGH.
BOING
AAGH

GET BACK!

EVEN THE COCKROACH HAS MORE DIGNITY THAN THIS.

THERE'S NO WAY I'M GETTING COCKROACH JUICE ALL OVER MY FAVORITE GENUINE-LEATHER SLIPPER!

YOUR WEAPON, SIR!

WELL, I GUESS SQUASHING IT IS THE ONLY ANSWER.

THEN TRY THIS.

NO, IT'S TOO SHORT.

STARE

THIS, THEN.

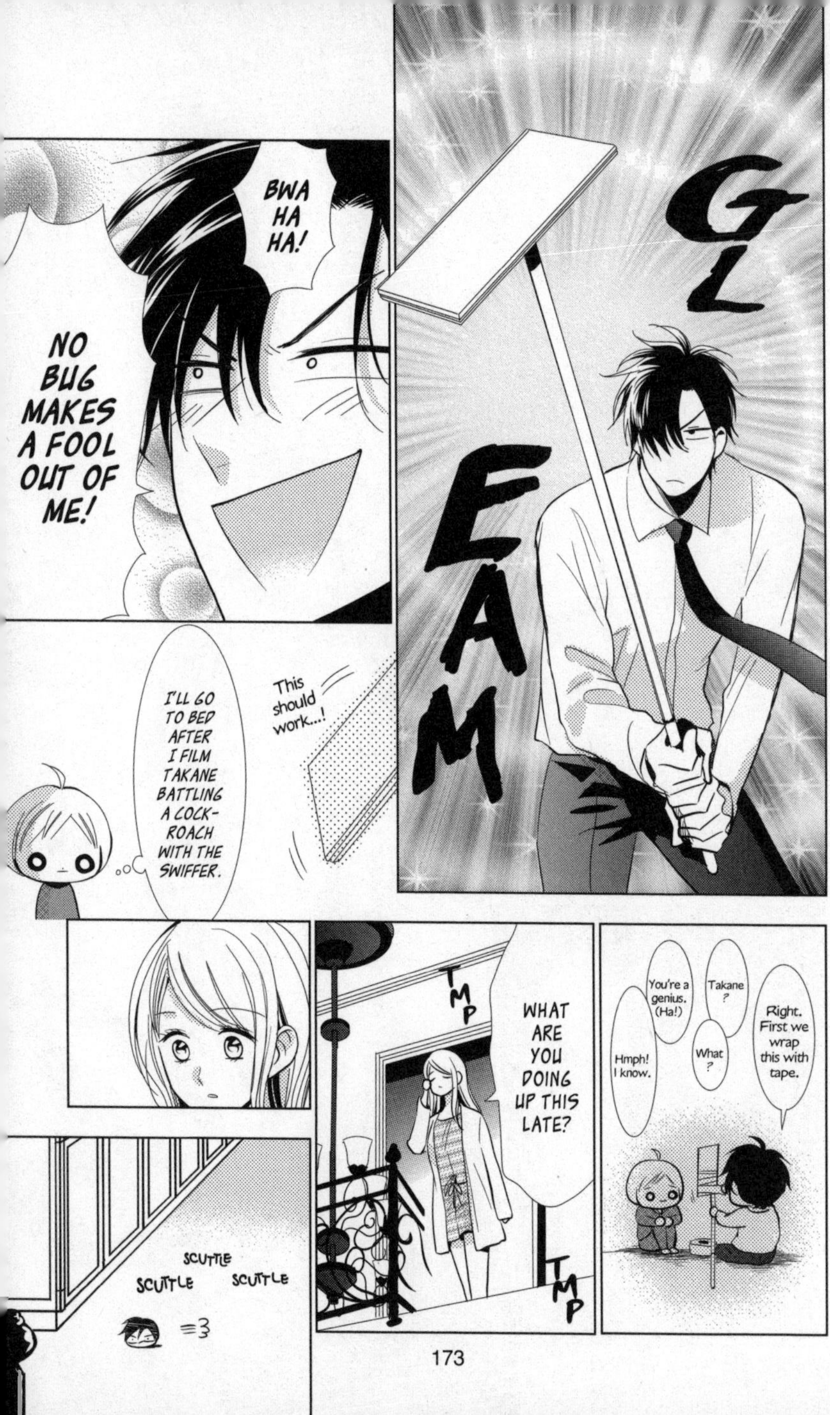
GLEAM
BWA HA HA!
NO BUG MAKES A FOOL OUT OF ME!
This should work...!
I'LL GO TO BED AFTER I FILM TAKANE BATTLING A COCK-ROACH WITH THE SWIFFER.
Right. First we wrap this with tape.
Takane?
You're a genius. (Ha!)
What?
Hmph! I know.
TMP
WHAT ARE YOU DOING UP THIS LATE?
TMP
SCUTTLE
SCUTTLE
SCUTTLE

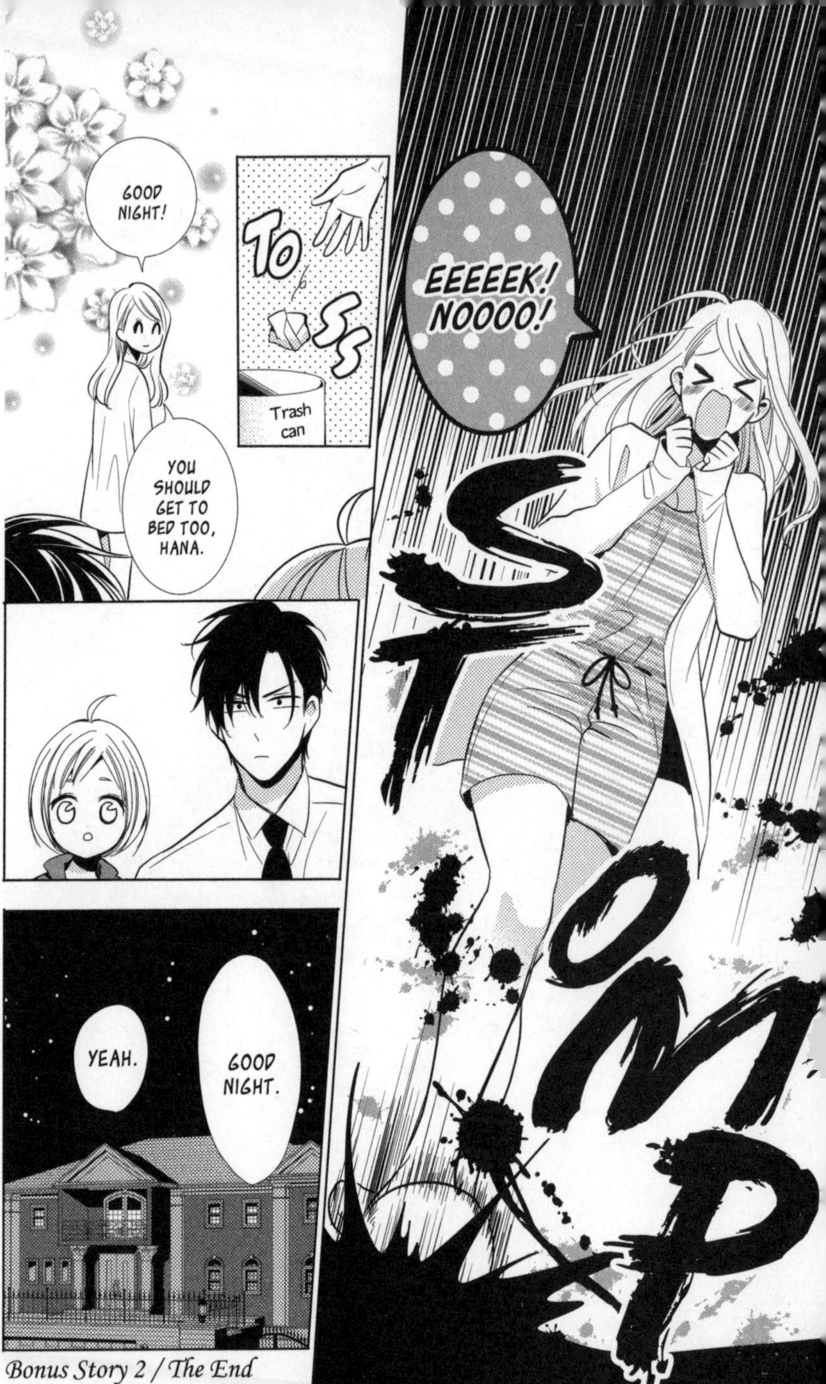
EEEEEK! NOOOO!
STOMP
GOOD NIGHT!
TOSS
Trash can
YOU SHOULD GET TO BED TOO, HANA.
YEAH.
GOOD NIGHT.

Bonus Story 2 / The End

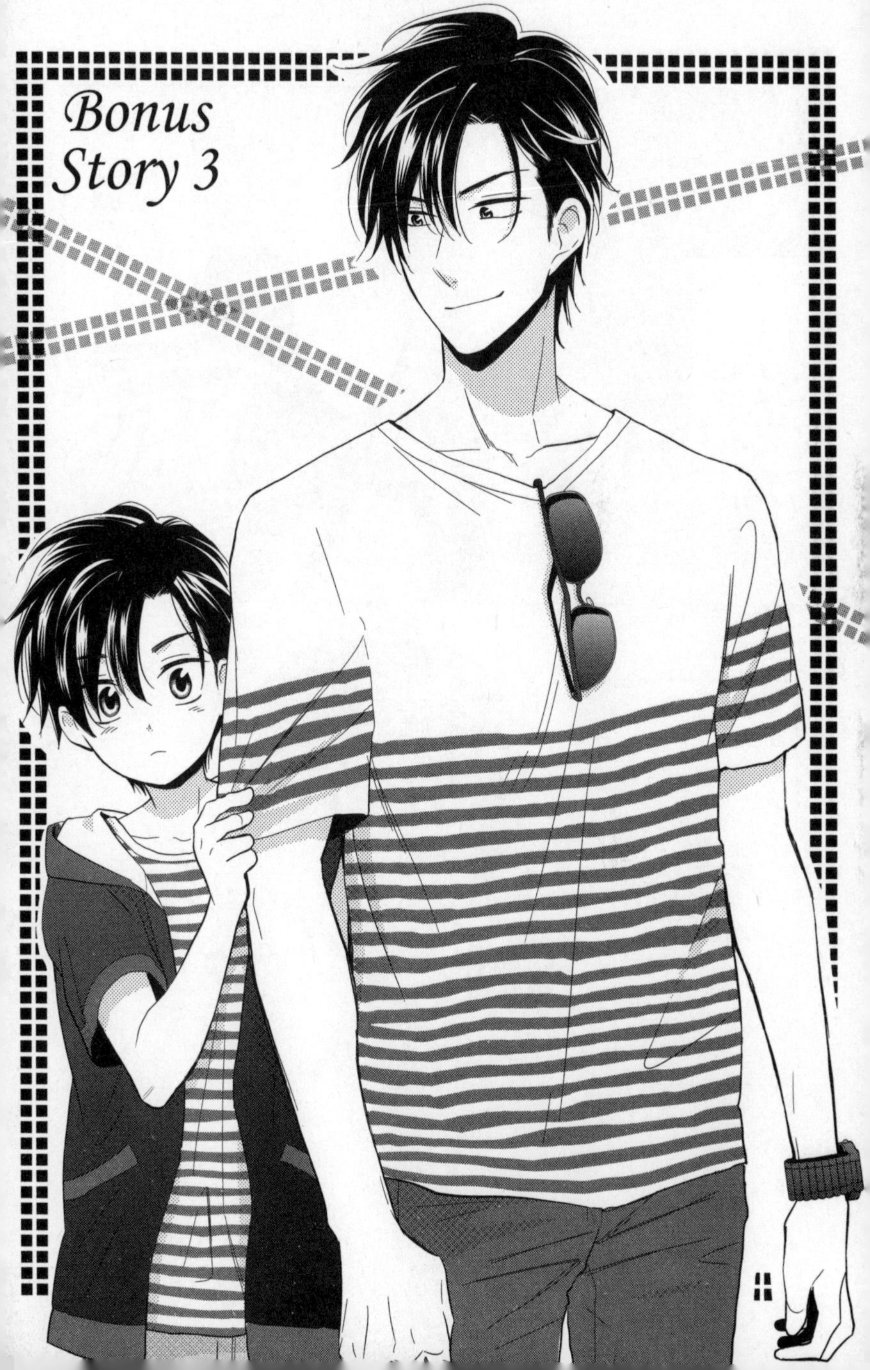
Bonus
Story 3

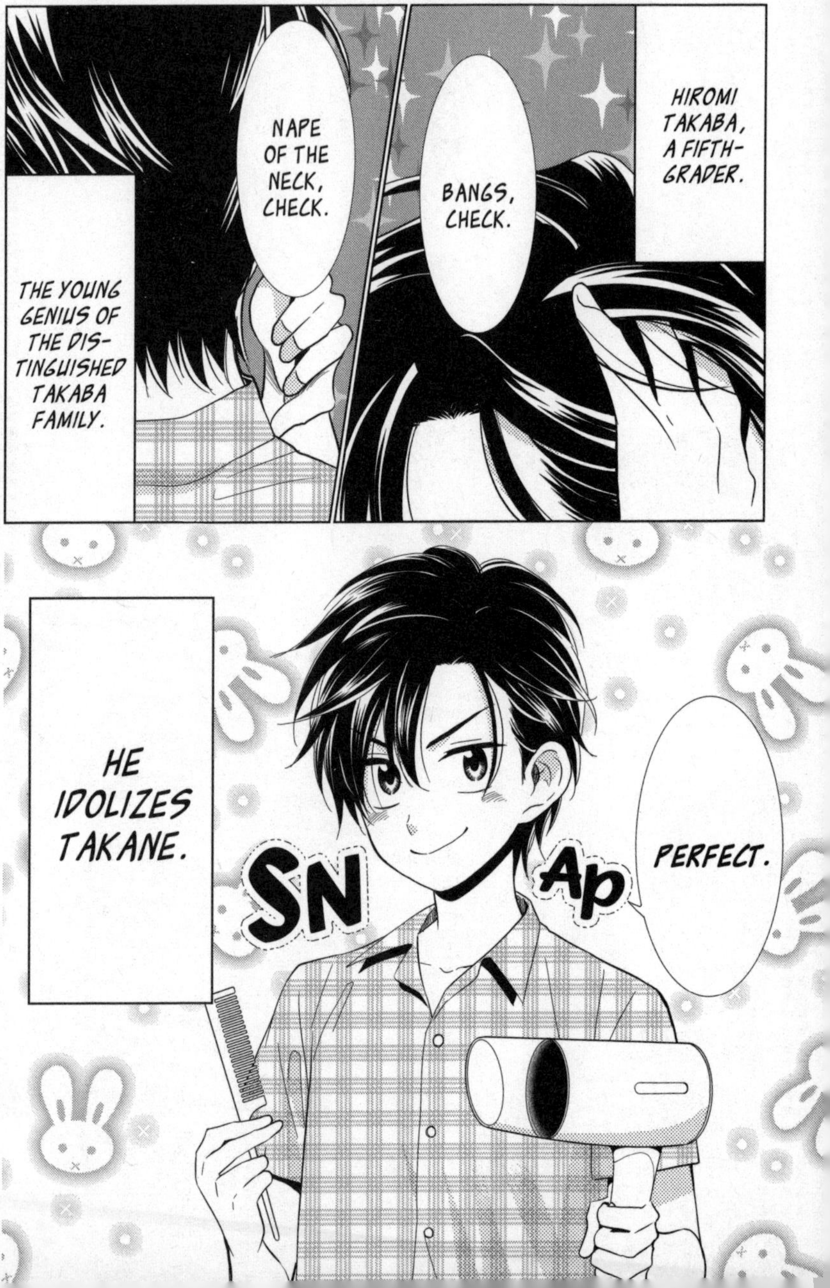
HIROMI TAKABA, A FIFTH-GRADER.
BANGS, CHECK.
NAPE OF THE NECK, CHECK.
THE YOUNG GENIUS OF THE DIS-TINGUISHED TAKABA FAMILY.
PERFECT.
SNAp
HE IDOLIZES TAKANE.

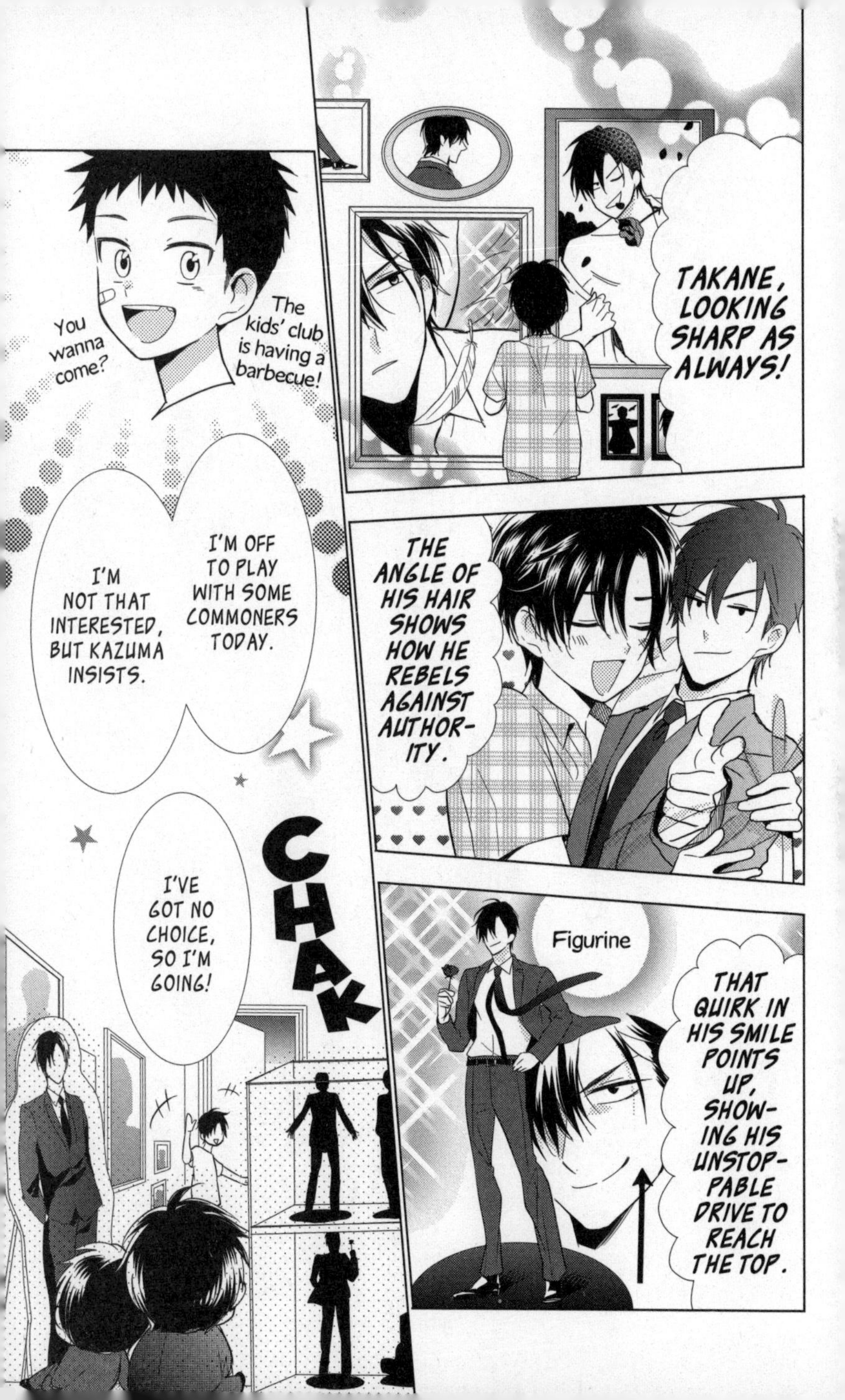
TAKANE, LOOKING SHARP AS ALWAYS!
THE ANGLE OF HIS HAIR SHOWS HOW HE REBELS AGAINST AUTHOR-ITY.
Figurine
THAT QUIRK IN HIS SMILE POINTS UP, SHOW-ING HIS UNSTOP-PABLE DRIVE TO REACH THE TOP.
The kids' club is having a barbecue!
You wanna come?
I'M OFF TO PLAY WITH SOME COMMONERS TODAY.
I'M NOT THAT INTERESTED, BUT KAZUMA INSISTS.
I'VE GOT NO CHOICE, SO I'M GOING!
CHAK

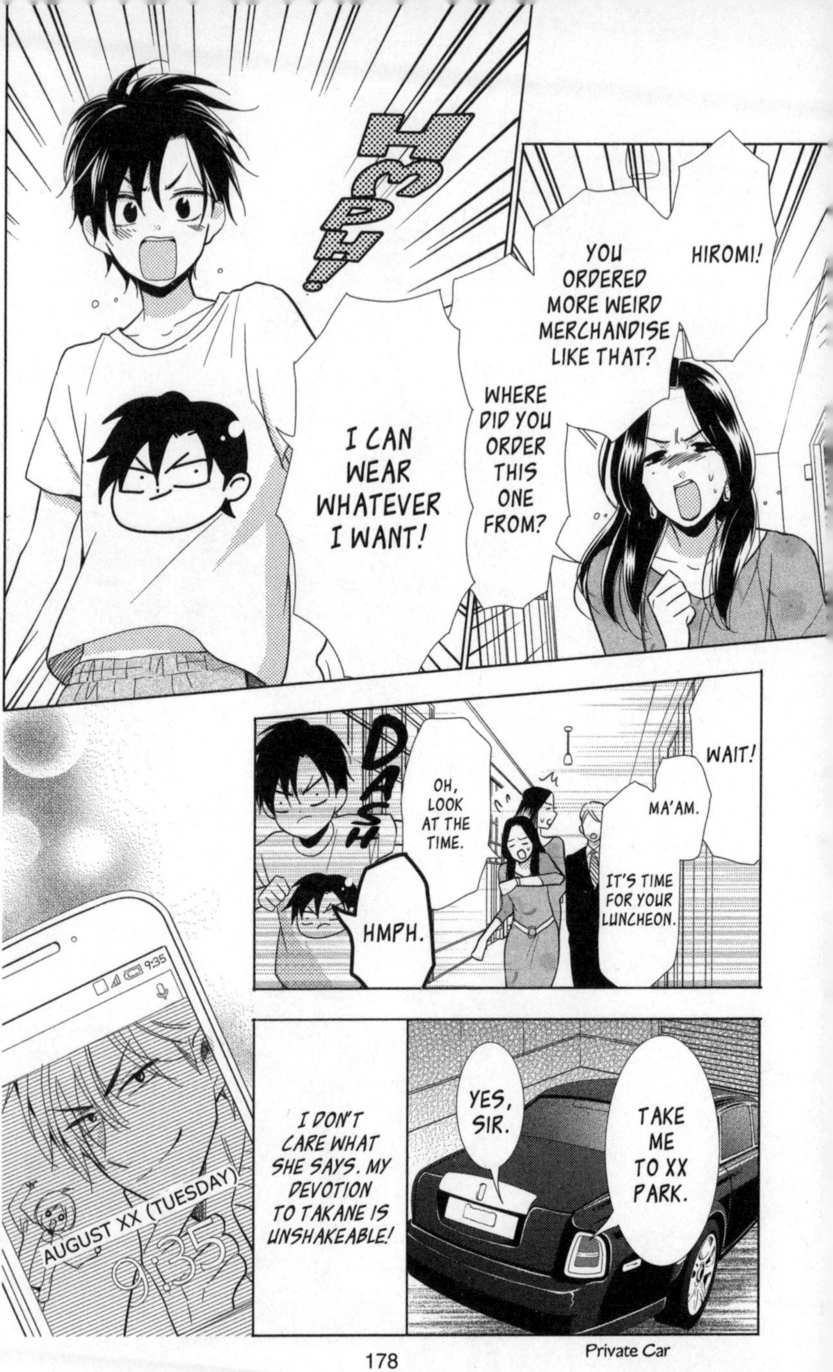

HIROMI!
YOU ORDERED MORE WEIRD MERCHANDISE LIKE THAT?
WHERE DID YOU ORDER THIS ONE FROM?
I CAN WEAR WHATEVER I WANT!
HMPH
WAIT!
MA'AM.
IT'S TIME FOR YOUR LUNCHEON.
OH, LOOK AT THE TIME.
DASH
HMPH.
TAKE ME TO XX PARK.
YES, SIR.
I DON'T CARE WHAT SHE SAYS. MY DEVOTION TO TAKANE IS UNSHAKEABLE!
AUGUST XX (TUESDAY)
9:35

Private Car

...

SIZZLE

OR SO I THOUGHT.

HEY!

I FINISHED MY JUICE.

THERE'S MORE IN THE COOLER.

YAY YAY

THE VEGGIES ARE DONE TOO.

OH, IT'S CUZ...

SHE'S TOO OLD TO BE IN THE KIDS' CLUB.

WHY'S HANA HERE?

I HAVE A TINY LITTLE CRUSH ON HER.

NOD NOD

IT'S NO WONDER TAKANE PICKED HER.

SHE STICKS HER NOSE INTO EVERYTHING, BUT SHE MEANS WELL.

AND THAT GUY'S HERE TO BABYSIT TENMA.

...drew me here.

The smell of a party... ★

...MOM AND DAD HAFTA BE AT THE RESTAURANT, AND MY BIG BROTHER HAS CLUB PRACTICE, SO SHE CAME TO HELP US.

OH.

GOSH, TAKANE'S A MILLION TRILLION TIMES COOLER THAN HIM.

YOU KNOW SO MUCH!

NO, IT'S BAD.

It's not food.

WHAT'S A SLACKER? DOES IT TASTE GOOD?

Do you eat it with mayo and ketchup?

WHAT A SLACKER.

CHATTER

CHATTER

LET'S SEE.

IN FIVE YEARS, I'LL BE AS TALL AS TAKANE!

YOU BET! I'M YOUR HEIGHT NOW.

YOU'RE TALLER!

HIROMI! IT'S BEEN A WHILE.

YEAH, IT HAS.

SH

UP

I KNOW WHERE I STAND.

Hey, Hiromi.

BESIDES, SHE'S TAKANE'S ARRANGED MARRIAGE MEETING PARTNER.

EMPHASIS ON THE "TINY" IN "TINY LITTLE CRUSH."

B-BMP

B-BMP

GROWTH SPURTS ARE GREAT!

WOW!

NO KID-DING.

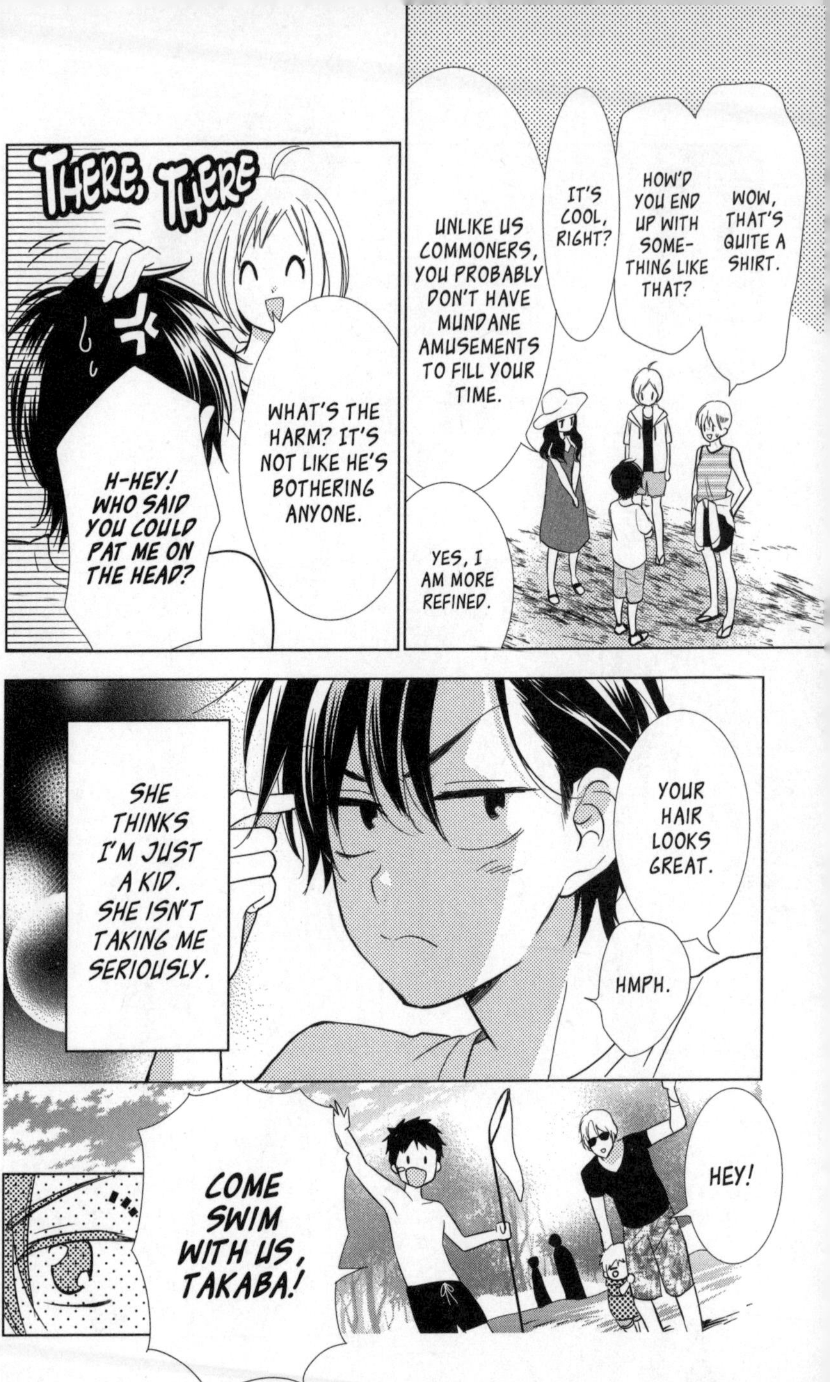
WOW, THAT'S QUITE A SHIRT.
HOW'D YOU END UP WITH SOME-THING LIKE THAT?
IT'S COOL, RIGHT?
UNLIKE US COMMONERS, YOU PROBABLY DON'T HAVE MUNDANE AMUSEMENTS TO FILL YOUR TIME.
YES, I AM MORE REFINED.
THERE, THERE
WHAT'S THE HARM? IT'S NOT LIKE HE'S BOTHERING ANYONE.
H-HEY! WHO SAID YOU COULD PAT ME ON THE HEAD?
YOUR HAIR LOOKS GREAT.
HMPH.
SHE THINKS I'M JUST A KID. SHE ISN'T TAKING ME SERIOUSLY.
HEY!
COME SWIM WITH US, TAKABA!

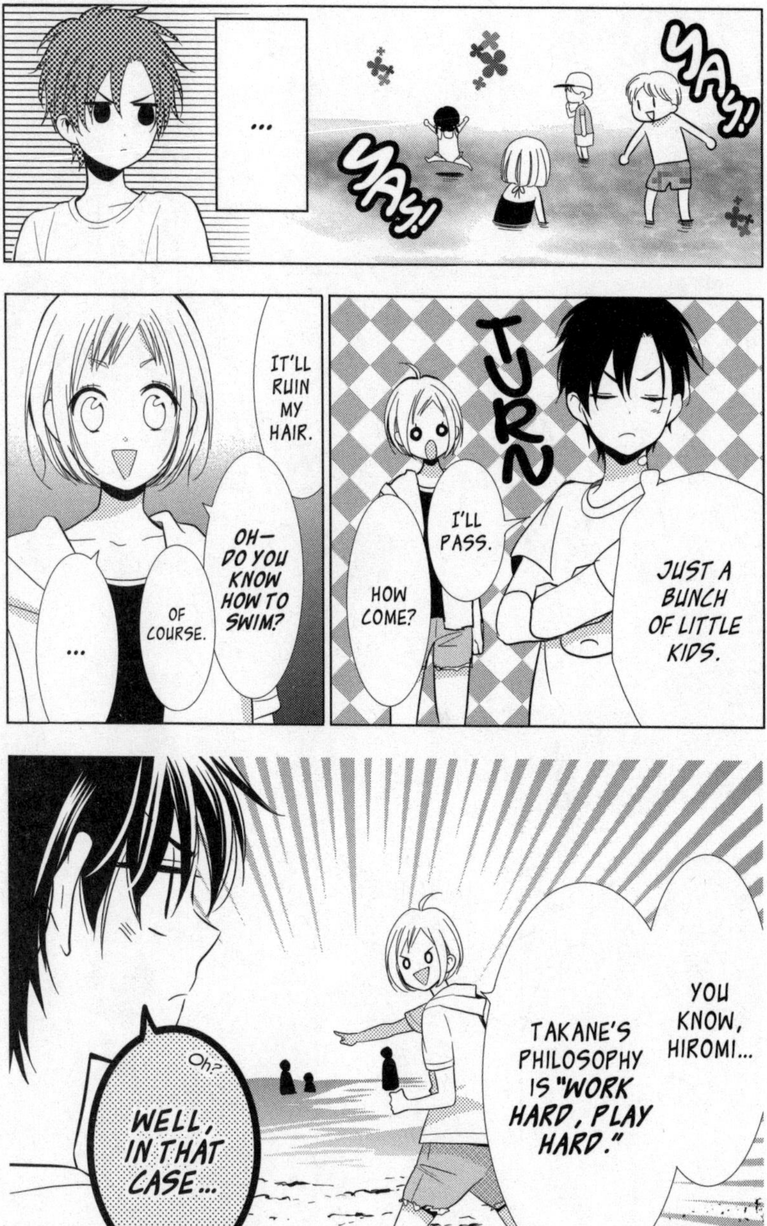
YAY!
YAY!
...
TURN
JUST A BUNCH OF LITTLE KIDS.
I'LL PASS.
HOW COME?
IT'LL RUIN MY HAIR.
OH— DO YOU KNOW HOW TO SWIM?
OF COURSE.
...
YOU KNOW, HIROMI...
TAKANE'S PHILOSOPHY IS "WORK HARD, PLAY HARD."
Oh?
WELL, IN THAT CASE...

YAY! YAY!

SHE'S GOING TO KEEP ON...

...TREATING ME LIKE A KID.

IRK

Ha ha ha!

NO MATTER HOW MUCH I IDOLIZE TAKANE, I CAN NEVER BE HIM.

Why are you running away?

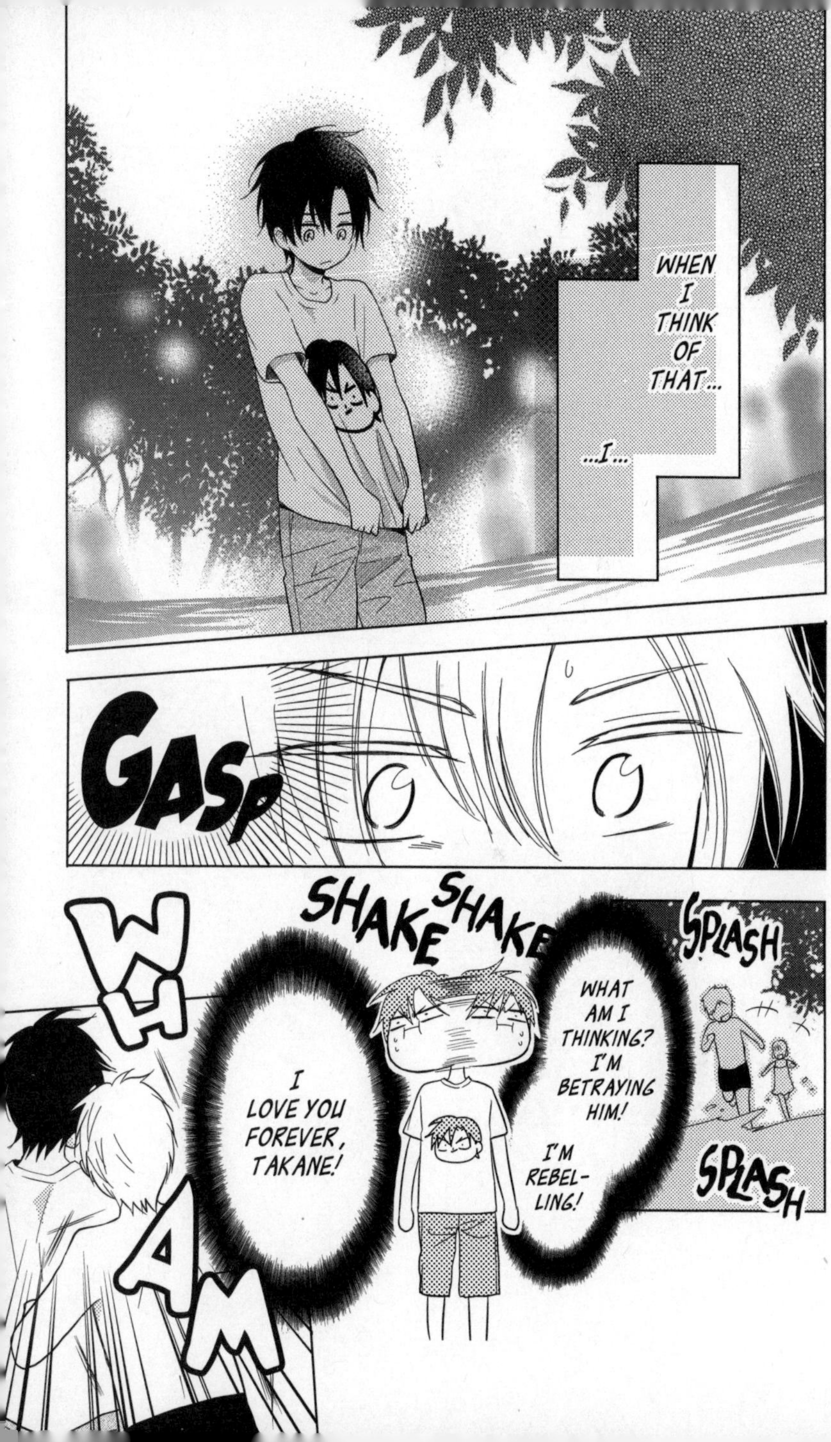
WHEN I THINK OF THAT...
...I...
GASP
SPLASH
SHAKE SHAKE
WHAT AM I THINKING? I'M BETRAYING HIM!
I'M REBEL-LING!
I LOVE YOU FOREVER, TAKANE!
SPLASH
WHAM

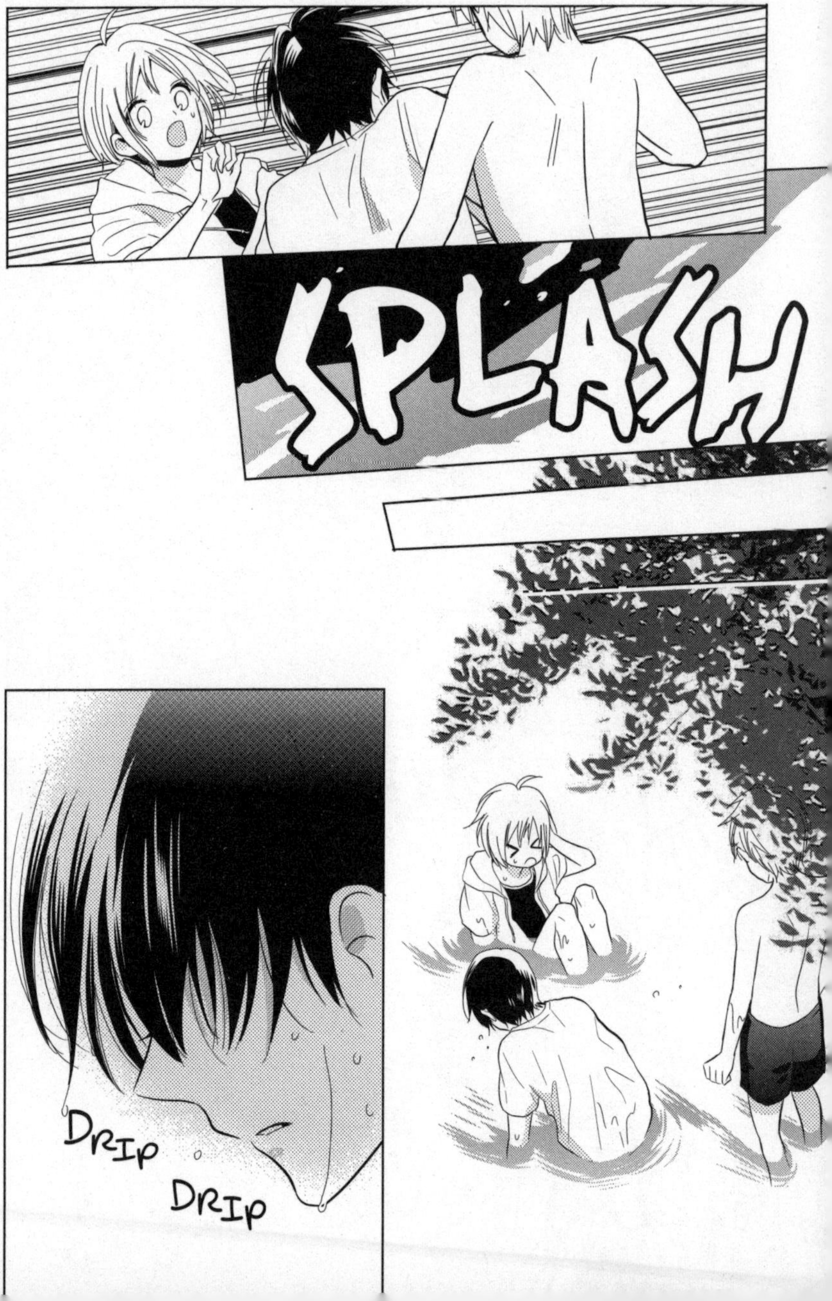
SPLASH
DRIP
DRIP

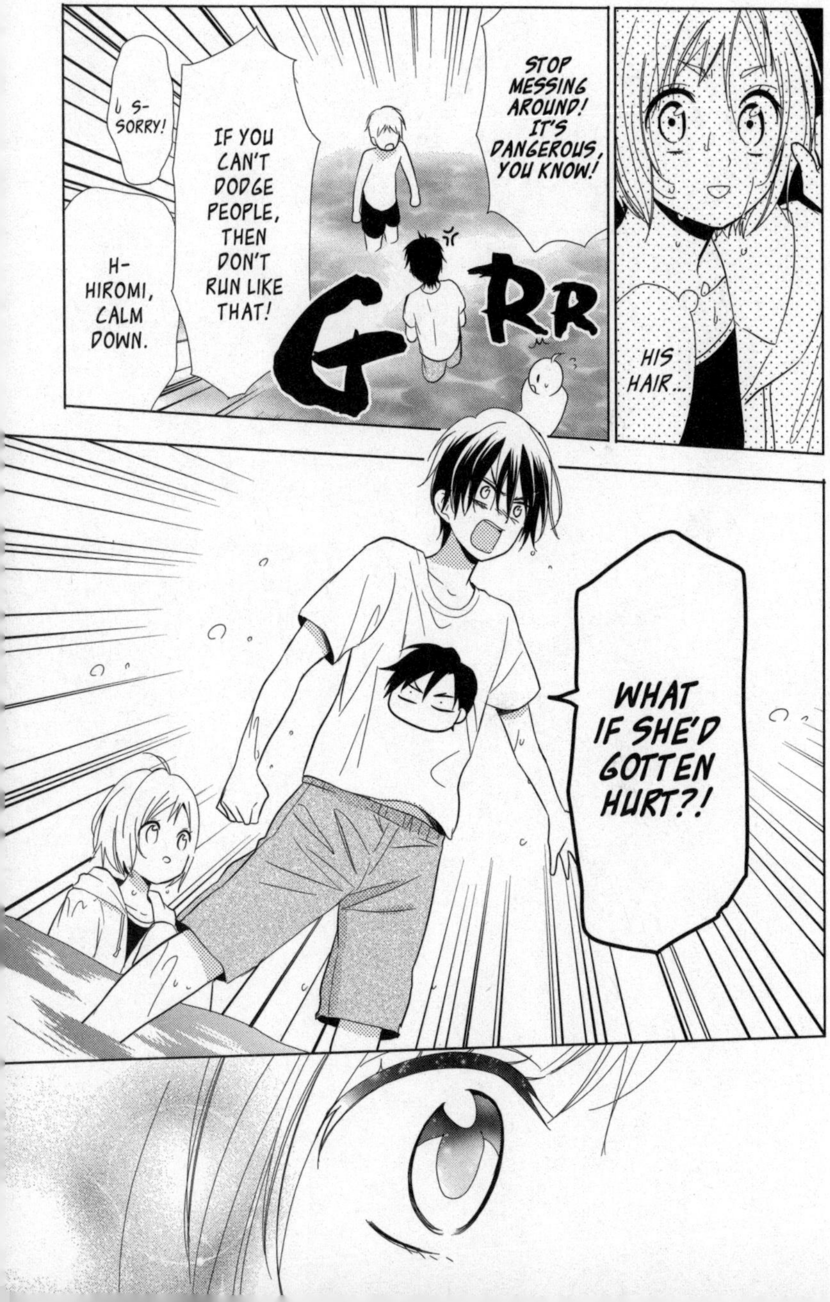
HIS HAIR...
STOP MESSING AROUND! IT'S DANGEROUS, YOU KNOW!
GRRR
IF YOU CAN'T DODGE PEOPLE, THEN DON'T RUN LIKE THAT!
S-SORRY!
H-HIROMI, CALM DOWN.
WHAT IF SHE'D GOTTEN HURT?!

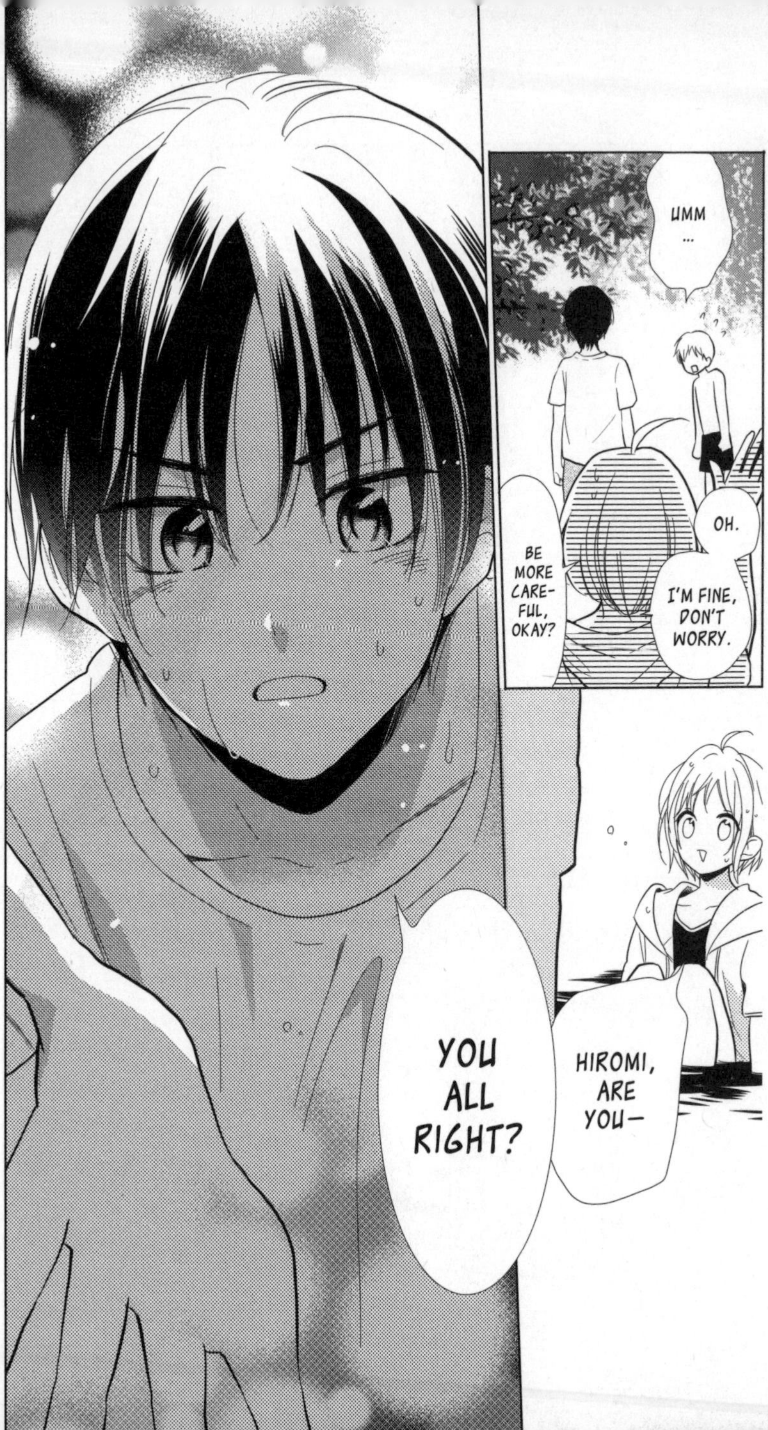
UMM ...
OH.
I'M FINE, DON'T WORRY.
BE MORE CARE-FUL, OKAY?
HIROMI, ARE YOU—
YOU ALL RIGHT?

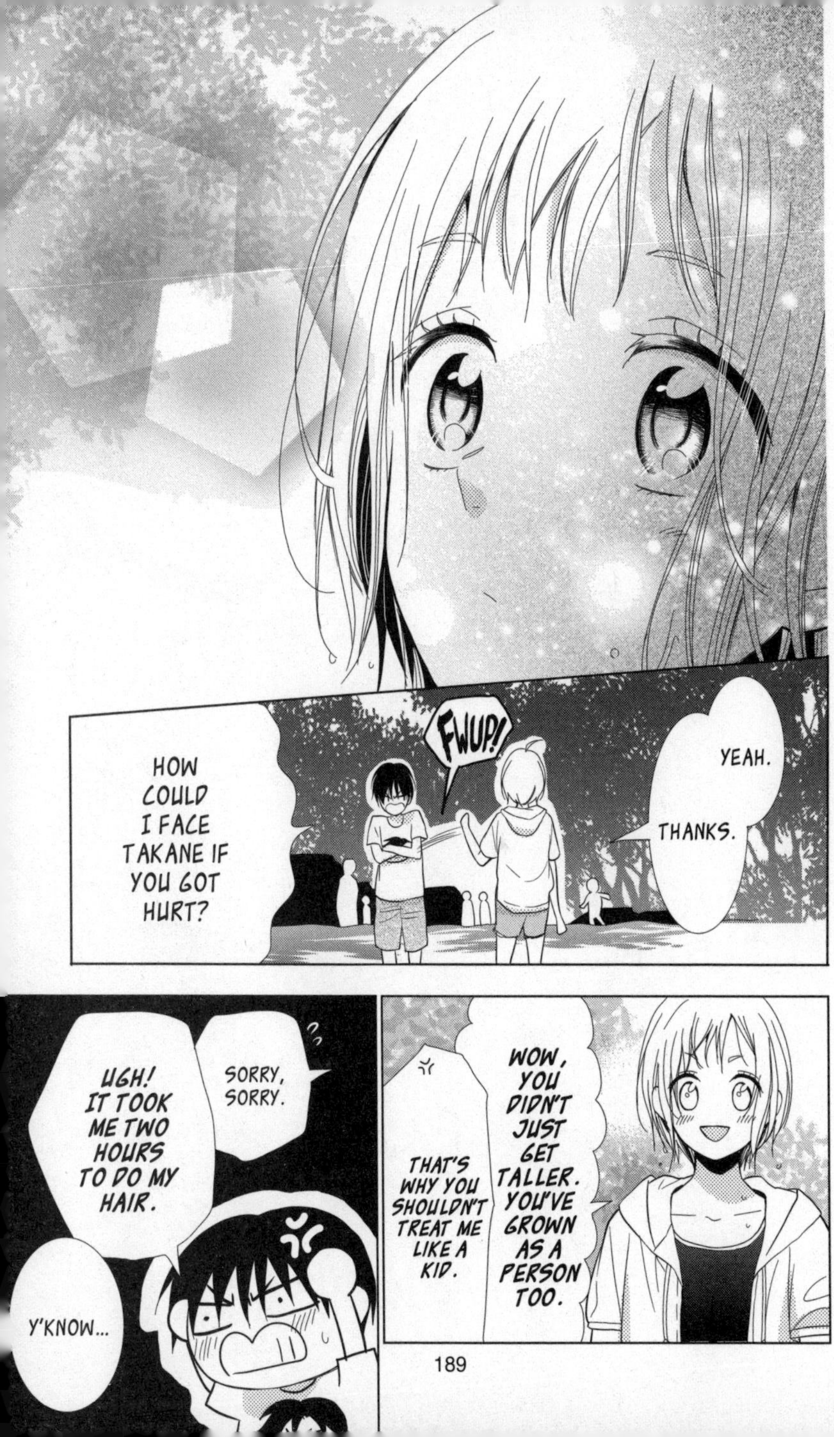
YEAH.
THANKS.
FWUP!
HOW COULD I FACE TAKANE IF YOU GOT HURT?
WOW, YOU DIDN'T JUST GET TALLER. YOU'VE GROWN AS A PERSON TOO.
THAT'S WHY YOU SHOULDN'T TREAT ME LIKE A KID.
SORRY, SORRY.
UGH! IT TOOK ME TWO HOURS TO DO MY HAIR.
Y'KNOW...

...PRETTY COOL THE WAY IT IS RIGHT NOW.

YOUR HAIR LOOKS...

You be quiet!

Quiet, you shrimp!

BUT IT'S JUST A TINY LITTLE ONE.

I MAY HAVE SAID I HAVE A CRUSH ON HER.

Bonus Story 3 / The End

James smiled and countered Mr. Blood's attack with a sequence that backed him up the steps and onto the quarterdeck. James finished with his boot planted firmly on the hilt of Blood's blade. Blood stood completely disarmed and at James' mercy. The shouts went up again for James to run the blackguard through.

"That would be bad form, gents." James smiled at Blood, ever polite, and released his hold on his opponent's saber. Blood seized on James' good form. As he moved to retrieve his weapon, he grabbed a gaff off a coil of line.

"James! The hook!" Jolly R cried. Instead of picking up his sword, Blood slashed at James with the gaff hook. Jolly's warning had given James just the second he needed to turn and grab Blood's arm, fighting to keep the sharp point from gouging out his eye.

"Your good form will be the death of you," Blood said.

"Someday," said James, "but not today."

Capt. HOOK

THE ADVENTURES OF A NOTORIOUS YOUTH

BY J. V. HART

ILLUSTRATED BY
BRETT HELQUIST

LAURA GERINGER BOOKS
HarperTrophy®
An Imprint of HarperCollinsPublishers

Capt. Hook
Copyright © 2005 by J. V. Hart
Illustrations copyright © 2005 by Brett Helquist
Published by arrangement with Great Ormond Street Hospital
Children's Charity. The rights to *Peter Pan* were given to the world-
famous hospital by J. M. Barrie in 1929. They continue to provide vital
funds to help change the lives of sick children everywhere.

Library of Congress Cataloging-in-Publication Data
Hart, James V.
 Capt. Hook : the adventures of a notorious youth / by J. V. Hart ;
illustrated by Brett Helquist.—1st ed.
  p. cm.
 Describes the youthful adventures of J. M. Barrie's classic character,
Captain Hook, from his days at Eton to his voyages on the high sea.
 ISBN-10: 0-06-000222-0 (pbk.) – ISBN-13: 978-0-06-000222-0 (pbk.)
 [1. Characters in literature—Fiction. 2. Eton College—Fiction.
3. Pirates—Fiction.] I. Title: Captain Hook. II. Helquist, Brett, ill.
III. Barrie, J. M. (James Matthew), 1860–1937. Peter Pan. IV. Title.
PZ7.H25663Ca 2005   2004027987
[Fic]—dc22   CIP
                                                          AC

Typography by Alicia Mikles
❖
First Harper Trophy edition, 2007

For David Hart and Michael Samuelson,
who blazed the trail to Neverland before us
and await our imminent arrival . . .

~ CONTENTS ~

CHAPTER ONE

HOOK AT ETON

I T WAS HIS EYES. The color of blue forget-me-nots, piercing, like two novas in a sky of dying stars. Profoundly melancholy, yes. Except when James was angry, at which time two red spots appeared in them and lit them up horribly.

James stood before the Burning Bush at the Crossroads of the Eton campus. Lean and blackavised, his hair hanging in long, raven-dark curls, twisted like candles. Collegers and Oppidans in their Eton suits, consisting of long trousers, tail coats, tall stovepipe hats, and starched white collars, hurried by in all directions. A few wore brightly colored waistcoats, marking the privilege of membership

in the Eton Society, or Pops, as they were called, their long tails flapping behind them as if propelling them along like fish fins. James studied their faces, all giving him the various as they passed by.

"How can God claim credit for this place? This is hardly Paradise. Hades. Bloody Hades. I hate Eton," he said.

"You were thinking maybe of Eden, Jimmy?" answered his aunt Emily. "Don't you be talking that nonsense and saying you hate it. Your father had to niffle you into this fine institution at great expense and greater risk to his reputation. You should be thankful."

James gazed at his aunt Emily and thought her beautiful. Gentlemen were forever turning to look back at her as they passed. James thought her worthy of a place in the Queen's court, worthy even to be the Queen herself.

Two upperclassmen, members of College Walk, reached out and thumped James' black curls cascading over his ears.

"And here I thought we were King's scholars, not Queen's," said one.

"If he scugs for me, he'll be bald soon enough."

Before Emily could stop him, James rapped his umbrella across the nearest Colleger's back. When the Collegers wheeled, James stood posed in the en-garde position, the tip of his umbrella in their faces like a sword. There was nothing playful about his action. His position and stance were those of a skilled swordsman. Survival was instinctive with James—that and a keen sense of good form.

"Oppidan," James corrected. "I am an Oppidan scholar. *Honoris causa.*"

"Oh, an Oppidan and a Scholar? I've never met one of those," the lesser said.

"A little less noise there, Oppidan, when addressing your superiors." The tall Colleger with the dashing good looks directed the tip of James' umbrella toward his lesser colleague.

"Sorry, scummy-chum, but that O.S. after your name does not mean 'Oppidan Scholar.' In your case it clearly means 'Obnoxious Scug.'"

The lesser smiled with an apologetic bow to Aunt Emily, who, of course, immediately attempted to apologize for James, but he would have none of it.

"Might I have your names, as it is my first day and I want to remember everyone I meet," James asked ever so politely. The blues of his forget-me-not eyes were beginning to flash red, causing the Collegers to squirm. The lesser tried to hurry the taller one away, but he would not budge.

"Darling," the taller one replied. It was not a term of endearment but his name. "Arthur L. Darling. And yours, Oppidan? You do have a name?"

James recalled the words of author Mary Shelley, the wife of the famed Eton graduate Percy B. Shelley, that his absent father had quoted in his letter informing James of his acceptance into this worthy institution: "Here were the future governors of England . . . the beings who were to

carry on the vast machine of society; here were the landlord, the politician, the soldier . . . "

"James Matthew . . ." As his mouth moved to form the words of his father's name, his courage failed him. And in that split instant, the Darling boy suddenly knew to whom he was talking. Everyone had heard about Lord B's bastard son coming to Eton.

"Right, James. Well, you might have to add a 'B' to the 'O.S.' after your family name then, won't you?"

"B" for bastard? Bad form, James thought, watching Darling and his accomplice join the stream of Eton Blues.

James entertained the mental image of his umbrella passing cleanly through the Darling boy's brisket and out his backside with a perfectly executed cappo ferro thrust. The fencing master who had tutored James in the skills of the sword during his childhood would have applauded his good form. Even with an umbrella.

James dismissed Aunt Emily at the doors of his residence, Godolphin House, a looming brick affair that was to be his home for the next few years. He kissed her politely on both cheeks, which was the absolute limit of any display of affection James would allow. Even if she was not his real aunt, she had always cared for him and raised him with a mother's love. Every holiday while he waited for his father to arrive for even the briefest of visits, Aunt Emily always remained cheerful and hopeful. The boy could count the number of times he had actually met his father on one hand,

When the Collegers wheeled, James stood posed in the en-garde
position, the tip of his umbrella in their faces like a sword.

with a frightening majority of his ten fingers never having to be used.

"He's not coming, is he, Em?"

"Some urgent business at the House of Lords today, I'm afraid, Jimmy."

"How unusual."

"But he sent these with his love."

Aunt Emily presented James with an official envelope carrying the official crest of the House of Lords and a leather purse tucked full of shillings and half crowns. James weighed both in his hands, deliberating. Letter? Money? Good form? Bad form? If his father was connected to nobles and nobility, as James had been raised to believe was true, then all he had experienced of this nobility was neglect and an allowance.

"I won't be needing his money." James returned the purse. When his distraught aunt resisted, James firmed his hands around hers, pressing the purse into them.

"Oh, please take it, James. It's your allowance. You'll need it."

Her eyes were sharp and bright with tears. Without Aunt Emily, James would be completely alone in the world. Yet there he was, severing his last tie with the one person who cared about him. He was at Eton. He was to be an Eton Blue.

"From here on I will take care of my wants and needs my own way."

James ripped the envelope into two pieces and presented

it back to her. "There is no name or address on this enve-lope. How am I to know this letter is for me?"

By this time Aunt Emily was acutely aware that several students moving their worldly belongings into Godolphin House had slowed their progress and were lingering about to watch. James actually played to the idle audience, openly enjoying himself.

"In the future, if my father wishes to communicate with me, he should have the courtesy to pen my full name on the envelope as any lord might be expected to do when com-municating with his son."

One rather rounded Oppidan set his bags down and applauded.

"Ripping. Absolutely ripping. Could you give my guv a bit of the same? Smashing—"

His name was Roger, an Oppidan who had been at Eton since age six—"Eton blood" they called a lifer. As he was most often jolly, James was soon to anoint him with the name "Jolly Roger," the one and only true friend there ever was to be in his lonely ascent to the top.

Jolly Roger assisted James with his trunk up the wind-ing, narrow stairs to the top of Godolphin House and James' small garret room.

"Roger Peter Davies. Of Kensington. Glad to meet you—" The fud-faced, redheaded rounder let his introduc-tion hang in the air, waiting for James to catch on.

"James Matthew. I don't need your help, but thank you all the same."

"That's it? That's all you've got? James Matthew? Is that your whole name?"

"Actually I prefer 'Jas.' King Charles II always signed his name 'Chas.' I rather like that. Quick. Precise."

"King Jas. it is then."

Jolly Roger overdid his bow as he opened the door, revealing the tiny room that was to be the King's new palace. Roger was suddenly not so jolly at the mess inside. Someone had been there before them, from the look of the wet paint on the bare walls. It was not the color that stopped Roger in the doorway, but the words the fresh paint spelled out:

James Matthew Bastard, O.S.B.

"I guess you do have a last name, King Jas." Roger laughed, making a trifle of the slur against James.

"I guess I do, my jolly Roger."

James wiped a long, tapered finger through "Bastard," then, looking in the mirror, smeared it carefully on his face just as the aborigines in Australia, the Africas, and the Americas customarily did before going into battle. The combination of piercing forget-me-not eyes, dark curls, and face paint all at once cut quite a startling figure in the tiny room.

"Swank. Topping swank"—this was the highest praise Jolly Roger could give to James.

James caught himself fighting back what can only be described as a smile. Here James had come up to Eton

with the full intention of making no friends, and yet he had managed somehow to find this one.

"Good form, Jolly R."

Being eager to put things right for this unusual new arrival, Jolly R offered to fetch the house matron to clean the offending wall.

"It's not a rotten den, King Jas. We'll fit it up nicely."

But James did not want the offending wall touched. "Leave it. It happens to be the truth." He preferred the words be allowed to remain intact as a reminder. "The end," he added after a moment. James punctuated many of his declarations with "The end." It had the effect of dropping the curtain on a moment he did not want the world to forget.

James Matthew Bastard, O.S.B.

Whenever the house matron stopped by to pick up or deliver James' laundry, the kindly woman would fold his clean items into his wardrobe and put fresh linens on his bed, being careful to avert her eyes from the "truth" on the wall. James liked to think of this controversial wall as the beginning of his notorious reign at Eton.

Until his arrival at this seat of higher learning, the most persons young James had ever dined with at once totaled the enormous sum of three: himself, of course, Aunt Emily, always—and on two, no, four, occasions, his father had made an appearance, but he was hardly there, so racked he was

with fear of being discovered. Then there were Em's cats, who did not quite qualify as humans, although Shelley, Byron, and Victoria were more human in many ways than the majority of the people populating the earth. Often an associate of Aunt Emily's would attend, bringing along a ravenous appetite, eating every crumb in Em's cupboard, including whatever James was not fleet enough to grab for himself. There were colorful characters from the theater and the opera; painted ladies reeking of penny perfume, who appeared as garish marionettes in the candlelight as they sang arias. And the men, oiled and bucked up by Em's sparkling presence and the sipping whiskey secreted in their tea, performed the great soliloquies of Shakespeare. James sometimes recited his favorite passages of *Richard III* instead of his prayers at night. "Now is the winter of my discontent . . . I pray the Lord my soul be bent. . . ." It was James' own version.

That first night at Eton, when Jolly Roger fetched James reluctantly from his garret exile and coaxed him down the stairs, past the wall of trophies and colors won by the boys of Godolphin House, and into the long, narrow dining hall, the sight of thirty-nine boys all seated along opposite sides of a great oak table while five Oppidan underclassmen "scummed" to and from the kitchen, serving, cleaning, and taking abuse from the prefects in their bright waistcoats, would have been enough to send a weaker boy fleeing.

But not King Jas. Even as all heads turned to embrace his entrance with thinly disguised agitation at his appearance, so un-Etonian was the boy, he was not deterred from making his way toward an empty seat at the far end of the great table.

"He looks like a baby who's grown out of his diapers."

The voice was loud enough for James to hear, along with several others. He realized the comment addressed the fact that he was not wearing "tails," as was every other boy in the hall who had reached the height of five feet four inches. James was fifteen years of age and much taller than that. Nor did he wear the telltale wide, stiff, white-as-sinless-snow collar that enslaved each boy's neck. James was still clad in a short-jacketed velvet suit with pants that buckled below the knee in the style worn by much younger and shorter boys. And of course, his long black curls, bombilating with each step he took, caused many to delight in the idea of shearing them from his head.

James gave his locks a good shake as he sat in an open chair between two upperclassmen, making sure they each received an annoying brush. The legs of his chair scraped on the aged oak floor as he righted himself at the table and began helping himself to the sea of food.

"You are late, James Matthew . . . whatever your last name is."

The sound of the voice rankled James. Sitting at the head of the table in the seat of power was Arthur Darling, Captain of the House.

"My apologies. I normally dine alone." James was never more sinister than when he was being polite.

"In my house, if you are late, you do not dine at all. And your choice of wardrobe is the shilpits. You'll wear the tails if you expect to school among us here."

James met Darling's gaze and continued to help himself to the beef and boiled potatoes, never averting his eyes or, for that matter, even blinking.

"Bread and water will not break me, and if you choose to isolate me, I shall only have more time to plot against my oppressors."

All Jolly Roger's discreet but futile warning signals from across the table were lost on James.

"We are dour and impenetrable, aren't we?" Darling gave his mouth a proper three daubs with his napkin, then rose, stiffening the cane in his hand, which seemed to be a permanent appendage, and approached. Two upperclass Whips, each with crater faces etched with the excavations of neglected skin eruptions, accompanied Darling down the long table toward James. One dangled a cricket bat at his side, and the other carried an intimidating instrument consisting of three feet of wooden handle with a thick bunch of birch twigs lashed tightly to it. The birches made a gentle swishing sound as the Whip twitched the thing nervously.

"Do you know what a scug is, Oppidan?"

James paused, considered the query, indicated that he did not, and continued loading his plate. "Sounds unappetizing."

"It is . . ." Jolly R whispered to James, risking his own

punishment trying to protect his new friend. James saw the signal—a pointed glance of Darling's eyes to his Whips, and suddenly the Eton birch sped in a blurring arc through the air, striking Jolly Roger on his bare left hand, causing him to spill his plate.

"Care to inform him, Mr. Davies? Enlighten our new O.S.B."

Jolly R was too consumed with trying not to yell out and reveal the intense pain shooting through his arm. The other boys of the house continued eating dutifully, all the while sneaking glances at the simmering confrontation quickly rolling to a boil.

"Right . . . A 'scug,' from the Anglo-Saxon, meaning a cheese leaving . . . a wee piece of the rind to be more precise . . . Mr. Darling."

"Good on, Roger. Now, tell us more. What good is a scug in the great scheme of things?" By now James was completely surrounded by Collegers, Arthur Darling's band of very unmerry men.

"Well, sir, a good scug keeps his master from getting all fagged out and tired like. A scug does anything his master needs—brings him tea, does his laundry, goes to chapel in his place, keeps the beaks happy in classes. See, it's against the rules for a senior, in his last halfs, to ever get tired. You know, fagged out. A scug's duty is to be tired for his master."

Jolly R received a condescending round of applause from the seniors. James continued eating, refusing to allow Darling and his bully boys to have any sway over him.

"How does that sound to you, James Matthew, O.S.B.?"

Darling unseated the boy across from James and sat down face-to-face.

"You're going to be my new scug, James. I will pay you the handsome sum of one farthing a day to tend to my every need and chore. I'm your new master."

James' cutlery striking the china plate was the only sound that could be heard in the silence that followed. Darling posed his offer again. James just stared at him, chewing his food with confident gnashing. Little red dots formed at the centers of his forget-me-nots, burning into Darling's eyes.

"If it's all the same to you, Darling," James replied in his politest and most eloquent diction, "I would rather suck a dead dog's nose."

Darling paled. The Whips gasped. Jolly R was the first to burst out laughing. Others joined him, unable to stifle their unbridled urge to laugh. Whatever bites of food or fluid held in their mouths went spewing, adding to the cacophony. It was as if James had tied each boy down individually and condemned him to death by tickling.

Darling rose, turning crimson and nearly upending the table. He glared at his Whips to make sure none had joined the derisive display. James had turned the entire house into chaos in a matter of minutes. He rose politely and bowed to his new master.

"Your wish is my command, Master Darling." His tone of voice and manner were as polite as they were dangerous.

"You're an impertinent bastard, James Matthew, O.S.B."

"A product of my breeding, which, sadly, I had no control over, unlike yourself, who must have mistaken his mother for a cow." The look on Darling's face should have been etched and bronzed, as the boys of Godolphin House began to moo like Darling's mother.

"You need a good swishing. I am afraid I have no alternative but to beat you."

The laughing and sniggering ceased, snuffed out by the House Captain's sentence. James accepted the pronouncement with an amused grin on his face. It must have been the insolence and rebellious quality of that smile that prompted Darling to point his hickory rod at Jolly Roger and inform him that he would be joining James on the flogging list.

Jolly did nothing to protest the injustice. James was outraged. What law had his friend flouted? What crime had he committed? James demanded to know. He could understand Arthur Darling's need to maintain his control of the boys by making James an example. But not Jolly Roger. His only crime was—befriending King Jas.!

JAMES GETS A SWISHING

ALL THE BOYS were sent to their rooms for lights-out. But none slept. Certainly not Jolly Roger, who was so shaken with fright over the coming beating that he sweated through his clothes as he sat curled up in a ball, seeking refuge inside his stifling wardrobe, hoping he would be spared. But there would be no praying for mercy from James. Waiting in silence in his tiny garret after lights-out, James contemplated his revenge even before the punishment was administered. He unwrapped a pair of handsome rapier blades from an oilskin bag and entertained himself, dispatching invisible foes with his own brand of unorthodox exercises and disciplines. He was at his happiest

when he was conjuring up schemes and devices of revenge against his oppressors.

According to the strict ritual, after evening prayers, the House Captain was required to pay a visit to the House Master in the company of his Whips. There the formal request was made.

"House Master, we wish permission to birch Roger Davies."

And the House Master, a man of some education and often a former teacher in the school, would properly reply:

"And why do you choose this discipline?"

"Because he has repeatedly failed to properly warm his master's tea water."

"Six strokes. Anyone else on the bill?"

"Thank you, House Master. There is James Matthew, a new arrival. Oppidan."

"Yes. Of course I know of him. And what has he done?"

"He is a subversive influence who must be punished."

"I leave him to you, House Captain."

Jolly R had explained to James how it would happen before they were separated to wait in their rooms.

"So the Whips—they run around the house, taking the longest route to your room to make you wait. They run their canes and birches along the wall panels and the staircases. That sends this clattering, whirring noise, all eerie like, bouncing through the house. If they start near your door, you know you are all right. Nothing bad is coming your way. But if they start miles away . . ."

Since then, James had been listening to the clicking and clattering wafting through the house, drawing closer and closer to him. Then it stopped. He could hear muffled voices and canes pounding on a door. Then the sound of the door being slammed open—

"Oppidan Davies!" the voice yelled. "You are wanted in the slab, now!" The Whips sent to fetch Jolly Roger to the slab, as they called the library, were not happy having to search for their victim, thumping and overturning furniture until finally the wardrobe doors were forced open—followed by Jolly's most unjolly voice—

"I demand to see my tutor! I'll tell my father!"

Father? *Whom would I tell?* James thought as he awaited his execution committee. The Whips made a racket escorting Roger down the long flights of stairs. "There's going to be a swishing!" the Whips loudly announced on each landing.

The candle James had lit to aid his sword ritual had attracted its first moth. James became fascinated as the creature flitted about the flame, so close, daring the fire to flicker at just the right moment to ignite its wings and burn it in a flash like a fuse on Guy Fawkes Day. Was it raw courage that powered the moth so close to a fiery end? Or just ignorance? The lack of a brain that could reason and weigh consequences?

The sound of a horrible meeting of wood against flesh thudded up from the library, breaking the silence that had swept through the house. Then the sound of heeled shoes walking a distance . . . stopping . . . turning . . . and then

walking again, picking up speed on the library floor, then running the last few paces before . . . that thud cracked louder this time. A cry of pain followed. A cry that wanted to scream louder but fought to swallow itself for all those prideful reasons the boy summoned. Then another. And another—

When Jolly Roger could no longer hide behind his pride, he shrieked. A helpless animal caught in a trap could express no greater suffering. Never had James heard such a horrible sound.

At the same instant, the moth dancing about James' flame dipped too close, and one wing caught fire. James struck with blurring precision, snatching the moth in his hands. He plucked the burning wing from its body, pinching the flame out with his fingers. He watched the single-winged moth struggling in his hand, flopping about with no escape possible. Another strike echoed from below. Another scream. James thrust the moth into the flame, putting the creature out of its misery. He held the flaming insect between his fingers, watching it char. He showed no pain as the flame brushed his fingers. Placing the blackened remains in his journal, he folded the pages shut, capturing the impression of the burned wing forever.

Beside the charred impression, he wrote: "Courage is the decision to fly straight into the flame while knowing the consequences."

James heard the rattling of birches and canes along the walls again, growing louder the nearer they drew. Now they

were on the narrow flight of stairs leading to James' garret door. Three firm knocks accompanied a voice attempting to sound deeper than it in fact was:

"You are wanted in the library in three minutes!"

James threw open his door, surprising Rupert Wainwright, one of Darling's cowardly custards, and the two other Whips dispatched to fetch him. He doffed his beaver top hat that Aunt Emily had purchased for a half crown on Keate's lane.

"I am more than ready," he said, bowing elegantly. "Why wait? I hear there's going to be a swishing!"

Taller than his escorts, he headed down the stairs as if it were Christmas morning.

James was left standing outside the library for five minutes according to the timepiece given to him by his father. The inscription inside read "Time is the final currency. Spend it wisely." No name. No date. Only the memory of a father who was not there at any time. The house was deadly silent save for the swinging of the pendulum in the tower clock guarding the door of the library. The turning of the internal gears accompanied the striking of the hour. At last it was nine o'clock. As the bells struck, the library doors opened and James entered.

All the senior boys of the house were assembled along the walls of books. James studied the cold faces staring back at him. Arthur Darling stood at the head of a gauntlet of Whips, his foot resting on the first step of the birching block where Jolly Roger and countless others had been

forced to kneel while being beaten. Two Whips escorted James to the block.

"Remove your hat in the presence of your superiors." Darling poked James' lopsided topper with his cane. James dutifully removed the offending item, making a mental note that the tradition of "capping" to a Colleger or a Pop would be the first to go in his new world order.

"Forgive me. I did not realize that is where I am."

"That is precisely why you have been summoned here, James Matthew, O.S.B." Darling crossed his cane in front of him, flexing it with both hands. "Explain why you are subversive to the honor and traditions of this house. Explain why you are a terrible nuisance . . ."

James' eyes caught a glimpse of the intimidating row of switches and canes standing behind the birching block, each more progressively cruel in design. "I am speaking to you, Oppidan. Do you have anything to say for yourself?"

Darling tapped James under the chin with his cane, raising the boy's flashing eyes back to his executioner.

"Twiddlepoop," James whispered.

"What? That's enough snash from you," Darling replied.

"Does your mother know that you are a Twiddlepoop?" James thinned his lips in the insolent smile that was quickly becoming his trademark.

"That smile is coming off your face. I am going to beat some sense into you," Darling answered, swishing his birch.

"I never turn my back on a learning experience."

Darling was spewing mad, pacing behind the birching block. Two holders forced James to his knees on the first step, leaning him over the high second step as if praying at an altar.

Two other Whips stood beside James, holding him firmly down on the block. Darling perused the switches and canes displayed inches from James' face, grasping each one and swinging it for weight and balance. None of the intimidating instruments suited the House Captain for the punishment at hand.

"I need something special for King Jas.," said Darling. "God demands his pound of flesh. Bring me the cat."

A Whip dutifully presented an ornately carved box of mahogany and opened it. There, coiled like a snake, was a braided leather handle. As the "cat" was raised into the air, nine trailing leather thongs unfurled, attached to it like tentacles. Each had barbed metal studs knotted into it along its length. When Darling swished the cat through the air, the studs clacked together like teeth. James offered no reaction to Darling's weapon of choice but fixed his gaze on the wall of books before him.

Aristotle, Chaucer, Defoe, Descartes—

Darling's first lash stung up through James' spine and down his legs like a hundred angry hornets. He uttered no sound but continued his library studies.

Descartes! Diderot! Dumas—

Darling, in his heeled boots, moved away from James across the wooden floor, paused, wheeled, then returned at a gallop, whirling the cat about his head until the precise

moment to strike, whipping the spiked tendrils through the air. James could feel the displaced air from the tentacles the instant before the cat tore through his trousers and into his hams with a sickening thud.

Dostoevsky! Fielding! Goethe!

Jolly Roger buried his head under his pillow to blot out the sound of heels rushing, the clatter of spikes hitting their mark, and the yells of excruciating pain to follow—but no yells of pain accompanied the strikes. He removed his pillow and listened. Nothing from James. Not even a muffled cry. Jolly dared to open his door and poke his head out for a better listen. Other heads peeked from doors, questioning looks across their faces. Why wasn't James crying out? They had the cat on him!

"Maybe they've gone and killed him," one frightened boy blurted out. Jolly R shook his head emphatically no. He sensed the power Darling and his senior Whips were up against. James was like no other boy who had ever entered the school. Eton would never be the same.

SHAKESPEARE! SOCRATES!

James had nearly completed his survey of the books before him, fighting off the excruciating pain burning through his body. And here in this moment of humiliation and torture, he had an epiphany.

When the knots tied into those tails of the cat strike me, he thought, *rather than crying out, if instead I focus my mind on the many methods I could employ to render my*

punisher extinct, then with each lash a new and better idea comes to mind. I am gaining knowledge with each blow! It is true then: I am having sense beaten into me! And, therefore, should only want more.

The sanguine smile that had found its way onto James' face with this realization unnerved the seniors gathered to witness his punishment. This had never happened before. New boys under the whip, regardless of age, screamed for their mommies. They begged, and promised to do anything if their betters would only stop.

"Where are your repentant tears? Why aren't you begging God for mercy?" Darling demanded. "This could not possibly be humorous to anyone with a right mind!"

No tears. No screams. Just James' smile haunting Darling, causing him to strike harder.

"The blood! Where's the blood?"

Seniors lining the walls echoed the question. Everyone wanted to see blood. James's trousers should have been crimson by now.

"He's not human—God save us all!"

Rupert, one of the pock-faced Whips, paled and was overcome to the point of fainting.

Others pushed for a look. Darling was shocked at the sight. James Matthew, O.S.B., was bleeding, no doubt about that. But he did not bleed red. Each wound inflicted by the cruel cat bled yellow!

Several seniors made a hasty exit without asking permission. Darling slapped the cat back into its box and

quickly wiped his hands with his handkerchief—

"Gad! You are a sick scug! Diseased! Some tropical malady, no doubt contracted from the swill you came from!"

King Jas.' smile exploded into a giddy cackle, one he hoped would follow him into adulthood, exuding an infuriating level of mischief, peppered with an air of superior intellect. Maddening. Frightening. The perfect equalizer.

"Stop that! Do you hear! How can you be laughing at a time like this?"

Eton Blues stood there in silence, squirming in their stiff collars and gaudy waistcoats, staring at James. He studied their privileged necks to determine in what order they should be snapped. Here he was in the presence of these gallant seniors—Collegers, the shining examples, who were to lead the scugs from darkness into the light of knowledge, replacing their betters someday as the leaders Shelley's wife, Mary Shelley, had spoken of—politicians, kings, and soldiers. They deserved an honest answer.

"Why do I laugh?" King Jas. smiled, pausing dramatically as he surveyed the lingering seniors clustered around Darling. "Because I know just how each of you is going to die!"

CHAPTER THREE

KNOWLEDGE IS POWER

EWS OF THE INFAMOUS SWISHING and the unusual properties of young James' peculiar mustard-
colored blood spread quickly and required none
of the usual embellishment that comes with the vivid
imaginations of young boys. Who could improve on the
truth?

James' yellow blood became the talk of the entire school.
How this happened to be is credited to Jolly Roger and a
handful of other Oppidan scugs who had posted themselves
outside the library in time to witness the chaotic exodus.
Seniors who had inflicted pain on their lesser Oppidans,
and enslaved them as scugs to do their bidding, now pushed

and shoved like mewling kittens to escape the library and James' yellow blood. Jolly Roger chided Rupert as the sickened Whip emptied the contents of his belly out a window onto the hallowed walkways of Judy's Passage. Inside, young James' maddening laugh became a rallying cry to the boys of Godolphin House.

The Eton *Chronicle* referred to the incident as "A GHAST FEST, THE 'KING JAS. VERSION.'" James Matthew, O.S.B., attained the status of royalty with the speed of a lightning bolt. Eton blood? If it was blue, the color of the moment was neither red nor blue but yellow. Those who had actually seen James' blood were hounded to tell their stories over and over again. Rupert could never manage to complete his retelling without being overcome with nausea.

And what of the Darling boy? He coined a new term, referring to James thereafter as the "mutant." He demanded that James be examined by the school physician, that his rare and no doubt highly contagious blood disease be exposed, and that James be turned out immediately with no provision for readmission. He simply was not suitable by any Eton standards.

Doctors poked and probed James for two entire days. He was quarantined in the clinic while various analyses were performed. During this time, several Oppidans paid regular visits and sent notes to James wishing him well, and thanking him for snashing on the Whips. James was suddenly a very popular fellow. This was something new and disturbing for him. With the exception of Aunt

Emily, of course, he had grown up believing himself to be loathed. And now, fame? That glittering bauble? He liked the taste of it. He liked it perhaps too much.

On the Monday following the swishing, James was discharged from the clinic and declared "healthy, although a bit on the thin side." As to his blood, it was reported to have high concentrations of odd yellow cells that regenerated at an alarming rate, which explained his quick healing powers . . . "an unexplained mutation." Arthur Darling's coinage of the word "mutant" to describe King Jas. was more than simply derogatory name-calling, but all too true. Regarding the color of his blood, it was described in his medical record as akin to the "color of lemon custard" with no further comment. This declaration caused the immediate replacement of lemon custard on every house's menu with a double helping of strawberry mess.

As a newly minted hero, James diligently set about his studies virtually unassailable by the beaks and masters and tutors, who could find no fault with his work. He was never punished for being late to div, as the classes were called, and his writings were posted regularly on the colonnade walls by admiring professors. The tails and pants that replaced his short trousers and jacket only added to his growing stature among the Eton Blues. That and the beaver top hat purchased in a thrift shop made him a striking figure walking across the School Yard between classes. The younger Oppidans followed him like sheep, adopting his manner

and his walk. Several stopped trimming their hair, so scraggly curls and bunches of locks began to appear among King Jas.' followers. So disturbing was this to Arthur Darling that he organized all the House Captains to denounce the "style of hair of women and pagans" being cultivated on the heads of Etonians. When the Provost's office issued an official ruling limiting the length of hair "not to exceed four inches below the earlobe," the Provost wisely excluded Oppidans sixteen years and older, knowing full well that lining older boys up to shear them like sheep would only be challenging the young, brash, bastard Oppidan to open warfare.

James' response to the "hairy edict," as the Oppidans named it, was to orchestrate a demonstration of astounding insolence. Right after chapel services one Friday, fifty-seven Oppidans gathered on the yard in front of the chapel, where, under the tutelage of Jolly Roger and other devoted followers, each boy's head was anointed with shaving soap and skinned near-bald with a straight razor, leaving only a furrow of hair down the center of the scalp in the fashion of certain native tribes inhabiting the Americas. A new style was born, one that conformed to regulations yet succeeded in being repugnant to the Eton bloods.

James made a public display of cutting his own dangling curls before his growing number of followers. His locks were placed in a can and burned, sending an acrid stench floating over the quadrangle.

"The hair is cut! Long live the hair!"

Darling and his Whips stood along the colonnade, powerless to stop the disgusting display of loyalty to the dark and sinister boy who had taken over the hearts and minds of Eton's young scholars. The resounding humiliation that James heaped upon his oppressors after shearing off his locks was doubled when overnight they grew back even longer, denser, and blacker than before!

Professor Pilkington, the bent-over tutor of classics who walked with a cane fitted with a nasty gaff for a handle, fueled James' growing list of accomplishments by posting his essays on the colonnade wall and by delivering them verbatim to all his divs and schools, Oppidans and Collegers—none were discriminated against. James' personal favorite was entitled "Knowledge Is Power." With knowledge, James planned to destroy every "imbecile" who passed through the hallowed Etonian halls. He spent hours in the library, making the great hall of books his personal fortress. Here James studied the great villains of history, who became his heroes. Alexander the Great, Julius Caesar, Nero, Ghengis Khan, Richard III, King John, Harry V and Henry VIII, Charles II, and Louis XVI with his marvel of capital punishment, the guillotine, which was used at his own execution. Villains made history. Villains changed the destiny of the world.

Where would mankind be if Eve had not taken a bite from the apple? What did she obtain from the experience of that succulent bite? Knowledge! James found Eve's

"reward" for obtaining knowledge unusually harsh. And what of Pandora? Her curiosity caused her to open the box given to her by the gods, releasing suffering and disease into the world. James concluded that injustice was the price of obtaining knowledge. Prometheus, the proud Titan, brought the gift of fire down from the heavens and gave its power to mortals. James could not imagine the world without fire. Yet Zeus punished his kinsman for sharing this wisdom with man and condemned Prometheus to eternal suffering. Why were the gods so set against mortals gaining knowledge? James wished to know.

"Knowledge is power," James wrote in his journal. The more knowledge he acquired, the more powerful James would become. He vowed to devote himself to acquiring all knowledge at all costs until he could plan his exit from this world to a more perfect one he would discover someday—and rule there as King Jas.

James rarely slept now. The dark dreams that haunted him were calmed only by the growing vision of this new land that had invaded his imagination. It was an island—at first a shapeless pool of teasing pale colors suspended in the darkness. Then, if James squeezed his eyes tighter, the pools began to take shape and the colors became so vivid that with another squeeze they would go on fire. Just before the point of ignition, the island . . . came true. And for a few moments James would sleep peacefully until, sadly, the vision would disappear.

He found the island again in his pursuit of knowledge. The study of zoological life and evolution, particularly the

studies of the rare, impossible, fascinating species that lived in the Galápagos in the South Pacific. Judging by the unusual collection of creatures that inhabited them, it appeared that all time was standing perfectly still there. It was a place where dreams could be born. He dubbed the dream island "the Neverland" and vowed to find it one day when he was the captain of his own voyage of discovery.

James' pursuit of knowledge made him a frequent visitor to the science laboratory. The avid arachnophile's search for the most poisonous spider in the laboratory's live collection was interrupted one day by Jolly Roger and two timid underclass Oppidans.

"King Jas."

"If you insist."

James turned to the boys while petting a palm-sized spider. Four pairs of large black eyes lined its head, and its thorax was covered in bright red fuzz laced with yellow dots that curved in the shape of a hook. The thing was, well, covering his hand—a good nine inches long! At the sight of the boys, the eight-legged nightmare reared back, flashing its poisonous mandibles. A high-pitched whistling came shooting out of its fanged mouth. The boys, Simon the Snash and Dicky Dongon, along with Roger, retreated hastily behind a workbench.

"A rare *Lasiodora parahybana*, from the upper reaches of the Amazon," said James. "That's just her way of saying she likes you. Not to worry. Electra won't bite. Unless I tell her to."

James blew gently on the spider's back, and to the amazement of the boys and especially Jolly Roger, the creature replied with a series of whistles, lowered her front end, reversed, and marched right up James' arm, stopping on his shoulder to perch. Two other equally unsettling arachnids revealed themselves, crawling over his back and taking up positions on his other shoulder and atop his head, the smaller of the species using his twisting curls to assist its rapid ascent.

"The wisdom of the spider is greater than that of all the world together," said James, quoting a traditional saying of the African folk legend Anansi, who was both spider and man. Everyone just stared at James and the spider collection. James tried again. "I've read that certain species of arachnids choose a location and wait for hours, even days and weeks, without moving, until the right victim happens along. Then they strike. The result: paralysis of their prey."

As impressive as James' eight-legged menagerie was, Jolly Roger had an entirely different agenda.

"James. . . ." Jolly Roger spoke tentatively. "You see, it's like this. I, I mean we—these gents and I—have a proposition that you cannot possibly refuse."

Each of the boys then produced a shiny shilling displayed proudly in his palm. "One shilling for one drop of your blood. Three shillings, three drops."

James eyed the wealth the boys offered. Quickly he penned a calculation of numbers and volumes and pints and other values on the bench top. And then he laughed. "I'm rich."

In a blur he snagged a lancet from the tool tray and stroked it across the tip of his thumb without so much as a wince. The pinch of a yellow bloom of blood James then presented to the first boy, trading it for the shilling.

"One for you, and you, and well, two for you since you are last and the smallest." He pinched the drops into each boy's tin and took their money, delivering two drops to the ten-year-old Dicky Dongon, who roared with approval.

"Topping swank, King Jas."

As the underlings tottered off, awed by the yellow gold they now possessed, James slipped one of the shillings into Jolly Roger's waistcoat.

"Good form, Jolly R. There's plenty more where that came from, eh?"

Jolly Roger was bowled over by the generosity of his King. He laughed so loudly at the potential windfall that could buy him almost anything his heart and stomach desired, the trio of spiders suddenly leaped from James through the air with great accuracy and took up residence on Roger's jolly face. Distraught with fear that he was about to be stung to death, Jolly all but ceased to draw air into his lungs until James gently removed each of his pets and placed them back in their cage. Except one—Electra, the large female with the jagged blaze curved like a hook on her thorax.

"I've got a special home for you, my beauty," he said.

The rare specimen of *Lasiodora parahybana* disappeared from the science hall that night. Electra's departure went

largely unnoticed except for the others of her species that had looked to her for leadership.

That night, after prayers and lights-out, James climbed out his narrow garret window and inched his way along the gutter forty feet up in the air to the corner downspout, then descended. At Darling's window James paused, assuring himself that Darling had gone on his rounds for the purpose of being absolutely positive no boy was out of his room past lights-out. Satisfied, James opened the window and stuck his head inside.

Electra, crouched atop his head, where she had been riding comfortably, jumped to the window curtain. James watched as she crawled up to the valence, reared again, and leaping to the headboard of Darling's bed, traversed up the wall, climbing over the collection of awards and colors Darling had won during his years at Eton. Then Electra affixed herself on the ceiling directly over the Darling boy's pillow—and waited.

Darling returned from his rounds a few strokes before ten. He sat at his study by his bed and made his entries of infractions into his flogging bill—

"Joyce three times forgot to light the fire for tea. . . . Geringer on the bill for knotted shoelaces. . . . That Barrie imp sleeping during prayers. . . . James . . ."

There was no entry he could put beside King Jas.' name. His very existence was an infraction that deserved a good lamming every day as far as Darling was concerned. The

only problem was risking another letting of yellow blood. The boy's stature had already been elevated beyond any acceptable level. He flaunted his mutancy like a coat of arms and mocked the traditions of Eton. And worse, the younger boys looked up to him. Darling would have to find some way to stop King Jas.' spreading reign at Eton. Perhaps the fencing team might afford Darling the opportunity he sought. After all, as school champion, Darling could be bested only by Lord Wellington himself, were he still among the living, and the member of the Kings' Fusiliers who regularly instructed Eton boys in the way of the sword. Perhaps a bit of poison on the tip of his foil could ensure a complete victory. It had worked for Laertes against Hamlet, had it not?

Only yesterday the bastard James was asked to be captain of games and join the house's Wall Game club. The humiliation would be beyond repair if an illegitimate love child of a member of the House of Lords led the Oppidans to victory over the Collegers in the traditional St. Andrew's Day Wall Game match. There, in the tangle of a bully-scrum, Darling knew, he would have more than one opportunity to knuckle James' pretty face into the bricks forming the wall along the narrow playing pitch. Even if knuckling drew Darling a penalty from the umpire, it would be worth it to smear the slippery nuisance into the mortar and brick of Eton. "The end," as James would say.

Darling so dizzied himself with his plans to end James Matthew, O.S.B., he did not see the *Lasiodora* descending

from the shadows of his ceiling. As he conjured visions of himself running James through again and again, the eight-legged nightmare landed on Darling's pillow and went straight for his exposed neck. There the spider affixed herself and sank her black fangs into his skin, repeatedly shooting venom straight into Darling's spinal cord. Before Darling collapsed and began to swell like a soufflé, he managed to slam Electra against the wall and was about to crush her eight legs to the floor with the Holy Bible always on his bedstand, when the poison invaded his gray matter and froze him stiff as a cricket bat. Electra managed to crawl out the window, up the downspout, across the gutter, and back to James' open window before Darling could muster a cry for help.

James, who had been waiting patiently in his room, rose up when his dark accomplice climbed back in through the window dragging one damaged leg. By the time the House Master and the matron had carried the Darling boy to the clinic, James had returned his arachnid friend to her cage in the science hall.

"The end," James said as he bowed to Electra.

Darling remained in the infirmary for a fortnight, burning with fever, his fingers, knuckles, joints, face, and head swollen like a patch of overripened melons. Every day James stopped by with Jolly Roger to look in on Darling and offer his aunt's homemade lemon custard as a certain cure.

And every day Darling looked at the custard, he was convinced it was James' blood. As a result, he hid under his

bedclothes. For the rest of his life Darling had an aversion to lemon custard and anything yellow. "Cowardly custard" became his nickname, which was freely used by even the youngest Oppidans, not only behind his back but to Darling's face as well.

After the incident of the spider, King Jas. dreamed of magical islands in the South Pacific where time stood still. His island was becoming more real with every recurring dream. Its geography grew more familiar with each appearance. The mysterious outcropping of earth jutted up from the misty blue like a great whale breaching from the depths. At its center a conical mountain of volcanic ash rose up to a smoking pinnacle. Animals and plants never before seen abounded in this paradise. Uncharted on any maps, it was as if the convenient little island had appeared by magic. His island. His Neverland. There, he would truly be King.

One night, after waking from a particularly vivid dream, James performed a delicate operation on his arm with a lancet he had liberated from the science laboratory, cutting a word into his forearm. The scar tissue, when healed, would permanently read "Neverland."

CHAPTER FOUR

THE WALL GAME

ALL BOYS ARE EXPECTED to play games at Eton. House Captains prided themselves on the performance of their house teams in cricket, rugby, rowing, the game of fives, the art of the sword—and then there was the Wall Game, Eton's own blood-and-mud event.

The field of play was as fraught with dangers as the rules were complicated. And those rules, it must be noted, had never been written down in spite of having originated over a century prior to James' arrival. The field was barely fifteen yards in width, traversing a not-so-straight brick wall some nine feet high and over a hundred yards end to

end on one side. A furrow not more than three feet wide marked the boundary on the other side. Two teams of ten would battle it out, attempting to move the ball up and down the field to score goals on either end of the pitch.

"How hard can that be? Seems simple enough. One side moves the ball down the pitch and scores while the other tries to stop it. Quite like any military conflict we study in history. Hardly as challenging as chess from the sound of it," James countered when Jolly explained it to him.

"Listen, James, there has not been one single goal scored in the Wall Game in the last hundred years. Plenty of broken bones and faces mashed in for trying, though. That's a bloody fact."

James had been elected unanimously to the Oppidan team by the underclassmen as a result of his heroics at his one and only swishing. In spite of his much-published loathing and distaste for sporting events—with the exception of fencing, a skill at which James was unsurpassed, having been trained from a very young age—he had become a threat to the Collegers. The hope was that the Collegers would be inclined to refrain from kicking him and lamming James' head against the wall for fear of his yellow blood gushing all over their uniforms. No upperclassman wanted to see James bleed.

"Then we shouldn't disappoint our betters, should we? My blood is yours, Jolly R."

"If it's all the same to you, King Jas., I'd rather you keep it to yourself."

"You want to win, don't you?"

On that there was no question. Winning, besting one's opponent, was the order of the day at Eton. At all costs. Rules are the folly of cowards, James came to believe. When it came to winning, one should be willing to do anything. Break all the rules, risk life, limb, reputation, honor, dignity—all for the glittering bauble of victory. Anything less was hypocrisy. But of course it all had to be done with good form. James would have his victories no other way.

"And what is our prize should we beat the Collegers today?" he asked.

Jolly Roger did not answer as he and James joined with the flow of Eton bloods heading for the wall.

"A golden goblet?"

"Hurry, Jas. There is someone I want you to meet."

"Ahh, a jewel. That's it. A jewel for my crown."

James followed Jolly Roger, who was in no hurry to respond to his speculations. At the point of thinking his friend was verging on bad form, James grabbed Roger by the back of his striped jersey and spun him around—

"Soap in your ears, Jolly?"

"Can't hear you, James. I've got soap in my ears."

He started to hurry on, but James extended his left foot, tripping him.

"Humor the Jas., Jolly. What am I to win in this contest of blood and mud? What is the treasure, eh?"

James' eyes were getting red. Not a good sign so early in the day. Jolly brushed himself off and blurted out the truth—

"A pudding."

"A pudding?"

"Yes, a pudding."

"We risk life and limb and my princely good looks for a spoonful of sweet sock?"

"If that is how you choose to view it, yes."

"I view it as a waste of time. The end."

Jolly Roger righted himself, dusted off his stripes, retrieved his cap, and hurried on.

"What about fortune and glory?" James was truly dismayed at this discovery.

"It's in the pudding!" Jolly Roger replied.

On this morning of St. Andrew's Day, the top of the wall was lined with Etonians sporting their colors, turned out in force for the match of the year between the Oppidans and the Collegers, or scugs vs. tugs, as the boys expressed it. Scores of old Etonians, who lorded as O.E.s, returned every St. Andrew's Day to celebrate the patron saint of Scotland and to relive their youth and glory days by watching these young boys tear one another apart. Many were fathers, James suspected, who had come to see their sons distinguish themselves in combat. James held little hope of his own making an appearance, although he studied the various groups of gentlemen who collected on the grounds that day. A lauded O.E. in his own right, his father had been a champion Wall Gamer and a winning wet bob on the rowing team. He should be there to see his son attempt to hold up the family tradition.

Jolly Roger's father had boated out from London on the Thames, piloting the family's private yacht. Roger had been so eager for his father and mother to meet his new friend that he convinced James to brave his aversion to water and row out into the river to greet them upon their arrival. James refused to immerse himself even in a tub to bathe, choosing the sponge method of bathing in the privacy of his room. He never explained his phobia to Roger, but there was little hiding it while sculling in the middle of the river. Every drop and splash from the oars might as well have been acid the way James recoiled.

"It's not like you're going to melt, King Jas."

"How do you know that for sure, Jolly R? After all, I am the one with yellow blood."

"I concede your point, King Jas. If you told me you could fly, I would have to be of an open mind on the subject."

James had gone strangely silent, no longer concerned about the drop or two of water that had landed on his sleeve. He had stopped rowing and was fixed on the sight dead ahead of them.

The seventy-foot yacht gliding their way was the most magnificent sight James could remember seeing in his entire life. Nothing else could possibly compare to the sleek hull carving the waters of the Thames, the billowing sails pulsing with life. James visibly struggled to understand the excitement surging through him. He had never been remotely interested in boats, because they required being near or on the water. Yet all he could think about, upon seeing this vessel,

was a longing to walk on its deck, to feel his hands upon the helm. James had seen larger ocean-going ships at anchor in Greenwich, but never in motion, never in the good graces of favorable winds and so close he could reach out and touch—

"Permission to come aboard, Father?" Jolly Roger's voice stirred James from his reverie.

An older and more weathered version of Roger leaned on the gunwales, regarding the two boys drawing alongside in their sleek rowing boat. The order to heave to had been given. The sails were dropped. The anchor was lowered with a splash as they rowed under the bow of the grand vessel. The figurehead affixed below the forward bowsprit brought a smile to James' face. Instead of the usual buxom siren, staring right back at James was the face of the devil. MEPHISTOPHELES, the yacht was branded along the bow. Had Jolly R's father made a deal with the devil to acquire such a dream of a ship? James wondered how much longer Jolly's father had before delivering his soul to the devil and thus perhaps passing on his claim to his son.

"Not so fast there, Oppidan," his father teased. "I'll not have just any Eton blood on my ship. Who asks, you scugs?" Roger's father glared at James. "With those tresses I cannot tell if it be a him or her."

James stood up, balancing himself in the rowboat, and announced proudly his full name.

"King Jas. we call him, Father," Jolly added. "He's my mate I've been writing you about."

James had seen the sour look before, when the cogs of the gears fell into place and the beholder had arrived at

the correct solution about *who* and *what* James was.

"Correct!" James found himself wanting to cry out. "I am the bastard Etonian you've read about! And your son is in my power now!"

Of course the polite course of action, the only good form that could be taken, was to be properly understanding, as Jolly Roger's dashing father stood there on the deck of the ship James coveted, making the reasonable excuse that the Wall Game was too close to commencing to allow young James a proper tour.

"Perhaps later, Master James."

"Of course, sir. She's an eyeful, sir."

"Jas., Father, he goes by Jas."

Jolly R rowed angrily back to shore while trying to make excuses for his father's rudeness. James showed not the least distress over the course of events. A desire had been opened in him unlike any he had ever imagined. He later thought what he was feeling might be the emotion people labeled "love."

"We'll call it the Jolly Roger," James announced quite matter-of-factly as he pulled on his oars.

"The Jolly what?"

"The ship. When we take it from your father."

Jolly R nearly missed the water with his oars as he keeled over, almost falling out of the boat. James had his eyes set on the yacht drifting at anchor, ripe for the picking.

Cheers went up from the boys on the wall as Jolly R and King Jas. joined their ranks. Random drums were beaten as the two rival teams approached the field from the

School Yard. The parade was led by pipers and drummers from the school corps who played the rousing Scottish anthem, "Scotland the Brave," droning across the grounds. Arthur Darling, still a bit green around the gills from his bout with spider fever, had only just been released from the clinic in time to captain the Collegers' Wall team against the Oppidans. Darling marched to the drums, carrying the Saltire flag of Scotland in honor of St. Andrew, the patron saint of all Scots.

Darling had ordered his Colleger tugs to paint their faces with the same colors as their game togs, which also matched the flag. They chanted fiercely, marching the length of the wall, rousing support from O.E.s and other Collegers massing along the field. Darling had to captain a win this day. He could not allow another humiliation at the hands of the odd Oppidan who was ruining his life. His academic standing had suffered during his incarceration in the infirmary. His authority at Godolphin House had eroded. Here, in the presence of royalty, he would distinguish himself. He had to.

Yes, royalty. Even James was impressed that the Queen herself should take leave from her residence at Windsor Castle and cross the Thames to Eton to attend their games. A gallery had been erected alongside the center of the pitch. And there, sitting under a great royal-blue and gold umbrella, was the Queen herself; her trademark hair, parted down the middle and tightly coiled over both ears, gave her the look of a schoolgirl, even at her advanced age of forty-odd

years. The dark tincture of her hair manifested the longevity of her Hanoverian bloodlines, refusing to gray or grow brittle regardless of how many ghosts of birthdays past she would entertain. The members of each team were required to halt as they passed and bow to Her Majesty. Her wave and near-imperceptible nod to the boys in between comments and chitchat to her entourage elevated this moment for an Eton blood to the category of legendary.

But it was the mysterious pretty face seated next to the Queen that each boy's eyes drifted to as he rose up from his bow. Ananova was her name, a Khanum Sultana of Turkish descent, a Princess. At only fourteen years of age, Ananova was living proof that goddesses do come from Greece. The Sultana had accompanied her father, the Sultan, all the way from the Grecian isles, where he ruled under the Ottoman Khan. Ananova was seeing England for the first time. Her instruction in proper manners to ensure proper behavior before the Queen and her Court was a source of great conflict between the Sultana and her tutor. Ananova had also tired of her father's endless efforts to prevent her from enjoying herself. Her father needed this diplomatic visit to go well with the Queen, due to the civil unrest among the Greeks and Cretans living on the many islands under his control. This meant that Ananova was not allowed to have any "adventures," as her tutors referred to them.

The Queen had been a girl once herself and knew exactly what the young goddess needed. There was a smile hidden

in her flawless features, but no one had yet found the code to unleash it. As soon as Ananova's father had departed to go hunting, the Queen suggested a visit to the most prominent boys' school in the world, just across the river from Windsor Castle and only a short carriage ride away. Ananova bit her tongue, wanting desperately to smile, but instead she curtsied politely without falling to one side or the other during the descent, then rose and excused herself to prepare.

Once alone in her chambers, the Sultana let out a squeal of unbridled delight. Boys! Eton men! Kings and Lords and Princes and Generals were born on the playing fields of Eton. A solid hour ticked by as she struggled to choose her attire. Then another hour to change, then half that to change her mind and be dressed in another costume. It took four attendants two hours to tidy up her chambers when Ananova was finally escorted away.

And now her ebony eyes roamed over the faces of the boys collecting before the gallery to pay homage to their Queen . . . and to Ananova.

"And what do you think of our selection of young English gentlemen, Ananova?"

The Sultana had developed an extremely bad habit of telling the truth, and this was no occasion for altering that policy.

"To be quite honest, Your Majesty, they all appear alike to me. I cannot distinguish between them. See how they wear the same suits, with their hair shorn in exactly the same fashion? One is just like the next."

The Queen must have been impressed with the young Sultana's display of gumption in daring to give such a truth-ful answer. The striking, olive-skinned girl from the lands of the Aegean had the true makings of a Queen in Her Majesty's eyes. She would require a very special matching from the ranks of young Englishmen. Finding Ananova's equal would be a challenge.

James stood out like a ghost marching with Jolly Roger and the other members of the Oppidan Wall team, his skin so pale it was almost blue in comparison to the others around him. One Colleger commented as the Oppidans passed by that James looked as if he had only just this morn-ing emerged from his coffin. The comment almost flew by James, who was still musing over the impact that the *Mephistopheles* had made on him. *Jolly Roger* was the only name for that craft. And it would be his someday.

"Oh, my coffin's not so bad actually," James answered, startling the Colleger. "The problem is there's nothing to eat. Not a scrap. Unless you go cannibal. It's a fact that if I do not ingest the beating heart of a Colleger before evening prayers, my head and arms fall off. Is that the beating of your heart I hear?"

James' elongated hand was a blur pressed against the tug's jersey, his talon fingers squeezing over the young man's heart as if poised to rip it from his chest cavity. The Colleger yelped like a hound on the hunt, he was so startled. The Queen noticed that Ananova was paying no attention

to the boys bowing before her but was more interested in something else entirely. The girl was finally smiling.

"Child?"

"Your Majesty?"

"You are smiling at something for a change. Which one?"

The Queen knew very well what had caught her charge's attention; it could only be one of the boys passing and bowing before the gallery.

"Point him out to me. I shall arrange for you to meet."

"Oh, no, Your Majesty. I simply couldn't."

"You can and will. I am the Queen, and I always get my way. It is the one benefit of being Her Majesty I cannot imagine living without."

Embarrassed, Ananova gestured rather than pointed.

"There. That one."

The Queen followed Ananova's pointed look to the boy bowing low before the gallery and dipping the Scottish flag in respect. Arthur Darling, Captain of the Collegers' Wall club, recent survivor of a venomous attack by Electra.

"My, my, he is a handsome bucko." The Queen summoned her aide with the tiniest curl of her finger. "Skeffington?"

"Your Majesty?" Skeffington spoke, but his mouth remained so tightly drawn, his voice must have come from somewhere else inside him.

"The lad there carrying the saltire—find out his name and his family background. See if he is a suitable acquaintance for our little goddess from the Aegean."

Skeffington, stiff-necked, set off on his thankless mission. And the wrong mission at that. The Sultana had not been studying Arthur Darling.

"No, no, no. Not him, Your Majesty. That one, there."

Skeffington stopped and watched as James' shiny black locks cascaded over his face as he bowed before the Queen's gallery with Jolly Roger and the other Oppidan gamers. When he raised his head and his long hair parted like a curtain, the ebony eyes of the Sultana held his forget-me-not blues, refusing to look away. Holding her gaze as long as he dared under the watchful eye of the Queen, James bowed again and moved quickly on.

"Who is he?" Ananova followed him with her eyes as he led his gamers onto the pitch.

"That one? Surely you jest? I doubt he should be playing in this match at all. A stick of straw would knock him over."

"He's the most unusual boy I've ever seen, Your Majesty. His gaze went right through me!"

Skeffington returned and bent discreetly to his Queen, speaking quietly. Her Majesty's face grew grave. She stiffened, her hands gripping the top of her parasol so firmly that her knuckles became white.

"Sultana Ananova." She spoke with the tone of an iceberg, causing everyone around her, especially the Sultana, to feel her chill. "I must forbid you ever to have any sort of contact, public or private, with the young man in question."

"What harm can there be in an innocent conversation with one of Eton's worthy—"

But the Sultana never finished her question. The sharp strike of the Queen's parasol down on the gallery floor, and the narrowing of her eyes as she swiveled her regal head to face the young Sultana, silenced every conversation within earshot.

"There is no innocent conversation to be had with that . . . Oppidan. Since I cannot command you, and he is my subject, any attempt by you to defy me will result in his arrest and removal from the school."

The Queen extended her hand for the Sultana to curtsy before her, a public sign of her submission to the Queen.

"Who is she?" James was still looking over his shoulder at the Queen's gallery, trying to keep the vision with ebony eyes in his sight.

"Never mind her, Jas. We've the entire honor of the Oppidan underclasses resting on us. She is just some Princess from Greece or Turkey or someplace."

"Greece? Turkey?"

"Or the isle of Crete perhaps."

"Crete. The site of the Minoan palace. Where Theseus battled the minotaur for the love of Ariadne—"

"You do know your Greek mythology, don't you, Jas.?"

"How long would it take to sail there, I wonder."

"Sail?"

"In the *Jolly Roger.*"

Roger tried to turn Jas. away from gazing back in the direction of the Sultana. James remained steadfast.

"We have a match at hand, King Jas. Could we worry about one thing at a time? Besides, the Ottoman Turks still cut off your hands if you are caught committing a crime."

"I am only thinking about winning. Not about committing a crime."

Jolly Roger looked at Jas., then at the Sultana, then back at Jas. "Besides, she is *just* a girl," he reminded his friend.

"Oh, no, Jolly R. You've gone blind. You are in desperate need of spectacles. She is not just a girl. She is a goddess."

James was so undeniably enchanted by the second vision he had seen this St. Andrew's Day that he failed to avoid walking right into the two-hundred-seventeen-year-old brick wall marking the game pitch. The impact was firm enough to send him reeling back—which placed him, for the first time since the swishing, in exactly the position Arthur Darling wanted him. The derision was instantaneous from the Collegers, beating their drums, blowing their pipes, and laughing at the downed King Jas.

"Well, well, look at the King!" Darling guffawed, and paraded around James, overacting. "Flat on his bummy-hunk, where he's going to be spending the rest of the day. The wall's been there only two hundred years, Jas.—ass. Maybe you should walk on water before you try walking through walls, scug."

Darling's tone was so rancorous that the hope every Oppidan sitting on the wall had brought with him for a victory evaporated. Collegers seized this moment of weakness and taunted the underclassmen up and down the wall,

yelling and beating the bricks, raising their appetite for the blood sport to a fever.

James remained flattened there on the field looking up at Jolly Roger, who was hard-pressed to live up to his nick-name at the moment.

"Bad form, Jas." was all Roger could manage to fumble out. "Listen to them."

James folded his hands behind his head and crossed one leg over his propped-up knee as if lounging at the shore.

"Oh, Jolly R, good century, the seventeenth. Good bricks. Am I bleeding yet?"

"No, thank the gods."

Jolly Roger was growing concerned that the blow against the brick wall had knocked James' canny sense out of him. Everywhere he looked, Collegers were laughing and jeering at James, while Oppidans were shrinking in voice and in number and the match had not even begun! James showed no sign of getting up, and no one was rushing to help him.

"Jolly R, I've seen two visions this day, and I do not yet know which one is the more important to my life. I intend to lie right here until that decision is determined."

The tone in James' voice was not threatening or de-manding, but no one—neither scug nor tug—made any motion whatsoever to remove James from the field by force. James had been bombarded by two surprising turns of events in almost as many hours. Not only had the sight of the *Mephistopheles* stirred his yearnings in a most unexpected direction, but now a Sultana? A girl whose

mere glance had so undone King Jas. that he walked into a wall? He had been raised by one female all his life, longing for the company of his father. But that a girl should have this effect on him . . . This was some kind of magic, some kind of sorcery that had captured him. Suddenly, there she was, filling up his every waking sense.

Ananova stood up in the gallery arching on the toes of her boots in an attempt to catch a better view of the wall and James. The Queen reached behind the Sultana and tugged on her cloak, sitting her down hard.

"Your Majesty, someone must help him," she protested.

"Royals do not stand on such occasions, Ananova, and a royal, when appearing in public, always maintains her composure and does not show her emotions, even at an execution." She offered Ananova a fan, indicating to her how to use it to hide one's expressions. Ananova snapped her fan over her face with a defiant look. The Queen did not see the young Sultana exhibiting her tongue like a serpent in the Queen's direction.

James had not yet responded to Mr. Pilkington, who now stood over him, jabbing him with his hooked cane. Pilkington had been the umpire at the Wall Game for as long as most O.E.s could remember. His hooked cane came in handy when collaring a fouler or a furker and yanking him from the field for an infraction of the rules. Now he asked James again if he was quite ready to play.

James rolled over and picked through the closely

cropped grass as if searching intently for some lost object.

"I demand that the mutant be disqualified for delaying the match, Mr. Pilkington." Darling's demand was echoed by the Collegers three deep along the furrow marking the wall-less side of the field.

"Muuu-tant! Muuu-tant! Muuu-tant!" they chanted. Darling's new word had caught on quickly. James lifted himself up like a cobra before a Hindu snake charmer, his head weaving from side to side, all his senses returned and ready. Then, knowing that the unexpected is a powerful weapon, James slithered to Arthur Darling and smiled treacherously. In his fingers he held a freshly plucked four-leaf clover, which he offered in the spirit of good form to Darling. "For luck," he said, still smiling.

"Good form."

Before releasing the charm completely to Darling, James plucked a leaf from the clover, removing any mysterious powers it might have had.

"Call me a mutant again, Darling boy, and I will rip your heart out in front of all your bloodthirsty supporters and suck it dry before you stop breathing."

James spoke this through a frozen smile of diplomacy. His forget-me-nots flashed a single red warning shot. Arthur Darling dragged a finger through his war paint and smeared a red dot right on the end of James' nose.

War!

"Stop talking!" Pilkington marched to the center of the field, whacking players with his cane.

"Are you ready?" He raised the oval leather ball over his head for all to see. Oppidans sitting on the wall cheered. Jolly Roger's father joined the Collegers and O.E.s pressed along the sidelines trying to get a view of the first bully. Oppidan gamers and Colleger gamers faced off on opposite sides of the orchard ladder that marked the center of the wall. Ten on each side. Twenty bodies now crowded onto the narrow pitch, all eyes fixed on Pilkington.

"The time of the contest is to be two complete half hours. No substitutions will be allowed. Any player injured, or ejected for repeated infractions of the rules, is not to be allowed to return to the match."

Darling was fixed on James, determined that the Oppidan would be leaving the match on a stretcher.

"Who calls for the Oppidans?" Pilkington raised the gold coin in his other hand for the toss. Jolly Roger launched James forward. Darling stepped up as Captain of the Collegers to witness the toss. Pilkington showed both sides to the crowd for approval. The Queen gestured from her gallery to proceed. Pilkington then readied to toss it into the air.

"Call it in the air please, gentlemen."

The coin tumbled up into the air seemingly for an eternity before gravity pulled it back toward Eton ground.

"Since Mr. Darling is so good at losing his—*heads*," James called as the coin landed on the ground. Pilkington placed his boot over the coin, concealing the result.

"This scug is mocking the sanctity of our tradition!"

Darling boiled. Pilkington admonished James for his conduct.

"I am not the one losing my head, Mr. Pilkington," James replied.

Rupert, the largest boy playing for the Collegers, had to lift Darling off his feet to hold him back. Pilkington removed his boot, revealing James' accurate call.

"Heads it is."

A cheer rose up and down the wall of Oppidans. Sympathetic O.E.s joined the hopeless crusade. Jolly Roger's father was not the only proud one present that day rooting for the Oppidans. A certain Lord B stood at the rear of the Queen's gallery, hidden in the shadows, watching intently from under the brim of his topper, the reluctant father of James Matthew, O.S.B.

During this demonstration Ananova hid her mouth behind her new fan and whispered to the Queen, asking if this demonstration of cheering meant that the Oppidans had won. The Queen allowed herself an uncharacteristic girlish giggle and pointed out how useful a simple invention such as the fan can be on such occasions. The Sultana had just saved herself from courtly embarrassment had anyone but the Queen overheard her absurdly uninformed question. The Oppidans had merely won the toss of the coin, allowing them to choose a goal—or "calx," as these zones were designated—to defend. Etonians took pride in calling things by their Latin names, *calx* being what is called "chalk" in the Queen's English; chalk was used to mark the boundaries and goals. There was the "good calx," that being

the goal with the garden door, and the "bad calx" at the other end of the wall, which was a scraggly tree. Of course, James chose the "bad" over the "good" in keeping with his reputation.

"I should have tightened my corset. We are in for a bumpy ride." The Queen was most matter-of-fact.

"Stop talking!" Pilkington called out, as if expecting some objection from the assembled Oppidans and Collegers, who were facing each other, crowded together now in a pack. Then, drawing three lines into the turf with the hook of his cane running perpendicular to the wall across the narrow pitch, Pilkington pointed directly at James and announced, "Heads." James took his place on the outside line and bowed as if performing a theatrical recitation. This, of course, precipitated spontaneous calls of derision and booing from the Collegers and their vast numbers of sympathizers. James got down on all fours and steadied himself against the wall.

"Are you ready?" Pilkington asked in his loudest squeal.

Darling and two other tugs, including the brutish Rupert, lined up opposite him in the few inches that separated them for the first bully.

"Coming!" Pilkington cried out in his scratchy voice; then he rolled the ball down the narrow space between them to the wall. James immediately covered the ball, latching it between his knees, and attempted to crawl forward. The pain was instant as Darling drove his head into James' shoulder. He was hit from all sides at once as the rest of the Collegers piled on behind Darling, attempting to push

James back and loose the ball. At precisely the same moment, Jolly Roger piled on behind James, pushing James with his head and shoulders, bolstered by the bodies of eight other Oppidans, all digging in in an attempt to shove James down the field with the ball safely between his knees.

The scrum of bodies and legs shoving and pushing against one another appeared as a giant turtle might if it had grown forty legs and could not decide which way it wished to go.

Fingers gouged eyes. Knees hammered against ribs. Heads speared into spinal columns. Of course, each of these punishing impacts qualified as an infraction of the rules and was subject to penalty. Pilkington was more concerned that no hands be allowed to touch the ball until it reached the calx ends of the wall than he was in preventing the bodily injuries that were mounting by the second.

The Oppidans lost their first linesman when Rupert drove a boy's face directly into the brick wall, flattening the scug's nose with the sound of a melon being dropped onto cobblestones from a great height. The boy was carried from the field by his fellow Oppidans.

In the tangle of the scrum, James and Darling had their faces pressed against each other from the driving weight of the collective bodies leaning on them. But James protected the ball as the scrum inched down the field.

Suddenly the ball was loose, rolling toward the furrow. James was in too much pain as he rolled on the ground, trying to breathe, to witness what happened next. Jolly Roger raced ahead of the tugs pursuing the ball and managed to

kick it down the field, bouncing it off the brick wall and rolling it toward the good calx. The Oppidans swarmed with the Collegers after the loose ball—leaving James doubled over.

Ananova was on her feet.

"Don't go hurting him, now! I'll have the fellow's head who touches him again!" she cried.

The rousing jeers that followed did not embarrass the young Sultana but only served to make her loathe this game. The Queen motioned to Skeffington, who inter-vened, placing his hands upon the Sultana's and then rais-ing the fan over her face. This did nothing to silence the boldness of her voice.

James could hear that voice above the din as he at-tempted to breathe again. His vision was a blur from the head buttings he had suffered. An excruciatingly painful effort was required to pull himself up onto his feet. The wash of faces yelling along the sidelines of the furrow had neither edge nor clarity to give them shape other than a mass of wagging mouths and waving hands—with one exception . . .

Ananova.

Every feature of her angelic face was crystal clear. "James," her eyes seemed to be saying, "you are destined to be greater. I see this as no one else does." He looked quite the goose standing there striped with mud and dirt, gawking into the gallery with a strange questioning smile on his face.

James' father, secreted in the rear of the gallery, had the sudden strange sensation that his son was looking directly at him. So unnerved was the gentleman by this mistaken assumption that he ducked his head and promptly left the premises without so much as bidding the Queen farewell.

"Bully on the spot!" Pilkington's voice broke the moment between the goddess and the boy. Play had ceased, and Pilkington was busy yanking boys from a pile by hooking the cruel handle of his cane through the necks of jerseys and the waists of leggings, heaving boys this way and that, until he reached Jolly Roger and Darling at the bottom, both fighting over the ball.

"There you are, you little furker." Pilkington yanked Jolly R by the neck, referring to the offense he had committed. "Furking outside the calx. Fifteen yards." Jolly Roger protested the accusation of making the illegal pass, but Pilkington was not listening.

"You should be ashamed of yourself, Jolly R." It was James politely admonishing Jolly as he strolled up as if on a lark. "Furking like that? Bad form."

James continued to wipe the mud and dirt from his uniform and his face, then tidy his hands on Darling's leggings. Darling batted away James' hands as he would a leper or a street urchin.

"Bully up, scug-mutant."

"Coming!" Pilkington crowed, rolling the ball again between the two opposing forces. Darling fell on the ball immediately. His fellows bullied behind him, rolling over the

Oppidans, grinding faces and hands and legs into the ground as the scrum inched back up the field toward their calx.

If a team could penetrate the ball into either calx area, then a "shy" could be scored. This was accomplished when an attacker raised the ball off the ground without using his hands and trapped it against the wall. A point would be awarded to the attackers, along with the opportunity to throw or kick a goal. James began to understand why a shy was rare and no goals had been scored in over a hundred years. The bully action continued for the entire half hour of the first period, and into the first seventeen minutes of the second half, and still no team had penetrated the other's calx or scored a shy. Certainly the account in the Eton *Chronicle* would have made for better reading had the young reporter been privy to the devious strategy the Oppidans had agreed upon to ensure them a certain win.

"Do you want to win?" James had asked Jolly R and his fellow Oppidans before the match. Jolly R and the others on the Oppidan Wall team were afraid to say yes to the tall, pale boy with the forget-me-not blue eyes and the long black mane. He had a plan, one that would guarantee the underclassmen a sure victory, but at what cost?

This was the fear James had to face throughout his days, that amorphous abyss between what people say they want and what lengths they are actually willing to go to, to risk achieving their heart's desire.

At the forty-ninth second of the seventeenth minute in the second half, James succeeded in delivering the ball into

the good calx area of the wall. This was achieved by allow-ing himself to be smeared along the wall like butter on a scone. James had managed to pin the ball with his back against the wall along one of its most jagged peppered sur-faces. Jolly R and the remaining Oppidans, the ones who had not been removed from the game with bruises and crushed fingers and elbows, placed their shoulders against James and pushed with all their might. Darling resisted with the superior opposing masses of Collegers' body weight to try to deny the Oppidans any further penetration toward their goal. The harder the tugs pushed, the flatter James became against the wall. By releasing all the resist-ance in his muscles and frame and going with the gravity being forced upon him, King Jas. began to skid along the brick surface. Like a wet sponge, the harder he was squeezed, the softer and more pliable he became, until he oozed along the brick facade as if made of mud. Behind James, trailing along the wall, a wet, sticky smear from his back charted his progress. Slippery to the touch, the smear was yellow.

Three Collegers shrieked like frightened children upon seeing the oily slick and retreated. This gave Jolly R and the exhausted Oppidans the edge they needed to move James closer to the calx zone. Darling dug in his heels, grinding against James. Rupert braced his shoulder against the middle of Darling's back and pushed with all his might.

"Darling boys—so you're afraid to see my blood, are you?"

"Bugger off, Jas-ass!" Rupert sputtered.

"Not me, mutant," Darling growled.

"Right. Good. How about your own?"

Before either of the grinding Collegers could decipher the threat behind the question, James opened his mouth wide and sank his teeth into Darling's right forearm. Before the shock of the bite had time to deliver the bad news to Darling's brain, James had released his powerful grip and savagely bitten him again.

Darling jerked and pulled and yanked with all his remaining strength, trying to free himself from the iron jaws of King Jas. With each effort James was pulled closer and closer down the wall toward the goal.

"Foul! He's biting me! Foul!"

O.E.s and Etonians lining the wall and the furrow watched in shock and outrage as Darling finally tugged his bleeding arm free. Calls of "Foul!" echoed across the field, but the Oppidans cheered.

"Blood. Blood. Where's the blood!" Oppidans chanted, mocking the Collegers' familiar taunt delivered during the swishings.

Pilkington, by the second bite, had waded into the bully, yanking scugs and tugs with his hook, trying to put a stop to the chaos. To the Oppidans' credit the underlings, under Jolly Roger's leadership, maintained their scrum, pushing James and the tangle of disintegrating Collegers into the calx area.

Sultana Ananova could no longer stand to be so removed from the excitement. She stood abruptly, waving her fan like a sword in battle, cheering the Oppidans.

"Sultana," the Queen cautioned, "the cheering of blood went out with the lions and Christians."

"Begging your pardon, Your Majesty, but I am from Greece." Sultana Ananova curtsied to make a hasty exit. "How do I get closer? I must see."

"Well, child, you must bustle."

"Bustling." This was the only word Skeffington was required to speak to send the Queen's Guards into motion, escorting the two royal ladies from the gallery and through the thick of the crowd with ease.

"I like bustling," Ananova whispered behind her fan as the boys of Eton fell back in her wake.

"GOT IT!" James called out from beneath the tangle of the scrum flattening him against the garden wall. This was followed by his mocking laugh, which only succeeded in fur‑ther infuriating the Collegers determined to flatten James into a greasy spot against the bricks. Darling had found his way through the tangle of torsos right to James' smiling face. James had no intention of showing any pain. Darling could see the ball wedged between James' legs and the stones of the wall. Jolly Roger's hand had found its way through the maze of limbs and was firmly set on the ball. As hard as he tried, Darling could not pry the ball free, so he did the most honorable thing a senior Colleger could do—he drove his right knee into the center of James' groin. And then he did it again.

"Shall I bite you once more, Darling? And suck your heart dry?" gasped James.

By the time Ananova and the Queen arrived at the furrow, the bully had all but stopped. Pilkington had successfully separated the two clubs from each other, with the exception of James and Darling, who stood frozen against the wall in a struggle to the death.

"Mr. Darling!" Pilkington spoke with what little adult authority remained on the pitch. "A shy has been claimed! This bully is ended!"

"Furking scrag bit me!"

Darling continued to drive his knee into James with no seeming effect.

"This is a gentlemen's game, Mr. Darling." Pilkington hooked his cane about the boy's neck. "And gentlemen do not bite or kick a fellow player while he is down. Which is, from all observances, precisely what you are doing. Noblesse oblige, gents, noblesse oblige."

Darling had to be physically pulled apart from James by his tugs, who had enough sense to act. Darling was in danger of receiving a penalty for dangerous play. Biting during a sporting contest was unheard of in Pilkington's view of the world. There was some conjecture after the incident that Pilkington was reluctant to inspect James' teeth for fear of being bitten himself.

James remained flat against the wall as if impaled on the ball. Truth be told, he was so on the verge of fainting from the pounding and mashing that he nearly missed the sight of Ananova standing at the furrow only a few feet from him. His vision had blurred so that he thought the woman

standing next to this goddess was his aunt Emily. Light-headed and completely oblivious to the voices yelling around him—"Shy! SHYYYYY!"—James remembered how often he had thought Aunt Emily reminded him of the Queen.

Jolly Roger led the chanting as every Oppidan on the wall and along the furrow joined in. Drums beat and pipes droned while Pilkington carefully inspected James' position. He was correctly holding the ball against the wall with the backs of his legs below the knee. No other hands save those of Jolly R had found their way through the tangle to touch the ball. Darling refused medical attention from the matron.

"The squeamish will send me inquiries on this one, mind you," the Queen observed. "It is difficult to imagine boys of Eton kicking and scratching, gouging and biting, breaking every rule of this honored game in order to gain advantage and win."

"Sounds very much like the English parliament, Your Majesty," observed the Sultana, never taking her eyes off James.

"SHYYYYY!" Pilkington confirmed, holding up the ball James had so dutifully pinned against the wall.

Jolly Roger was the first to leap, punching the air with joy.

Darling fumed, pacing at full bristle. Rupert and his fellow tugs protested along with the scads of Collegers up and down the wall. Jolly Roger's father had pushed his way to the furrow and joined the O.E.s, who suddenly felt brave

enough to cheer the Oppidans. The man actually held up currency and called for a wager!

James removed himself from the wall and the wet, oily slick that marked his path and paraded back to his team. Ananova, now completely beguiled, wanted to know every-thing about the game. She asked the Queen about this term "shy," wanting to know its meaning, since clearly there was nothing shy in manner that could be attributed to any of the players, especially James Matthew.

"Skeffington—shy," was all the Queen needed to say. Her devoted aide commenced to recite the rules of the Wall Game that to that day had never been written down. "A shy is when an attacking player touches the ball with his hand below the wrist, the ball being supported against the wall, fully off the ground, by any player on his own team with any part of his leg below the knee, and the team claims the shy with the words 'Got it!'"

Ananova acknowledged excitedly that James had screamed precisely those words.

"The hands and feet of the player supporting the ball, the player touching it, and the ball itself must be fully inside the calx line." Jolly Roger's hand had indeed touched the pinned ball, and James' body had been shoved and smeared down the wall well inside the calx line. As Skeffington droned on, both teams were lining up opposite the ball once again.

"When a shy is claimed, the bully must stop moving at once and break as instructed by the umpire. The umpire calls 'Shy!' if he is happy the claim is a fair one."

"And this is a good thing?" Ananova had become completely vexed by Skeffington's interminable explanation. The Queen matter-of-factly reached out and covered Skeffington's mouth with her fan.

"Ah, yes, because now you see the Oppidans have the opportunity to score a goal, which would humiliate the Collegers for eternity. You see, child, no goal has been scored in the Wall Game in over a hundred years."

Now Ananova looked upon James and Jolly Roger and the younger, smaller Oppidan team with new respect and understanding.

"GOOOD FORM, OPPIDANS!" she cried. "MAKE THE BLOODY GOAL AND KNOCK THOSE COLLEGERS ON THEIR SCRAGGY ARSEEEEESSS!"

Even the most liberal of Etonians in attendance went slack-jawed at that one. Skeffington stopped breathing until the Queen thumped him with her cane. Every eye had turned to Ananova—until the Queen smiled as if nothing had happened and made a little circle with her hand indicating that the game proceed.

Jolly R jostled James, breaking his trance. "You heard what the lady said, James. All you have to do is take the ball, give the tossy a heave through the garden door there—" he said as he twisted James' head so he was facing down the wall to the garden door some twenty-five yards from where Pilkington had placed the ball—

"—and you'll go down in history."

All the Oppidans echoed Jolly R's assessment. James surveyed the Collegers now pacing like animals, cornered with no face left to save. Darling stood like a statue over the ball, jersey barkled with blood, fists clenched tightly. His eyes reminded James of a drawing he had come upon in his biology studies—the dead eyes of a shark.

"Look at them," said James. "In the event you have not noticed, our opponents are no longer afraid to see me bleed. In fact it is my blood they want. . . . Do you want to win?" James spoke with the calm of a great commander about to send his troops into battle. "Then for the next thirty seconds, you must be prepared to die."

"But . . . King Jas., it's just a game." Dicky Dongon was near tears, he was so badly bruised and banged about.

"Dunderwhelp," Jolly Roger corrected. "This is no game. A bit of sock pudding is not what we've been slogging it out for against that pack of quoobs. James has got it right. Fortune and glory. I want my name on that wall. Next to Lord Wellington, and Shelley, and James Matthew. And nothing less will satisfy, ever again. When I'm an O.E. someday, and I come back on some St. Andrew's Day, I want all Oppidans, from every house, to be talking about this match and how the Oppidans drubbed the Collegers into the Thames."

James had never been more proud to call Jolly R friend than at that very moment. The runty, undersized band of Oppidans placed their hands together in a circle and swore to death before dishonor. "Someday our foes may win."

James grinned. "But not today!" The cheer rose up from the ranks up and down wall and furrow as the Oppidans closed ranks.

The Queen had given in to the tide of the noise and joined Sultana Ananova in what came to be known as "yell leading." First, the spelling of "Oppidan" as loud as one's vocal cords would permit (the Queen could not speak at full gale for three days after the event, having lost her voice completely), followed by Ananova's colorful and memorable—

"GOOD FORM, OPPIDANSSS, GOOD FORM!"

Several Oppidans in the crowd struck their drums sharply after each repetition of this phrase, producing a rousing, syncopated chant.

"GOOD FORM, OPPIDANSSS, GOOD FORM!"
Bammity bam!

Had Pilkington had any notion of the severity of the Oppidan team's commitment to win or to die, he might have called the contest a draw on the spot, instead of risking a bloody massacre and no doubt his retirement as umpire of the famous Wall Game. Neither team held weapons concealed in their jerseys or leggings or shoes. No, weapons would not be necessary. Desire was the only ingredient required. The desire to win—

James knew he would be the first to die. He had every reason to believe that given the opportunity, Arthur Darling would not so much as wince at breaking his neck, if necessary, to prevent James from scoring a historic goal.

This is precisely why James chose to receive the ball as the designated scug who would attempt the twenty-five-yard heave at the garden-door goal. It seemed strange to James that such a nothing piece of wood and frame, so badly in need of a coat of paint, posed in the middle of an old brick wall, should hold such significance in the universe. Yet there it was. The entire galaxy to play in, and he was standing at the very center about to change the laws of nature . . . or die trying.

"Quiet!" Even Pilkington could not conceal the enormity of what was about to happen. His voice cracked on the "et" syllable. The air was, for the moment, deathly still. The bleating of a lone sheep grazing on the Six Penny fields took on the qualities of a cry for help.

"Ready!"

James stole a sidelong, aching look at Ananova. She was hiding behind that convenient fan the Queen had insisted she incorporate into her life. What now, James thought, is she not even going to have the decent courtesy to witness my glorious end? Then her eyes rose above the arc of the fan to meet his.

The ball rolled across the field from Pilkington toward James. No defender could touch the ball until the attacking team had attempted its shot at the goal. However, once it was touched, the attacker controlling the ball could be charged. James picked up the ball and spun on his heels to race down the garden wall to the door—his target. Then he waited—and waited. Darling leaped across the calx line, leading his mates in a stampede toward James.

"What is he waiting for? They'll trample him!" Ananova bobbed up and down behind her fan, trying to decide whether to watch the massacre or not. All along the furrow and from one end of the wall to the other, voices screamed at James to do something, do nothing, score, die, bleed, go home, win, lose—and yet James waited for Darling and his horde. Then they were on him. James smiled, refusing to put up the least resistance, and heaved the ball backward over his head! Then he curled like a burned match as bodies crashed into him. As he fell, he twisted to catch sight of Jolly Roger reaching up to catch his toss. Firm in his hands—safe!

It was too late for Darling and the Collegers to adjust. Jolly R had control and was surrounded by a scrum of snarling, yelling Oppidans, all ready to die for the goal. Jolly R wheeled to face the garden wall, planted both feet, reared back, and heaved the ball tumbling through the air toward the garden door.

"*Floreat Etona!*" James yelled as if it were his last wish. Hearing the phrase stunned many onlookers. "May Eton flourish" had the ring of an epitaph.

James never saw the result of his sacrifice. His face was pounded into the hallowed ground, pummeled by Collegers' feet trampling over him. The ball curved off course! It was going to miss! Groans and cries were on the lips of Oppidans lining the wall. Then it happened. The ball caromed off the wall—instead of deflecting to the ground, it boosted into the air and tumbled end over end, thumping into the

garden door and coming to rest on a patch of hogwort right in front of the aging goal.

Jolly R had scored!

So flustered was the crowd that not a sound, not a word, was uttered. Pilkington, too, lost his ability to speak. There was no official signal given confirming the goal.

O.E.s were dumbfounded up and down the field. James was spread flat on his back, his forget-me-nots hidden behind his sealed eyelids. By all appearances he was ready to return to his coffin. Finally, the dumbfounded silence broke. Pilkington called out, "GOALLLLLLLL OPPI-DANSSSSSSS!" The first in a hundred years! The man was on the very verge of tears. Oppidans stood up on the wall, waving their colors, calling out the names of their scug heroes. "Jolly Roger," "Naffing Napier," "Simon the Snash," "Dicky Dongon," and on, all nicknames that would go down in Eton history, names that would be etched into the chapel hallway alongside those of Wellington and Shelley and Walpole and Pitt the Elder.

King Jas. received the loudest *huzzah* of all. A thin, sat-isfied smile crossed James' semiconscious face when his name was called. His eyes remained closed; he preferred to continue in his deathlike repose, lying there on the field in his moment of glory, entertaining himself with the images playing on the backs of his closed eyelids. What reality could possibly compete with his imagination? Why should he not enjoy these moments in the privacy of his own mind? He could see Darling, his dishonor turning him into

a monster of untold ugliness. He could see the Eton Blues, who only minutes before had cheered Darling and placed the weighty history of their school honor in his capable hands, now hurling stones at him, driving him from the field for the shame he had brought to the Collegers. He could see how they lifted him up and carried him, not as a conquering hero to the gates of Eton, but straight to Sheep's Bridge, where they heaved the once lauded House Captain who had suffered the first defeat of Collegers to Oppidans in the history of Eton into the River Thames.

James opened his eyes to the blue sky and puffy, white-tailed clouds. Oppidans lifted him up facing the heavens and carried him across the field with Jolly R in the lead. James' euphoria suddenly plummeted as he watched Jolly R receive a warm hug and strong pat on the back from his father, Captain of the *Mephistopheles*. Echoes of "well done" and the word "son" reached James' ears over the din of drumming and yelling. "Son." How nice, James thought, to have his father there to share this moment of victory on the very fields where, as a young man, he also had distinguished himself. How proud James imagined his own father would be—if he had only bothered to come! And how sad James would have been had he known Lord B had been there but had left out of fear of discovery before his victory.

Jolly R's grin was blinding. He reached over and grabbed James' hand, raising it high with his to more rousing *huzzahs*.

"Fortune and glory, James! Swill it down!"

James shook his black curls and crowed. Cocks of College Walk. There just might be something to this fortune and glory.

Sultana Ananova enlisted Skeffington and several willing O.E.s to join in a traditional Greek circle dance. The poor man was on the verge of collapse when the Queen finally had the Sultana discreetly restrained just as the mass of Oppidans carrying James and Jolly R and the rest of the team on their shoulders passed by.

She wanted desperately to wave to James when he passed, but she was not permitted. Two royal fusiliers were suddenly on either side of her, escorting her quickly away. The Sultana retired with the Queen to a waiting carriage while the conquering heroes continued their parade, moving like a giant centipede across College Field.

Lord B called to his driver to stop his carriage. He climbed out to satisfy his curiosity at the clamor he thought he had heard competing with the clatter of his horse's hooves on the road to Windsor Castle. The heights where the great castle sprawled had a commanding view of the Thames and the town of Eton below. William the Conqueror had chosen the site on the edge of a Saxon hunting ground over seven centuries earlier to guard the western approaches to the city of London. Now the sounds of drums and cheering echoed over the playing fields and up the steps to Windsor as if another invader threatened the fortress. Lord B could make out an irregular procession making its

way through the streets of the village from the gate of the college. Calling to his driver for his spyglass, Lord B climbed atop his carriage for a better view.

Oppidans, scores of them, carried the Oppidan team on hands and shoulders, chanting and cheering. But why? Lord B asked himself; they could not possibly have beaten the Collegers. Then his spyglass found what he was least expecting: There, draped in the colors of a victor, was one Jas. Matthew being carried in a hero's walk on the shoulders of his schoolmates. His son had risen above the shame of his questionable origins to this exalted status of hero. Why had he left the competition?

The shrill blast of a trumpet interrupted Lord B's moment of pride tempered with self-recrimination. The Queen's royal coach was ascending the road to the heights, her cavalry escort in the lead, bearing down on Lord B's carriage. Quickly, his driver steered the carriage aside as the royal escort passed by. Lord B bowed while still standing atop his carriage. The Queen herself poked her head from her coach window.

"Lord B," she called out, "you missed a splendid match."

"Your Majesty, so I gather."

"That scraggy lot of Oppidans up and made a goal."

"Good God!"

"Good Oppidans!" the Queen corrected. She rapped the side of her carriage with the palm of her hand. *Bammity bam.* "One in particular I should have thought would hold a certain interest for you, Lord B."

The Sultana, unable to contain herself, shoved her head out the other window and seemed to be telling the world along with Lord B—

"Oppidans one! Collegers nil!"

Yes, Jolly R had scored a goal . . . the first in over one hundred years, thanks to Jas. Matthew, who had suddenly achieved the status of a legend.

Why had Lord B not stayed to share this moment with his son?

THE PUDDING PROOF

THE ENTIRE OPPIDAN TEAM and any other members of Godolphin House who could pry themselves into James' top-floor mouse hole of a room squeezed and squished until thirty and seven had actually cleared the doorway. Jolly R led the pig pile of bodies throwing themselves onto James' bed until it collapsed onto the floor. Waves of laughter accompanied the jostling and wrestling. Suddenly, Jolly R began searching the covers and bedclothes in a panic—

"James? Hullooooo! Where's he off to, the villain?"

"Perhaps the slubbery lot killed him with adoration," said James from his superior perch in the garret window,

where he sat calmly sipping a cup of tea, his tall silk hat cocked atop his curls.

"Boys, have at it!" Jolly R signaled to Dicky Dongon and Simon the Snash. Both boys produced jars of paint and began to brush it madly around the slur "James Matthew Bastard, O.S.B." that had greeted Jas. on his first day at Eton.

"That's my shrine, Jolly!" James protested. "I prefer it not be fumbled with. I see it every night before I wink out."

"Have a little patience, James. Just making a few improvements." Dicky signaled that the job was done. Jolly commanded everybody wedged into the tiny space to stand as best they could and show some respect. Naffing Napier then commenced to blow a truly awful fanfare. Jolly and Simon prodded James off the windowsill and marched him the two whole steps to his bed—where Dicky stepped back to reveal:

<u>KING JAS. MATTHEW BASTARD,</u> O.S.B.
Keeper of the Wall—Lord Protector of the Pudding

James studied the additions in silence, his forget-me-nots fixed and staring straight ahead. Jolly R had a sinking feeling that he had miscalculated the boundaries of James' sense of humor. At last James reached out with his finger and touched the wet paint forming "King," then smeared the paint across his forehead and under his eyes as he had done the first time this freshly painted slur confronted him the day he arrived at Eton.

"Good form." James was suddenly all smiles, stem to stern. In all his bastardly days, with the exception of his second birthday with his Aunt Emily, he had never felt as if he belonged anywhere or with anyone until this very moment.

"Topping swank good form, scugs!"

The explosive feeling of camaraderie and goodwill that filled the tiny room received an even bigger boost when James opened his pantry and revealed a tin of sweet buns and chocolate biscuits, which he offered freely to his mates.

"Sweet sock from Aunt Emily."

Hungry hands quickly reduced the treats to a few crumbs in the bottom of the tin. Dicky, his cheeks bulging with an entire sweet bun, stopped in mid chew to reflect.

"Aren't we a band of gundyguts now! Shouldn't we be saving a biscuit or two for our old chap, the tug Darling? Or is it Darling Tug?"

The caterwauling was as barbed as his question.

"Naaaa—he's still soggy from his dunking in the Queen's pond," Simon the Snash offered. A multitude of rude noises from the Oppidans followed this pronouncement, but James remained neutral during the demonstration and name calling.

"Stow the clatterbox, scugs. King Jas. has something to say!" Jolly yelled, banging on the empty sweets tin.

Every head was suddenly turning to stare straight at James.

"Arthur Darling is the Captain of this house," James

cautioned sternly. "Think about it. When you are all swank Seniors in a few years, how might you feel when a bunch of underclassmen give you the boot from your lordly perch?"

The thought was sobering, even terrifying as it took hold. Suddenly the sock from Aunt Emily seemed to taste less sweet.

"Arthur Darling is true Eton blood," James continued. "Therefore, he is now more dangerous than any reptile or spider in the London Zoo. I know—had I been in his shoes today, I would be."

Just then an eerie whirring sound rattled through the house. Canes and birches being run along the walls, panels, and staircases. Darling's Whips on the hunt—

"We must be on the bill to a man."

Now heels clomped on the stairs, canes and switches rattling closer.

"But we gave him a real lamming. We drubbed the lot of them mulligrubs into the ground."

"That is why we're going to get a hiding. For beating the buggers."

"Darling is still in charge. He can give us a swishing for whatever the quiff he chooses." Garret stairs clattered as the delegation of Whips arrived and pounded on James' door. Rupert Wainwright filled the frame, red-faced and boiling. Three Senior Whips backed him up, their birches flitting and smacking the door frame.

"Oppidan scugs! You are wanted on the slab!"

James smiled and bowed politely.

"Thank you, Rupert. We'll be along in a bit. Care for a cup of tea? I've got a tin full of homemade sock. Sweet buns and honey. My aunt Emily makes the sweetest—"

Rupert stared at the empty tin in James' hand. His voice dropped from his usual screech to a deep, unholy whisper.

"Now, scugs."

James gathered his tall hat and led his mates from this crowded room, following Rupert and his Whips dutifully down the stairs. The collection of hard soles clomping on the wooden steps drummed a cadence echoing all over the house, this being of course due to the additional Oppidans who joined the ranks following James, Jolly R, Dicky, Simon, and the Whips down to the slab and to whatever fate awaited them.

When the doors were thrown open to the library, Whips ushered the Oppidans in to face ranks of Collegers lining the walls. Not a pretty sight, given the long frowns and grim looks that greeted James and Jolly R. At the opposite end of the oblong room four pipers and two drummers from the Eton corps sounded a fanfare, when a death march might have been more appropriate. Whips and switches were raised in the hands of the defeated Collegers, but not to strike. As James and Jolly R, Dicky, Simon, and the others passed, Collegers hammered their weapons of massive swishing on the four-hundred-year-old oak floors over and over again. The tugs were paying tribute.

"I've got a rather bad feeling about this, Jas.," Jolly R whispered to James from the corner of his mouth.

"Smile, nod to the natives." James showed his pearly teeth, nodding his curls this way and that. Doors opened at the opposite end of the library. Darling entered with the rest of his Whips. All were dressed in tails, smart trousers, formal waistcoats of many colors, crisply pressed and cinched tightly. Every single hair was in place and gleaming with Macassar oil. Darling's eyes fixed on James with an unblinking predator's gleam. He held his birch switch braced in both hands across his waistline. At a snap of that switch, Collegers ceased rapping their canes and birches on the floor. Rupert carried the colors of St. Andrew and Eton Blues draped across his arm. Darling relieved him of the raiment and held it forth to James and Jolly R. There was no falter in his speech, no air of concession. If pride was lost, Darling showed no signs of it.

"Oppidans, these are the colors of St. Andrew, our patron saint. The colors have been part of Eton since the year fourteen hundred and forty, when King Henry VI founded the college. Every year they are passed to the winners of the Wall Game on St. Andrew's Day."

Darling spread the colors with the help of his Whips, displaying the saltire flag of Scotland and the coat of arms of Eton. He cleared his throat.

"I doubt it ever occurred to King Henry or Saint Andrew that a bunch of Oppidans could possibly triumph against the Collegers," he began. "But, to quote Professor Pilkington, 'History is filled with unexplained miracles—and tragedies.'"

James remained facing Darling as Jolly R accepted the colors.

"As the House Captain," Darling continued, "I say to you, Oppidans, good form. You won. Do not get used to it. Your victory is only temporary."

Amid nervous laughter among the Oppidans, Darling extended his hand to shake with Jolly. Then Darling turned to King Jas. They stared at each other. James extended his hand. Darling did not, choosing to adjust his tie rather than touch the "mutant."

"I assure you and all the lauded and noble Eton Blues who have come before us," said James, lowering his hand but not his eyes, "that we will uphold the honor of the colors even if we are lowly Oppidans. More important, old chum, where's the pudding?"

"Pudding?"

"*The* pudding."

The pudding reception was held in Headlam House, the meeting place of the Pops—the prefects who made up the Eton Society. After this day, James was a certain candidate for invitation to join the society. There would be only one obstacle. Arthur L. Darling, president of Pops and a senior prefect, had rededicated himself to the cause of ending James' visit to this waking life before the end of term. In keeping with the St. Andrew's Day tradition, parents and family were welcome guests, Jolly R's father being the most audible and demonstrative of any present. In the history of

Eton never had such a reception celebrated an Oppidan victory over the Collegers in the Wall Game. But the unforeseen Oppidan victory put a severe damper on attendance at the ceremony by Collegers and their families. James was first to notice, upon his arrival with Jolly R, Dicky, Simon, and his Wall gang, that no Colleger they had faced in the match was present. In truth, no Collegers could be seen at all amid the collection of tall hats and stick-up collars. The tugs were all off licking their wounds.

And Arthur Darling was otherwise engaged at the fencing pavilion, using a particularly cruel swept-hilt rapier to severely punish his inanimate foe. The padded effigy offered no resistance as Darling sliced and chopped it to shreds. The stringy locks of a housemaid's mop adorning the dummy's head properly identified the Oppidan Darling imagined he was eviscerating.

"'Vengeance is in my heart, death in my hand, blood and revenge are hammering in my head!!'" Darling bellowed out the quoted lines with violent thrusts, driving his rapier completely through the effigy of King Jas. The vengeful young man had discovered a universal truth that his adversary had known since his early days with Aunt Emily entertaining her theatrical friends—for every life situation there is a fitting quote from the hand of Shakespeare.

At the very moment Darling was gutting him in effigy, James had but one thought occupying his mind and a singular image filling his field of vision. The pudding! The massive mound of sweet sock was the size of a keg of

brew, and it required four pudding bearers to parade the confection into the hall. Festooned with plums and berries and creams, smeared with glaciers of chocolate covering its rounded crown, the monstrous sock seemed to have a life of its own. Rows of spoons circled the pudding in several concentric rings, shined and ready for the boys to stab into the sweet beast. No plates and linen serviettes for this sitting. The pudding would be consumed in barbarian fashion by all members of the venerated tribe of Oppidans spooning mouthfuls of the sugar dragon until only a carcass of crust remained. Surprisingly, this heavenly pudding was no longer the object filling James' mind and eye.

"She is here, Jas. Your Sultana," Jolly R whispered as Dicky, Simon, and the rest of the Oppidans bowed one after another.

Ananova! The Sultana herself was all James could absorb into his six senses, wishing he had a seventh so he could fill that as well. Ananova followed regally behind the pudding cart, chaperoned by Skeffington, who appeared to have been embalmed especially for the occasion, along with two royal guards on either side.

The scent of her wafted over him, laced with the perfume of the pudding. Ananova scanned the gathering from behind her fan, searching for the true reason she had subjected herself to the scrutiny of this collection of Eton males. Skeffington pounded his staff and began:

"On behalf of her Majesty the Queen, who sends her heartiest congratulations to the victorious members of the

Oppidan sporting club on their historic good win over the Collegers this Saint Andrew's Day—"

The din was instantaneous. Every Oppidan in the hall erupted in some form of cry or shout. Several alumni struck up the Eton hymn, performing loudly and substantially off-key.

James remained silent, his entire focus directed at capturing the attention of the Sultana standing not four feet away on the other side of the pudding. Her eyes darted everywhere, studying every boy in the room—with the exception of James himself. Her eyes finally met his . . . and did not look away. And then she smiled. There it was again, James thought, the same sensation he had experienced upon seeing the *Mephistopheles* at anchor on the Thames—a foreign lightness of being invading every muscle, every nerve in his body. But Ananova was not a sailing ship. She was, as Jolly R had observed, "just a girl."

"The Princess Ananova Ariadne, Sultana of the Ottomans and the house of Majiid, guest of our Queen, has graciously made herself available to honor the champion Oppidans. To the victors goes the . . . pudding."

"Just a girl?" James remarked quietly to Jolly R as Ananova began at the head of the receiving line that had been hastily formed, as was the custom when being presented to royalty.

"Right, just that."

"Then why are you sweating?"

"Well . . . because . . . I have never met a royal before."

The Sultana stopped before each member of the Wall

team, who bowed before her. She would then offer an inane nicety, to which the lowly subject was expected to respond politely and briefly.

How do you find the weather? Did you suffer any injuries? What is your favorite school at Eton? Have you read Shelley? Do girls play the Wall Game in England? How do you find the weather? James could hear her voice asking the simpleton questions of each of his mates and their equally shallow responses as she drew nearer to him and Jolly R, both standing at stiff attention at the end of the formation. Jolly R's knees almost buckled as he performed his bow. He leaned on James discreetly to keep from toppling over.

"I understand you all chose the Captain of this team. Would you approve of females serving as Captains?"

This was the last question Jolly R had expected, having mentally rehearsed his weather comment ad nauseum. As a result, he quite simply went silent.

Skeffington immediately moved to usher his charge away, but the Sultana stood her ground and nodded her head as if she understood every move Jolly R made. James had underestimated her. She was more than just a girl goddess, she was a compassionate human being, an example of the species James was not sure he had ever encountered except in Aunt Emily. Titters and whispers radiated through the gathering. Jolly R's father turned red.

"What my good friend means, Your Highness—" James' voice reverberated through the room. "If I may continue, Sultana Ananova?"

Ananova nodded regally with a gesture of her fan. Skeffington's attempt to stare James into silence had no effect. Not once did James remove his eyes from the Sultana as he spoke.

"What my friend means is that women represent the triumph of matter over mind, just as men represent the triumph of mind over morals. . . . 'Captain' is a label we men and boys need to make us feel less inferior . . . to you."

The Sultana stopped breathing for an instant, not knowing whether to be affronted or to bow before this mysterious young man holding her in place with his haunting blue eyes, like the invisible threads of a spiderweb.

"And may I add the heartfelt hope that the scandalous weather in our country does not dampen your spirits," James continued, interrupting Skeffington's mimed but insistent signaling that this audience was indeed over. "My injuries will heal, thank you for inquiring. I read Shelley daily, and I am a devoted servant of history and the natural sciences. And when I am done with Eton, I will rule a small country with a Queen destined to be a dish for the gods."

The blade of a broadsword could not have severed the spellbound gaze between them. Skeffington had never witnessed such outrageous behavior in all his years at court, yet he stood mesmerized by this young man's precision of logic woven into the words of a poet. This was reckless behavior that violated the Queen's own command that the Sultana have no contact with Lord B's bastard son. Her hand

snagged a spoon from the cart and presented it in royal fashion to James—

"Pudding?" she asked.

"Pudding," he replied.

James plunged the spoon deep, nodding to his mates to join in. Jolly R recovered, leading the feeding frenzy that attacked the mountainous sock from all sides by an army of spoons gouging and digging away the creams. Dicky used two spoons like shovels to fill his face. James, ever polite, offered his first spoonful to the Sultana. The sweet disappeared into her mouth, causing her almost to swoon. It was so delicious that she licked the corners of her mouth to prevent even the slightest trace from escaping.

"Dish for the gods . . ." James murmured quietly to himself. "Will the angels envy us?" Ananova did not hear his quiet question, she was so enjoying the freedom of devouring the monster pudding in the company of Eton's Blues.

Skeffington would have to order the royal guards to pull her away, but he suddenly did not have the heart. Perhaps just a pinch of pudding?

Arthur Darling, quite by coincidence if there be such a thing in the universe, chose this moment to deliver a violent reversi tondi with his sword, striking a forceful horizontal blow across the neck of his mop-headed effigy, sending it flying end over end through the air to the floor. Overwrought, he fought for breath, his heart beating to a dangerous cadence. Then, traversing the distance across the

floor, Darling thrust his weapon, extending his torso and legs and skewering James' likeness through the charcoal-dust eye. Without interrupting the momentum, Darling opened the firebox in the corner and tossed it in.

" 'Hamlet, thou art slain. No medicine in the world can do thee good.' " Darling did not move from his vigil until every strand of the mop hair had curled and charred and the effigy was no more.

CHAPTER SIX

DANGEROUS RENDEZVOUS
AT THE QUEEN'S EIGHT

T HE SPARKS AND STATIC ELECTRICAL CHARGES
that passed between James and the Sultana
Ananova at the infamous presentation of the pudding could not possibly have gone unnoticed even by boys
most immune to anything that smacked of romance and
girls. Skeffington, in spite of his favorable impression of
James, was obliged to advise the Queen immediately of the
potential scandal that could result from any consorting
between Lord B's bastard son and the Sultana Ananova,
daughter to the Sultan and Ottoman ruler of the Grecian
Isles. The Queen took little time to deliberate the situation

and ordered the Sultana confined to the castle during the remainder of her visit, with no contact permitted with Eton boys unless prior approval was granted by Her Majesty personally. The one freedom Ananova insisted on was to continue her horseback riding, her archery, and sword training with her tutor, a skilled Marxbruder of German descent, who came from a long line of duelists whose expertise in the use of hand weapons was unequaled.

The Queen consented but confined Ananova's training to a tiny secluded island upriver, and only under the strict supervision of the trusted Marxbruder. In this sanctuary, Ananova could leave the confines of the castle behind for a few moments of freedom.

In the service of King Jas., Jolly, turned spy, obtained clandestine intelligence through his father's clerk as to Ananova's complete training schedule and when she would be traveling on the river to and from the small island, nicknamed the "Queen's Eight." James, should he develop a sudden interest in rowing, could at least be on the river at the same time to catch a glimpse of his beloved Ananova.

"You are the epitome of good form, Jolly. It's official. I will be the best rower in Godolphin House. Four miles to the Queen's Eight and back in record time. If I live long enough."

"Live long enough? Is there something you're not telling me, Jas.?" Jolly asked.

James handed Jolly R a formal note sealed with a wax crest. Jolly R recognized the seal as that of Arthur Darling.

At James' request, Jolly opened the message and read the contents. Short and to the point was Darling's challenge. The duel was to be held at a place to be determined and at a time to be mutually agreed upon. "Death before dishonor" was Darling's closing line. James was so taken with the phrase that he logged it into his journal with the likes of "Knowledge is power" and "Someday my foes may win, but not today!" Jolly R was uneasy about James' enthusiastic reception of the invitation to a duel. It was strictly against the rules. The Provost would bounce him the instant word got out. And given Darling's prowess and reputation in swordplay, there was the distinct possibility of serious injury or worse. . . . Only one duel had ever been fought by Eton blues while attending the school, and no one official ever spoke of the incident. There were no records or mention of the event in any history of the school. Had James informed his Oppidan friend of his training with the sword during his childhood, the beads of worry that appeared on his round noggin would have rolled like a tidal wave down his nose.

But whatever thoughts of melancholy and doom had gripped Jolly and James after the pudding affair completely dissolved now with this news of Ananova and the promise of a deadly duel. With that superior laugh, James placed his hands on his friend's shoulders and spun Jolly R a half turn to face the wardrobe.

"None of that snash, Jolly," he said, wiping his friend's brow. James unlatched a complicated series of locks on the

wardrobe doors. "Or you shall not be the height of fashion with yours truly this season."

With that, James opened wide the double doors, revealing the most startling sight. A dozen spiders of James' favorite *Lasiodora* species were busy at work spinning a dense web, but not just at random. This was a web spun over a tailor's mannequin—its headless torso the precise size and shape of King Jas. James' pet spiders were weaving him a waistcoat!

"Ah, but not just any waistcoat that any prefect can sport about in." James delighted in the amazed and bewildered look on Jolly's generous face. "This one has unique properties. Allow me to demonstrate."

James took out his vintage wooden flute, a baroque period piece, and played five very precise notes.

Suddenly every spider stopped working—just simply froze where it was on the web. Astounding. A second series of five notes startled Jolly R. The tones caused the spiders to animate again, marching together with their eight legs in unison as they retreated to the top of the wardrobe, where the arachnids lined up in formation and waited.

"*Quid est?*" James posed the question in Latin, thoroughly enjoying himself. "What is it? What in nature is it?" Jolly R could only shrug and watch, slack-jawed, as James carefully removed the webby waistcoat in progress and slipped it on. Marvels. A perfect fit—

"How comes later, my friend. En garde!" James flipped one of his prized rapiers to Jolly and grabbed one for himself. He slapped Jolly's blade impatiently.

"Attack, Jolly. Come on. Attack! You know you cannot match me! I've had the best masters in England tutor me in the art of the sword. Come on—advance!"

"I don't like this game, Jas. These spiders—this thing—"

"No game. I am invincible in this magic suit of armor, Jolly. You cannot harm me."

Jolly was not convinced. James pressed, slapping his blade across Jolly's legs and hands and finally his cheek. Jolly reacted, flaring a thrust to counter James' annoying flicks. In a blur, James dropped his guard and spread his arms in submission, letting the full force of Jolly's thrust drive the blade into his chest. James reeled, staggering with the force. Jolly dropped his sword, horrified at what he had done. Again James laughed that infuriating cackle and struck a pose, inviting Jolly to inspect him.

"No blood. Red or yellow. See?"

James was right. Jolly R smoothed his hand over the spot on the web waistcoat where the rapier had surely pierced James' chest. A small indentation could be felt, nothing more.

"That is quite impossible."

"Not if you believe in the possibility of the impossible." James carefully removed the waistcoat and returned it to the dummy in the wardrobe. Then, after he had tooted five more notes on the flute, the spiders descended from the top of the wardrobe in unison on precision webs and resumed their task, whistling, as this species was known to do, while they worked.

James laughed again at the incredulous look on Jolly's face. "Jolly, oh Jolly, good Jolly—this flimsy webbing can withstand the strongest winds, the most powerful typhoon, even fire. It can entrap prey one thousand times its weight and more. Woven into enough layers, I wager my fancy waistcoat could stop a pistol round at fifty paces. So you see, Darling is wasting his time. *I am invincible.*"

Jolly R remained silent for several moments, unable to speak and scarcely able to breathe. Then he pulled James aside as if the wrong ears might be listening in and whispered:

"Think the ugly little buggers could make one to fit me?"

James smiled. "Why not?"

James had managed to delay Arthur Darling's eagerness to cleave him to his brisket by pleading a need for conditioning for the grueling duel. James manipulated his nemesis with a stroke of diabolical genius, convincing Darling that he would not want to win over James too easily. Such a victory would be hollow. No, if Darling was going to defeat the "mutant," it had to be a fight that would live in legend and be recounted by every Eton Blue who wore the colors. Since both would clearly be dismissed from school forever, it had better be worth the trouble.

Darling all but destroyed the Eton Society meeting hall, he was so vexed, but he could not possibly disagree. A fortnight was agreed to. And then they would meet as gentlemen and fight until they could fight no more. Swords were

the agreed weapon of choice. The location would not be agreed upon until a half hour before the appointed time to avoid drawing a crowd.

In the center of the Queen's Eight, alone in the meadow, grew a small hawthorn tree several hundred years old. It stood covered in bits of ribbon and string and dangling pieces of tin and glass that tinkled like bells in the night breezes, left there for luck as offerings to the field faeries that some believed lived beneath the trunk of the old tree. On midsummer nights the oaks and firs surrounding the open meadow sparkled and twinkled with a thousand tiny lights. Locals were convinced the Queen's Eight was haunted by faeries, a belief fueled by the periodic appearance of Faerie Rings on the island, perfect in shape.

Ananova's fleet white Arabian followed the circular paths trotting in endless rings around the meadow. Pandora, the Sultana's aptly named mount, was, like her namesake, nothing but trouble. The beautiful silver-white mare traveled the four miles from Windsor Castle upriver past Eton and onto the Eight tethered on a flat sailing barge accompanied by Ananova, her sword teacher, the stocky imposing Marxbruder, a member of the famous sword masters' Fraternity of St. Mark, from Frankfurt, and the horse's groom sent from the Queen's stables. Pandora bucked and kicked and whinnied over every inch of water.

Rowers from Eton sculled up and down the Thames with ease, knifing the narrow boats through the waters.

The river was so crowded around Eton that Ananova was forced to remain inside the small pavilion erected on the barge's stern to hide her from view.

James and Jolly drew plenty of wry looks from the piloting wetbobs as the pair clumsily rowed their two-man scull up the river. James had recommended a goodly distance pass between them and Ananova's barge before they gave chase, so as not to draw attention to themselves. Their uncoordinated strokes sent laughter rippling through the ranks of the more advanced rowers speeding by. But the two enthusiasts were slowly gaining on Ananova's sailing barge.

"If we had your father's boat, we could overtake her in a flash, board her barge, and carry her off," complained Jas.

"Right. There is one gaping hole in your logic, King Jas.—we don't know how to sail my father's boat. We can't even row a decent stroke."

Jolly toppled over backward from pulling too hard and spattered James with more of the Thames.

"At this rate we may catch her by spring."

But James was not daunted by their lack of efficiency. This was but another of life's numerous problems. It was there to be solved. He pulled the solution from his rucksack and began to play. The notes from his flute that had charmed his army of spiders set a rhythm that Jolly could not resist. He began to pull to the melody. In seconds he fell into a smooth cadence with each stroke, propelling their craft faster and faster. When James instructed him to hum the tune, Jolly readily obliged, sculling faster with each pull on the oars.

The music of James' flute reached Ananova's barge. The melody was almost buried by the noise Pandora made as the horse tugged and pulled at her tethers. Seeing the struggle her groom was having controlling the white mare, the Sultana made a hasty exit from her pavilion onto the deck of the barge. She spoke soothing tones to Pandora in her native tongue, calming the horse with a tidbit and her familiar touch.

"*Passen Sie auf*, Sultana, you must remain in your tent. I have strict orders from the Queen." The Marxbruder did his best not to bark at Ananova, for suddenly she was in full view of boaters and rowers passing by. As the stocky man guided her back to her quarters, Ananova heard the flute and managed to sneak a look astern through the opening of the flaps of her pavilion. The music drew her attention to a particular scull moving rapidly upriver not a hundred yards behind the barge. Eton Blues. One rowed and the other . . . played the flute. She recognized his gangly frame and his telltale black curls flapping in the breeze.

"Pudding boy." She smiled warmly, whispering, "Come on. Catch me if you can. . . ."

As if her voice had reached his ears, James put down his flute and began rowing in cadence with Jolly R, both of them humming the catchy melody at the top of their lungs. At last the boys drew up alongside the barge, panting and puffing. The Marxbruder glared at them suspiciously, put off by their loud humming.

"*Anhalten!* Look out! You're scaring the horse. Keep

your distance." The Marxbruder waved them away like annoying horseflies. This only prompted James to slow his cadence and guide the scull closer.

"She is a rare beauty, sir." James was staring right at the pair of eyes peering back at him from behind a flap in the pavilion as he spoke. "Arabian, I believe. What's her name?"

"You ask too many questions, *Junge.* Take your singing and your sculling elsewhere. *Schnell!*"

"On our way, sir. Like lightning bolts we are, sir." Jolly R splashed the man with his intentionally clumsy rowing as they pulled away.

"Did I mention she is a rare beauty, sir? Runs like the wind from the looks of her."

The Marxbruder roared angrily, raising his arms as if running off a stray dog.

Ananova snapped the flap of her tent shut as James looked right at her and smiled.

Her boatsman steered the barge toward the leeward shore of the island. James and Jolly quickly corrected their course and rowed up the left fork of the river. They were soon out of sight, protected by the dense groves of trees marking the top and bottom of the Queen's Eight. Jolly R was reluctant to put James ashore alone. This was supposed to be a simple adventure to get a glimpse of the Sultana on her boat, not a plan to invade the island while she was in residence and risk being discovered.

"It will be your arse if you get caught," Jolly warned.

"And mine, too. What do you propose to do when you see her?"

"Read her a poem, kiss her, then—kidnap her I should think."

"What? WHAT? King Jas., are you completely potty?"

James leaped to the shore, pushing the scull back into the river with the force of his jump. He smiled sanguinely.

"Not completely. . . ."

"Right. Good. I feel so much better now!"

James sent his accomplice on his way with instructions to circle the island and pick him up at the downriver point in half an hour. Under no circumstances was Jolly R to leave the scull and come ashore. Then James entered the dense grove of ancient oaks and headed for the center of the tiny island.

All in all, the Queen's Eight was the perfect-sized isle, he thought, large enough for a castle, yet small enough to rule without the necessity of massive armies protecting the borders. The Thames offered access to London and the mighty oceans beyond. Now all he needed was a Princess, and his kingdom had begun.

If they were each trouble apart, now Pandora and the Sultana functioned as one, barely grazing the beaten path with each powerful stride. From his secret perch up in a great oak overlooking the meadow, watching horse and rider go around and around the circle, it appeared to James as if the duo might lift off and fly.

The Marxbruder stood in the middle of the meadow, walking around the ancient hawthorn tree, tracking his charge and her progress. His husky voice barked commands, drawing an instant response from both horse and rider. Pandora would change direction at a gallop, turning sharply, yet Ananova remained calm and steady in her saddle, ready for the next obstacle. James was dazzled by her skill. Now the groom raced about, setting up higher and higher jumps, until horse and rider cleared a six-foot rail with ease.

James stifled his urge to applaud and shout, "Brava." Silently he descended the tree to a lower branch, giving him a closer view—too close.

The Marxbruder trotted toward the outer ring directly in James' direction. He was armed with a short bow and a quiver of arrows. Had he seen James lurking in the tree near the ring? Suddenly the sword master issued a command and swung the bow from his neck with one hand, grabbing an arrow in the other. He nocked the shaft and pulled back on the bow. Was he going to take aim and fire? James flattened into the foliage, trying to make himself invisible. The Marxbruder loosed the arrow into the ground at his feet. The man trotted ahead of Ananova and fired another arrow into the ground. Then another, and another. As Ananova approached each arrow sticking up from the ground, she lunged down, holding one hand fast to Pandora's mane, and snagged the arrow with the other. Then, pulling herself back up in the saddle, she clenched each new shaft between her teeth before collecting it in the quiver slung from her

belt and readied herself to snatch another. With each success the Marxbruder grunted, urging her on. At the end of the circle the man dropped the short bow flat on the ground and stood inches from it. Ananova bore down on her prize. The Marxbruder showed no fear and no sign of moving as the horse and rider headed straight for him. With no expression on her face, Pandora's hooves tearing up the path, Ananova raised the short bow, nocked an arrow from her teeth, and fired backward over her shoulder—at a straw effigy hanging from a low tree limb—the very limb directly below James' hiding place! The arrow arced right at him. If James moved, surely he would be discovered. If he did not . . . The arrow impaled the straw effigy, tearing it from its tether, and ganched it fast to the trunk of the tree.

Ananova thundered around the ring, firing more arrows at targets hanging in the trees or standing on the ground. None survived. As she reined into the middle of the ring, James concluded that this girl was not to be trifled with. As accustomed as he was to winning, he realized he would have to kill Ananova to win any argument against her.

Instead of praising her, the Marxbruder dressed her down and criticized her faultless performance head to toe. The horse was the star, not Ananova. The only reason she had a horse of such magnificence was because of her royalty. She could never ride in the Sultan's cavalry, even if she were a man. James had to control an urge to leap down from the tree and defend the Sultana against this disrespectful bully.

"*Verdammt!* Gather your arrows. *Das Pferd,* the

Pandora, I'll see to her. Find every one if you expect to continue with me. I don't have a care whose *Prinzessin* you are, I am not a nursemaid."

Ananova dutifully acknowledged his authority with a polite bow of her head. As soon as the Marxbruder turned his back to tend Pandora with the groom, Ananova thumbed her nose in the man's direction. Muttering under her breath in her native tongue, the Sultana began the mindless task of collecting her spent arrows.

James held his breath as she stood beneath him attempting to loosen the straw effigy from the first arrow that had drilled it to the tree trunk. The shaft was deeply embedded. The Sultana hiked up her leg, placing her boot heel against the trunk, and with both hands tugged and pulled at the stubborn arrow. James nearly fell from his perch. Though covered in a proper layer of hosiery, this was still the most of any female James had ever seen. He made himself look away, but a sudden thud of body against ground returned his attention to the Sultana. Now flat on her back, her entire dress riding up over her head, both legs kicking, Ananova was sputtering dust and dirt from the riding ring. But she did have the uncooperative arrow firmly in hand. The cackle that erupted from the trees sat her up in a flash.

"Who's there?"

The Sultana looked back to the river. Her groom and the Marxbruder had their hands full loading and securing her horse on the barge. Pandora was making all kinds of

misery for her handlers. And then there was James, hanging from the tree limb by his hands.

"Forgive me for dropping in unannounced, Your Highness." He landed lightly on the ground beside the tree. "But you look as though you could use a hand." Which he offered to her and bowed—

"Your obedient servant."

She batted his hand away, jumped to her feet, and shoved him back into the cover of the trees.

"Do you have any idea what will happen to you if you're caught?"

"I'm invincible."

"Oh, really?"

"I had to see you again."

Ananova looked over her shoulder and shoved James deeper into the bush. James took her hands in his, successfully halting her efforts to push against him. She was indeed a strong girl!

"I propose to have my own island someday and rule it as a King or a Pasha. Maybe a Sultan. And I would like you, Sultana Ananova Ariadne, Sultana of the Ottomans and the house of Majiid, to be my Queen." James spoke sincerely.

The flush traveled from her cheeks down her neck. For the first time since she had uttered her first syllable as a baby, Ananova could think of nothing to say. Her response was involuntary, like breathing, or the beating of a heart. Her hands found both sides of his pallid cheeks, and she held his head firmly but gently between them. She arched upward, balancing on the balls of her feet in an attempt to

raise her face to his level. Then she pulled him down to her until their lips met. The kiss, their first, was brief and unforgettable. . . .

"'O, she doth teach the torches to burn bright! . . . Beauty too rich for use, for Earth too dear. . . .'" James was not sure he had actually spoken the words, but Ananova heard them and smiled her approval at being compared to Juliet. She gazed into his forget-me-nots and touched her fingers to his lips.

"The angels will envy us," she whispered, then found his lips again.

"PRINZESSIN!"

James opened his eyes to see the Marxbruder racing from the river across the meadow in a rage. The Sultana shoved him deeper into the underbrush out of sight.

"I'm not leaving you!"

The Marxbruder now had his blade drawn and was coming fast, thrashing through the trees.

"This is not the time, James Matthew," she gasped.

Ananova drew her bow and aimed an arrow point-blank at James—

"Go!" Her voice was desperate and most convincing. James obeyed. He turned and ran. The bushes swallowed him up instantly.

"Wer ist da? Where'd he go? He is a dead man, Princess!" The Marxbruder shielded his charge, his sword at the ready, backing her from the trees into the meadow. "Who is he? Have you seen him before? Eton boy?"

Ananova glared at him.

"I don't know what you are talking about, Herr," she said, regarding the Marxbruder with convincing contempt. "Shall I inform the Queen my sword master has been in his cups and can no longer be trusted to watch over me?" Ananova paraded toward the barge in a royal snit. "I'm tired. Take me back to the castle. Enough of this." The Marxbruder began to doubt himself.

"This will not stand, Your Highness," he warned, but his voice held no conviction. He scanned the trees surrounding the meadow, then hurried dutifully after the Sultana.

James had no way of knowing how Ananova had saved him from certain discovery and capture, but he knew in his heart that she had. He hid with Jolly R along the banks of the Queen's Eight until nightfall before they rowed undetected back to the rafts at Eton. Jolly Roger could not accept that his friend and King would allow such a revolting thing as a kiss to occur. Even more upsetting was that he would risk life and limb for one. Jolly would rather face a duel with Arthur Darling than pucker up for a Princess.

James wanted nothing more said about the incident. He had the overwhelming feeling, as they returned to Godolphin House that night, that after this day his life would never be the same. All that he had planned for his days at Eton was quickly unraveling. With one exception . . .

Up in James' cramped quarters, inside the wardrobe, the team of arachnids continued to spin their webs and weave the magical waistcoat. . . . King Jas. would indeed be invincible.

CHAPTER SEVEN

DUELISTS, A DAMSEL, AND THE GUILLOTINE

EXAMINATIONS AND TRIALS approaching at the end of the Michaelmas term brought the traditional chaos of mad studying and cramming that consumed the students of Eton. The panic infected the boys' houses like the plague. In the middle of the night, screams of horror would echo down the halls from some Oppidan who had been startled awake from a fitful sleep trying to remember the answer to an obscure question regarding ancient history or math. Math was the universal nightmare among the majority of underclassmen. But Darling was not bothered by such trivia as academics. He was itching to have a go at

J. M. Bastard before the holiday. Every day he could be found at the fencing center punishing sparring partners with saber and rapier. He was obsessed with ending the reign of the mutant.

News of the impending duel between Eton's leading Oppidan and Colleger had remained a surprisingly well-kept secret from the Provost and the host of teachers and professors charged with the boys' education.

On the other hand, the indiscreet rendezvous Sultana Ananova was rumored to have had with an "unidentified Eton student" was not a secret. In fact, the story of Ananova being caught in a compromising position with a "wetbob" had quickly found its way around the entire Eton community. The gossip was ignited, of all places, in morning chapel before classes, when the chaplain delivered a lesson on the temptations of the flesh. How the proximity of females could sway a weaker man from his course in life, and how study habits and performance in trials and examinations could be adversely affected by exposure to female companions, even mothers. The story of the hour was Adam and Eve, and the message was clear—that Paradise would have been better off without Eve! This was presented to the boys as the very reason Eton had been founded in the fifteenth century by Henry VI to educate deserving scholars—exclusively boys. Girls were strictly forbidden as students within the hallowed halls of Eton.

At the noon break between schools, Oppidans and Collegers crowded around the posting board at the north

end of the School Yard to read a notice authored by the Provost—

> BE IT KNOWN TO ALL STUDENTS
> CURRENTLY ENROLLED IN A TO G LEVELS
> AND ALL KING'S SCHOLARS AND
> COLLEGERS, BY ORDER OF HER MAJESTY
> THE QUEEN, THAT ANY PERSON OR
> PERSONS ACTING ALONE OR IN CONSORT
> WITH ONE ANOTHER WHO MAY HAVE
> DISGRACED ENGLAND AND THE
> INSTITUTION OF ETON BY CAUSING GRAVE
> OFFENSE WITH THEIR ACTIONS SHOULD
> IMMEDIATELY PRESENT THEMSELVES TO
> THE PROVOST FOR REPRIMAND AND
> FORMAL APOLOGY. ALL PRIVILEGES AND
> RANKS OF ALL STUDENTS ARE HEREBY
> SUSPENDED UNTIL THIS MATTER IS
> RESOLVED.
>
>   PROVOST OF ETON COLLEGE
>   FLOREAT ETONA

The reaction was immediate all over the Yard. Collegers accused Oppidans. Whoever among them was to blame for this outrage should come forward and accept the punishment. Oppidans, fueled by their victory over the Collegers, lashed back, blaming the senior tugs for abusing their privileges of rank. Dicky Dongon, Simon Napier, and J. M.

Bastard's "Wall gang" got into a heated debate with Rupert and his tugs. Dicky cited Rupert's plummeting academic standings as reason enough for him and other Collegers like him to leave before they dragged the whole school down. The suggestion was made that Rupert and his classmates should apologize to the Queen.

The Provost fueled the rising tensions and charged all House Captains to deliver suspects to his office within twenty-four hours to avoid any further humiliation to the Queen and the school. Details of the crimes committed were not disclosed, but the implications were clear that Sultana Ananova, daughter of the Sultan, ruler of the Aegean, had been involved.

Arthur Darling knew exactly who the villain was: the same Oppidan scug he was set to face at the other end of a dueling sword. Darling's indefatigable duty as House Captain would require him to name a suspect. But if Darling made the case to the Provost, the mutant would surely be dismissed from school and Darling would never get to fight his duel. There had to be another way. If James would continue to refrain from giving himself up, then Darling could go after another who no doubt shared the mutant's guilt.

Darling's Whips intercepted Jolly R on his way to evening mess. Each of the seniors rattled the banisters with their birches and flexed them in a visible show of force. Rupert led the delegation, showing no decorum or tact in declaring the purpose of their meeting.

"Jolly R—gaucy name for a gaucy Oppidan, don't you agree?"

"Are you referring to me, tugface?" asked Roger innocently.

Rupert shoved his birch rod into Jolly's stomach.

"Giving a senior the various, eh?" He shoved his rod harder into Jolly, causing him to bend over in pain.

"Bugger off," Jolly moaned.

Rupert signaled. The other Whips grabbed Jolly R by the arms and pinned him against the corridor wall.

"I'm putting you on the bill, scug. You're due a good swishing."

"I haven't done anything!"

"Oh? Really? What about your mutant bastard friend? Word is you and he did a little dashery with that Sultana. Got the Queen's hackles up, haven't you now."

"Why don't you ask him?"

"Nobody can find him. Skipped his schools and hasn't been in his room all day."

Jolly R shrugged, feigning ignorance, and struggled to walk away. Rupert slapped him hard across the backs of his legs, buckling his knees.

"You're our suspect, Oppidan Roger. You're going to the Provost—unless you take us to where J. M. Bastard is hiding."

Jolly would not have revealed his friend's whereabouts, even if he had known, regardless of swishings and other tortures the tugs might threaten him with. But in any case he

could not tell. As soon as Jolly R had gotten word of the Queen's ire, he had gone looking for James, only to find his King had disappeared. All the usual haunts turned up empty. He thought he was sure to find James secluded in the basement of the science school, finding sanctuary assembling their secret lab project, a working, full-size guillotine. All to be found were several doll heads and a sack of old potatoes that had been cleanly halved by the apparatus' blade.

Jolly's fears for his mate, especially with Darling on his trail, worsened as the hours passed with no word from James. Jolly R could only hope that James had not done anything drastic. No names had been put forth by the Provost. The Sultana must be protecting James, refusing to cause him any harm. An honorable thing for a girl to do, Jolly had to admit to himself, in spite of the chaplain's view on Adam and Eve as the reason no females were allowed to attend Eton.

Darling and the other prefects were waiting in the house library for Jolly. The swishing was, as Jolly expected, severe. But, inspired by the growing Eton legend of James' method of pain endurance, Jolly R fixed on the names of his favorite authors visible on the shelves before him, just as James had done. Although this time the blood ran red, the theory held. Oppidan Roger Davies did not so much as utter a whimper during the entire beating.

Upon learning of the edict, James had wanted at first to rush straight to Windsor Castle and demand to see the Queen. He would apologize to Her Majesty and to the Sultan, but not to Ananova. To the Sultana he had given

no offense except to enjoy the sight of her—as well as the touch of her lips and the smell of her hair. For that he would not apologize. Ananova could have at any time prevented him with a simple command. He would have obeyed. Now their innocent tryst had resulted in the virtual captivity of the entire Eton population—unless James gave himself up.

Halfway across the footbridge connecting the village of Eton and the environs of Windsor Castle, James had an epiphany. He had been so blinded by the mix of guilt at having brought this on his mates and his anger at the Queen's actions that he had not considered that if Ananova had revealed his name, the royal guards would have come straight to him and arrested him without such a public furor involving edicts and notices. She was protecting him! That had to be the case. James could only imagine what pressure and threats were being placed upon her to identify him. The protection of virtue, especially that of a Princess, was carried to ridiculous extremes in the realm of Kings and Queens. Wars had been fought, Queens been beheaded, lovers drawn and quartered and left to rot in public markets over indiscreet affairs. Ananova could at this very moment have her life on the line over an innocent kiss. The insanity escalating through the school and the village because of his obsession with the girl could turn barbaric unless he acted wisely.

The opportunity to take action came in the form of a beggar wrapped in a tattered, hooded cloak who approached James—the man's eyes blinded by the tortures of the dungeon now appeared as dark holes crusted over with time.

James took no pity on the man. A fair transaction that served both was in the offing.

"A ha'pence, a farthing for a blind soul, guv'nor?"

"Oh, so you can see me, citizen?"

The blind beggar swabbed his hands onto James' face memorizing his features. One hand slid down to James' chest. Suddenly the beggar withdrew with a crackling laugh.

"I can see a black heart, guv'nor. I should hope to meet the devil instead o'you."

"The devil is on holiday. I'm just filling in. I'm in the market for a cloak. This should cover your inconvenience." James folded a coin into the blind man's callused paw, sealing the deal. The beggar's greed got the better of him. Demanding more money, the man refused to give up his cloak, appealing to James' charitable nature. James demonstrated the dark depths of his black heart by jerking the cloak from the beggar's back, leaving the pitiful creature lying on the cobblestones, clutching his half crown.

"I'll see you in Hell!" the beggar yelled after him.

James headed for the castle trying not to gag from the stench in which he had enshrouded himself. Here he had given the beggar enough money to supply himself with food for a week and the lout wanted more. James was sure he would later step over the man lying in a drunken stupor on the road.

Windsor Castle sprawled across the top of the steep hill overlooking the Thames and Eton to the west. Near

impossible to assail from this direction, even with a vast army, the fortress was virtually impregnable on its remaining three sides as well. James appeared small and insignificant against the massive walls as he approached the main gates. The Queen's coat of arms flew atop the gate turrets, indicating Her Majesty was in residence. Good, James thought, that meant Ananova was more than likely still inside somewhere. The number of guards at the gates would prevent him from storming the castle, but not from entering on official business. The challenge came quickly from the guards as James approached. Pikes dropped, barring his path.

"I'm here to see the Queen. On business."

That claim brought only laughter from the sergeant at arms, who turned James around and gave him the boot, sending him on his way. James spun right back and walked again toward the gates with a determined stride. The sergeant, tired of this folly, drew his blade. James continued his course until the point was pressed firmly against his chest. Before the guard spoke again, James held up the Provost's notice he had snatched from the school, and spat with a thick peasant's accent—

"If y' be loyal to our Queen, she be wantin' to know 'at I got the goods on the piece o' snash wot done wrong to the little Princess who's Her Majesty's guest from abroad."

The guard snagged the notice, squinting at the writing.

"I could read it fo' ye, if y' like, Your Worship."

The sergeant glared at his own men, who laughed at him. James bowed low as he backed away across the drawbridge.

"I'm sure a man o' your rank will make sure the Queen's let know I stopped by. Ifn she wants to know the whereabouts of this bloke, she can send her man to meet me at the wharf off Weir's Lock. I'll be waitin' one hour. And if the likes o' you and your mates show up, I skin outa there. The Queen's man. Alone. . . ."

No beggar had ever given orders to the sergeant at arms, and he was not going to set a dangerous precedent by letting this scraggy one make a fool of him in front of his command. Hastily, he called the alarm. Royal guards poured through the gate.

"The devil with you!" The sergeant lunged to grab this drunken beggar, who was surprisingly agile and leaped nimbly aside, using the guard's forward momentum to send the man careening over the drawbridge rail and splashing into the waters of the scum-infested moat.

"Twice have I been likened to his satanic majesty. Who wants to see me in Hell!?" His angered voice, combined with his wraithlike appearance in the dark hooded cloak, slowed the guards just long enough for James to escape.

Racing along the side of the moat, he quickly outdistanced his heavily laden pursuers. James reached the edge of the steep hill that fell away from the western walls, and he kept right on running. He pointed himself straight down the sharp incline, spreading his cloak behind him. The tattered material billowed out like a sail. His feet never left the ground completely, but James did not stumble, running like the wind down the embankment,

the beggar's cape acting like a sail, stabilizing his speedy descent.

Fog whispered over the canal boats and sailing vessels moored along the Thames at Weir's Lock. James hid himself easily in the drifting walls of mist rolling up the river. He chose the bowsprit of a river schooner and perched atop the figurehead, which gave him a superior view of the fogbound wharf, and waited. Was he being an idiot, he wondered? Was any girl worth even the slightest of risks? He had to know what this fluttering presence was that had taken up residence in his heart since the moment she had come into his life. His future was damned to hell because of her. It was only a matter of time before he would be banished from Eton. What could he possibly gain by this dangerous course he had set forth on? A moment to look into her eyes and say . . . "Good-bye"?

The sound of hooves and the clatter of a carriage penetrated the fog. James shrank back as mists parted like a curtain to reveal horses and a carriage carrying the royal seal of Her Majesty the Queen. The carriage pulled to rest in front of the schooner. The Queen? Had his bold rendezvous brought him the prize? The figure that stepped from the carriage was far too tall to be the Queen. A man. When the carriage and team had again been swallowed up in the fog, the man walked slowly along the wharf, his identity still a mystery. James leaned out from the figurehead to get a closer look through the mist.

"I assure you we are quite alone." The man's soft-spoken voice ripped through James like fangs, nearly causing him to topple from his hiding place. He could not be sure until he heard the voice again.

"James Matthew? I'm here at the behest of Her Majesty."

It was the man himself! It had to be! And then the word that sent James into a flash sweat—

"Son?"

The man fanned the fog away from his face and stepped into the lamplight, revealing himself. Lord B, James' father by blood. The boy flattened himself against the figurehead, his heart pounding. What was *he* doing here? A universe of questions flooded his mind, overwhelming him.

"Lord B." James' voice echoed up from the fog, alerting his father. The man turned his head from side to side, trying to fix James' location. "Are you the Queen's man?" James echoed again.

"I serve the Queen in many ways."

"I've nothing to say to you!" Anger and shock filled James' voice.

"Listen to me, James—they know it's you, the boy Sultana Ananova was seen with. . . . I'm here to help you. I've struck an agreement with the Queen. You must listen to me." The fog grew denser, His Lordship more desperate.

"Did she tell—?"

His father stared into the mists rolling around the bow of the schooner for the voice. There he was, standing up on

the figurehead, looking down on his father like a wraith. James' anger and pent-up hatred toward his father for the life he had been forced to live poured through him with such force that a vortex formed around him, driving the fog away from the space he occupied.

"DID SHE?!"

His father shook his head in silent response.

"The Sultana refused to name you, James. She refused your name even to her own father."

James felt the surge, the same feeling he had experienced watching her ride Pandora, or spooning pudding into her mouth. And then the dark cloud returned, the doubt and anger.

"You both share the confidence and arrogance of youth. I envy you, James."

Now his father moved toward the edge of the wharf, closer to the ship and his son. James drew back beside the figurehead, his mind racing.

"You'll forgive me if I do not envy you." James' voice was hard and without a trace of charity. "How was I known then?"

"You're one of a kind, James. No two of you alike in this world."

The description by Ananova's Marxbruder along with her groom's had immediately been recognized by Skeffington and the Queen. His long black curls, the pallor of his skin, the color of his eyes, and that praying mantis frame that carried him like a great elegant bird above the lesser flocks. He stood as an original among minions of ruddy-faced,

toffy-headed Eton bloods. Even a beggar's cloak could not hide him.

"You've made quite a name for yourself, son. Academic excellence. Your historic victory in the Wall Game. You've cut your own wake. Why throw it all away now? For a few moments with a girl you can never have—"

James shook his head, holding his ears with his hands.

"Like you? Isn't that what you did . . . *Father*?"

Lord B was silent.

James had lived and suffered with his oddities and differences, growing up a bastard in a closed society. His successes had been hard won, but were they worth the price? As he stood there before his father, the only thought clear in his mind was Ananova.

"I must see her. . . . "

Lord B sighed wearily. "James, if you cooperate, and apologize to the Queen and to Ananova's father, you will be allowed to finish the year. If you refuse—"

James' burning eyes pierced the mists. "Apologize? For what? For existing? I didn't ask to be born. The Queen wants me publicly humiliated and removed from Eton. Ananova's father wants me thrown in the London prisons to rot. Why? Nothing remotely scandalous happened between the Sultana and this bastard in the time we were together. I have been condemned to the block by a Queen who does not approve of my lineage, nothing more! I've been tried and convicted all my life, sir; there is nothing new here. I am an accident of birth."

"She leaves in the morning, James. Her father is returning her to her home. You will never see her again."

His Lordship could not see James through the fog, but he could sense the anguish this news had brought his son.

"James . . . let her go. Make the apology and get on with your life."

James' sardonic laugh cut through the mist. The fog parted, and suddenly His Lordship was face-to-face with his son, who was now perched like a gargoyle on the bowsprit, grinning at him—a predator ready to pounce.

"And whose life would that be, Father? The bastard's? Or the life of a distinguished Lord's son who can visit his real mother on holidays? And take tea with the Queen? And hobnob at the Prince's cricket pitch? A respected alumnus rooting at the Wall Game. That sounds just topping swank, doesn't it, Father?"

Lord B guarded his anger.

"Yes, well, it's up to you, James," he said, a steely note coming into his voice. "There will be an apology for you to sign at the Provost's come morning. No reprimand. No public notice."

"Good form, Father. Keeps your name out of the scandal and you remain the Queen's man. Good form."

"And you may remain in school, subject, of course, to any further unfortunate events. . . . I've done all I can for you."

James laughed again bitterly. "Then 'all you can' is not enough," he said, giving himself the last word as the sound of horses interrupted their conversation.

The cart approaching remained buried in the fog, but its cargo was clearly visible. The white Arabian's head poked through the mists, traveling effortlessly through the air, like the mythological horse Pegasus, winging his way amid the clouds. Ananova's mount—Pandora! Lord B retreated back into the shadows as the cart rumbled past and stopped at the schooner's gangway. His Lordship threw a worried look back to his son—but James had vanished from his perch on the bowsprit. Quickly, he looked up and down the wharf. No sign of James. It was impossible to see anything more than a few yards in any direction.

Pandora jerked her head violently about, snorting and baring her teeth in a threatening display as her groom and another handler struggled to lead her from the cart up the gangway onto the schooner.

"Dunno which is worse, this bit o' 'ell on four legs, or the Sultana herself."

"Maybe the bloody nag just don't want to leave England."

Pandora reared, pawing her hooves at her captors. As soon as the Arabian's forelegs clomped back to the wharf, her hindquarters lashed out, kicking the handler and sending him tumbling into the river. James had scurried higher up the rigging when the cart arrived. Out of sight, he watched Pandora as more crew hurried down the gangway to help the groom try to control the wild-eyed horse. Ropes were looped around the animal's neck. One sailor grabbed a torch and waved it about, causing the Arabian to bolt up the

gangway kicking and bucking onto the deck. The groom shouted angrily at the crew to leave her be. They were only frightening the poor animal. The burly boatswain's mate cared neither for the groom's opinion nor the cargo he was charged with.

"We be the ones that 'af to sail halfway round the world with this devil in the hold, not the likes o' you, ducky." The boatswain slapped Pandora across the nose with a lead-filled sap. The horse reeled on her haunches, stunned. It was all James could do to restrain himself from leaping down on the villain. The groom acted quickly, throwing a saddle blanket over the animal's head, blinding her to anything that could frighten her more. He calmed the white mare with strokes and quiet words.

"Be clear about this. The Sultana will not set sail without this horse. Make sure she is well cared for if you value your station." The groom settled the gleaming white animal as he hobbled both Pandora's front and rear legs to prevent her from bolting. Then, with the blanket still covering the animal's eyes, the groom fed her carrots and eased her back into a stall that had been built on the main deck. The boatswain headed aft trailing a flood of curses.

James decided then and there that if he was forced to kill the others, the groom was worth sparing. He would be needed for the long journey when James rescued the animal and his Sultana and sailed her away from all this injustice. If he was the best and brightest Eton had to offer, which, in his own opinion, he undoubtedly was, then surely he could

conjure a successful intervention that would best the Queen's will—and bring him together with Ananova forever. A spell had been cast. Even the meeting with his own father, longer than any from his earliest years, held no sway over James.

James remained undetected up in the rigging. The carriage that had brought his father soon appeared from the fog and paused to retrieve His Lordship. A passenger leaned from inside. The glow from the carriage lamps outlined the face of Skeffington. The two men shared a few sharp words. Skeffington was visibly annoyed at Lord B's news. His Lordship took a last look around the wharf and then climbed in. The carriage again vanished in the fog, bearing the Queen's men back to Windsor.

His Lordship had chosen to live by the rules of society and hide in the shadows from fatherhood rather than honor his bond. He was the Queen's man. James decided then and there that he would be, now and forever, his own man.

Ananova had entered a self-imposed vow of silence since her father had declared his decision to "deport" her back to their homeland for conduct unbecoming a member of his royal family. Food served went untouched by the young Sultana. Confined to her quarters until she was to set sail for the Aegean and her island home, Ananova sat down to write a brief note to the strange young Eton boy of dubious origins who had kindled a feeling inside her that she would never forget—and never wanted to—or grow out of as her

father said she would in time. Given her father's order that she set sail in the morning, she was determined to leave James a letter to be delivered after she had gone, in the hopes that he would forgive her for leaving without saying good-bye. How could she prepare herself to become a ruler someday if she was not allowed to make her own decisions and rise or fall on the merits of her choices? If James was such a low form of life, then whatever was he doing at Eton, the bastion of Britain's finest? She resented the Queen's intervention—and her drastic measures to capture this boy. Had a kiss the power to create such scandal? Could a single embrace be more threatening to her father than a multitude of enemy armies? She remembered the story of a certain Helen, whose face was so beautiful that it launched a thousand ships.

So far Ananova's face was responsible for launching a single ship. Perhaps a thousand would follow. . . .

CHAPTER EIGHT

A GENTLEMAN'S RESOLUTION

JOLLY R HAD NO TIME to scream. The gloved hand muffled him tightly. James leaned over him, a long, tapered finger standing at attention across his lips, signaling for Jolly R to remain silent.

"Jas. They're looking for you. Everyone—" James jammed a pillow over Jolly R, who continued to babble in incomprehensible muffled tones.

"Right, yes, Jolly. I know. I'm a popular fellow. Darling wants to run me through. The Queen wants my head. Even my father came and found me. I'm sailing for the Mediterranean come morning, and I just wanted to say farewell."

Jolly R bolted upright, forcing the pillow away from his mouth.

"What?"

"With the Sultana . . . of course."

"Oh, by all means. And what does her father the Sultan have to say about this?"

"Nothing, really. He doesn't know . . . yet."

"Ripping. And the Sultana?"

James shook his head in the negative and laughed, giddy at the idea.

"My father, His Lordship, actually expects me to sign an apology to the Queen. Tomorrow. Provost's office."

"You spoke to him?"

"Yes. But I won't be speaking with him again after tonight."

Jolly R flopped back down in his bed and covered his face with his pillow, voluntarily this time. Then he showed his round face, pantomiming a scream.

"You've gone batty."

"Completely."

"So, for this awfully big adventure, do we have a plan?"

James smiled wickedly.

"We?"

"You think I'm going to stay here and be Darling's whipping boy? They gave me a swishing tonight, Jas. I'm your accomplice. Why, next time I could break under torture and scream out your name to the Queen!"

"You bastard—"

"Not me. That's you. I'm coming with you, Jas. Matthew Bastard, Oppidan Scug."

"Good form, Jolly-o. Here. See if this fits."

With that, James presented him with a finished, shiny, web-silk waistcoat. Complete with a pocket for his watch and a hanger sash for a sword. Jolly R stared slack-jawed at the garment. He slipped it on eagerly. A perfect fit. He turned and spun, fending off hordes of imagined evils with an invisible sword. The waistcoat stretched and molded to his frame with every move. Then he stopped short and removed the protective shield and handed it back to James.

"I can't. You'll need it more than I will."

James stifled a laugh as he raced through the buttons of his long coat and threw open his lapels wide, revealing an identical waistcoat spun from the impenetrable silk.

"Seems Electra and her cohorts have already spun one."

The two mates stood side by side admiring their magical vestments woven by James' pet spiders.

"Topping swank, Jas., topping swank."

Jolly R broke into a jig, high kicking and pirouetting about. They were invincible!

One hour before dawn, Arthur Darling was awakened by a quiet knock on his window. Jolly R reveled in the perplexed look his presence brought to Darling's face. He stuck out his tongue. The startled Colleger rifled his bedclothes, searching for a weapon to protect him from the mad

Oppidan grinning at him from outside his window four stories above the cobblestones below. Jolly fanned his hands behind his ears and stuck his tongue out even farther, which indicated to Darling that this boy on the ledge was completely daft. Finally Darling wrapped his hands around his birch rod and rapped it against the glass in hopes of sending Jolly R on his way. Instead, the scug applauded and produced an envelope, which he flattened against the window for Darling to see. Light from his night candle revealed Darling's name penned in the elegant hand of Jas. Matthew. Jolly R tucked the envelope into the shutters, contorted his features into another appalling face, which involved rolling back his eyelids and spreading his nostrils like a pig, then made his way along the ledge and disappeared.

Darling fetched the letter with his scone tongs, handling the envelope as if it might contain a disease. Inside in elegant hand was what Darling had been waiting for—

> Master Arthur L. Darling,
>   Your presence is requested for an arbitrament of the sword, to be held at first light this day on Agar's Plough. Your Second is welcome. The contest will conclude when one or both parties are incapacitated or have expired.
>   To good form. . . .
>
>   Respectfully yours,
>   James Matthew, O.S.B.

The duel was on!

Darling shuddered with anticipation; in a very short time he would at last be meeting his nemesis at the other end of a sword—not a blunted fencing foil but a blade that could pass through the viscera or slice flesh with the ease of carving a juicy beef Wellington. This mutant bastard, who had been the bane of his existence at every turn since the day he had arrived at Eton, would meet his fate at last. Yellow blood be damned. Darling had fretted that the Queen's edict would cause King Jas. to be revealed and force him to be removed from Eton before they had settled their score. Whatever was afoot, all that mattered to Darling was the chance to avenge the humiliations he had suffered and restore his family name. He dressed methodically, going over his training and strategy in his mind. James would certainly be defeated. Darling had superb confidence in his skills and no doubt as to the outcome. But there would be repercussions. There would be inquiries. He could be expelled forever from his beloved Eton. But the shame of expulsion was nothing compared to the happy image embedded in Darling's mind of Jas. Matthew Bastard lying on the field of Agar's Plough in a pool of his own yellow blood.

The Provost received an identical invitation a few minutes later, as did the Captains of the boys' houses surrounding the Eton campus. The deliveries were each accompanied by a loud knock from a phantom messenger, who then quickly disappeared. The messenger posted one on the pole

at the Burning Bush in the middle of the town as well. The secret duel was no longer a secret. . . .

Ananova received a knock on her door in the early hours of the morning. But no invitation to Jas.' duel was presented. She was astounded to see the Queen standing in her doorway. Her Majesty had knocked smartly to awaken her. But Ananova had not been sleeping. She had not slept all night, as the letter she sat to write for Jas. had completely consumed her and the hours of darkness until her departure. She had hurriedly completed her thoughts and dusted the ink dry, hastily sealing the letter and hiding it on her way to her chamber door. The Sultana and the Queen stood silently for a suspended moment, neither knowing quite what to say. Finally, Ananova curtsied in proper submission.

"Your Majesty . . . I was not expecting you."

"Ananova . . . nor was I expecting to be here. May I come in?"

"It is your castle, Your Highness."

The Queen could tell Ananova had passed a sleepless night. Already her trunks and personals were being loaded onto the ship anchored on the Thames. All that remained was for the Sultana herself to board. The Queen had not found sleep that night either, and admitted so to the Sultana. It was not the Queen's decision to send Ananova back to her island homeland, she explained. This was her father's choice. She was happy to have the Sultana stay on as her

guest. But formality of office, proper protocol, and the saving of face had carried the day.

"I am not so old that I cannot remember the feelings I once had for a special young man."

Ananova did not want to show interest in anything the Queen had come to say. She had come to the conclusion that all grown-ups believed they knew about everything in life and had a story to prove it. She was silent. The Queen went on:

"In spite of his bad reputation, the opinions of my advisers, and his lack of royal blood, I was in love with him. Quite truly, madly, and deeply . . . in love."

The Queen surprised herself at the emotions these memories still evoked in her.

Ananova's resolve was weakened by the tears that suddenly sprang to the Queen's eyes.

"What happened to him?" she asked.

"It's best we not talk of these things . . . forgive me. It all ended tragically. Really, child, I want only what is best for you. This young man is not for you. But you will need his memory many times in your life."

The Queen embraced Ananova, then removed a precious necklace from around her neck and folded into Ananova's hands.

"Write him a letter, child—put your heart into every word. Record every feeling and memory you want him to share . . . then burn it. I made the mistake of not burning mine. And that letter still haunts me."

The Queen gathered herself to leave. Ananova bent in a curtsy. The Queen stopped her with her hand and gazed on her beauty. Then she kissed Ananova on the forehead and left, closing the door quietly behind her.

Ananova remained motionless for a moment, giving in to her tears, holding the necklace the Queen had given her. Another knock on the door. Skeffington. It was time. The downriver currents would be swift.

DARLING'S REVENGE AT AGAR'S PLOUGH

AGAR'S PLOUGH SPREAD to the north of Eton, butting up against the Willowbrook. A thin layer of mist coated the large field, hiding the ground that had been a palette for hotly contested cricket matches between the many houses that made up the Eton bloods. This morning the first rays of sunrise stirring mists across the field would unmask a contest to the death.

Arthur Darling stretched out his hamstrings, limbering up his legs and thighs with lunges and low cappo ferros, offensive tactics intended to carry Darling's rapier under his opponent's and drive his blade through the heart of

James Matthew. His second, Rupert Wainwright, sharpened Darling's weapons with a whetstone, honing the edge to a fine gleam in the dawn's first light. Darling was growing impatient. It would be like this mutant to play some trick, he thought, violently slicing the mist in visible twos as he cut and carved his way around Agar's waiting for the appearance of his foe. But he had never pegged James for a coward. Surely he would show up.

The mists parted as a lone figure approached. The tall hat of an Eton blood cruised like the stack of a steam train toward Darling and Wainwright. Darling exulted, slashing his blade about, calling out to the figure drawing nearer—

"You're late, scug. I've already disemboweled your rotty carcass a dozen times in your absence. I have one more in me for the scum of you that's left. Tell me, Oppidan, did your lordly father bed a swine to bring such a filthy animal into this waking life? Is that how you explain your miserable existence, you rutting bastard?"

Two more silhouettes separated the mist, flanking the tall, hatted figure. Then another. More figures dotted the Plough, amassing from the fog. Rupert visibly blanched at the surprising number of Etonians who had been informed of this secret duel.

"Are you speaking to me?"

Darling paled, his rapier hand going limp as the Provost of the college emerged from the rapidly dissipating fog, his tall hat splitting the beams of the rising morning sun.

"Master Darling? I repeat. Are you speaking to me?"

Oppidans and Collegers collected around Darling and Wainwright, waiting for a duel that was not going to happen.

"Yes, sir, no—I mean, no, sir. . . . We—I was just rehearsing." Darling improvised as prefects surrounded them. A prefect from Dumford House removed the rapier from Rupert's hand and confiscated it for the record.

"Rehearsing, are we? So early in the morning?" The Provost held up the sample of Jas. Matthew's elegant hand. "'Your presence is requested to attend an arbitrament of the sword. . . .'"

Darling stood speechless before an impromptu jury of his peers. There was no place to hide. Nothing he could say could absolve him from guilt. His intentions were all too obvious. He was preparing to participate in a duel, a practice forbidden by the college and one punishable by severe disciplinary action and dismissal. And he had been led straight into this trap by the cunning and conniving of King Jas.

"And in this said rehearsal, did you win, Master Darling?"

Darling had no choice but to allow his rapier to be turned over to the Provost. There would be an inquiry. Arthur Darling would be put on probation, given his long history at the school. Rupert Wainwright would be given over to a master at Godolphin House for a fit punishment and possible expulsion. Jas. Matthew Bastard had emerged the victor without ever having drawn his sword.

CHAPTER TEN

THE UNINVITED GUESTS

THE TOWERS OF WINDSOR CASTLE drifted leisurely by as the schooner cast off and glided along Weir's Lock into the currents of the Thames. Ananova did not wave good-bye to her father and his attendants watching her depart from the shore. Their final words to each other had been brief and harsh. Nothing she could say had swayed her father from his decision to return her to her island home. For the next fortnight she would be trapped on the small schooner with her nurse and tutor, the Marxbruder, who was charged with her safety, a handful of skilled sailors, and her beloved Pandora. She thanked the gods that the Queen had made arrangements for her and

her magnificent animal to travel together. Pandora tossed her head and whinnied, greeting the Sultana. Ananova stroked the animal, finding the warmth of Pandora's coat comforting against her cheek as she nuzzled her neck. The stall was small and confining. The deck would offer no opportunity to gallop on Pandora's back, but there would be many days at sea for the Arabian and Ananova to train together. If she had to return to her homeland in disgrace, she intended to arrive on the back of a horse fit for a Queen.

The chapel bells were clanging the early hour. Ananova tried to lighten her heart by thinking that maybe James had climbed up into the chapel belfry and was ringing her a farewell. The letter she had written him was secreted away in a leather pouch, where it would remain close to her heart during the voyage. She had no intention of forgetting him. Ever.

Belowdeck, barrels of drinking water filled much of the cramped space. There were no separate sleeping quarters for the crew, only hammocks slung between beams. Ananova and the Captain had the only cabins, located aft. The Captain had graciously offered to accommodate her nurse and tutor. The hold was taken up by Ananova's collection of trunks, containing an extensive wardrobe she rarely wore. Once she was on board and the ship was heading downriver, she ordered one of her trunks to be brought to her so that she could change out of the formal dress she had worn for her departure and get into her riding garb. She was not going to be told how to dress for the next two weeks.

* * *

Whispers issued from one of the trunks resting in the darkness of the hold. Then the trunk began to shake and rock from side to side. The blade of a dagger poked through the side, carving out a hole. A lone forget-me-not eye peered through the opening from within. A stowaway—

"Jolly?" James whispered, hoping to avoid drawing attention from the main deck. He could hear footsteps of the crew as they hurried about to the boatswain's orders. He called again a little louder. No response. James' dagger sliced through the leather hinges, then the cinch straps. Slowly he stood up in the trunk, raising the lid with him, then carefully set it aside.

The light seeping down between planks on the main deck and through an open hatch gave enough illumination in the hold for James to see the problem. Ananova traveled with far too many trunks and cases. He moved quietly to each one, knocking gently and calling Jolly's name. His friend had to be here somewhere. James had waited on the wharf, watching the cargo being loaded, until the last possible moment, when he had to choose a trunk or run the risk of never getting on board. Jolly R had arrived from delivering invitations to the duel as the last of the cargo was about to be loaded. He had not been able to let himself leave Eton until he had seen the look on Arthur Darling's face when the Provost arrived along with half the school to witness the "arbitrament of the sword." He was sure Darling would keep the lot busy while he and James made their great escape. James was forced to stuff him into a trunk full of

froufrous and then sit on it to get the lid fastened while Jolly chattered giddily on about the particular angle of Darling's slack jaw and the big baby tears tug Rupert had shed. It had been worth whatever risk he was taking to witness that moment. His only regret was that James had missed it.

At this point in Jolly's epic tale, James quieted him and hid himself away in the remaining trunk. The crew had returned to the wharf to load the last, and the heaviest, of Ananova's cargo into the hold. One burly mate swore the very trunk hiding Jolly R smelled of a dunghill. The mate concluded within the confines of his limited gray matter that the Sultana was transporting horse flop as well as the horse to go with it. From inside the trunk James overheard the Captain discussing the voyage with his pilot—how long the tides would run, when they expected to reach Greenwich and London before heading for the English Channel and on to Gibraltar, course headings, and the like. Then the sound of Ananova's voice filtered down from above as she conversed with Pandora. James just lay there in the cramped space of the tiny trunk and let the sound of her melodic voice carry him away.

"Jolly? Where are you?" he whispered again. Footsteps approached from above, coming down the stairs, approaching the hold. Then he heard it. A snorting . . . like a piglet. James followed the sounds of the snort right to the trunk containing Jolly R.

Two crewmen climbed down into the hold with a lantern, searching the trunks. James had to work fast. Quietly he

used his dagger to pry the trunk lid loose. Jolly R was curled inside, covered with lacy froufrous, snoring. James reached down with his thumb and finger and pinched his friend's nostrils together. The baby pig stopped snorting. Jolly R popped open his eyes, staring right into James', who smartly held up two fingers forming a V. He inverted the V and walked his fingers like people through the air, then he pointed. The crewmen were picking their way through the cargo right toward them. Jolly pulled some lacy pantaloons over his head and ducked back into his box. James eased the lid shut and rolled into the shadows as the men approached.

"What does herself fancy this time?" The taller of them had to stoop to avoid colliding with the deck beams as they slid trunks apart, searching.

"Long as she don't get m' ration o' rum, she can 'ave whutever the diddle she wants."

"That'll be the day. 'Adn't you 'eard? There ain't no rum on board this planker. Not a drop. That Sultan bloke, he didn't want no liquor around his lass. Nothin' but water and tea, mate."

The barrel-shaped crewman shook as if struck by lightning. When his senses returned, so did his anger at this shocking twist. No self-respecting seafaring man would put out to sea without his share of rum to get him through the tedious nights and grueling days. The irate fellow lashed out, kicking and slamming the trunk containing Jolly R. His shipmate backed him off, pointing to the very trunk he had pummeled and identified it as the one herself's nurse had

requested be brought topside. The foul-smelling one to boot.

Inside the trunk Jolly bit down on a mouthful of ruffles to squelch his fear. This was not proceeding according to the ingenious plan James had schemed up—two lowly Oppidans, empowered with superior intellect and the confidence of youth, subduing twenty men good and true, taking command of the ship, and then sailing away with a willing, beautiful Sultana. The "willing" adjective admittedly being the big unknown in King Jas.' scenario. With Ananova, James was definitely sailing into unknown territory. And if James did not do something in the blink of an eye, then Jolly R would surely be discovered prematurely and bring the wrath of the Queen down about their ears.

The two men bent to get a grip on the trunk and give it a hoist when a voice from the dark hold startled them. It had the sound of the grave, hissing and guttural as it moved in the darkness, changing locations—

"Who's there? 'Allo? Show yourself, now."

"We'll call the Captain, we will!"

"I am the Captainnnnnn!" The voice hissed again.

Both men got the shivers, flashing their lanterns about, trying to catch a glimpse of the shadowy figure.

"What do you want? There's no rum, ifn 'ats your game."

The hull creaked and moaned as the ship heeled with the wind. Gravity sandwiched the two crewmen together. Now the voice hissed behind them.

"I want your souls. . . ."

The bolder of the two drew his dagger, turning with the darkness, following the slide and clomp of the thing's twisted form.

"Scugs! Your size? What are you?" the voice asked, completely befuddling the tars with the offhand question. The piggy squeal that squirted from the trunk spooked the men even more—suddenly the trunk lid burst open! A ghost rose up from inside festooned with froufrous and frilly garments and smelling like a piglet. All the Jolly apparition had to do was "oink" and the two turned to run. The dark demon from the grave was waiting. The bigger crewman instinctively stabbed his dagger into the demon's chest. The crewman's hand recoiled as if hitting a stone wall. In the lantern light the men stared in shock at the bent blade.

"Coooo—'e's a bleedin' ghost."

James smiled politely and knocked the wind from them with the wooden capstan spoke, doubling them over. A whirling whack to the backs of their grimy necks and both men dropped to the deck floor, conked cold.

"Good form," James whispered to the unconscious couple. He had removed the smaller man's pants and shirt while Jolly was still untangling himself from the ghost of froufrous. James tossed the pants to Jolly, then the man's sweat-stained shirt.

Ananova's nurse answered the knock on the Captain's cabin door, a bit put out at how long it had taken to bring up the Sultana's trunk. She was amazed that the two lowly

crewmen had actually retrieved the correct one. She directed the two men to set it down. The pants on the tall, lanky sailor were clearly too short, stopping at his knees. Telltale locks sprang from James' hat as he set his end of the trunk down. He quickly tucked them back inside, avoiding any eye contact with the nurse. Jolly, lugging the front of the trunk, gaped at the panoramic view of the Thames through the wall of windows that spanned the fantail of the great cabin. The waters were swiftly carrying the schooner farther and farther from Windsor—still visible on the cliffs high above Eton. Then it too was gone as the ship followed the current around the bend. His sweat-stained jersey was stretched taut over his belly. The knitted watch cap filched off the oily head of the bound and gagged crewman down in the hold did little to hide his young age, but just enough. Their thin disguises had allowed the boys to exit the hold and maneuver the Sultana's trunk past the Captain with not even a glance. As a veteran of the Royal Navy, the less this Captain had to do with the Sultana or any of her possessions, including her most unseaworthy mount, the better this voyage would be.

James had dared to steal a glimpse of Ananova as they hefted her trunk up the quarterdeck steps. Separated from everyone aboard and seeking solace in the stall with Pandora, the Sultana refused to speak or acknowledge anyone except her white Arabian. Why couldn't she look his way just for a glimpse? Surely she could feel his presence? She had to know that he would not just let her sail away. Couldn't she

stop paying attention to that horse long enough to return his glance?

The nurse interrupted James' thoughts, shooing him and Jolly out of the cabin. Jolly bowed and scraped, trying to delay being sent back out on deck. The plan was to keep the woman busy, giving James time enough to reach Ananova. Beyond that, James had not informed Jolly of his intentions—except to say that the ship they were about to seize would be named after him. *The Jolly Roger!*

"Will there be anything else, mum? Shall I unpack it for you? Are you and the Sultana comfortable? Could I open the window for you, let some of that fresh air in? Ahh, good for the constitution, it is."

Then he said the magic words, "Oh, mum. Pardon my asking, but what color are your eyes?" James could always count on Jolly R. He could occupy the hagborn nurse for the next hour without her even thinking about her duties to the Sultana. That was all the time that James would need.

Pandora's back rippled to Ananova's brushstrokes, the animal's muscles twitching. Her white coat undulated from her tail across her back, up her withers and mane as Ananova groomed her, singing in soothing tones in the language of her land. Ananova let herself go, dancing traditional steps of her homeland as she moved around her horse, brushing with rhythmic, alternating strokes. She reached for a horse comb resting on a stall post to untangle Pandora's mane, but the

comb was not there. Without missing a beat, the Sultana reversed her direction to search for the missing comb and was at once face-to-face with the oddest-looking crewman, smiling at her with the blue of forget-me-not eyes.

"Do you believe in magic?" James half whispered. Ananova was so dumbstruck, she could scarcely breathe. James smiled, waved his empty hands—in a blur the horse comb magically appeared. "I do, Your Highness." James bowed in the proper courtly gesture and presented the comb to her. The Sultana backed away hesitantly.

"I believe . . . you are mad."

"Take the comb, Your Highness," James whispered from his lowly position, eyeing the main deck. So far no one had paid them any mind. Ananova quickly retrieved the comb and began stroking Pandora's mane.

"The other side," she instructed James. "Quickly! Pandora will hide you."

James circled behind Pandora to face the Sultana over the horse's neck. Pandora craned her head around to get a look at James. She nudged him with her snout, nibbling at his face. Ananova had to stifle her urge to giggle.

"Pandora likes you . . . James."

"I hope that makes two of you."

Ananova smiled as she combed out Pandora's mane.

"I thought never to see you again."

"Ah, see, no faith. I always knew I would see you."

"You're right—I have no faith."

She flushed and shied away, ducking down beside

Pandora out of James' view. He lowered his lanky frame to meet her under Pandora's belly.

"Oh, why would you take such a foolish risk just to see me?"

Her thick twist of black hair drooped from her head like a wilting flower.

"Give me a brush. I'm just your groom. Nothing more."

Ananova nodded. Reaching under Pandora's neck, she passed James a brush. Their fingers grazed and lingered for the fleetest of moments. She pulled back, catching herself, and shivered. She began to brush her side of the horse vigorously, avoiding any eye contact with James. He imitated her strokes on the opposite side, trying to exactly match her moves and pace.

"My life is already planned for me, James," she said.

"You believe in fate, then?"

"It never sounds like any fun . . . 'Fate.'"

"Good form. So let's try destiny."

"I don't know what I believe."

Their hands reached the top of Pandora, and side by side they stroked the animal's great back. With each sweep of the brushes, their hands touched and stayed in contact from one end of the stroke to the other.

"There is an unwritten law in the universe that wills celestial bodies in motion to alter their course, so they may collide in the heavens," James whispered across Pandora, never taking his eyes off Ananova and holding her in his hypnotic gaze.

"And what happens when those bodies . . . collide?" Ananova looked away, frightened by the sensations surging through her. She looked toward the crew and the Captain, praying none would hear her heart pounding and rush over to spoil this moment. James slid his hand in the motion of the stroke onto hers, folding his fingers through hers as they completed the course of her brushstroke together.

"The energy of their union is of such power that a new sun is born into the galaxy."

Ananova covered his hand with her own and drew the brush back down to Pandora's withers and shoulders, guiding it in circular motions on the animal's white coat. Then she looked James right in the eye.

"Did you make that up just to impress me, or did somebody important write it? Socrates? Alexander the Great? Gallileo?"

James' usual mischievous grin spread into a smile of admiration. This Sultana was no gullible girl.

"Does it matter, Ananova?"

James realized he had never before spoken her name to her face.

"They will probably kill you when they find you," she said sternly.

"Did it never occur to you that I will kill them if they try?"

Ananova smiled at James, so fearless and seemingly invincible. Impulsively, she bowed to him and, placing her lips on the back of his hand, she held them there, pressing against his long, tapered fingers, a gesture fit for

Kings and Dukes and Princes . . . not for bastards.

The Captain's voice broke the moment. Ananova saw him approaching across the deck, suspicious of her actions with the tall crewman. Before James could react, Ananova suddenly grew venomous with James, grabbing both his hands and firming them around the brush. Forcefully she drove his hands along Pandora's back.

"Oh, you idiot! That's no way to brush a horse. No wonder you English have to beat your animals to obey you."

The Sultana was very convincing, even to James, who took her verbal browbeating, curling himself lower and lower as she slapped him about the arms and shoulders with Pandora's tether.

"Now muck out the stall and be done with you! Throw yourself overboard for all I care!" She continued with grating conviction, shoving him deeper into the stall, causing Pandora to go skittish and whinny. Before the Captain could draw too close, Ananova slammed the stall gate and marched to meet him,

"Shilpits! All of you English," she barked at the Captain. "There's not a decent groom on the whole boat—"

"My deepest pardon, Sultana. My men are sailors. And this is a ship, not a stable. Let's try and make the best of it."

The Captain made an attempt to get a closer look at the sailor mucking out Pandora's stall, but Ananova turned the Captain right around and herded him forward, laying it on. James marveled at her powers. Even though she was tiny in stature next to the Captain and veteran crew, the men fell away from her path like wheat before a scythe. She

had provided James an opportunity to escape undetected. Get Jolly and over the side and . . .

But the opportunity was short-lived.

A commotion rose up amidships. The two crewmen whom James and Jolly had subdued and stripped of their outfits had been discovered. They had been brought up on deck in their skivvies, which, by the scuddy sight and smell of them, had not been laundered over several voyages. The two crewmen babbled out their story of a "demon who wanted their souls and their clothes." Ananova played a convincing performance, accusing the two sailors of smuggling rum on board and being drunk with their talk of demons in the hold.

But the Captain was taking no chances. The crewmen had been found bound and gagged. He ordered the Sultana to her cabin until the intruders were ferreted out. Ananova's Marxbruder went on alert immediately, rousing himself from his nap on the fo'c'sle deck and strapping on his weapons. Since that incident at the Queen's Eight, the Marxbruder had been the subject of criticism over his performance as Ananova's tutor and trainer. This time he had no intention of letting any scoundrel who would threaten his charge escape.

Pandora became skittish at the sudden activity sweeping the ship. She began to buck and kick the walls of her stall as Ananova was brusquely ushered toward her cabin. The Sultana broke away and quickly returned to the stall, hoping she would find James gone. To her relief, he was nowhere to be seen.

CHAPTER ELEVEN

AN AWFULLY BIG ADVENTURE

JOLLY R HAD ENTERTAINED the nurse in James' absence—at least by Jolly R's new definition of entertainment. The poor woman sat at the Captain's table, horrified as Jolly whistled and clapped. There, on the tabletop, performing on command, was James' prized *Lasiodora* silk-spinning spider. Electra reared up, displaying her horrible fangs, whistling an eerie response that caused the nurse to shudder and whimper. The furry thing pivoted and walked backward, erect on her rear legs, ending with a high back flip and landing on all eight legs, ready to pounce. To Jolly's surprise and distress, the nurse fainted dead away, slumping in her chair.

James knocked their secret pattern. Jolly unlocked the door and was nearly bowled over as James hurried into the cabin and bolted the door behind him. Jolly R was instantly on the defensive.

"I didn't touch her, King Jas., I swear. Electra was absolutely smashing. . . . "

James was not interested in reviews and critiques. In a matter of seconds the Captain's men would come to search for the "demons" who had infested the ship. James explained this to Jolly R as he forced open the latch on one of the great windows facing astern. They would have to jump.

The two friends stared at the wake the schooner was carving in the swift current of the Thames. James fought against his revulsion and fear of the water, but the phobia drained the courage right out of him. Jolly R buckled, offering no help or encouragement.

"You go right ahead. Be a wetbob," Jolly said in full retreat. "I'll be staying here and taking my chances, Jas." Jolly R retreated back to the table where Electra crouched waiting for her next command. "I can't swim, Jas. Never learned."

James almost burst out laughing at his round friend. "If I can squash my phobia, Jolly, you're jumping."

Jolly was adamant, shaking his head in a determined negative. The first knock came at the door. The Marxbruder's voice announced to the nurse that the Sultana was in his company and to please open up. Jolly raised the

woman's chin. Her head lolled about on her neck like a rag doll's. She was comatose from fear. Electra shrieked.

"I suspect we don't have adequate time for Electra to knit us a boat, do we, Jas.? Just a small bit of a scull, eh?"

If James had not known Jolly so well, he would have cuffed him a good one for making cheap jests at such a dire moment. But Jolly R was serious. James whistled to Electra and plopped his hat on the table. The creature crouched and jumped into the crown of the hat, which James promptly secured back over his curls.

"Then we fight our way out."

"Fortune and glory, James. Fortune and glory."

The Marxbruder pounded again, threatening to break the door in if the nurse did not answer.

"You're frightening the poor woman," Ananova intervened, rapping quietly on the door, calling gently. "It's all right, Gwenny. Take your time. I am not in a hurry to disturb you."

James looked around the cabin. They needed a diversion.

"I'm afraid I'm not at all decent at the moment, m'lady. Just slipping on my frock. Won't be a moment—" Jolly answered in his best falsetto perfected over years of playing the female roles in Eton's Shakespeare festival. James threw open the trunk containing Ananova's froufrous. The linens and cottons and silks would do nicely. He snagged the lamp hanging over the table and dumped the oil into the frillies, setting them afire. Smoke billowed up immediately from the oily fabrics—

"Oh, my goodness! Fire!" Jolly yelled on cue and in character, shrieking and fumbling about, knocking over furniture to add to the chaos. James heaved the comatose woman over Jolly's shoulder, who toted her toward the door. The cabin filled quickly with smoke.

"Somebody save me!" Jolly had embraced the role of an imperiled woman with opening-night fervor.

The Marxbruder slammed against the door again. James and Jolly readied themselves on either side of the entrance. The door buckled under the next impact, bursting from its hinges. The momentum of the stocky sword master carried him careening into the cabin. Blinded by the smoke, the Marxbruder collided with the Captain's heavy oak table, leaving him stunned. Jolly and James spilled out the door with the nurse onto the quarterdeck and right at Ananova's feet.

"You English have extremely odd ideas about courtship. Takes some getting used to."

James quickly rose and bowed.

"Yes, but we have manners and good form. Sultana Ananova, may I present Jolly Roger Davies, my dear best friend—correct that—my only friend in the entire world."

James regarded Jolly R as if realizing this fact of their friendship for the first time. Jolly managed a feeble bow under the weight of the nurse, who was coming to.

"Your Highness. She'll be all right. Bit of a scare—"

"I'll see to Gwenny. Quickly, over the side with you while there is still time." Under other circumstances, the Sultana

would have politely asked Jolly what his favorite subjects were, how life was at Eton, the flavor of his favorite cake, all the important things he had done, and the like, but this was not one of those circumstances.

Sailors hurried up the quarterdeck stairs carrying buckets of water to douse the flames. The Captain headed across the main deck barking orders.

"Jolly, take the helm." James grabbed the first bucket of water to arrive and heaved it into the smoking cabin as if he were part of the effort to extinguish the flames instead of the fire's cause.

"Me? My father never let me take the helm." Jolly was astonished at this turn of events.

"Take it, Jolly. Steer us as close to shore as you are able." James gave the order, paying no attention to Jolly as he took the next bucket and tossed it into the cabin. The sailor with the bucket stopped cold face-to-face with James. It was the stout fellow on the short side James had spooked in the hold—still in his skivvies. The man paled and completely panicked.

"It's the demon. It's 'im!"

James took the bucket and, putting his boot to the man's chest, shoved him tumbling down the stairs, rolling other crew with him. James heaved the bucket of water into the smoking cabin. The contents doused the Marxbruder on his way out, coughing and rubbing his burning eyes and flailing about blindly.

"Go, James, go. Please!" Ananova tended her nurse,

trying to shield her from the brigade of feet and buckets passing around her. James kneeled down.

"Someday my foes may win, Sultana Ananova—*but not today!*"

Watching him as he turned to the task at hand, even Ananova could not dispute his claim. He had the confidence of kings, the belief that he was invincible. James placed his hands on the railing; then he called out to the crew racing about in the smoke.

"Abandon ship! The fire is out of control. Save your-selves!"

By lowering his voice, James did sound convincingly captainlike. Remarkably, the adage "Where there is smoke, there is fire" still had some teeth among the crew. Several immediately sent themselves diving over the side. Others retreated to the bow and began to break out a jolly boat. Ananova marveled at her view of the chaos from the quar-terdeck.

Jolly R, who had delayed carrying out James' orders, suddenly found the courage he needed. He marched up to the rattled helmsman at the wheel and saluted politely. "You heard the Captain. We're abandoning ship. Right, I'll take over. Go on. Be quick."

The helmsman needed no further convincing. He gladly turned the wheel over to the round lad and hurried away. Way beyond any rational sense of danger or basic survival instinct, Jolly was in a state of complete euphoria as he stood before the vacated wheel. First his right hand firmed around

the wooden peg on the wheel to starboard, then his left curled around the grip to the port side. He could feel the tension of the wind filling the sails, singing through the array of ropes and rigging wound and tied and all converging on the wheel tugging at his hands. Before him the deck and masts heeled and bobbed at the motion of the wind. Beyond the bowsprit, the river Thames, and beyond the river . . . the sea was waiting.

"I'm sailing," Jolly R whispered to himself. "Wish my da could see me now! Haaa!"

The Captain had completely lost control to young James Matthew. Many of the crew were abandoning ship. With the exception of one, the Marxbruder.

"*Feuer gelöscht*—the fire is out," he reported. "Only a trunk of the Sultana's— Halt there! I know that face. *Wer bist du?* Who are you?" The Marxbruder drew his sword and gully knife, instantly en garde.

"Your worst nightmare, I'm afraid, sir." James bowed. As he rose, the Marxbruder slashed at his head, knocking his hat off. Great coils of black curls sprang down, framing his smile.

"You! The bastard. *Bist du das Dämon?*"

"The same." James whistled shrilly. Electra crawled up the back of his curls to the top of his head, trained her huge black eyes on the Marxbruder, and leaped, landing squarely on his face. The sword master reeled back, dropping his weapons, slapping at the eight-legged monster. Electra's high-pitched whistle sent Ananova retreating down the

stairs. James grabbed the Marxbruder's sword and followed. For an instant Ananova doubted James. Who was this strange boy really? Perhaps he was some kind of demon prince, with attacking spiders at his command and yellow blood. Through the waning smoke Pandora's anxious snorts and cries summoned the Sultana. She turned her back on James and fled.

Pandora had all but kicked her stall to pieces. Ananova finally managed to cover the horse's head with a blanket, preventing her from seeing the chaos caused by the smoke. James was suddenly there, holding the horse's halter rope taut, steadying the animal as Ananova moved around Pandora calming her.

"Sultana . . . we can take it—the ship—to wherever you wish."

She gazed at him and her fears fell away. Then she silenced him by pressing three of her fingers to his lips.

"Take me away, James . . . far, far away," she said. "To an island where the skies and waters are the same color, pure and clear as light. And flowers bloom year-round, even in the snow."

James stared at her. She was describing *his* island—his Neverland!

"I know the place," he said. "We could rule together there and never grow old."

"Yes," she said. "Someday."

"Someday"—the word floated between them like the ocean of time that he would cross to win her. Their hope

was in the future, he realized, not the present as he had dreamed. She was a Sultana. Someday she would be a great ruler. By sending her home, her father was protecting her from the one thing that could redefine her destiny. In Sultana Ananova's life, James Matthew had arrived too early. Someday—

The force of the Marxbruder's headlong charge tore James away from Ananova and slammed him into the stall, driving the breath from his lungs. Pandora bucked, kicking at the two men in a panic. Ananova maneuvered the Arabian to the back of the stall, fighting to keep control. Her pleas to stop went unheeded. Her official protector was seething with rage, his face swollen with fresh spider bites. Before James could recover his breathing, the sword master was on him again, using his momentum to hurl James tumbling to the deck. The sword he had taken from the Marxbruder slid across the deck, caroming off the capstan. The man suddenly drew a long dagger concealed in his back sheath and charged! James fought the burning in his lungs and scrambled to retrieve the blade just in time to block the attack by the Marxbruder. The clang of their blades drew the attention of the last crewmen, who only moments before were prepared to abandon ship. James was no match for this superior swordsman as he struggled to defend himself. The sword master was toying with him as crewmen followed the pair battling around the deck.

Jolly R had a clear view of the duel from his spot at the helm. He had turned the ship, now heading for shore just as

James had commanded. A stout wind abeam heeled the ship over, dropping the masts toward the water. The sudden pitch of the deck caused Pandora to fall back on her haunches, pulling Ananova with her. Both horse and Sultana splintered the stall gate and rolled onto the deck.

"Release the helm!" the Captain yelled, furious at Jolly R, as he and the first mate climbed to the quarterdeck.

"Can't do that, sir. Orders." Jolly R held fast, causing the angle of the deck to pitch more. The first mate grabbed Jolly R, pulling him off the wheel. As soon as his hands were freed, the wheel spun like a top in the reverse direction. All the sails luffed with the radical course change. The massive jib swung across the quarterdeck, sending the Captain arcing out over the Thames, clinging to the spar. Now the ship careened out of control toward the shore.

The tilting deck sent James and the Marxbruder sliding across the surface as if on ice skates, bumping into the gunwales, grabbing at any rope, cleat, or spar. Ananova held on to Pandora's mane as the horse fought the changing pitch of the deck to remain on her feet.

"Good form and fighting with foils is for schoolboys, *Junge*." The sword master, his spider-bitten face a landscape of boils and welts, locked James up in a bind. "I have the authority from the Sultan to end anyone who threatens the Sultana, or I give you a lesson, and then I kill you. What say you? *Du*, bastard? Lesson or death?"

The answer was obvious to James as he lay there staring up at the grinning face yelling insults in German and

threatening to extinguish him. James was an excellent competitive fencer, trained by fine sword masters when he was just a boy, but certainly he was no match for this hardened veteran. Where he was headed he could not fathom. Outmatched, separated from Ananova and Jolly R, facing the frightfully real possibility that not only his days were numbered, but possibly his minutes and seconds as well—

"Lesson first—then death, I should think," James stated casually. "You go first."

"Right!" The man puckered his welt-ridden face and spat right in James' forget-me-not eyes, then drove his boot hard, sinking deep into James' groin, sending him rolling on the deck. Cheers from the handful of sailors still on board clamored through James' head. He clenched his teeth to wait out the white-hot pain shooting up from his groin, fragmenting through his brain. The Marxbruder stood over James, a carnivore's gleam in his teeth and eyes, a predator ready for the kill.

"Lesson's over, lad."

The sword master measured his blade at James' heart. James closed his eyes and took in the sounds swirling around him. The straining and moaning of the ship and sails. The waters of the Thames thrashing at the hull. The voice of Jolly R calling out his name above the cacophony of the crew. The braying whinny of Ananova's horse. The staccato clatter of hooves. The imagined flapping of great wings as seraphim made their journey down from the heavens to retrieve another lost soul. And then James knew the answer

to the question that he alone had the knowledge to ask. He opened his eyes and stared into the angry, tormented face forcing the tip of a sword into his chest, right over his heart.

"Are you afraid of death?" James asked in priestly tones.

The Marxbruder cocked his brick of a head, flummoxed at the bold question from this boy who was at his mercy.

"Me? It's you who should be answering that question."

"I know the answer." James smiled and lunged his chest against the sword. His protective web-spun vest deflected the blade, startling the veteran swordsman.

"What magic is this?" James slammed his heart again against the blade with the same result. Now the Marx-bruder grew frightened. "What are you?!!!! *Was bist du?!!*"

"Lesson's over." James smiled and whirled in a most unorthodox blur that sent the Marxbruder's weapon flying over the side, leaving him defenseless. James flicked his blade to the man's throat, then bowed and backed away.

Crewmen fell back at the primal wails of Ananova running beside the pounding hooves of the white Arabian galloping across the deck toward James. With the fluid motion of a ballet dancer, Ananova hung on to Pandora's mane and swung up onto her mount bareback. James watched the mystical sight as the dream horse carrying his Sultana reared up on her powerful hind legs, pawing her forelegs against a backdrop of sails and rushing water. Sailors poked and stabbed at the mount, to grab her down. Pandora snapped her neck back and forth, butting her tor-mentors with her forehead like a bull. Ananova steered the

horse through the men, yelling at James to jump on.

James leaped to his feet, dodging grabbing hands, then vaulted up, grabbing the ratlines leading to the mizzen-mast, timed his attempt, and jumped.

At this very same moment, Jolly R, mustering his courage, leaped onto the first mate, twisting his ear until he released the wheel, begging for mercy. Jolly looked up just in time to see the ship's bowsprit buckle and snap as the hull struck a sailing barge trying desperately to maneuver out of the way as the craft plowed into an array of hog boats moored at a ferry wharf. The repeated collisions shuddered the schooner to a near stop.

The impact catapulted objects not securely battened down toward the bow, carrying men and equipment with them. Jolly grabbed the wheel as the Captain and the first mate sailed past him off the quarterdeck, crashing to the main deck below. A sharp crack traveled up the mainmast. A century's growth of oak separated, sending the mainmast toppling toward the fo'c'sle, hauling down rigging and sending canvas cascading across the ship into the waters of the Thames.

Pandora used all her instincts and graceful agility to stay erect as crew and objects rushed by. She galloped up the heaving deck, running in place as the ship tipped forward. Ananova clung to Pandora's mane, hugging the horse's flanks with her knees. James hung on behind, wrapped around Ananova. Pandora's iron shoes struck the deck in a blur of speed, leaving a trail of sparks behind her.

The Marxbruder held on to a halyard, watching the surreal sight of the white horse galloping up the deck, leaving hell's fire in her tracks. And there was James with the Sultana astride Pandora, heading right for him!

"A demon he is. God save us all!"

Ananova urged Pandora on faster, stretching her out. Pandora pushed off with her powerful rear flanks, leaping right over the Marxbruder, over the fallen mast, and into the air as if the Arabian would sprout wings and fly!

Jolly R clung to the wheel, petrified at the sight of the great white horse carrying the Sultana and King Jas. over the side of the listing ship and splashing into the Thames, sending a crescendo of spume into the morning sky. He unpried his fingers from the spokes. Spikes of adrenaline moved his feet thumping across the quarterdeck toward the gunwales. If he was breathing, Jolly did not know it. Fear of losing King Jas. overcame his fear of drowning, that being the most logical fear one can possibly have when one cannot swim across a teacup.

"Jasssssss! I'm cominggggggggg!" All the way down he yelled until his voice choked on the Thames rushing into his throat and up both nostrils, stinging his lungs as they filled with the briny water. His body screamed for air where there was none. He clawed and tried to climb back to the surface, but he only sank deeper as the waters closed around him. Jolly R twitched and contorted, his eyes wild with a terror he had never known. Then he sagged, rolling silently with the current.

Jolly R clung to the wheel, petrified at the sight of the great white horse carrying the Sultana and King Jas. over the side of the listing ship and splashing into the Thames. . . .

Turbulence in the currents suddenly buffeted Jolly. Churning legs appeared through the waters. Pandora's powerful flanks paddled up alongside Jolly's inert form. Then that magnificent white head poked down from the surface, blowing air bubbles from her snout. Baring her teeth, the Arabian clamped down on Jolly's spider-silk waistcoat and pulled him up from the depths. James reached down from astride Pandora and slid Jolly R across her crowded back. Ananova guided the animal downriver, carried along in the swift current.

"Jolly, you bloaty codfish, you really can't swim!" James was beside himself, slapping Jolly, shoving his hand into his friend's distended abdomen. "Breathe, Jolly, breathe. We've got an awfully big adventure ahead of us—"

Jolly blew like a great sperm whale, spewing the Thames through his nose and mouth, coughing back to life. He was alive! Pandora tossed her head and whinnied. Ananova grabbed James' hand and squeezed it tightly. Together they held Jolly R, keeping him from slipping back into the river. Jolly blinked the water from his eyes and took a long look at his saviors. Ananova glistened wet, her hair trailing behind her like a mane. A goddess, a mermaid on her rounds. Then his eyes found James hovering over him, cradling his head to keep him from swallowing any more of the Thames.

"If this is Heaven, then you're the ugliest mucking angel I have ever seen," Jolly blurted out between gasps.

Ananova's crystal laugh rang out. It was a moment out

of the blue for James—a rare, improbable moment with friends. He had never cared for any other person in his life, save Aunt Emily, enough to fear losing them. He had never had anyone to lose but himself. Here, straddling a snowy white Arabian swimming down the Thames, fleeing from a Sultan and a Queen from separate worlds who had long ago lost their youth, he could not imagine going on in this life without his friend, his true friend, Jolly Roger. Jolly had shown good form from the very first moment they had met. Even James' scandalous origins had not sent Jolly running to join the ranks of those who viewed him as less than human, a mutant who did not deserve to share the privileges of Eton bloods. The round, soaking-wet Oppidan spread across the back of this horse had risked everything—even his own life—to be James Matthew's friend.

He cradled Jolly in his arms, rocking him and laughing from sheer relief that his friend had not drowned. They were alike, he and Jolly. Brothers brought together by the need to dwell on the fringes. James vowed in his heart to protect Jolly R, to always keep him close and never again to let him suffer because he had chosen to be James' friend.

"Hey! You're choking me, James!" Jolly sputtered in James' tight grip. "I could've done *that* drowning."

"Just didn't want to lose you again, Jolly."

A familiar whistle echoed as Electra crawled from inside Jolly R's wet waistcoat and perched on the boy's head. James laughed and loosened his grip on his friend as the loyal spider shook herself dry. Ananova caught his eye. He held

her gaze. Her eyes were impenetrably deep and fearless, the royal indigo scarf she wore around her head holding back her mane, giving her the appearance of a pirate princess. She belonged on his island, his Neverland. Someday he would take her to that glassy-smooth lagoon he imagined, sheltered from the wind, where time stands still and they could be forever young. Sometimes James believed that if he imagined the island hard and long enough, it would appear. Right before his eyes . . .

And James knew then and there that he could not lose Ananova ever or his life would be over.

Ananova pressed on the back of Pandora's neck. The Arabian responded, swimming faster into the center of the Thames. Behind them, chaos reigned. The schooner had impaled two sailing barges, dissected a row of hog boats, destroyed a ferry pier, and run aground on the shore. The Captain cursed them from the quarterdeck amid the wreckage of his command. Ananova's nurse wept as she waded among the trunks with her Sultana's belongings floating in the river. James caught a last glimpse of the Marxbruder rowing one of the ship's jolly boats after them, refusing defeat.

Ahead, the river would carry them to London, then to Greenwich and the sea, where the awfully big adventure awaited.

TO THE VILLAIN
GO THE SPOILS

A

CCORDING TO THE CONSTABLE of record, a trio of young miscreants and an aggressive arachnid believed to be poisonous were taken into custody at Kingston upon Thames for attempting to commandeer a privately owned sailing ship at anchor named the *Mephistopheles*. The would-be pirates were identified as two students from Eton. A third, a female also taken into custody, remained unidentified. Names were withheld until family and relatives were notified. Sir Michael Spencer Davies, the owner of the vessel, was summoned from his estate nearby to witness the charges, only to discover that

one of the perpetrators of this crime was none other than his son, Roger Peter Davies, a sixth-form student at Eton. Sir Michael refused to comment. He was convinced that this incident was the result of some end-of-term prank, in the great Eton bloods' tradition, that had gone terribly awry. The damages for this bit of skullduggery had reached hundreds of guineas and were still climbing. A schooner that had run aground and inflicted significant damage up-river from the scene of their arrest was also linked to the spree of river piracy instigated by the young "buccaneers."

Jolly Roger had cheered out loud in the presence of the Magistrate when the constable used that phrase to describe the young criminals. His father batted him down repeatedly, and admonished him to show some respect for the laws he had violated and the private property he had destroyed with his fellow criminals. James remained stoic throughout the humiliating process of the arrest. They had been manacled hand and foot like galley slaves, or criminals condemned to the executioner's block for high treason against the Crown.

James reviewed a parade of images invading his mind: French peasants lined up in chains before the guillotine for stealing a loaf of bread . . . a child laying her head on the block, arranging her dolly next to her, to wait for the blade to fall. James imagined the horror as the blade fell and was himself disturbed by his own dark imagination. Surely, he thought, the heads who should be placed on the block, ending any further threat they could be to society, should not

be the lowlifes and the oppressed, but those of the ruling class who had the power to turn an innocent kiss into an international diplomatic scandal. Now, the punishment of two young, curious hearts had resulted in these catastrophic events that affected many, including Jolly Roger. And why? A bastard, no matter how intellectually, academically, or financially solvent, and a Princess of any magnitude, were forbidden by class and protocol to have any kind of a relationship. Again, James asked himself why.

He could find no sensible answer in the Magistrate's sickly expression, or in the constable's rum-rutted self-satisfaction in having done his duty by apprehending the young "buccaneers," and certainly not in the angry, chiseled visage of Sir Michael Spencer Davies, whose business interests in shipping and sailing ships made him rate piracy the worst crime a human being could commit, more severe than murder or crimes of the heart. Sir Michael wanted James thrown in prison for inciting his son to commit these disgraceful acts.

The only face that held the answer for James was Ananova. And she was gone. Now only the memory of her remained.

When asked if he had anything to say to the Magistrate, James resisted his urge to deliver a cold diagnosis of the disease he could see was eating at the man, which would soon be the death of him. The deep-red discoloration of the man's lower eyelids, the yellowing of his fingernails and the tips of his fingers, told the tale. But James chose to remain silent.

The Magistrate could rot as his liver slowly poisoned him.

The Magistrate ruled that reparations for all damages would be the responsibility of the accused. Other charges could come from the owners of the schooner. If these costs could not be paid, the boys would find themselves in prison for a very long time.

Jolly R was escorted from the chambers by his father. He was allowed to return to his family's estate in Kingston in lieu of the constable's accommodations with rats the size of kittens, and a smell so foul that drowning might have been preferable to breathing the stench. Jolly was relieved of his chains as his father led him away. Whatever punishment was to be awarded James, Jolly R wanted exactly the same.

"King Jaaaas.!" he shouted as he was dragged from the chambers. "Someday our foes may win . . ." His voice echoed as a heavy wooden door clanked shut, separating them. James sat in silence. Jolly's voice continued to echo over his father's admonishments. And then he was gone.

". . . but not today. . . . Good form, Jolly R." James spoke quietly, a slight smile returning to his melancholy face. James had every intention of living until he caught up to Ananova once again, even if it took forever. As he studied the sick Magistrate struggling to fill his lungs with his next breath, James considered the amazing possibilities an eternal life might offer. Why had James never understood this before? It suddenly became clear to him sitting there, cloaked in chains and humiliation before this all-too-mortal Magistrate, that the single most important purpose for the

seeking of knowledge was to learn how to become immortal. All mathematics, the study of the stars and heavens, all science and philosophy, religion and the theories of man's evolution and origins, even myth and fairy tales, were knitted together with one universal uniting purpose—the quest for immortality. James felt that his brain was about to explode with this revelation. Even his chains could not contain the power he had just unleashed inside his own mind. A great scientist, a Gallileo or da Vinci, would not have to die before completing his world-changing discoveries. Had da Vinci been immortal, would he have discovered the secret to human flight? Might James be flying about like a bird with his own wings had da Vinci lived? Would Shakespeare's thirty-eighth play have surpassed the genius and tragedy of *Hamlet* or the comedy and mirth of *Twelfth Night?* Would the Bard's one hundred fifty-fifth sonnet unlock the key to love's secrets had he lived to write the words? If time stood still on his magic island, he and Ananova could live forever. Forever young. There, in his Neverland, he would find the secret of immortality. There all waters would run from the fountain of youth and everyone who drank of it would live forever in Paradise. His Paradise . . .

"King Jas.?"

The Magistrate's voice snapped James from his reverie. He was studying James over his spectacles.

"Your partner in crime called you King Jas."

James gave a perfunctory nod, as if the question were annoying.

"A fond endearment, no doubt."

"No, your worship," said James, staring at the man. "He *knows* I will be a King one day."

"I've had enough of you, King Jas." The coughing fit flattened the man in his great chair. "I shall spare the rats in the constable's keep the pleasure of your company. There is something dangerous about you—beyond boyish mischief. I have never met a young man quite like you, and I hope never to do so again."

The Magistrate called for his bailiff and ordered that James be escorted back to Eton with his arachnid pet and turned over to the Provost with a record of the complaint. He was sure the Provost and the good chancellors of Kings College would know what to do with their "King Jas." and his lab specimen.

"And what of Sultana Ananova?" James demanded as he was being led out. "What has happened to her?"

The Magistrate looked at him with jaundiced eyes.

"She has been returned to her people. English law has no jurisdiction over royalty from a foreign country. You will not be seeing her again in this lifetime, King Jas.," the Magistrate answered. For imparting this news with some joy, James decided that the Magistrate would be the first to lose his head to the guillotine he intended to use when he was crowned King.

"If that is the case, your worship, if I am never to see her again, then I am a condemned man. And therefore I do not

need the noose of English law around my neck to decide my fate. My course is my own. And I shall set it."

His voice remained steady and cold as the constable linked his chain to James' manacles. From her small cage Electra hissed an angry whistle at her captors as the constable led them away.

ETON BLUES

THE VIEW FROM JAMES' TINY GARRET window at Godolphin House looked particularly bleak. Confined to his cramped room, he awaited the inevitable knock on his door. Colleger escorts would accompany him to the disciplinary council, where his fate was being determined by beaks and peers with small minds and smaller hearts. Darling had been suspended for dueling—for the intent to duel, in truth. The disciplinary council could not punish him for something he had not done. And in light of his intended duelist, Darling got off lightly. One-term suspension. He could still graduate the following year with all the honors and colors earned during his eleven years at Eton.

Many of the council privately conceded they wished the duel had taken place and that Darling had been the victor.

Jolly R had already been disciplined. Dicky Dongon passed the details along through a note he slipped under James' door. The beaks had barred Jolly R from attending the Lent term, forfeiting all his class hours and study credits for the previous term. He could possibly return in the fall to start his sixth level over again if he passed a careful review by the Regents and the Provost. His father, Sir Michael, had agreed to pay all the damages to the ship chartered by Ananova's father and all the collateral damage to the other boats involved in the incident. But the worst blow to Jolly was learning that Sir Michael had been forced to offer his treasured ship, the *Mephistopheles*, for Ananova's passage to the Mediterranean.

It had been two days since James had seen his friend. Jolly R had been isolated by his father at the family estate near Kingston to prevent him from having any contact with James. "Evil," Sir Michael had called James to his face. "The world would be a better place if you'd never been born."

James acknowledged that his own father would most likely agree. His Lordship could have been spared the social embarrassment. And his poor mother, whoever she was—had he ruined her life by being born? But Aunt Emily would have suffered without James in her life. He was all she lived and breathed for, devoting herself to his upbringing, taking him to the theater and teaching him the classics. At least there was one in the world who would not have

been better off had James not lived and breathed. No, two.

James rejected the idea that Jolly R would be better off in his life without their friendship. Jolly R and the Oppidans had won the historic Wall Game against the Collegers and chiseled themselves forever in the annals of Eton—a proud legacy even for Sir Michael. Had Jolly even known the true meaning of friendship before James came along? Certainly James had not.

James had come to Eton suspicious and critical of everyone who spurned him for being different. And when Etonians had not wanted him, he had, with Jolly's help, conquered the Eton bloods on his own terms. He had left an indelible mark on the tradition of the school that could not be denied. But had it not been for Jolly, James admitted to himself, he might never have had the heart to make so proud a stand.

When the royal guards had arrived at the constable's with the Marxbruder and Skeffington, James and Ananova had already been separated. A convenient slit allowed them glimpses of each other, so narrow only one eye at a time could see. James spoke quickly, his mastery of words failing him. There was not much time, and he had much to tell her. Hearing the horses and carriage arrive, and the voices of the Marxbruder and Skeffington entering the constable's jail, James suddenly found himself begging Ananova's forgiveness for all the difficulties and problems he had visited upon her since the moment he first laid eyes on her. Her voice barked at him with regal fury, like the ruler she could be someday.

"How dare you ask forgiveness of me, James. You risked everything—your friend, your position, your future—for me! What would I be forgiving you for?"

It was a question he did not have the words to answer. James did not completely understand the feeling in his heart. Or why his mouth went suddenly dry. The voices were louder now. Ananova turned away from the slit, speaking in her own language. Her phrases were sharp and angry. Was she talking to her father? Then she turned back to James, urgent, sadness in her eyes.

"Find your island; then maybe you will come for me. Good-bye, James."

Her eye disappeared. James could see her stuffing something into the slit, blocking the view. He slid his hand in to remove whatever was blocking it. The object was soft to his touch. He pulled out the long indigo silk scarf Ananova had worn about her head on the schooner. The smell of her was still captured in the silk. He tied her banner around his neck, cursing himself. They had all been together, standing on the deck of their pirated ship! He and Jolly R and his Sultana. Looking at Ananova beside him as they placed their hands together on the helm, he could no longer distinguish between the rush he felt being with her and the indescribable thrill of being Captain of his own ship. And finally it did not matter. He was alive, so much so he was afraid that he might actually explode into a sizzle of sparks. Together they would learn how to sail her. What they did not know, they would pick up from the wisdom and

experience of the sailors who would join their enterprise. The island was waiting for them to discover. Nothing was going to stop them. After all, they were invincible— The rock crashing against his garret window shattered his musings.

"Mutant!"

There was no doubt who belonged to that voice. Another rock glanced off the window. James threw open the sash and craned his head out to look below into the alley.

"This is not finished, mutant. I'm not done with you!" ranted Darling.

James could see Rupert and two other toffs in his company wearing masks tied around their faces. One waved an effigy hanging from a broomstick. The long, stringy mop hair had been dyed with ink to resemble James'.

Darling was tearing the effigy apart, stomping the stringy hair, while Rupert and his fellows wrestled him down the alley before a prefect spotted them.

James calmly closed his window. There was no avoiding Darling now—James knew that. A true duel was inevitable, and James was determined to be ready for Darling. He recalled his study in Birkin's history class of the three hundred Spartans who had charged hundreds of thousands of invading Persian soldiers at the battle of Thermopylae, and how the young General Leonidas led his Spartans, killing multitudes of the invaders from behind their wedge of shields before they all perished. A splendid, glorious death. What an adventure. James prepared himself. He would not go down without a fight.

He opened his wardrobe. Electra was in the throes of herding her army of *Lasiodoras* into ranks ready for battle. James was overwhelmed by the sight. Fifty-plus very scary-looking large arachnids reared back on their hind legs and pawed their forelegs in a salute, whistling some lost chord in tribute. James bowed, displaying his waistcoat for all to see. They had served him well. He lamented that this could possibly be the last time he would see them gathered. He did not wish to see them exterminated after he was gone. He stroked Electra on the back of her furry thorax and whistled a thankful response.

Locking his wardrobe on his spider mates, James pulled a rapier from under his bed, tucked a cruel-looking dirk down the back of his britches, adjusted his fair lady's scarf about his neck, and struck a pose, taken from the best of the actors who had entertained him at Aunt Emily's when preparing to recite from Shakespeare: his right foot advanced ahead of his left, his fisted left hand placed on his hip, with his elbow at a jaunty angle, his right hand firmly grasping his sword, the tip of his blade touching the ground, head erect, and long, flowing curls framing his unforgettable forget-me-nots. A hero's stance, elegant and evil. How could one not help but take up a heroic stance when portraying Henry V giving his St. Crispin's Day oration just before his archers, armed only with longbows and gray-goose shafts, destroy the vastly superior French army at Agincourt?

Footsteps arrived at his door, and the butt of a birch rapped smartly. It was the Duke of Gloucester who answered.

"*'Tis not my speeches that you do mislike, But 'tis my presence that doth trouble ye. Rancor will out.'*"

The two Whips who opened the door were not impressed with James' acting ability; but the rapier that blurred in his hand, and just barely missed touching the bases of their throats before they could react, made up for any shortcomings in his thespian training. Unnerved, one of the Whips dropped his birch switch, sending it clattering down the steps.

"You'll have to kill me to beat me," said James.

"Good God, James, we've only come to tell you there's someone to see you."

James remained with his rapier en garde as methodical steps ascended the staircase.

"*Henry VI*, part two, act one, scene one, I believe. At least you've learned your Shakespeare. As well as your art of defense with the sword, I see." The head that appeared first rising up the stairs was covered in a dark, wide-brimmed beaver-fur hat, but the voice was not a mystery.

"Twice in the same week my own father seeks me out! If I started a war, would you invite me home for Boxing Day, Father?" James forced his father to stop at the threshold of his door before he retired his blade.

"If you were trying to get my attention, you've succeeded," said His Lordship dryly, waving the two Collegers away and sending them gratefully half leaping down the stairs. James retreated, allowing his father to enter his tiny quarters. The man's eyes surveyed the appointments and

items his son had found important enough to put up on his walls or pile about in corners and on shelves. He looked everywhere but at his son. He lingered over the yellowing portrait of Charles II hanging above the coal fire, the King's curls identical in style and presentation to James' coiffure. Then the scathing bit of penmanship on the wall:

KING JAS. MATTHEW BASTARD, O.S.B.
Keeper of the Wall—Lord Protector of the Pudding

"Tea? Hemlock?" James busied himself putting a kettle on his coal fire.

"Not for me, thank you. Good news and bad news, James. How would you like it?"

"There is probably not much difference. I leave it to you."

His father produced an envelope from his topcoat, complete with an official wax seal, all proper and intimidating. Addressed to "James Matthew" and nothing more.

"Your dismissal. I've assured the Provost and the Queen that you will be gone from Eton within twenty-four hours."

James studied the envelope and handed it back to his father.

"When my entire name appears on the envelope, I will accept it."

"That would not change any aspect of the situation."

"It would for me."

"I didn't have to come here. I did not have to intervene on your behalf after your despicable conduct. Have you any

idea of the cost of what you have done? Monetarily . . . morally . . . socially? Even the politics are fragile—"

"Mmm. Despicable. Am I to live with you?"

"No. Not possible."

"Of course . . . Aunt Emily? Will she have me back?"

His father gathered himself and produced a second, thicker envelope.

"Since you seem obsessed with sailing ships, I've arranged for a position on one of my merchant vessels. You'll start as a first mate's apprentice on the *Sea Witch*. Her Captain has been in my service for a long time. After seven years at sea under his command, not only will you learn a trade, but more important, you will learn discipline."

James held the envelope, struggling to comprehend the overwhelming news. His hands shook.

"Seven years? At sea . . . ?" James could barely speak. He was elated.

"You leave me no choice, James," His Lordship said sternly. "No matter what I do for you, it is not enough. Maybe seven years before the mast will give you something I cannot."

James was beside himself. He wanted to shriek with unbridled joy. Here his father was punishing him with the very severest of penalties just this side of the executioner's block. James was being condemned to heaven. The sea! Oceans of time! To learn firsthand how to command his own sailing ship!

"Without discipline and laws and rules, we are no better

than the savages. I'm sorry, James. There is no other way."

James fought to remain sullen but had to turn away from his father to mask his glee.

"And those savages we have slaughtered by the thousands in Africa and the Americas—what does that make us, Your Lordship?"

Lord B held his son's piercing gaze as James turned back to face him. For a moment his father wondered if he had mated with the devil's concubine instead of James' unfortunate mother.

"You are insolent, sir," he answered. "Use that tone with the Captain of the *Sea Witch* and you will see where it gets you." The man folded his topcoat, pulled his hat down to shield his identity, and turned to make his exit.

"My man Broadbent will be around tomorrow to organize your orderly exodus." He paused. "Son, should I never see you again . . . I hope you find what you are looking for."

Lord B's boots clacked down the steps, his black fur hat finally disappearing below the horizon of the staircase.

It was all James could do to keep from crowing in triumph. James Matthew Bastard, O.S.B., Lord Protector of the Pudding, was going to sea!

CHAPTER FOURTEEN

ENDGAME

DICKY DONGON AND SIMON the Snash Napier had the honor of delivering the letter that King Jas. had written to his friend Jolly R. The boys had tucked it in among the personals and books and things Jolly R had requested from his room at Godolphin House. The Davies manor house was a grand prison. Though Jolly R luxuriated in the appointments of a Prince and had all the diversions in the world at his beck and call, he had little energy to live up to the nickname King Jas. had dubbed him. Dicky and Simon had a fine meal and stuffed themselves with sweet sock from the vast stores of chocolates and pastries on hand. Jolly was even allowed to take his friends on

a horseback ride around the estate grounds under the watchful eye of the tutor his father had put in charge of his studies, but the tutor was on hand mostly to ensure that Jolly R received no news of James.

Beyond a brief statement from Skeffington regarding the need for improved relations with the Sultan's country and a report of the river accident, there was no mention in the public record of the daring piratical acts of King Jas. and Jolly Roger Davies and their spectacular attempt to kidnap the Sultan's daughter. What good was being punished for such an amazing piece of dazzle if you could not tell the world about it?

After Dicky and Simon had returned to Eton, Jolly waited until he was in the sanctuary of his room, away from the prying eyes of his father's staff, to read by candlelight the brief epistle from his friend.

> *Good Jolly,*
>
> *If you are expecting an apology from this scug for all that has befallen you, then do not bother to read on, as time is our most precious currency and I will spend no more of it dwelling upon the misguided judgment of the mentally defective Provost who has exiled us from Eton. Be warned. Unlike yourself, I am a selfish fellow who will do whatever is required to get what he wants.*

*I haven't any scruples. But even a pirate can
miss a friend, and I will miss you, Jolly.
Yours truly is to vanish like a phantom on
the winds of the sea, never to return. My
father, His Lordship, has condemned me to
seven years aboard the Sea Witch, now
anchored at Greenwich, which will sail on
the tide the day after tomorrow. Therefore,
this being my last night at Eton, once I
have settled my accounts, I assure you there
will be no record of my existence as an
Oppidan except in the memory of you, my
friend, my only friend, and Ananova. The
ocean will be my mother, the Sea Witch
my home. I trust you will remember my
oath to you, to captain our own ship
someday. To Neverland!*

> *Fortune and glory—*
> *Floreat Etona—*
> *KING JAS.*

Jolly R could clearly hear King Jas.' voice, with all his
eloquence of diction. He was filled with dread over the startling news of James' departure. What would the world be
like without King Jas.? It was the next question that flooded
Jolly's mind. He wrestled with it for the rest of the night:

How could he let his friend and scug mate go off on this
awfully big adventure alone?

ETON BLOOD

JAMES HAD A MAD VISION of a guillotine standing in the School Yard when his father's man called for him the next morning. He knew it was mad, and yet—the guillotine seemed an efficient and economically frugal method of removing the undesirables from society. Instead of rewarding the mere handful of outstanding scholars with colors and more paper to hang on their walls, why not indeed reward those intellects who were dragging down the scholastic standings of the various houses and the schools of the college with a good lopping?

It was, of course, not his own noodle he imagined on the executioner's block, rolling across the yard, and being kicked

about in the Wall Game, but Arthur Darling's rotty noggin, as well as the beans of all the beaks and prefects whose
sole mission in life was to inflict pain and misery on Oppidans and bastards like himself. Queens' crowns had rolled
from the slice of the guillotine, and Kings', so why not the
lesser minds, the puny posers who everywhere lowered the
Etonian standards of excellence.

On his last night at Eton, he was, in fact, the top Oppidan Scholar, chosen among the academically most distinguished to be a member of Pops, the Eton twenty-one,
ranking just below the Captain of the school, all rather fan-
tastic achievements in his short-lived reign, and yet he,
King Jas., was to be banished just like that. Somewhere in
the stack of Eton journals yellowing in the corner of his garret was a contribution entitled "A Dissertation on Roast
Pig." The essay graphically described the slaughter and
butchering of a pet pig at the hands of the boys of Dumford
House. James detailed how the boys had turned into animals, stabbing and cutting the creature to death as they
chased the squealer all over the School Yard. It was not an
incident the Provost or the chaplain had wanted publicized.
James' article had brought a flood of complaints from parents, who were horrified at the news that their boys were
carrying out ritual sacrifices like packs of heathens. What
would they think of a guillotine in the School Yard? It
would be the perfect scandal. He would assemble the guillotine that very night in the basement of the science lab. His
public proclamation would call for the execution of all Eton

bloods whose academic standings were below the standard. By the time his bit of anarchy was discovered, he would be well on his way to Greenwich, never to return. What a glorious exit!

And when his fame as a pirate and gentleman of fortune was so much the height of fashion as to be poised on the tip of every scug's tongue, Eton would claim credit for having spawned such an illustrious former student. The Chancellors would offer up Jas. Matthew Bastard's scholastic record as proof of his time there. But none would be found. James had a plan to destroy every trace of his existence on his way out. His only dilemma was how to say good-bye to Arthur Darling. He knew he could not leave Eton without a proper farewell to his devoted nemesis. But what would it be?

As soon as darkness enveloped the campus and the lamps were lit by the village lamplighters, James liberated his loyal *Lasiodoras*, releasing them in waves down the garret stairs into the bowels of Godolphin House and down the waterspouts to find new homes in the sewers and cellars of Eton. He could only imagine the look on the face of some poor scug waking to find himself wearing a new nightshirt spun from indestructible spider silk. He quietly hoped a few would find their way to Mr. Pilkington. He wasn't such a bad egg as far as beaks went, and he deserved a fine waistcoat that would last longer than his lectures.

Dicky Dongon and Simon the Snash would know what to do with the *Lasiodoras* if a furry lot crawled into *their* window. Simon had fancied a helmet for the Wall Game,

something lightweight and durable that would enable him to drive his head through his opponents, batting them aside like tufts of cotton. His webby helmet could inspire a whole new fashion for the sport as well as protect him from nasty head injuries.

James would miss Electra most of all. But her last service would be her most important. She would pay a visit to Arthur Darling to notify him of James' departure and tell him where to rendezvous to settle unfinished business. With a farewell whistle, James set Electra on her path down the waterspout toward Darling's window. He would be gone when she returned.

James surveyed his room, grabbing the few things that mattered to him—the cat-o'-nine-tails, a stolen souvenir of his triumph; his tall crooked hat; the dried pudding Ananova had presented him after the victorious Wall Game—stuffing them all into a valise. Then, fetching a tightly coiled ball of spiderweb his arachnid tailors had spun into a wire-thin cord, he heaved the unfurling line down to the School Yard and fastened the other end to his bedpost. Before he tucked his rapier into his belt, he paused and sliced the blade across the insulting words painted on his wall until all that remained legible was "Lord Protector of the Pudding."

The spiderweb line could have held a hundred times his weight. James lowered himself and his suitcase quickly to the ground, then headed down the alley with a confident gait. He tipped his hat and smiled warmly at the first group of Collegers, asking them if they liked roast pig as he passed, but not waiting for an answer as he headed up

toward Common Lane. Arthur Darling would hear of this sighting in a matter of minutes. The endgame had begun.

Rupert, skating on the wafer-thin edge of scholastic probation, found Darling in his cups at McIndoe's Public House down by the river, a haunt of Collegers since the days of Shelley, where an ale or two was considered one way to make ready for a game of Fives against Harrow or to take the edge off the pressures of term trials and examination sittings. Darling had spent most of the afternoon at the pub fortifying himself against the shameful truth that he would not be returning to finish the term or graduate at the end of Trinity term until the following school year. Rupert and his mates would be moving up without him. His father, a recent electee to Parliament, was so vexed by the dishonor his son had brought against his own ambitions that he informed Arthur there was no honor in a challenge that went unresolved. Calling someone a liar, or otherwise impugning his honor, his courage, or his name, was a challenge in itself and must be resolved. Wars were fought over questions of honor. And fathers sent sons off to die in them. Duels were no different. Just less noisy and less costly. A good wounding was enough in most cases to satisfy the injured party.

In spite of laws forbidding dueling, the lethal contest remained a popular method of settling disputes, especially among schoolboys and the young aristocracy. Pistols were out of the question, except in the duels of adult men over infidelity and insults to an individual's integrity.

The word was that the mutant was on the prowl, ready to fight. Darling took the time to finish draining his pint of stout before leaving with Rupert to fetch his weapons for the inevitable duel. Darling was confident his Whips would conveniently look the other way rather than make any attempt to prevent him from leaving the house carrying a sword and dagger. Entering his dark room, Darling walked right into a dense, thick web of Electra's handiwork blocking his doorway. Instantly he panicked, his flesh rippling with the memory of what his last encounter with a spider in his room had brought him. He knew this was the mutant's work as he thrashed about, pulling at the sticky chains clinging to him. But Darling encountered no poisonous arachnid, its fangs filled with paralyzing venom. Electra watched from her upside-down perch in the corner of the ceiling, her obsidian-black eyes filled with multivisions of Darling as he brushed her web violently from his arms and face. Rupert, who had entered right behind him, had the quick wits to light a lamp and inspect Darling, assuring him that nothing was crawling on him. Then Rupert saw it, knitted into the webbing crisscrossing Darling's shoulder blades, a small scroll of rolled-up parchment, small enough for a spider the size of Electra to carry, yet large enough to bear a message. Darling stripped away the webbing and viewed the message in the lamplight. This time there were no flowery words, simply a crudely drawn map of the school and a bold X marking the spot where the mutant would be waiting.

CHAPTER SIXTEEN

CODE DUELLO

DARLING MADE NO EFFORTS to conceal his presence, nor did he attempt the use of stealth to approach the rendezvous. His boots clicked urgently on the cobblestones as he turned down the narrow street leading to a dark mews behind the science building. Rupert, acting as his second, marched beside him. A proper duel involved seconds and surgeons and even witnesses and referees to raise the combat above an armed assault on a victim. Even though dueling was illegal by law, the code of the duel, Code Duello, was strict. Not every duelist would be an expert swordsman. Energy often exceeded skill with the blade and enabled a lesser duelist to down his superior with the right

thrust. Arthur Darling was the best competitive fencer in the school. He had won countless bouts. But he had never fought for blood and certainly never killed another human being. To win tonight, to survive, he would have to overcome the fear building in him as they walked. His heart was already pounding at the apprehension of a clash with primal chaos. His weapon of choice was not a foil but a straight sword thirty-one inches long and weighing a quarter stone, three and a half pounds, with a blade just under two inches wide with razor-sharp edges that could slice through James' guts with the ease of cutting freshly churned butter.

The blades in leather sheaths protruded from their long-cut coats, appearing with each stride, then disappearing again under the coattails. The dim tallow lamps they carried offered little illumination in the pitch darkness of the mews. Only the brightly colored waistcoats of their status as prefects reflected in the murky light.

Ahead, blade metal scraped across the cobblestones, tracing a flickering trail of sparks; then the glow vanished. The blade scribed an arc again on the cobblestones to their right, momentarily illuminating boots moving beside a rapier blade. Then *whoosh*. Gone. Darkness, opaque and seductive, returned.

"Mutant . . . ?" Darling whispered expectantly, moving cautiously toward the darkness where the last sparks flashed. Boots kicked up more sparks on the stones circling to Darling's left, the dark figure remaining just beyond the dim reach of the lamp.

"He's moving, Arthur—" Rupert lost his nerve and drew his sword. He slashed out at the darkness. "Come on, you leaky bastard!" A blade flashed, striking the stones again, kicking up sparks. A whip of steel cut through the darkness. A sharp sound like a melon being sliced made Rupert recoil; he clutched his sword hand in excruciating pain—

"Ahhhhh. He cut me. Bastard—"

Rupert's sword dropped clanging on the cobblestones. Darling pulled Rupert's hand into the lamplight. The blade had cut cleanly across the back of Rupert's knuckles as if it were a surgeon's lancet, so sharp that only after a moment did the thin plume of red emerge along the slice from beneath the surface and begin to spill onto the street.

"Is this an ambush? Or a duel?" Darling addressed the darkness angrily. The superior giddy cackle James had perfected to annoy just about everyone who had ever heard it echoed behind the two Collegers. Darling turned, whipping out his sword and pointing it into the night.

"Dish hilt sword. German design, favored by the Mensurs." James' voice echoed from the darkness, bouncing off the mews walls. "Little heavy for you, my Darling. Those Deutschy boys play by the first-blood rule. If you subscribe to such cowardly measures, then this contest is over."

James shoved his face into the dim light, slapping Darling with the hilt of Rupert's sword, then retreated into the darkness.

"It's not my blood you drew, mutant!" Darling spewed

as Rupert whimpered like a kitten. Wobbling there, looking at his bleeding hand, Darling's second crumpled in a heap on the cobblestones in a dead faint.

"Ohhh, bad form, Darling. Your second's gone sterky from a mere cut. A light scratch. Now *we* shall have to fight."

James vanished from the lamplight and dashed across the mews, down another alleyway. Darling turned his fleeting attention to Rupert lying on the cobblestones, then rushed after James, slashing the shadows. The clash of metal in the dark ignited a cry of exhilaration from Darling.

James extended both his sword and Rupert's purloined blade, dragging the tips along the claustrophobic walls of the passageway, scoring sparks like the tails of comets trailing behind him. Darling followed the cosmic glow along the narrow, twisty passageway, yelling and cursing for James to stand and fight. The passageway opened onto a dark courtyard. James danced around the open space, sweeping his blades along the walls and sending sparks that ignited oil torches protruding from sconces. One after another flames spouted, revealing an eerie sight that stopped Darling cold, a structure jutting into the night sky from the center of the yard.

Three triangulated oak posts rose ten feet into the air. Braces at the bottom and top supported the shaft tower. A broadax blade was raised in the shaft and counterweighted by a cut quarry stone, waiting to fall on its victim. Wooden stocks at the bottom of the shaft stood empty, awaiting a

victim. James leaped up on the platform and readied Rupert's sword to strike the rope to release the blade.

"Off with your head!" James howled, laughing. "I've always wanted to say that."

"You're mad, mutant." Darling pointed his blade at James, his hand trembling with surges of panic spiked by the horror before him.

James smiled, facing his opponent.

"It takes Madame Guillotine only a blink of an eye to fall. And then bliss, after the half minute it takes for the body to die. By the sword, death is much longer and more painful. From here I cannot see any difference between you and a butcher's swine. Except, of course, the pig does not know that it is about to die. Have you given any thought to the consequences of what we are about to do this night?"

Darling fixed on James' pointed steel for the first time, its glinting sharp point magnifying until it filled his vision, dwarfing everything around them. Heart-pounding apprehension filled his head. The sword's edges flickered in waves of torchlight, prepared to change Darling's physical appearance forever with one slash.

"Are you schooled enough for savagery?" James purred. "Can you imagine how it will feel when your blade thrusts with such force that your hilt crushes into the breastbone of your enemy?" James punctuated his challenge by throwing open his web-silk waistcoat and shirt, revealing his bare chest to the sharply honed point of Darling's sword, daring him. The blood pounded in Darling's head.

"Strike true! Death is the ultimate adventure!"

Darling collected his anger and fear into an explosive thrust, driving his blade at James' heart. But James was too quick. Like a ghost he dodged away, letting Darling's sword bury itself in the oak post of the guillotine. James flicked his blade, cutting Darling a nick across his forearm just enough to enrage him with its sting. Darling instinctively attacked with an overhead chop at James' skull. But again no James! Darling's edge cut cleanly through the rope holding the guillotine blade secure.

With a squeaking, teeth-gnashing rush, gravity pulled the blade down the shaft. It stopped with a sickening thud. Imagining his own head there, Darling reeled back in a wave of nausea, losing the ale souring in his stomach all over the cobblestones. He grabbed an upright post on the contraption to steady himself. Then madness took over, the fever of the kill. Darling began to laugh, a giddy, maniacal cackle. James exulted. The bloodlust had taken firm hold. Then, drawing the proper distance from Darling for the beginning of the duel, and rolling his right hand, tilting his steel slightly downward, he rested his blade against Darling's.

"'And never erring in the shaking hand, the sword rules itself as if it were a living spirit,'" James quoted with conviction.

"You know your masters." Darling could not help but be impressed by the obscure quote from the German duelist and author of *William Tell* and *The Maid of Orleans*, Friedrich von Schiller.

"Then you must know William Tell was a far better swordsman than he was an archer."

Darling and James nervously circled the guillotine, caressing each other's blades, ready to engage.

"If you put an apple on your head, I promise to miss."

James loosened Ananova's soft silk kerchief at his neck. Both sets of eyes stayed locked, waiting for the first to move. James knew he must keep his focus on his opponent's hand holding the sword. Wherever the hand moved, so went the sword.

Now James slipped Ananova's silk scarf from his neck and wrapped his sword hand with it. Death. He catalogued the possibilities. The end from a cutting slash could result in exsanguination, a massive hemorrhage, or embolism, air in the bloodstream. A mortal wound could suffocate the duelist, asphyxia, or readily collapse a lung, pneumothorax, resulting in the victim's slowly dying like a fish out of water fighting for air.

Suddenly Darling lunged with speed and certainty, throwing a half-high quarte at James. James quickly defended the move with a tierce and countered with a full fleeting inside quarte, pushing Darling back across the courtyard. Their blades whistled through the night air like steel horsewhips. Their boots clacked over the cobblestones, punctuating their deadly dance.

The sword master whose methods James had studied had instilled in his acolytes that their steel was the medium through which the duelist accessed not only the workings of

his opponent's brain, but the foe's heart as well. James nimbly parried Darling's thrusts and countertempo thrusts, reading full well his opponent's dark intent and also his weakness with the ease of reciting the alphabet. Darling was a fencer, trained in the Italian style and use of the foil, a fragile sword. Fencing was fought with rules and rigid forms. Darling had no experience in combating the unorthodox dueling style of French courtiers or English buccaneers, who had invented the rapier and the cutlass. And James, predicting Darling's every move, was about to give his exasperated foe a lesson in the unorthodox—Darling threw a half-high quarte that James skillfully parried with a circular cavation, and before Darling could recover with a reverso, James thrust his sword straight as a shot into Darling's dish hilt and catapulted his sword into the air—up ten, fifteen feet. Darling followed the flight, tilting his head up as it hung in mid space.

"Bad form, bastard."

James took the opportunity to slice his blade across Darling's belt line. His britches succumbed to gravity and dropped to his knees. As the humiliation sent him grabbing his pants, the sword, whistling down like an arrow, slammed into the cobblestones inches from Darling.

"Wrong. *That* was bad form."

Darling's moan was agreement enough. James secured Rupert's blade in his belt, flicked Darling's sword up into his grip, and weighed it, feinting and slashing the blade inches from Darling's face and arms, moving around him

with lightning feints and reversos. Darling dared not move for fear of losing an ear or part of his nose.

"Your Italian teachers of defense have failed you, Master Darling. Where are your stoccatas, your imbroccatas, and your mandrittas?" James recounted the dialectic natters of the English sword master George Silver, who had incapacitated many an Italian opponent with his cleverly barbed insults as well as his blade.

"Your punta reversas are too genteel for combat, Colleger. And what of your stramazons, passatas, and incartatas?" James mocked each fencing position as he danced around Darling, accentuating the silliness of the fencer's footwork. "You hate me, don't you?"

Darling was too frightened to answer.

"I asked you a question, Colleger." James flicked the two weapons with blurring speed, shredding Darling's colorful silk waistcoat without so much as scratching his skin.

"You have everything—blood lines and proper family—why risk all that with an inferior weapon and hopeless Italian training against the skills of King Jas.? Why?"

"Because . . . you're a mutant . . ."

"And so is my style. And you're afraid if you do not rid the world of me, that I will breed and populate the Earth?"

"You think you are smarter than the lot of us, don't you?"

"A genius, in fact. . . ." Jas. touched his blade to his temple as if in deep thought. "What is genius? 'Men of genius are meteors intended to burn to light their century.'"

"Napoleon said that. You compare yourself to him? Give me my sword and I'll shut that wormy-tongued mouth of yours!"

James stopped his dance around Darling and considered the claim. He balanced the Colleger's blade and sighted down its shaft to see how true its maker had forged its lines.

"Napoleon also said genius is the infinite capacity for enduring pain." Saying that, James presented Darling's sword to him hilt first, then stepped back and spread his arms wide, exposing his chest as a willing target.

"So give me your best imbroccata. Your strongest scannatura." James posed, pointing to a spot on his spider-silk waistcoat for the entry of each blow and thrust he described. Darling curled his fingers around the hilt of his sword and warily measured the blade distance between himself and James' chest.

"You are mad. . . ."

"Mad mutant genius." He spoke the phrase as if inventing it out of the thin air. "I like the sound of it. Make it good, Colleger. Your most excellent incartatas. If you fail, I will end you. Your epitaph will be my exit from Eton."

Darling lost all good form and charged James with his full force, an enraged bull expecting to jam his blade cleanly through James' sternum and crush it with his hilt.

But his steel did not penetrate James' impregnable waistcoat. Not even the slightest dent was made in the skin over his breast. Instead, the power of Darling's thrust bent the blade double and broke it cleanly in half with a

resounding, ringing snap, the point striking the cobble-stones tip first, bouncing end over end, resulting in more tinkling musical notes. Darling stood in shock, staring at the half blade trembling in his hand, the other half lost in the darkness. Completely unscathed, James fingered the slightest tear in his spider-silk as if just losing his best friend.

"Awwww . . . you tore it. My favorite waistcoat."

His sanguine grin returned, visible in the flickering torchlight, his forget-me-nots flashing that dreaded red.

"My turn." The evil eloquence of these two simple words turned Darling on his heels to run. But James was too quick. Like a coiled snake he struck, slicing Darling's leg with his blade. Darling cried out, unable to flee. James grabbed his foe by the back of his collar and shoved him across the courtyard, swatting him with the flat of his blade, driving him like a pig to slaughter.

"Squeal, pig. Let the world hear your last words of wisdom. Oinkkkkk! Weeeweeeeeweeehhhh!" James was possessed, demonic, as he dragged Darling, who had gone completely limp, quivering with fear, shoving him against the guillotine.

"Please don't harm me. . . ."

"*Please don't harm meeeeee!!*" James mocked as he pinned Darling's arm in one of the locks.

"What are you doing? You're insane!" Darling pulled and yanked to no avail. James pinned his other arm and slammed the other lock shut. With that he raised the blade and tied it off securely.

"You've nothing to worry about. After I relieve you of your noggin, you will no doubt just grow another one." Darling opened his mouth to scream, but no sound came out. James shoved Darling's head down into the neck block and dropped the heavy bar in place, locking it fast. Darling craned his neck, barely able to glimpse the broadax blade hanging above him, ready to fall.

"Feel free to soil your trousers, Darling old chum. I read that is what the majority of the forty thousand souls did who lost their heads during the French days of tyranny. I won't tell. Promise."

James knelt before Darling and slowly raised the rope so that it hovered above. Darling's pupils were dilated wide with fear. He shook all over.

"What is the moment of death like? Is there life after . . . ? Just think, you will be the keeper of all this knowledge forever. I am almost jealous. You will actually know the answer."

James moved Darling's chin up and down several times indicating "yes" as a puppet master would a marionette. Then, without hesitation he unwound most of the guillotine rope from the cleat, careful to prevent the blade from falling, and wrapped the loose end around Darling's right hand.

"Try not to get sleepy, Darling, and whatever you do, don't lose your head."

James laughed as he stood, bowed—ever the gentleman—tipped his crooked beaver hat, and finally punctuated his

superb manners by elevating his boot and kicking the cleat repeatedly until it broke away from the guillotine, releasing the last wind of rope. The blade plummeted with metallic squeaks. The slack was taken up as the blade fell, jerking Darling's hand up against the block, which stopped the blade abruptly, five feet above the Colleger's neck. Darling screamed bloody murder.

Yes, Arthur L. Darling was alive!

But he had gratefully soiled his britches.

CHAPTER SEVENTEEN

EXIT FROM ETON

THE ACID DRIP HAD EATEN its way through the thick wood covering the ash pail filled with pyrite and phosphorus. The container had been secreted away in a corner of the hall of records amid the rows and stacks of thick, bound ledgers. Pressed among parchment leaves and pages dating back two centuries was the name of every Oppidan and every Colleger who had ever dipped his cup in the learning pool of Eton blood. Their entire history—colors won, awards received, punishments incurred, honors, and failures—all recorded in careful hand by dutiful registrars to preserve Eton's history for the ages. When the first droplet of acid leached down through the wood and

landed in the pyrite, the laws of nature demanded the inevitable. The chemical reaction began. Acrid fumes coiled up in tendril billows. The second and third droplets penetrated deeper into the elements. A flash of green phosphorescent light—then the ash pail exploded, spraying gelatinous flames out in radiating waves. Ledgers and brittle parchment went up instantly. Great aging pages of recorded lives were consumed in a great wall of fire.

Darling craned his still-intact neck just enough to glimpse the eerie glow of the mysterious fire churning above the School Yard. Bells clanged through the village as Etonians rushed to the fire roaring through the hall of records. Collegers joined villagers forming a bucket brigade up from Jordan Creek, passing water buckets hand to hand in a futile attempt to douse a corner of the blaze. Spitting onto the flames would have done as much good.

Rupert hurried along the cobblestones toward the courtyard leading his Whips, each armed with a birch and saber. His lacerated hand, wrapped tightly in a piece of bedding, held a torch high, lighting the way. Darling's screams hurried them into the courtyard. The victorious Colleger they expected to see standing over the skewered carcass of one mutant Oppidan was instead bent over, locked in the stocks, seemingly dangerously close to losing his head. Fumbling hands and panicked voices, attempting to free Darling from his perilous situation, accidentally loosened the rope in his hand. Darling reeled back shrieking as the guillotine

slammed the blocks loose with a metallic thud. The once powerful and respected Captain of College Walk crabbed backward on all fours away from the horrible tableau, squealing like a pig.

Fire curled through the current year's register, vanquishing names until reaching the name James Matthew . . . the last name obliterated by the flames, curling ink and parchment into nothingness.

And then King Jas. was no more in existence in the recorded history of Eton.

CHAPTER EIGHTEEN

THE *SEA WITCH*

THE ISLAND APPEARED off to starboard at first light. At first just a shapeless pool of teasing pale colors floated suspended in the darkness; then if James squeezed his eyes tighter, the pools began to take shape, and the colors became so vivid that with another squeeze they would surely go on fire. Just before the point of igniting, the island's distinctive profile became clear, with its mysterious outcropping of earth jutting up from the misty blue like a great whale breaching from the depths. At its center a conical mountain of volcanic ash rose up to a smoking pinnacle.

A quick survey through his spyglass revealed fruit groves of *Mangifera indica*, as mangos are properly known,

and drupe and pome trees. Massive green sea turtles, *Chelonia mydas*, were so numerous that their shells, the size of boulders, formed their own island in the lagoon. Dolphins and porpoises cavorted like children around his craft. Abundant game was visible everywhere on the island. A monotreme astounded James as he studied a furry, duck-billed, web-footed creature sunning itself with a group of sea lions. And there were primates galore shunting up and down tall palm trees as they gathered coconuts. Baboons and gorillas lived side by side without any signs of conflict. A small group of goats munched on browse and foliage right before a magnificent great maned *Panthera leo* that let the billies and nannies eat in peace. Flocks of exotic plumed birds filled the skies. James was amazed at his recall of their proper Aves classes and orders from his science lectures: *Struthio camelus*, or ostriches, strutted like pompous professors, craning their long, scrawny necks, then burying their beaks in the sand, rooting out small crustaceans hiding under the surface. Quantities of brightly colored *Psittacidae* skrakked and screeched from the trees. Parrots! James could teach them all insulting phrases to send scurrilous messages to his enemies!

James was witnessing the cradle of creation spread before him. His thoughts carried him to Ananova, and now he found himself longing to share with her these seas full of great blue whales. Never had such an ark of life been encountered around one tiny scrap of volcanic ash and sand in such a remote corner of the ocean. Uncharted, it was as if the little

island had appeared by magic. A Neverland. A dream . . .

Even the weather was unique. Oddly, it seemed to be snowing at one end of the island. Snowing? On a tropical isle? The other end was awash in the sunshine of a perfect summer's day in Brighton, with one peculiar exception—two suns hung in the sky: one on the rise, the other sitting on that invisible meeting point between sea and sky, bathing the west end of the isle in a perpetual sunset. It was as if all time had stopped dead still. Time, ticking away—its fleeting sparkle had flooded James' every waking thought since he had escaped Eton. His most tortured dreams were all about time. If only he could live forever. If . . . only . . . wait! There was something else on the island that drew him closer to the jagged reefs—

Singing—

Not the dissonant babble of annoying Collegers, but haunting and vexing, the songs of Sirens beckoning to lost sailors . . . The wooing enchantment seemed to be coming from the other side of a rocky formation just beyond the reach of James' telescope. The singing intensified, causing James to clutch his head in unbearable pleasure.

Suddenly there was a thrashing and churning of water around James' craft. A powerful tail rose up and swatted him like a fly. His cries for help were muffled as powerful forces yanked him under and dragged him beneath the boiling surface toward a mysterious-looking rock. The face of a beautiful vixen was there under the waters, calling to him, pulling him deeper and deeper—

There was no turning back. As his lungs burned for air, the unseen choir of enchantresses filled his head. He was being pulled like a fish into a net. The maw of Mother Ocean gaped like a great toothed serpent's mouth that could swallow an entire ship. And then, oddly, he could breathe! His lungs filled with the purest air he had ever tasted—sweet, like the smell of a Christmas pudding. The great funnel of the sea splashed him down on waters as blue as forget-me-nots—the very same color as James' eyes. And then he drifted, blown on the breezes of time, toward the shimmering face of Ananova, capturing him in the net of her smile and the enchantment of her singing.

James squinted at the shapeless pool of colors forming around Ananova. "Go on, James . . . ," she called to him. "Angels will envy us. . . . " She beckoned him closer and closer.

Sailors' tales of mermaids were legion—how the she-fishes could enchant a man and cause him to drown himself by chasing the fin-goddesses into the deep to steal a kiss; how their voices could drive even the best sea pilots off course until they drove their ships right onto reefs and rocks.

But here, on this island of Never, a nation of mermaids existed for real. And suddenly the rocky maw took complete and heavenly shape. Rainbows arched over the waterfall, sending up mists and spray, and James saw hundreds of them, sunning on the rocky shelf or engaged in playing a water game, batting about bubbles of as many colors as could be splashed in the water with their tails.

Ananova continued to beckon until a horrible darkness snatched her from his sight and sucked her down into the deep abyss.

"Ananovaaaaa!" he cried, gagging and choking on the seawater filling his lungs.

James awoke, spewing water. He was drifting, collapsed over the oars of his scull, his head half immersed with each wave that rolled his craft, carried by the currents of the river.

The island of Neverland was gone.

And there was only one sun rising in the early-morning sky.

James resumed pulling on the oars of the purloined scull he had propelled down the River Thames all through the night, aided by the currents, toward the port of Greenwich and beyond. He was determined to put as much distance as possible between the glow of Eton burning in the night sky and any trace of his existence. He had to buy himself enough time to reach his ship of exile before it set sail for the open sea . . . and freedom.

"Buy himself time . . ." There it was again, he thought. Time being referred to as a commodity one could purchase at the smoke shop, or by the flagon at the local public house. Could there ever be enough time? Would he run out of it before he could find her? Or before the glittering bauble of fame was held securely in his hands?

James fought his fatigue and stinging muscles in the chilly morning air. These games of the mind and daydreams

dulled the throbbing pain eating through his body with each pull of the oars. Even as he rowed, he imagined that he might already be the talk of all Eton.

Once the local constabulary had managed to extinguish the flames of James' joyful pyromania, there would be a search of the smoldering remains for any unfortunate victims. He imagined the mixed emotions certain Eton bloods would experience upon discovering the clues and objects James had carefully placed that would lead to the conclusion that he had perished in the fire. Beak Pilkington would take this news with a philosopher's air, giving some quote to the Eton *Chronicle* that would no doubt give James Matthew Bastard martyr status in the annals of Oppidans.

"The King is dead. Long live the King of the Wall Game."

That is how he would be remembered. Fitting headlines for an Eton Oppidan who had shone so brightly and too briefly.

And Arthur Darling? He would refuse to believe the claim at first.

"The mutant? Burned to a crisp? That's a jookerie. He can't be killed. A ranking demon, he is."

Darling would rifle the still-smoldering ashes of the Hall of Records, desperately digging about for any sign of King Jas., wanting to believe with every burned and charred object that his nemesis was nothing but carbon dust. And then Darling would find conclusive proof that Jas. Matthew Bastard was history . . . his tall beaver hat listing to one side,

charred in the heat of the blaze, but unmistakably the property of the former King Jas. James chortled to himself as he rowed, conjuring up Darling in his mind—the humiliated high priest of College Walk. The mutant had perished, burned alive in the holocaust of records. Then, when offered the opportunity to touch the scorched hat, Darling would back away and refuse, claiming respect for the dead— when in fact it would be Darling's paralyzing fear that James might spring to life beneath the tall hat and reconstitute himself from his own ashes. There James would stand, a macabre Humpty Dumpty put back together again, with that goading laugh of his, explaining to Arthur with great glee how, due to circumstances beyond Master Darling's control, James Matthew Bastard had become immortal. Yes! And how grand it would be that now James would possess all the time in the world, empowering him to devote eternity to making Arthur L. Darling's life completely miserable!

"Topping swank," Jolly R would say.

James had to stop rowing, he found himself laughing so hard. His mocking guffaw echoed across the river, grating against the melodic calls of the morning birds and wildfowl feeding along the shores and cruising the eddies and backwashes for minnows and salamanders. James needed to laugh. He desperately needed a purging from the gravity of all that had transpired over the last few days of his Eton reign.

Only in this moment, far down the river from the

scenes of his faux demise, having literally burned his one and only bridge, did James think of the impact on his friend. Jolly R. would take it the hardest. He would blame himself for the loss of his King. . . .

Chimes of church bells broke James from his thoughts. He went immediately on alert like an animal. Again the bells echoed. Not a peal or two but a wave of clarion strikes sending a wall of stirring sounds up the river to meet James. The bells of Saint Alfege. The church at the port of Greenwich. The church where Henry VIII was christened. Greenwich! James had made it! He rowed faster, ignoring his fatigued and aching body, his blistered hands of no concern as he drew toward the sounds of the bells echoing in the morning mist. Ships' masts spiked the sky's first light.

Suddenly, a beautiful maiden loomed before him, her gown painted in the colors of the Union Jack. The figurehead protruded from beneath the bowsprit of a massive three-masted square-rigged frigate directly in James' path. He rowed right under the figurehead, hugging the curve of the hull to avoid detection by the watch. Shipping his oars, James drifted beneath the twenty-odd gun ports lining the port side of the great ship. It was no doubt a pirate hunter in its day, returned from chasing the dread pirate Bartholomew Roberts or the ghost of William Kidd. All was eerily quiet on board and around the harbor at this early hour.

Dozens of sailing ships at anchor emerged from the parting mists, dwarfing James' scull as the port of Greenwich

opened up before him. Single-masted sloops bunched together near the docks, the swiftest ships on the sea. A twin-masted schooner spread directly ahead, its narrow hull and sleek lines conjuring the image of speed on the high seas. Somewhere among the collection of ships and the miles of rigging and the thousands of square yards of canvas sail, the *Sea Witch* was anchored. James's new home.

Elevated above the village of Greenwich, perched at the edge of Blackheath, the golden-domed Royal Observatory lorded over the port. James had always enjoyed a peculiar connection to the brick and copper framed building, designed and constructed by the famed scientist and architect Christopher Wren. King Charles II, whose infamous long, curly hair King Jas. emulated, had written the royal warrant appointing Wren to construct the observatory on the zero-degree meridian marking the center of the world and all time. Time. Again, time. Everywhere and nowhere, but always slipping away . . .

The *Sea Witch* rested at anchor south of the Church Street landing. She did not have the grace of the *Mephistopheles*, but she was a close second. This was an elegant witch, hardly hagborn. James had to admire his father for His Lordship's taste in ships. At two hundred and twelve feet long and forty-eight feet in the beam, this schooner could carry a crew of seventy-five; it had eighteen cannons and a cargo space twice that of smaller sloops and corsairs. The *Sea Witch* was no lumbering merchant craft. This

vessel was built for speed on the open seas and rigged for quick maneuvers. Her shallow draft would allow her to go into gunkholes, small coves, and dock at shallow quays. Her twin masts could be hung with square sails for quartering in the wind, or added staysails for windward sailing. The fantail of the ship protruding out over the lower stern was angled off like the macabre head of a coffin. And ahead to the bow, the figurehead mounted under the bowsprit was sculpted straight from Dante's *Inferno*. Her demonic features were bright green, and from her wanton mouth there curled a serpent's tongue. In her demon hands the *Sea Witch* held her very own spiked tail. And she was leering.

This demented work of art being invitation enough, James shouldered his bag, stood up in his scull as it drifted under the figurehead, and jumped, barely managing to grab onto a support timber and pull himself up until he was face-to-face with the witch.

"And a fractious good morning to you, Madame Siren. James Matthew, formerly of Eton, at your service. Forgive my rudeness—are you a good witch? Or a bad witch?"

Pulling himself along the bowsprit, James climbed with his bag onto the fo'c'sle. There he stood on a floating island once again, and his thoughts went immediately to Jolly R, who should have been there with him. He missed his friend. The sway at anchor, the cry of gulls, and the breeze luffing at the furled sails above were the only sounds.

"Should I ring the Captain's bell and announce my arrival?" James thought. But the rumblings of his empty

stomach overruled any mischief James was considering. He could announce himself later. The Captain would, of course, have been informed of his coming by his father. He just prayed that they would set sail before any news of the fire at Eton reached his ears.

James almost doubled over below to avoid braining himself on the lower deck head beams. Cannons rested on their four-wheel carriages, secure at their ports. He maneuvered past scores of crew hanging in hammocks like slabs of meat at Shepherd's Market in London. Arms and legs dangled. Heads lolled back and forth with the gentle movement of the ship at anchor. The smell of rum in the air was overpowering. He could scarcely breathe in the cramped quarters. Bathing was obviously not a regular part of a sailor's life. One particularly begrimed foot he encountered was so squalid, his entire olfactory system revolted, and he had to cover his mouth to stifle his gagging. He managed to shove his head out a gunport for a broadside of fresh air just in time. Taking several deep breaths, he summoned his courage and continued his search for the galley.

The first mate's cuddy, a hole of a cabin, found at the stern under the poop deck, was even smaller than James' garret room in Godolphin House. At least it was spotless and had the pleasing odor of incense. Here was a seaman who had found a way to cope with the foul smells James had just encountered. A wedge of barrel cheese and a half-eaten loaf of dark bread sitting on a trunk appeared slightly more

appetizing than the rank collection of feet racked out in the outer hold. After a fastidious nibble, James was unable to stop himself before he had devoured the entire lot. He was in the act of licking his fingers for every last trace of the cheese when it hit him. His peeled and raw palms from rowing . . . his aching fatigued body . . . the fire . . . a clash of blades . . . Darling's head in the stocks . . . the guillotine . . . James and Ananova leaping into the river on Pandora's back . . . Jolly sucking down sweet sock pudding after the Wall Game victory . . . Ananova's beguiling eyes peering at him through the slit in the jail cell door . . .

James hit the berth like a sack of potatoes, his body and mind spent. He plummeted into a deep, comatose state of exhaustion.

The island was just shimmering into focus—

Yes, there it was—

Waiting . . .

A tumble to the hard wooden floor from the berth shocked James awake. Then a stab of pain in his buttocks startled him even more. There it went again. James fumbled himself over to face his attacker. The face staring down at him over smallish round spectacles seemed years older than the childlike eyes would have suggested. The scrumpy little man held an unusual serrated dirk with a serpentine curly blade like a corkscrew pointed right at James.

"Told ya, Johnny. This scug's alive. Good thing you

finally woke up. We been droppin' mates wi' a touch of the yellow j-j-ja, er, the yellow fever. Can't be too careful, eh, Johnny?"

The little man addressed his curvy dirk as if it were alive, stammering in his excitement.

"I beg your pardon—" James managed.

"Little late for that, b-bo-bo, ah, bucko. I been trying to budge you off m' bunk for nigh on a quarter hour. Thought y' was a deader, bein' as blue gill as you l-l-loo, from the looks of you."

The little man pointed at James' almost-blue skin with his dirk.

"Sorry, it's . . . genetic. A condition . . . inherited from . . . my . . . ancestors."

"What? I was about to open you up like a mutton pie with Johnny Corkscrew here to see if you was expired. You could be usin' a bit of sun from the looks of you." James concluded that the "Johnny" the little man referred to was his blade and politely pointed it away from his gut.

"I am very much alive, thank you. Or quite close to it." James pulled himself up to a commanding height above the little man and braced himself at attention—bending just enough to avoid colliding with the deck head.

"James Matthew reporting for duty. Permission to come aboard, sir . . . Captain . . . sir. . . ."

The scrump behind the spectacles crinkled into a mad smile and cackled like a hyena, drawing in great gasps of air so that he brayed instead of laughing.

"Don't let the Captain hear you make that kind of mistake. He'll have your hide for sure. He's fond of the cat-o'-nines to satisfy his need for a good flogging now and then." The little man brayed, extending his hand to James in friendship. "Bartholomew Quigley Smeethington. Smee to the Captain and the crew of the witchy woman. First mate."

"Smee?"

"That's me. And you are again—?"

"James Matthew . . . signing on as first mate's apprentice . . . I believe."

Smee, in a sudden state of awe, circled James slowly in the tight quarters.

"Ah, yes, James Matthew. The b-bast-bastard."

"That would be me."

"Sons of virgin bitches. Are there two of you? Haven't got no impersonator running about, by chance, have y' now?" The little man reached out with the hands of a classical pianist and pinched James' bluish cheek to ensure he was in fact real.

"Two of me? I should hope the world could do with only one of me. This is all very confusing. You see my"—James hesitated before describing his benefactor as his father and corrected his course—"His Lordship who arranged for my assignment aboard the *Sea Witch*—"

While James prattled on trying to be very official, feet clattered on the main deck above. A shrill whistle blew. Voices shouted. Smee didn't pay attention to this, or to James, as he fished a journal from his worn leather satchel

and began riffling pages with a lick of his finger, mumbling through a host of entry names and dates.

"There!" He pointed to the page emphatically. "Perhaps you can explain how another James Matthew has already signed on the ship's manifest for the duration of the v⁄voy⁄ trip? See, Captain's cabin boy. You can read, can't ye? There. Is that your mark?"

James stared at the page full of X markings underneath the crew's names. The one educated signature was affixed below his block⁄letter name in the registry log.

"Jas. Matthew . . ." James half whispered it to himself in complete confusion.

"He entered his name as 'Jas.' Said it was a nod to His Majesty King Charles II. Said the King preferred 'Chas.' Seems a bit of odds bods tinker and tongs if you ask me. Can't be havin' no impostors on board now. Cap'n Creech, he hates snools, weevils in his bread, slotterhodges, and impostors."

"Could I by chance meet this impostor?" asked Jas.

Smee scratched his head.

"Who's to say *you* ain't the impostor?" he asked, winking slyly and very pleased with himself for stating the obvious.

Drums now beat on the deck above, breaking the moment. The boatswain's whistle piped a shrill command. Smee's eyes inflated, dwarfing the rims of his spectacles.

"Flog me dead, it's the Cap'n!"

The blood drained from his ruddy cheeks as he fumbled

anxiously, stowing the ship's register, slicking down his unruly eyebrows. He paused for a panicked moment studying James—

"That your dunnage?" Smee pointed to James' bag, which James confirmed was his property.

"These your best togs? Going to sea in this, are we?"

James smoothed his rumpled and stained long day coat and the starched collar of his Eton shirt, which by now appeared more of grimy beige than the sparkling white populating College Walk.

"I left in a bit of a rush. What about this other James?"

Smee pushed and herded James from his small cabin, passing where bodies in hammocks had previously festooned the lower decks. Now not a single smelly, squalid hammock was to be found. Again the boatswain's whistle piped above.

"All hands on deck. All hands on deck—"

The drums beat faster as James climbed the stairs toward the light of the hatch leading to the main deck. Smee lagged behind him, searching every pocket and possible hiding place in his clothes for something important he had forgotten.

"And that goes for you double, Mr. Smee!"

The booming voice echoed down from above through the open hatch. Smee hastily retreated below, muttering to himself, leaving James alone at the mouth of the hatch. The pounding of drums, the shrill whistles, voices calling out commands ricocheted around the ship. James took a deep breath and slowly poked his head up through the hatch for

a clandestine glimpse. Feet blurred by, heading in every direction—still grimy and smelling of bilge, but now moving with speed and purpose. Many were shod in well-worn boots, others wore a style of slipper worn by Asian merchants and vendors James had seen on the streets of London with Aunt Emily. James tracked a sailor wearing these slippers as the spindly fellow scaled the ratlines to the tall mast rising above James' hiding place. Members of the crew stood along the crosstree spar, spanning the mast like a flock of birds perched to fly. More lined the topsail spar above the mainmast, at least ninety feet above the deck.

None of the men bore a consistent mode of dress. The order of the day was baggy galligaskin trousers and blousy shirts, a far cry from the spit and polish of the sailors on the *Mephistopheles* and those in the Queen's Navy. Faces that appeared for a moment in James' field of view to shout a command, utter a guttural response, and then blur away to their duty offered James a weathered, craggy landscape of beards, mustaches, and valleys of scars and wrinkles charting each man's time served on the high seas.

"You there! Scug! Can't you understand the Queen's English?"

The voice bellowed again almost directly behind James. The roar belonged to a pair of frightening eyes that were fixed upon him, peering from under the shadows of a tricorn hat—one roving gray eye, the other completely white with no center. They appeared to be the eyes of a dead man. He wore the blue jacket of the Queen's Navy, part of his glorious

past, no doubt, from the condition of it. In his hands he held a birch rod identical to those the Whips sported at Eton, causing James instinctively to duck back, holding the edge of the hatch with his exposed hands.

"I said ALL HANDS ON DECK!"

James' knuckles burned with the slash of the birch across them inflicted by Dead-eye. In the minutest particle of time that it took for the pain to register in James' noggin, he had already countered with his own discipline to overcome the searing torment. Rather than cry out, James focused all his mental faculties on the many methods he could employ to render the remainder of the man's being as dead as his eye. That unnerving, serene smile appeared on James' pale face. Youth and insolence were all that the dead-eyed quartermaster read in his look as he raised his birch to strike again.

"Wipe that smile off your face and get your bum on deck, or you can entertain the fishes. Be quick, scug." He rattled his birch along the railing just like a house Whip.

James surmised that this husk of a man either knew his identity and his Eton pedigree, or perhaps had himself attended the venerable institution and had been sentenced like James to a life at sea. Or, more likely, Dead-eye had been rejected by the colleges and held persons like James in the lowest contempt.

"If that is an order, you need not strike again, sir. My threshold for pain is formidable. The more you beat me, the more my insolent manner will annoy you."

His maddeningly polite superior diction gave Dead-eye serious pause. Billy Blood, for that was his name, had been elected by the crew to be the quartermaster of the ship and was in fact the ranking crewman whenever the Captain was not aboard. Blood was always elected to this post, and he always ran the ship, no matter who was Captain. Above all, the quartermaster's duty was to maintain order among the crew and mete out punishment for violations of the code of conduct at sea. Mr. Blood laid his birch across his waist, flexing it with both hands. Slowly it dawned on him that this was the bastard from Hell he had been forewarned would board his ship one day, not some young recruit to be bullied.

"Mr. Smeeeeeee!" Blood bellowed, never interrupting the standoff between his dead eye and James' blue ones. Smee reappeared, trundling across the deck toting the leather register, mumbling about dressing in his more formal attire, hopping now on one foot, now on the other in an attempt to pull on his knee-high striped hosiery.

"Coming, Mr. Blood, coming. Oh, fubbery and blast—"

"I'm putting this mumruffin under your command, Mr. Smee."

Smee raised his tiny spectacles and squinted at James.

"Brimstone and gall. Why me, Mr. Blood? I've already got one just like him."

Blood thumped each of Smee's legs, pointing to the mismatched colors and stripes of his hosiery.

"He's a sodding nonconformist. Just like you, Mr. Smee."

Mr. Blood left the two nonconformists to sort out their

differences and duties and climbed to the quarterdeck, striking his birch along the balustrade just as the Whips had done in Godolphin House.

"*Floreat Etona.* I feel so at home." James' irony was lost on his keeper, who still struggled to affix his socks to his knee breeches.

"Do you now? Wait till you meet the Captain. He's got some strange ideas about home and the like. You'll see firsthand. There's a touch of true e-e-evil in him. He lives for suffering. That's the canker that gnaws at his dark soul."

James heard this warning from his shipmate with more curiosity than alarm. Perhaps the Captain of the *Sea Witch* would afford James an opportunity to acquire even more knowledge and further enhance his darker talents.

"Prepare to receive the Captain!" Blood bellowed over the drumming. Crew had formed ranks on either side of the gangway. More lined the booms and spars. Smee led James to a spot in the ranks facing the crew opposite. The two drummers pounded directly across from James and Smee. All eyes were on the gangway, anticipating the Captain's arrival. A jolly boat approached from the docks, pulled by the heartier of the crew. Seated in the middle of the skiff, the Captain remained hidden in the shadows of a large parasol held by his roundish cabin boy.

"So where is this imposter Jas., Mr. Smee?" James surveyed the assembly of freaks, frauds, fugitives, and thieves for any semblance of what might be mistaken for himself.

Either James was blind to his own ugliness or the face that looked back at him in the mirror was an elegant impostor. Smee shushed him and pointed to the Captain's entourage ascending the ladder onto the deck.

"There's the cozener now. Jas. the second is accompanying the Captain." Smee snapped to attention, causing his hosiery to slide down his spindly legs. "Don't be going and making a row over 'im in front of the Cap'n."

The boatswain braced and blew on his whistle.

"Captain Everard Creech, formerly of Her Majesty's Royal Navy, master and commander of the maritime merchant ship *Sea Witch*," he announced.

First came the four crewmen from the jolly boat carrying two heavy strongboxes, each fitted with a formidable lock. Boulder-size men struggled under the weight as they passed the laden trunks down into the hold.

James peered over Smee's shoulder as the nervous little man scribbled notes in his register detailing "two strongboxes gold to be accounted for."

"Gold? That is our cargo?" James asked, trying to sound unimpressed.

"Not hardly. We ain't got no dunnage putting out. It's the cargo we purchase with that gold that's our concern. We'll be counting every piece of gold, you and me, before it gets spent."

"Mr. Smee, I did not sign aboard this vessel to be a clerk."

"I see. It's emptying the Cap'n's chamber pot you prefer, then?"

Smee tilted his head back to take in the tall young man standing beside him, his long, black, regal locks twisting over his shoulders. His profile cut against the blue sky as confident and constant as the cardinal points of a compass.

"Aye, o' course not. Let me take a wild stab. You come on board to let's see . . . be a Cap'n? Hmm?"

A Vatican priest's wide-brimmed hat appeared bobbing up the ladder, shaded by the wide parasol from the jolly boat. The long, black robes of a Jesuit grew taller as the figure stepped through the opening in the bulwark and onto the ship. The tall priest held a Bible clutched to his chest. He raised his free hand to bless the crew as if he were the Pope himself. His pronouncement was in Latin, a chant that James translated with relative ease—*"May God have mercy on this vessel of sinners and fornicators and hold back his wrath and vengeance against the lost souls on our voyage. Send us, Lord Almighty, sleepy seas and fair winds until we reach our destination."*

James struggled to understand how such a prayer would be a comfort to the crew. According to the priest's request, given the shamefully depraved status of the crew members, at the end of the voyage their reward was a Heaven full of God's stored-up wrath and vengeance. Is that all he had to look forward to?

The entire crew echoed "Amen," even those perched on the topgallant mast. Smee spiked James an elbow to the ribs, prompting him to join the chorus of *Amen*s. James was still ruminating over "wrath and vengeance." He had

not been expecting a priest to come on board the ship.

"Is that priest shipping out with us? Or did he just come to curse us, then return to the mainland?" James was feeling a ripple up and down his spine as the man of religion reviewed the ranks of the crew. There was something dangerous emanating from the man that James could not decipher, only sensed strongly.

"What bit of snash would you be talking now? That *is* the Cap'n."

James stared incredulously at Captain Everard Creech, man of the cloth. The Captain forced a crewman down on his knees in front of everyone and demanded that the demon possessing the lost soul be cast out. As the poor crewman begged for forgiveness, Mr. Blood was instructed to use his birch across the man's back as encouragement for the demon to hurry its departure.

"You're an abomination of God's creation!"

"Aye, Cap'n. I know it, Cap'n. Can't help m'self. Mercy, Cap'n!"

"There is no mercy on my ship for sinners. You're a sinner, and so is the woman who made you!"

"I never knew me mum, Cap'n. Mercy!"

In that respect James and this unfortunate crewman shared the same sin, if it could be called that. James did not know his mother either.

Finally the man prostrated himself before Creech and pulled a green bottle from inside his vest, offering it in shaking hands. Creech gestured a silent command to

Mr. Blood, who seized the bottle and smelled its contents. A nod of his head and a look from his dead eye were all the confirmation Captain Creech required. Raising his hand to the heavens, Mr. Blood obeyed the Captain's silent command, tipping the bottle and pouring its contents over the side and into the water. The yellowish-green liquid glowed in the rays of the sun as it streamed down into the Thames. Absinthe . . .

"The green faerie that lives in this bottle has eaten your very soul. Sucked the life out of you and condemned you to a living Hell!" Creech circled the quivering man, the impact of his wood-heeled boots the only sound save the morning breeze animating the rigging. There would be no drinking of liquor on board Creech's vessel. Any man caught in possession of spirits after the anchor was weighed would be punished severely. The Captain, a self-ordained minister of the faith, had been abstinent for more than twenty years. He was bitterly intolerant and made no exceptions once under sail. Drunkenness could be a death sentence on the *Sea Witch*.

"Waste o' good absinthe, y' ask me," James heard the mate next to him mutter under his breath.

"Not to worry. I got me peg leg full of bumboo. I got a feelin' we'll be needin' a nip or two on this voyage." The one-legged sailor next to the mate shook his carved wooden leg. James could hear the rum-and-sugar solution sloshing about inside.

Having run his course of patience on the matter, Creech,

surprisingly to James, blessed the crewman quivering before him.

"Take the wretch below until the demon possessing him is unable to scream."

The man began screaming immediately, an indication that his demon was not the least bit exhausted and would not be done in for many hours. The screaming continued all the way down below deck, as the man was dragged away by his heels with the assistance of Mr. Blood's two muscled thugs, who vanished the lost soul into the bowels of the ship.

James made two mental notes on the incident, which he swore silently he would never forget; one, to never let his lips touch or consume absinthe, rum, or any other libation; and two, that when he became Captain of his own ship, he would never invoke the name of his creator to punish and humiliate any other living being. He had seen this in the cowardly actions of Arthur Darling and his Whips. All in the name of "our father who art in Heaven." He was revolted then by their hypocrisy just as he was by the Captain's. No god should ever be invoked to inflict harm.

James watched the Captain ascend the steps of the quarterdeck, shaded by the umbrella in the hands of the nervous cabin boy. Clearly, the man preferred the sanctuary of dark places to the revealing light of day.

"Stand by to make sail!" Mr. Blood yelled out the command that immediately lifted every man's spirits. Drums beat again as the crew scattered quickly across the deck,

ascended ratlines, and manned the windlass to raise anchor.

"Make ready to weigh anchor!" Voices echoed the commands. James was completely caught up in the energy that seemed to swell through the entire ship like blood pumping through a human heart. He could feel his own blood racing, his adrenaline rising with the rush of bodies in motion around him. Suddenly he longed to be a part of the crew. Above him, crew standing on the crosstrees loosened the plaited gaskets holding the great sails on the topgallant mast.

"Leave way the staysail. Leave way bowsprit sail!"

Crew monkeyed across yardarms and crosstrees, untying the beckets. The canvas on the smaller forward sails furled out, searching for the breeze that would carry the ship downriver to the sea.

The second mate released the brake on the windlass. Crew manning the capstan began to turn the drum of the windlass, which cranked the anchor from beneath the water up to the surface, one chain link at a time.

Through the blur of bodies passing back and forth in front of him, James swore he glimpsed a familiar face. There it was again. James caught his breath, not believing his own eyes.

"Jolly R?"

It could not be. Here? On board the *Sea Witch*? He was convinced his eyes were playing tricks on him. Smee tugged at James' coat, attempting to steer him out of the chaos.

"You're just in the way here, sonny. You come below with me."

"Please, Mr. Smee—I know him!" James pointed through the crowd up at the fo'c'sle. Once again the unmistakable face of Jolly R peeked at him from behind the umbrella shielding the Captain from the sun's beams.

"Ahoy! Ahoy, Roger!" James was beside himself with unexpected pleasure. "Jolly!"

On his next peek, Jolly R beamed a smile across to James, then ducked quickly back to Creech, who scowled at him, bringing instant discipline. Creech adjusted Jolly's hand on the umbrella, guiding it to block the sun.

"I know him, Mr. Smee. He's my . . . friend." "Friend" sounded so foreign to James as he said it, an incredibly happy word.

"Doodle and dash—that's a good one. You ought to be knowin 'im. 'E's you."

James queried Smee with his look of amazement.

"Signed on yesterday, he did."

"Jas. the second." James cackled his giddy laugh with the understanding that Jolly Roger had used the name James to sign himself aboard the *Sea Witch*. His familiar laugh reached Jolly R, who could not control his own. The Captain became more irritated and finally snatched the umbrella away from Jolly, dismissing him with a look of disdain.

Jolly practically fell down the quarterdeck stairs and pushed across the deck toward James. The only sight that could have possibly raised James' spirit more would have been Ananova galloping across the deck on Pandora. But for now the rather round Oppidan, Roger Peter Davies of

Kensington—and late of Godolphin House—standing before him grinning widely was a true life-giving tonic.

"King Jas.?"

"Jolly R?"

Neither could decide which impossible question to seek the answer to first. Mr. Blood made the decision for them.

"You two there—mewling scugs. Make yourselves useful. Get on that anchor chain."

As if they had been at sea all their lives, the former Oppidans from Eton snapped a Royal Navy salute and shouted out—

"Aye, sir. Right away, sir!"

The two friends crowded onto a capstan bar and pushed with the other sailors winding the anchor chain about the drum in the hold below. Between the groans and chanting of the men as they raised the anchor, James learned that Jolly R had made the decision to run away and sign on the *Sea Witch* after his father had informed him that he would not be returning to Eton for the next Michaelmas term. Or ever. The family humiliation would be too great.

"I couldn't let you go off to sea all by yourself."

"I seem to have plenty of company, King Jas. II."

"It was the only name I could think of when Mr. Smee asked me my name."

"Then we will both need new names. Jas. Matthew, formerly of Eton, died in the fire."

James could tell from the cryptic look of complete dismay on Jolly's face that he had not a clue of the meaning behind his comment. He had no knowledge of the fire at

Eton or the cause of it. James had indeed been successful. He had vanished without a trace.

"You're here, Jolly R. We both are!"

"Topping swank, James!"

James' gratingly superior laugh prompted the big sailor pushing the windlass behind them to yank James' locks like the reins of a horse and urge the two to haul their weight.

"Put your bony carcasses to the wheel, y' cherry bums, or we'll be dragging anchor to the shores of Tripoli."

James growled like a seasoned sailor, and so did Jolly R.

"Someday our foes may win!" James yelled to the men around him.

"But not today!" Jolly R completed the refrain as they turned and turned the capstan, chanting with the other seamen until the tonnage of the great hook cleared the water and was pulled to rest against the hull. The last umbilical cord binding the *Sea Witch* to Mother Earth had been disconnected. The ship caught the current and headed down the Thames. Now the mizzen canvas was unfurled. The mainsails were raised, catching the wind, pushing away from the trees of cross spars, yardarms, and masts until the canvas surfaces bowed taut.

James and Jolly climbed out on the bow with the rest of the old salts and veterans and stood waving goodbye to Greenwich, to England, and to their old ways and lives. . . .

"Jas., this is going to be an awfully big adventure," said Jolly R.

Of that James had no doubt.

CHAPTER NINETEEN

BLUE WATER

JAMES' FIRST NIGHT AT SEA would not go down among his happiest. In truth, this night could, with less than even the slightest prompting, easily have been his last. Certainly Jolly R considered bringing his life as a sailor to a fast and merciful end. With every run of the ship down the backside of a swell, followed by the gravity-defying rise up by the stern, Jolly donated the contents of his gut overboard to Mother Ocean. Unable to stay below-decks, where the world turned upside down with every wave, Jolly R secured himself to the fife rail encircling the mainmast and watched the *Sea Witch* dizzily pitchpoling in twenty-foot swells.

James was holed up in Smee's cuddy under the poop

deck counting gold sovereigns under the command of the eccentric first mate. Each strongbox of gold coins had to be counted and recounted, weighed and reweighed, while the entire ship was attempting to defy gravity. He marveled at Smee, who attended to the task paying no attention to the objects sliding about his tiny cabin, or to the shifting stacks of gold coins, which James had to catch and imprison one at a time back in the strongbox. Smee counted aloud, mumbling each number, which he then wrote down in his register. The little man was completely unruffled, refusing to be interrupted in his important task by the topsy-turvy force of the sea. Impossibly, Smee stood up from the table and strode out across the lower deck with his head buried in his ciphering. He walked on such an even keel, James was convinced that he could have balanced a tankard of ale on the little man's head and not spilled a drop. James had to hold on to every beam and bulkhead as the deck shifted and pitched beneath his feet to keep from spilling the coins. Not so for the venerable first mate. His spindly legs bearing striped stockings of differing colors stretched and bent like rubber, seeming to shift and change lengths as they absorbed the pitching of the ship. With some miraculous and instinctive understanding of physics and balance, Smee never missed a count of a coin into the strongbox.

"Mr. Smee," James gasped as he slammed into a bulkhead balancing the box. "Couldn't this wait for calmer seas?"

"Aye, and we'd still be waiting for that mirrorglass a year from now. The smartest thing we could do is throw this lot over the side."

James was shocked—heave a respectable fortune in gold into the ocean?

"Then the Captain couldn't work his black magic with it." Smee remained standing straight up while James staggered backward until the deck seesawed the other way.

"Black magic? Isn't that against his religion?"

"Not this kind. When we get to our destination, the Cap'n is going to take this yellow gold and turn it into black gold. Then we'll all be payin' a visit to Hell."

The sinister sound of Smee's words piqued James' curiosity. He began attempting to match the spring-loaded pattern of Smee's leg movements with his own to keep up with the little man.

"Black gold? What is this riddle?" James had drawn beside Smee and was near matching him with each yaw and sway as they crossed the deck. Smee peered at James over his tiny spectacles.

The scrumpy first mate deftly steered James away from an answer.

"Admiring my sea legs, are we now? Getting some of your own."

James continued his balancing act in an attempt to steady himself like Smee. "I am trying. How do you do that?"

"Quite simple actually: I always make it a point to stand at an angle of ninety degrees to the rest of the ear-ear—the world."

James had to marvel at the idea. To be perpendicular to the rest of the world, always standing straight! A constant

truth. To always be in balance with the world instead of fighting against it—the forces of nature, the power of gravity, even the passage of time was of no consequence as long as one maintained a ninety-degree relationship with the rest of the planet.

"Ninety degrees to the rest of the world. That way you consistently maintain an even keel." James was suddenly as at home on the pitching deck as a ballerina is onstage.

"Mr. Smee, you're a genius!"

"Nonconformist, actually," Smee corrected. "The Captain don't take to geniuses on board his ship. Same as bumboo rum and women. You should be rememberin' that if you know what's good for y', Jas. Mind your tongue if you don't want to lose it. Speak too smart, and your life won't be worth a dead man's dinghy." Smee took the box of gold from James and locked it inside the lazarette in the stern.

"With you it's not gettin' your sea legs under you I worry about," Smee concluded darkly. In the brief instant following the cryptic comment, James noted that Mr. Smee was perhaps the most perceptive nonconformist he had ever met.

On deck, the helmsman held his course bearing southwest from the English Channel toward the Iberian Peninsula, then west toward the outer bulge of the African continent. Captain Everard Creech prayed constantly in his cabin with his Bible open to a verse that he spouted aloud above the crashing of the seas.

"Your male and female slaves are to come from the nations around you; from them you may buy slaves. You may also buy some of the temporary residents living among you and members of their clans born in your country, and they will become your property. You can will them to your children as inherited property and can make them slaves for life. . . ."

Before him on his spartan table the Captain spread the tentacles of a cat-o'-nine-tails, each of the leather strips latticed with steel barbs and bits of broken glass tied fast, more lethal than the stinging whip James had met with at Eton.

Mr. Blood slept standing up on the quarterdeck, impervious to the rolling of the main deck as the *Sea Witch* stayed its course, south. His dead eye remained always open, deceptively giving his gargoylelike features the look of being on constant watch.

James tried out his newfound sea legs, walking the deck until he found Jolly R clinging to the fife rail around the mainmast. Jolly was as green as old cheese. James offered his friend a fresh dip of water, which Jolly promptly spewed onto the deck, already slippery with sea spray.

"You look as if you will have to die just to get well."

Jolly summoned a sickly smile, taking James in as he paraded around the deck showing off his sea legs.

"Can't you do anything wrong, James? Here you're supposed to be the boy who hates the sea and I'm supposed to be right at home on it. My father would make me walk the plank if he saw me spewing my bilge."

James needled Jolly with a sadistic dash of irony, suggesting that if he should drown himself, his father would no longer be a worry to him. Instead of laughing with James, Jolly R suddenly panicked, looking frantically about the ship.

"You don't think Father will come after me, do you? Perhaps he'll try to stop the ship and snatch me home? Do you think so? He wouldn't get His Lordship to set sail after us, would he? I'm not going back. Never. I'm done with that life. I won't go. I won't—"

James firmly grabbed his friend by the shoulders, looking him in the eye to calm him.

"Jolly! You're raving, man. Do you think he cares? Do you really imagine your father's out raising an army to fetch you back? You're not exactly a face that could launch a thousand ships, now, are you?"

James' reference to the beautiful face of Helen, the legendary cause of the Trojan War, sobered Jolly R. His King's forget-me-nots gazed sadly back at him. His own father had banished him to sea, a blessing in James' mind. Jolly R recalled his last moments with his father—the disappointment and the disgust in his voice as he described the humiliation of having to explain to the Queen how his son had tried to kidnap the Sultan's daughter, the enormous costs to him personally for the financial loss, not to mention the public drubbing he was forced to take from the O.E.s in his class at Eton. The confrontation had been all about his father and the cost to him of Jolly's relationship with "that

Oppidan bastard." His father had never once considered Jolly. But disgrace and his father's disgust were not the only forces that had prompted Jolly R to leave his life behind. His loyalty to King Jas.—the honor they shared, from the victory at the Wall Game to the noble attempted rescue of Ananova—this force was too strong to be shattered by mere Kings and Queens. Good form in life was far more noble than social status. And it was good form to risk everything you had for a friend.

"Ananova's father sailed her away with an armed escort to protect her from the likes of me!" James' voice commanded Jolly's attention over the roar of the sea. "Wouldn't you like to have a father who would do that for you? Wouldn't that be *nice*?"

Jolly suddenly began digging madly in his waistcoat as if trying to ferret out an infestation of bees that had chosen him for a hive.

"I saw her!" Jolly cried, now burying his hands in his trouser pockets and pulling out an envelope wrapped in oilskin. "Ananova! She gave this to me . . . she wanted you to have it. . . ."

James went numb all over. His hands mechanically folded over the letter with the care of touching some ancient document passed down by the gods. He stared blankly at the parchment as Jolly R described the few moments he had had with Ananova before her Marxbruder escorted her to the *Mephistopheles*, which Jolly's father had been forced to provide for her crossing.

Jolly had been confined to his room on his father's estate until his fate at Eton had been determined and a proper punishment could be prescribed. When Jolly had learned from the loyal Oppidans, Dicky Dongon and Simon "Snash" Napier, that James was being sent to the *Sea Witch*, Jolly R was determined to find a way to join him. On the night of his planned escape, as he dressed as one of the servants, Jolly had an unexpected visitor.

Skeffington stood properly and bowed, taking in Jolly's head bandage. Fastidiously polite, he asked after Jolly's injury, "suffered in this most unfortunate catastrophe." Jolly assured Skeffington that he was in "good form" but went on to say that he was surprised to see the Queen's man present in his father's house, given the embarrassment Jolly had personally caused Her Majesty by his "deplorable display." Skeffington allowed a slim smile, confessing to Jolly that the Queen had no knowledge of this visit and that Jolly must promise to keep things that way or there would be "repercussions." He punctuated his ambiguous threat with a single raised eyebrow, this being the man's sole flag for anything distasteful. Gout, execution, wrong choice of clothes—all received the same arched brow.

Jolly paused, letting the gravity of the Queen's adviser having a clandestine meeting with a freshly defanged student rather than some head of state or powerful member of Parliament sink in. Jolly fixed on the page standing behind Skeffington, who was staring directly at him.

"And what about your page, Master Skeffington? Is he sworn to secrecy as well?"

Skeffington smiled again, then laughed, enjoying himself.

"Hardly necessary. I am utterly positive *she* won't tell a soul."

Jolly stared again at the page, dressed in a waistcoat and knee breeches. Her eyes were the giveaway. No page in the entire royal palace possessed such fiery eyes.

"She has a message for your King."

Ananova stepped forward and opened her official-looking leather pouch. Jolly accepted the charge, then bowed and kneeled to her. Ananova stood him up, shaking her head emphatically, her eyes flashing. She kissed Jolly gently on his lips, completely shocking him. Then whispered—

"Take this to him for me, *o agapitos mou philos.*"

She presented him an envelope bearing the royal seal of the Sultan.

Skeffington left Jolly standing there in the great room all alone, as he led his "page" out with apologies.

"Urgent Queen's business, time of night, whatevers and wherefores," he mumbled. Although Skeffington would never admit it, performing this particular diplomatic service to keep the balance between the rulers of two civilized countries did not come from blind duty to his sovereign, the Queen, but from that secret soft spot he harbored in his barnacled old heart for these young adventurers. Skeffington bucked his innate cynicism with the sincere hope that

James and Ananova and Jolly R would somehow prevail by the sheer power of their youth.

James held the oilskin envelope in the dim flicker of a tallow candle. He had left Jolly abruptly on the main deck without so much as a "thank you" or a "good form," so driven was he to be alone and treat himself to its contents. Wedged among the frames that ribbed the hull under the poop deck, away from the elements, James opened the letter with the care reserved for great religious relics. Her hand writing and choice of words evidenced the gifts already at her command. He could hear her voice speaking to him as if she were indeed standing there before him, sheltered from the wind and sea, calm but forceful.

> James . . . I am not allowed to speak your
> name but I write it. I am told that you are a
> traitor, a criminal of the lowest order. But I
> have learned that your father is a Lord and
> that you have been denied your station
> because of the unfortunate circumstances of
> your birth. Why should this prevent you or
> anyone from being treated as my equal? I
> am not like my father. I measure the value
> of a human being by actions and deeds, not
> by bloodlines. In my country there is
> fighting over who is the rightful ruler. I will
> lead an army if I must, but your island

sounds so much more inviting. My only sanctuary is dear Pandora and my memories of you and Jolly R. I envy your friendship with Jolly. Now I return alone to my island. You can find it by gazing at the stars. If you look to the east, find the constellation Lyra. It is shaped like a lyre with a bright-blue star at its center. The story goes that Orpheus, son of Apollo, played the lyre so beautifully that all the animals of the wild and all the forces of nature were enchanted by his music. But his music could not save Eurydice, the woman he loved. Orpheus descended into the underworld to save her. Because he played so beautifully, the god of Hades released Eurydice to him on one condition—that he would not look at her until they had journeyed out of Hades. Her beauty was great, but Orpheus resisted looking at her. All went well until they neared the upper world. Eurydice protested that he must not truly love her, since he had refused to look at her even once. Orpheus could not help himself and looked back at her to explain, only to see Eurydice recede into the shadows and be lost forever in the underworld. Orpheus still searches for her. As a tribute to their love, Zeus placed the

lyre in the heavens, marked by the stars.
Find the big blue star. My island is right
under the second star to its right and then
straight on till the morning sun greets you.
    Panda ime i agapiti phili sou. Ya
hara. . . .

James read the letter again. With each sentence the image of her took on more clarity and definition; he would never forget her face. "*Agapiti phili.*" Her closing was in Greek and could be translated as "loving friend."

Sultanas had no place in the life of a sailor, he told himself. Females were bad luck on board any ship. James resolved to put Ananova out of his head. He had seven years before the mast to become master and commander of his own fate. He had no time for Ananova now. James prepared to tear up the letter, but hesitated. After all, she was the very reason he and Jolly were sailing for adventure! James rushed back up on deck with every intention of declaring his loyalty to Jolly R, of beginning to perfect his skills as seaman without such things as Sultanas blowing him off course. Instead, he found himself eagerly searching the skies for the blue star marking the constellation Lyra. He was too late. The sky had already started to brighten as the coming sun peeked over the whitecaps. His long first night at sea had passed. He folded the letter carefully back inside the envelope and tucked it in his shirt, entirely too close to his heart.

* * *

"Permission to speak to the helmsman," James blurted out, rushing up the poop deck steps and practically over-running Mr. Blood. Ever on watch, the quartermaster opened his good eye and glared at James.

"State your business, scug. First bell's not for another half hour."

"Sir, could you tell me which way to the Greek Islands?"

Mr. Blood rippled his entire frame awake and crossed the poop deck to look James in his forget-me-not eyes.

Mr. Blood pointed to the binnacle housing the ship's compass affixed beside the helm.

"It's a bloody long way from where you're standing," he said.

Mr. Blood folded his hands behind him, his dead eye back on watch. That was all the answer James could expect.

"Now, seeing as how you're on deck with the rising of the sun, get that mate o' yours off the fife rail. Empty the Captain's chamber pot, then swab the quarterdeck."

"Aye, sir." His insolent salute prompted Mr. Blood to turn his back on James and spit over the fantail. James descended the steps to the main deck and was heading for Jolly R, passed out on the fife rail, when he slowed and looked to starboard. The sea was turning from the black of night to indigo as the sky lightened. There was something missing in his field of vision all the way to the horizon—an island, a coastline, a hunk of England. . . . There was noth-ing. Just blue water as far as his eyes could see. For the

fleetest of moments he felt dizzy. Was it possible? James wheeled. Ignoring the snoring Jolly R, he crossed the deck to the portside bulwark, peering into the glare from the east. He shaded his eyes. The sun was rising from the sea, not from behind any mass of land on the horizon.

"Jolly! Look at this!"

He shook Jolly R, pinching his cheeks. Jolly had nothing left in his stomach, so all he could do was groan. James half dragged and half carried him to the foredeck, jostling and pummeling him awake.

"You are missing it, scugo!"

Jolly finally focused on the view before him. James pointed beyond the bowsprit aimed like the needle of a compass. . . . Blue water . . . and sky . . .

"Do you see it?"

James turned Jolly R slowly for a three-hundred-sixty-degree view of the ocean stretching out on all sides of the *Sea Witch*.

"What?"

"Open your beady eyes, Oppidan. What do you see?"

"Nothing . . . absolutely nothing. . . ."

James exulted, opening his arms to the heavens.

"Look at it, Jolly. It's magic. Somehow, overnight, by some miracle of nature, the earth has become completely covered by Mother Ocean!"

Jolly R panicked when he realized there was not a speck of earth in sight. He grabbed the railing, whipsawing his head about. Everywhere he looked, the big blue filled his

view. He convulsed, trying to catch his breath, as James howled. No land in any direction.

"What happened? Where did the land go to?"

James howled again. Jolly's shock melted gradually into the laughter more readily heard from inmates in a lunatic asylum. He turned in circles on the deck with dizzying speed, pointing and gesturing at the endless sea surrounding them.

"We did it! We're free, King Jas. Unhooked from Mother Earth and sailing on Mother Ocean!" The sight of the two landlubbers making fools of themselves on the fore-deck prompted chides and catcalls from the crew as they began appearing from below for their morning tasks. None of the name-calling slowed Jolly R as he danced his dizzy jig. Smee joined Mr. Blood on the poop deck.

"Mr. Blood . . . "

"Mr. Smee . . . "

"I was thinkin' about the first time I b-b-blue-watered."

"Is thinking about such things good, Mr. Smee?"

"Don't you remember your first time?"

"I try to forget. Every cursed, goddamned day."

Smee watched Jolly try futilely to stand on his head so as to view the ocean upside down and turn it into the sky. Smee took in the two boys whooping with joyful abandon. He had known the feeling . . . once.

"Not me. I envy those two. I do."

James rocked back on his heels, taking in the huge bowl of the infinite sky. A lone gull winged overhead, matching the speed of the *Sea Witch*.

"The only place that could possibly be better than this would have to be up there," said James, watching.

Sailors scaling the ratlines aloft jeered.

"Well, why don't y' just fly up there and see for yesef, y' pewling little spawn!"

This was one of the more polite suggestions in the barrage of derisive curses from the gathering crew. James struck his characteristic regal pose, his left hand on his hip, his right hand raised before him with fist clenched. He addressed the sailor on the ratline.

"What's to stop me?" he asked in a commanding voice. "Man walks the earth and sails the seas. Why not soar through the skies?"

For a moment the wind snapping at the sails and the parting of the seas around the prow of the *Sea Witch* were the only sounds as the crew fell silent. The logic of his proclamation and the confidence with which he spoke seemed unassailable. Then a sailor let go a rooster crow, shaking the ratline. The jeers and scurrilous remarks were turned on the crewman who had challenged James. Doodle-doos rippled through the crew until everyone was crowing.

"Fair enough, Master James. When you learn how to fly, will y' teach me?" The crewman flapped his arms on the ratlines, taking the larking from his mates in stride. More echoed the request. "I want to fly like a floggin' bird!" "Take me wi' y' when you learn!"

James paraded the foredeck, bantering with the crew with far too much swagger for Mr. Blood's liking.

"Right! Enough of this babble. To your tasks while the wind's fresh. Make sail! All the canvas she'll take!"

James stood like a statue on the other end of the ship, facing Mr. Blood as sailors and crew scrambled about the deck and up the ratlines to their duties. Smee chuckled and made a private entry in his register, unwittingly recording one of the last good moments of the voyage worth committing to memory.

"Wouldn't that be nice? Flying. Like a little bird. I'll have some o' that."

"Whales!"

Jolly R was in the midst of serving tea and biscuits to Captain Creech in his quarters when the cry echoed from the lookout up in the crow's nest. James practically dragged Jolly R onto the deck to witness an unbelievable sight. During the night the *Sea Witch* had sailed into a pod of whales! The ship was surrounded by hundreds of humpbacks. Their great heads plowed the surface of the sea, forming a powerful wake, then submerging and rising again like horses on a carousel. With each rhythmic motion, the spray from a multitude of blowholes filled the sky, and the breathing noises of each whale combined in a cacophonous blast of sea and air. The *Sea Witch* had no choice but to continue east, unable to change course against the bump and rub of the magnificent creatures surrounding the ship. James joined some of the more daring of the crew as they hitched themselves to a halyard, then walked down the side of the hull

alongside the whales. One by one, sailors ran along the backs of the beasts as they rolled up to the surface, hopping from one to the next, then pulling on their safety line and climbing back up for another pass.

James earned the respect of the crew that day as he stood over a blowhole and let himself be lifted into the air by the full force of a behemoth's blast.

"I'm flying!" he cried, then descended on his line and waited for another spew to turn him euphoric and weightless again.

But by the next morning, the giant elephants of the sea were gone.

On the fifth day human carcasses floated by the *Sea Witch*, followed by a ghost ship, a small single-masted sloop drifting aimlessly on the waters. Two men could be seen hanging from the yardarm, the life choked out of them by the sheets twisted around their necks. Gulls had picked away at their flesh, leaving their bones exposed to the elements, and the deck was strewn with a dozen other corpses.

Mr. Blood steered a course far clear of the death boat, then ordered the master gunner to man the *Sea Witch*'s sixteen pounders and blow the boat out of the water. James protested. There could be men still alive on the vessel. They should be rescued. Smee pointed to the yellow-and-black flag flying from the jack staff on the bowsprit of the doomed ship.

"The plague. Yellow jack, maybe. Or the black sickness. That's what took 'em. Probably the drinking water got the taint. Bully beef stores spoiled. That and poor seamanship. You don't give respect to Mother Ocean, she'll pluck your heart out. Those men hanging from the yardarm . . . probably hanged themselves. Better fate than the plague for sure."

James and Jolly R learned much that day. Both served on their first gunner's crew as powder monkeys, loading the black powder charges into the cannon before firing. It took only one fusillade from the starboard battery to sink the ghost ship. Sharks that had been circling the floating coffin wasted no time swarming over the carrion feast.

CHAPTER TWENTY

BLACK GOLD

WHEN THE LOOKOUT CRIED, "Land," Jolly stilled like a statue in a museum as he sorted through the past seven days at sea until the Captain's stinging voice snapped him from his reverie. Jolly had continued to pour the hot tea into the Captain's cup until it had run over and scalded the Captain's hand. With his unburned hand Creech grabbed Jolly R by his coat collar and shoved him toward the door, threatening him with the wrath of God if Jolly did not do penance by pouring scalding water on his own hand. Nothing Jolly could say or do had any effect toward reversing the Captain's command. In his confusion, Jolly inadvertently set the hot pot down on

the Creech family Bible, a book that never left the man's side. The leather-bound heirloom smoldered with the smell of burning hide.

"Off the port bow!" the lookout called again.

The ship's bell clanged. A rumble of voices filled the silence between the Captain and Jolly R as both stood immobilized, watching the Good Book as it cooked. On deck, the boatswain's whistle screamed like a kettle on the boil. Creech lunged for the teapot, forgetting his scalded flesh.

"Captain! No!"

The shell of the pot seared Creech's bare hands as he grabbed the hot vessel off his precious Good Book. The pot clattered on the plank floor, spraying hot water. Creech forced the scream of pain back down his throat. Refusing to yell, his hands curled raw, he set his murderous eyes on Jolly.

"Sorry, sir. Your book, sir."

He held the book up in offering to Creech, a perfect circle burned into the hide of the old volume. Jolly might as well have handed the man his own death warrant.

Jolly R was doomed and he knew it. Creech held up his crucifix in one burned hand while fumbling open the wooden box and lifting out his cat-o'-nine-tails with the other.

"Jackal!!! I cast thee out!"

Fueled with fury, Creech snapped back the cruel tentacles to strike. A polite knock on the cabin door and Smee's dutiful voice were all that saved Jolly.

"Begging your pardon, Cap'n. We're there if you care to have a look-see. We're awaitin' your orders—"

The calamitous noise of Creech lashing his cat-o'-nine-tails had prompted Smee to crack the door and peek in. Jolly had taken refuge under the Captain's great table. The Captain was yanking and lurching, trying to free the studded tentacles of his whip now embedded in the tabletop.

"And if a man smite his servant, or his maid, with a rod, and he die under his hand, he shall be surely punished. But if he live on a day or two, he shall not be punished: for the servant is his own property!"

Smee dropped to his knees, crawled quickly across the cabin floor, and joined Jolly R under the table. Calmly the little man pointed to the door, then walked his fingers through the air signaling Jolly to make his exit. Jolly nodded, terrified, as the Captain freed the cat-o'-nines and struck again, this time shredding the Chinese silk curtains festooning the fantail windows.

"Let's l-le-leav—bustle while the Cap'n's still in a dodgy mood." Smee shooed Jolly on his way as if putting out a cat. Jolly R squinched his eyes tightly, gritted his teeth, and scurried toward the door.

"And if a man smite the eye of his servant, or the eye of his maid, he shall let him go free for his eye's sake. And if he smite out his manservant's tooth, or his maidservant's tooth, he shall let him go free for his tooth's sake."

Smee stood up, startling the Captain.

"Time for your medication, I do believe, Cap'n. You'll be wanting to be at your best when you greet the new p-pas-passengers." Smee retrieved a chemist's bottle and

glass from the cupboard. Unruffled by the Captain's murderous tirade, he proceeded to pour a tablespoon of the putrid-looking contents.

"Passengers?" The Captain caught himself in his rant as if snapping out of a seizure. He stared at Smee for a moment, giving the impression he did not recognize him. Smee took this opportunity to shove the spoonful of medicine into the Captain's mouth.

The lookout, Mr. Toon, who had verbally jousted with James on the issue of human flight, had seen fit to invite this newly respected member of the crew aloft on his dogwatch to get a gull's-eye view of the world. Far up in the air above the decks, James felt as if he were almost flying. Gulls bucked against the wind, matching the ship's speed until Mr. Toon sailed a piece of hardtack into the sky and watched the birds dive for the crust, snatching it out of the air.

"The more gulls, the closer the land," said Mr. Toon, instructing James. "Do you see it yet, Master James. There? Off to port?"

James squinted into the distance. The waters were turning purple as the light from the setting sun faded behind them.

James gestured to the spyglass hanging around Mr. Toon's neck. "I could if you'd let me have a look through the glass."

The man grinned, flashing a brace of gold-plated teeth. "Not till y' sees the terra with your nekkid eyes first.

Follow the gulls. They'll be showing ya land sure as a compass."

James framed his hands over his forehead, blocking out the sky. He followed the swirl of seabirds circling and weaving out over the ocean. An aerial ballet of grace and speed. When they were but specks on the purple horizon, he saw it—a strip of a thick shape where no ocean waves rolled. James followed the dense strip stretching farther and farther across the horizon.

"I see it—there it is. It's a topping big island, Mr. Toon!"

"Aye, it's more than that."

Mr. Toon handed over his spyglass and gestured for James to take a look. James hesitated before raising the eyepiece.

"I'm not sure I want to see land," he said. "The ocean's quite the better place from where I sit. The whales and the dolphins and gulls—and all the fish in the sea—they seem to have it better in life than men do."

The *Sea Witch* all at once felt very small and insignificant floating on the vast ocean surrounding it.

"Then you're a wise lad, Jas. A mite heedful, more than many of the men who captain ships. Go on. Yell it out. Tell the world."

James raised the glass to his eye, studied the image at the other end of the spyglass, and hailed—

"Land hoooooo! Off the port bow! Land hooooo!"

He twisted the glass, bringing the image at the other end of the tube into focus. For a fleeting glimmer of a

moment his island was there. Beckoning to him to come. The turquoise lagoon shimmering under the two suns. A splash of fins as mermaids formed a greeting party, swimming out in schools to meet his arrival. Onshore, the trees filled with rich tropical fruits. Sandy beaches glowed, white as snow. Maybe it was snow. His island was that unpredictable. Then the dark narrow strip of earth stretching across the horizon became clear. It was not his island. There were no mermaids. There were no mountains of exotic fruits and pure bleached sand.

"What is this place called, Mr. Toon?" James did little to hide his growing trepidation.

"Africa," Mr. Toon said with equal dread regarding the rugged shoreline. "The Gold Coast they call this stretch of the dark continent."

Pirates, ivory traders, and worse ruled these waters. James was still mulling over the gravity of Mr. Toon's pronouncement when he could feel the entire mainmast shudder and vibrate like a harp string, followed by the rumble of a sixteen pounder firing from the forward portside gunport. A billow of smoke and flames belched from the hull of the ship. Gulls scattered, shrieking wildly. James saw a white plume of ocean erupt three thousand feet from the ship, as a cannonball splashed harmlessly into the water. Below, drummers took to the quarterdeck pounding out "beat to quarters."

"Are we going to be attacked?" James looked to Mr. Toon with excitement.

"Depends on which side of the deck you're on. We're just

lettin' 'em know we're here." Then Mr. Toon ordered James below. Mr. Blood would have his gold teeth for bringing a lubber aloft on his watch. James was reluctant to leave his superior perch, but he did not want to be the cause of Mr. Toon's losing his golden smile. The ratlines were already crawling with crew climbing up to take positions on the crosstrees. Toon unloosed his stayline and snapped it taut.

"Y' said you wanted to fly, eh, peacock? Well, this is your next lesson." He handed the line to James. The leather becket wrapped around the rope would protect James' hands from being burned raw. "Don't be getting your curly locks caught on the way down." Mr. Toon laughed as he boosted the boy over the side. James grabbed the line to keep from falling. Instead of hanging, the smooth leather slid down the rope, taking James with a rush.

James landed on the fo'c'sle with a skid, dropping on a pile of cordage. Sailors bustled around him. On the main deck, Mr. Smee was overseeing the breaking out of arms— Enfield muskets, hangers, and cutlasses. There were even crossbows from another era. The men were preparing for action of a most serious kind. James skimmed the crew trying to find Jolly R. His round face was not among the sailors taking up weapons and readying themselves along the port gunwale. Other sailors winched a large black cauldron up from belowdecks. James had to move quickly aside as the men swung the heavy iron pot and set it amidships with a ringing thud. Mr. Blood's hand landed on James' shoulder.

"Get below and keep your gundy-gutted friend out of

the Captain's sight." James considered asking the quarter-master for an explanation, but the preparations for battle and the chance of riling Mr. Blood carried the day.

"Aye, sir. What's all the fuss, sir?"

"We've reached our destination. Taking on cargo."

James eyed the crew lining the bulwarks ready for battle, then the large iron pot looking strangely out of place on the deck.

"Are we expecting trouble or guests for dinner?"

Mr. Blood read his skeptical frown.

"There's always the unexpected, scug. I gave you an order."

Mr. Blood planted the metal tip of his birch rod squarely on James' chest. James did not budge. Instead, he produced his insolent version of a salute, then disappeared below.

The air belowdecks was already thick with the smell of sweat and gunpowder. The master gunner, a one-eyed, grizzled veteran everyone called "Cyclops," paraded up and down the gundeck checking each of the nine cannons on the port-side battery.

"Open the ports!"

The order was repeated, echoing down the line to the aft gun, where James had taken up a position. Looking through the square opening into which the cannon would fire, he noticed several jagged rock mounds jutting up from the sea in the sundown gloom. Masses of gulls roosted on the rocky teeth. The *Sea Witch* had drawn closer to the African shoreline clearly visible beyond the jagged rocks. James had

still not set eyes on Jolly R anywhere on the gun deck.

"Number nine. Draw a bead on that first rock and make it a bit shorter. Put on a little demonstration for the locals."

"Be my extreme pleasure, it would."

The gunner's mate and loaders at the number-nine cannon in front of James set to loading and priming the piece.

"Right. Let's lob 'em a grenado. Figger a ten-second fuse ought to do it." The gunner's mate took the nod from Cyclops to proceed. The rammer jammed wadding down the barrel with his oiled pole. The loader cut a length of hemp fuse from a roll on his belt, fitted a sixteen-pound cannonball from a rack into the cannon, and waited. All the choreographed activity suddenly stopped. The gunner looked around the crowded deck.

"Powder! Where's me boobin' powder monkey? 'Allo?"

James recognized the rounded shape trundling among the gun crews, lugging shoulder sacks bulging with canvas canisters packed tightly with black powder. Loaders grabbed powder charges as he passed. Gunner crews chided Jolly, squawking and making faces.

"Be watching that flame there, monkey boy. Don't want to be blowin' us all to kingdom come just yet." Cyclops closed the glass door on a single flaming wick burning in a pot of oil as Jolly R edged by, holding the powder charges close to his chest. This being the only source of light allowed around the gunpowder, the gunners had to be extremely careful when priming the cannon.

James relieved Jolly R of one of the powder bags. His

friend was distraught and sweating like a roasting pig.

"Mr. Blood said to keep you away from the Captain. What did you off and do?"

"I was just making him a cup of tea. I swear I was."

James looked at his old Eton chum and shook his head.

"I would have thought you'd have learned something at Eton. You're lucky you're not being shot from one of those cannons. The end."

Jolly R continued to sweat. He had risked everything to follow James to sea. He worried that James would tire of his stupid mistakes and abandon him to the Captain's whims.

"Do you know whom we're going to fight?" Jolly desperately reached to regain some footing with his King.

"Mr. Blood said we're taking on cargo."

"I was down in the hold, James. The men are hauling out chains . . . with fetters and manacles on them. And what's that big pot on the deck for? Answer me that?"

Before James could fully weigh Jolly R's perplexing revelation, they were both called into action. Grabbing the rope lines on each side of the number nine, the boys pulled with their gun crew, rolling the thousand-pound cannon forward into firing position at the open gun port. The loader lit a wick at the oil lamp, quickly closing the protective glass on the flame. He stood over the firing chamber on the cannon while the master gunner sighted out the port. The rammer held the sixteen-pound grenade, waiting for the fuse to be lit. As the ship heeled to port on the swells, the guns were lowered below the jagged rocks. On the following swell to starboard, the

guns rose, bringing the target into view. James marveled at old Cyclops as he sighted down the barrel out the port, timing the movement of the ship to bring the target into line.

"Fuse!" Cyclops spoke in his graveled rasp.

The loader lit the fuse on the grenade. Immediately the rammer placed the ball in the barrel.

"Count us off, scug. We've only got to ten—"

"One one thousand, two two thousand—"

James counted the seconds, trying not to hurry but to give accurate time. If the cannon misfired and failed to propel the grenade to its target, it would explode in the barrel, which could ignite the powder, sending the entire gun deck up in flames.

"Five five thousand—"

The rammer gently shoved the grenade down the barrel and stood aside.

"Ready on the nine."

"Seven seven thousand—"

Jolly R was about to embarrass himself by throwing up.

"Let her rip!" Cyclops bellowed. The loader touched his wick to the powder hole. The bright flash was sucked down the cavity with a whoosh. The thousand-pound barrel jerked, rearing back like a bucking horse. Fire spewed from the muzzle. The roar was deafening as the gun deck filled with acrid black smoke.

"Eight eight thousand!"

Before James could reach the count of ten, the top of the jagged rock exploded with a direct hit, sending shards and

frightened seagulls scattering to the winds. A cheer went up across the gun deck, lauding the skills of old Cyclops. The gunner's mate with the wooden leg full of booze passed his appendage around to the gunners for a quick nip in celebration. When the leg came to James, he smelled the contents and politely passed it on to Jolly R, who rocked back and downed a huge pull, to the loud approval of the men.

"A little less noise down there!" Blood stomped on the deck above, immediately quieting the gunners. James was incredulous at hearing these words. The ghost of Arthur Darling was still with him. Blood was an O.E. He had to be.

The crew waited in tense silence, quietly passing around their rum. In the distance, the echo of another cannon rolled from the shoreline. A plume of water mushroomed several hundred yards short of the *Sea Witch*.

"That's it. There's the signal." James and Jolly R remained in the shadows as the men clambered above.

Captain Creech exited his cabin carrying his Bible and took up his position on the quarterdeck beside Mr. Blood. Smee followed, carrying the Captain's carved box containing his dreaded cat-o'-nines.

"Mr. Toon!" Mr. Blood called up to the crow's nest. "Give us your report, man."

Mr. Toon peered into the darkness with his spyglass. Fiery glares dotted the shoreline, growing in size.

"They've lit the signal fires."

Mr. Blood turned to Captain Creech. He noted the

Captain's hands were bound in bandages. A look to Smee warded off comment.

"All clear, sir. No British man-o'-war or American frigates to interfere with our enterprise." Blood awaited a response from Creech. The Captain drew his Bible to his lips, closed his eyes, and raised his arms to the heavens.

"Then let us pray and give thanks to our heavenly Father for delivering to us this bounty that we are about to receive." The God-fearing men among his crew bowed their heads in reverence. Some knelt where they were. Then there were the few who dreaded the bounty the Captain prayed for. Smee, the nonconformist, did not close his eyes and was oblivious to the Captain's words. He peeked discreetly, remaining fixed on the fires along the shore now burning bright. Way up in the crow's nest, Mr. Toon, who was also watching the glowing shoreline draw closer, said his own prayer.

"Deliver us from evil . . . deliver us from evil . . . deliver us from evil." He whispered the phrase over and over, like a spell for warding off demons and devils. On the foredeck a mate cast overboard a line attached to a grappling hook, letting the halyard slip through his hands until the hook reached bottom and the line went slack. The mate then hauled the hook up rapidly, counting the knots tied in the line at measured intervals.

"By the mark, twelve fathoms!" The mate called out the depth of water beneath the ship. They were heading into the shallows as the *Sea Witch* drew closer to the shoreline.

"Hold your course." Mr. Blood steadied the helmsman,

peering into the coming night as the Captain continued to pray for deliverance. "Reef the mainsails," Mr. Blood called aloft, sending sailors in the rigging monkeying along cross-trees and furling the main- and mizzenmast sails.

James and Jolly R had, mercifully, missed the Captain's prayer. The mate's next call, "By the mark, ten fathoms!" was of no import to them. The two young adventurers had stolen below to the lower hold, a dank, dark place deep in the bowels of the ship reserved for cargo and barrels of drinking water required for the voyage. The single oil lamp offered virtually no light at all, but enough to reveal to James and Jolly R a perplexing sight. The length of the hold had been partitioned into large shelves approximately six feet wide. The space between the shelves was less than three feet. Four of these partitions had been fitted into the dark place. Ham-mering and pounding of metal clanked in the dim light. Swabbers, three of them, were hammering iron stay rings into the rib beams supporting the shelves. Manacles and fet-ters were being fitted to each ring by the three men.

"Here, you two scugs. Make yourselves useful. This is not the time to be taking in the bloody sights." Starbuck, the coxswain, startled the two boys. Mr. Blood's second in command approached, lugging long lengths of chain. He dumped the coils at their feet with a clank that echoed through the empty hold.

"Run these along the footers through every one of the stays. And be quick about it." He demonstrated feeding one end of the long chain through a ring at the foot of a wide

shelf. "Want the place to be all hospitable like, don't we?"

Jolly R was shaking so severely, the length of chain rattled in his hands.

"I don't like this, James. Not a smidge."

James curled his hand about the chain. With the other he fitted a manacle around his ankle.

"Neither will the poor souls who have to wear these. The cargo we're taking on . . . they're men!"

Suddenly, Jolly R heard the cries. He thought it was his mind playing tricks on him, caused by James' chilling declaration. But then James heard them as well—cries of human suffering.

Bonfires illuminated the strip of scrubby shoreline in a hellish glow. The *Sea Witch* had come close to the shore and dropped her two bowers in the shallow waters. A pontoon quay jutted out from the beach through the gentle surf over a hundred yards to the ship. The screams came from people being driven onto the beach and out onto the floating wharf heading straight for the *Sea Witch*. Their ebony skins were shiny with sweat in the light of the fires. Whipped and beaten, they were being herded like cattle. The warriors tried to shield the women and children from the sting of whips and clubs.

James and Jolly R stood at the bulwarks, both sickened to the point of nausea. This was the "black gold" to which Smee had alluded.

James stood devastated as the dreadful truth became

clear. . . . Could his father possibly know how his ship was being used? Was Lord B, his father, a slaver? Slave trading had been banned years ago by Parliament. The United States had forbidden the import of slaves as well. How could this be?

Mr. Blood had descended a gangway to the end of the quay in the company of two burly thugs, the ship's surgeon, and half a dozen others, all bearing sidearms. Each African was paraded before Blood for a most inhumane inspection. Lips were pulled back and teeth bared. Eyes wide with terror were examined for jaundice and signs of the yellow jack fever. Body parts were poked and prodded. Any of the captured with open sores, poor frames, or thin musculature were turned back. Some of them were shoved into the shallows and left to wade ashore. One proud young warrior refused to let go of an elderly sick woman who must have been his grandmother. When the whips struck him, he refused to cry out, glaring instead at the white man who was beating him. There was such hatred in his look and such dignity, James could not turn away as the young warrior took the beating. Mr. Blood stopped the driver, jerking the whip from his hands. This specimen was too strong and fit to torture. The young warrior was herded with his grandmother to the loading area, where "keepers" selected to board the ship were marked with a stripe of whitewash by the coxswain and loaded by the score into a cargo net. Hoisted onto the deck, the Africans were lowered directly below to the hold, where they were manacled, chained, and

forced onto the shelves side by side, like corpses in coffins.

A net full of captives swung overhead, passing by James and Jolly R. Fingers clutched the robe webbing. Eyes stared out at the crewmen who were guiding the net down into the dark hold. Women and young ones wailed, shaking the net and struggling to tear the heavy hemp loose. Others sagged under the weight of the bodies piled on top of them, resigned to their fate, their eyes already dead. James felt the young warrior's eyes on him, burning with hatred, before the net twisted away. James watched the African descend into the dark void until he disappeared. James' anger swelled.

"This cannot stand." James headed aft, paying no attention to any crewman who might be in his path. His eyes turned red with rage. Jolly R pursued.

"Jas., please. Don't be going off half-cocked about all this," he pleaded.

"This cannot stand," James repeated. "Someone will answer for this!" James shoved the barrel-chested coxswain from his path, riling the man.

"Bugger off, y' little rutter." James had removed the coxswain's cutlass from his sash and had it at his throat before the man took his next breath.

"If I spare you, you must swear you will learn to speak the Queen's English properly." Even though he was a boy, his stature and the demon eyes backed the sailor off at once.

"James?" Jolly R was shunted aside by the handlers maneuvering the next cargo net. He watched helpless as

James stormed the quarterdeck steps, cutlass in his hand, ready to strike. The Captain, hopelessly possessed, ranted loudly from the railing, spewing scripture and praying for the slaves' salvation. Smee sat on a stool counting the gold with two of the lighter-skinned men from the shore. One, the head slaver, was dressed in expensive silks and sat on a sedan chair tended by four Africans. His face was covered with pockmarks. The other, an olive-skinned skrag of a foreman James had seen herding slaves on the beach, read the look in James' eyes and went immediately for the cruel leather whip coiled on his belt. James deftly swiped the cutlass, severing the whip. Without missing a stride, he stopped before the slaver in silks and threatened him with his cutlass.

"This is a crime against the laws of England and all human decency. Stop this in the name of the Queen!" James was on fire, using all his self-control to keep from splitting the dandy from his throat to his bum. The slaver simply laughed at him.

"Continue the count, Mr. Smee. Your Queen's laws mean nothing here."

Mr. Smee swallowed twice, trying to find his voice, but all that came out was the clacking of his ivory choppers. In a blur, James flicked the strongbox lid shut with the tip of his blade.

"I suggest you tell me what authority you have to sell these people. Can you prove you own them?" James was now flanked by two other slavers flashing knives and

daggers. They chattered back and forth in an Arabic dialect.

"I have the higher authority, sir, and you shall feel my wrath!" Captain Creech had broken from his endless sermon to complicate the standoff. "The book of Genesis commands it. Chapter nine verse twenty-five: 'Cursed be Canaan! The lowest of slaves will he be to his brothers!'— Thus saith the Lord!" Creech held his scorched Bible over his head as if he were Moses carrying the Ten Commandments down from the mountain.

"There you have it!" The slaver was fearless, blowing smoke rings from his cigar. "Insh'allah." God willing.

James grabbed the silver holder from the man's mouth and ground out the burning end of his cigar on his own arm, showing no pain.

Mr. Blood, hearing the shouting, hurried back aboard and made his way to the quarterdeck.

"Scug, stand down before you are locked away yourself," he yelled.

"My father owns this ship, Mr. Blood. He is an English lord and cannot be a party to any of this. These are free men and women. This gentleman cannot sell what he does not own. I demand he be placed in irons."

Mr. Blood could see members of his crew slacking off the loading of the cargo.

"I'll have you charged with mutiny!" he threatened.

"Not yet. I haven't taken over the ship. Give me a few more minutes," James retorted.

Mr. Smee audibly gasped at the boy's recklessness.

Jolly R felt the overwhelming urge to cheer from the position he had taken up. Hiding below the poop deck, he could witness the goings-on. Mr. Blood tapped his birch rod in his hand, flexing it as he circled James, trying to get the upper hand.

"Free? I don't see any free men. They have been bought and paid for with this gold." Mr. Blood held up a fist full of the coins from Smee's count. "Smee, show the young Oppidan bastard the deed of ownership."

High up in the crow's nest, Mr. Toon watched the fight with keen interest. He knew the boy had pluck, but he had never expected him to go up against Blood and Creech. Toon hiked himself to the ratlines and descended for a closer view. Smee, muttering to himself, searched all his pockets and pouches for the deed, putting off the inevitable as long as he could. The little man could not look James in the eye. Mr. Blood snatched Smee's tricorn from his bald little head and handed it to Smee, giving him the dead eye.

Smee fished out a document tucked into the crown of his hat. "Oh, bugger me dead. Here it is. All legal and proper." Mr. Blood snatched it and presented it to James, snapping it taut for him to read.

"Go on, bastard. Read it."

James read silently, and the words raced through him like a burning fuse. One hundred eighty-eight consignees between the ages of ten and forty "fit and able to travel by sea to—" had been purchased for the sum of three thousand

gold sovereigns "on behalf of—" James closed his eyes, not wanting to believe the names affixed to the bottom of the document next to the red wax seal.

"If I turn them loose, how do I explain to your father what happened to his cargo and his gold?" Mr. Blood was enjoying his little moment of victory over James.

The young man remained completely still, trying to make sense out of all that had happened. He had hated his father all these years, loathing his denial of James' existence, but the man had still exhibited affection enough to send him to the finest school, provide him with an allowance, pay for tutors. Even Aunt Emily was provided for in a comfortable fashion. This benevolence, however cold and distantly administered, had left in James an ember of hope that his father might someday profess his love for his son and grant him his station in life. His Lordship was not capable of the inhumanity James had witnessed. Yet there was his seal and the name of his trading company.

"My father is not a slaver! He is not!" James shook his head in a vain effort to convince himself.

Jolly R slunk down in complete despair. He held his head in his hands.

"Enlighten the maggot, Mr. Smee." Mr. Blood clicked his birch along the balustrade of the railing around the deck. The noise sent sharp pains through James as he recalled his beatings at the hands of Arthur Darling. In this moment of devastation and despair, James found strength in the pure clarity of knowing exactly how Mr. Blood was going to die.

"Now, Master James, I don't want to be upsetting you," Smee said soothingly, "but seeing as things has come to this, there be a few facts of utmost importance concerning certain individuals—"

Mr. Blood exploded, rapping the little man across his bare forehead with his birch. "Tell him! Or I'll gut you!" Mr. Blood's hulking thugs held James in check with a brace of pistols aimed right between his eyes. Smee retrieved his spectacles from the deck and managed to continue.

"You see, your father, His Lordship, owns sugar and tea plantations in the W-W-Wes—the Indies. That being the case, he needs help harvesting all the spices and sweets to ship home to England. Especially since he's had a bit of trouble with a recent revolt among his . . . property. The workers from home just melt and die in the heat. But these, these . . ." Smee gestured to the last of the slaves being loaded onto the *Sea Witch*. He struggled to find the right word to describe them. "Consignees." Smee conceded, "Well, they're suited to the climate. They can work in the full sun in the full heat and sing about it. Without them to harvest the tea and sugar, think what would happen to all of England's sweet tooth." Smee trailed off.

"My father enslaves free Africans so that our Queen can eat sweets and petit fours with her afternoon tea?" A volcano was about to erupt inside James as he faced down Captain Creech and Mr. Blood.

"This is your father's money. We spend it in the manner he instructs, as we do God's work and bring his teachings to

these heathens." James openly laughed at Creech with all the disdain he could muster.

"Someday my foes may win. . . ." Then he ripped the deed cleanly in half and threw it to the ground.

"But not today!"

James rushed Mr. Blood, angling for a head slice. The quartermaster's stiff demeanor melted. He deftly parried the quick kill blow with his cutlass, binding James up and locking their blades.

"You think you can free them? Fool!"

Before James could counter, a well-placed blow to the base of his neck with a belaying pin swung by Blood's hulking thug paralyzed him long enough for Mr. Blood to look him right in his red eyes—

"Your father's a floggin' bloody slaver. And so are you."

James crumpled to the deck in a heap like a marionette. Jolly bounded up the steps yelling his name. Smee hurried to the fallen boy's side. His eyes, again deep purple, stared blankly at the seagulls circling in the night sky. He had a single clear thought—he should be looking for the blue star in Lyra. He had the vaguest notion that Ananova had told him he could find her island under the second star to its right. But the sky was all dark . . . there were no stars . . . and no island. . . . Then his eyes closed. Blackness embraced James and pulled him down, down into the dark.

CHAPTER TWENTY-ONE

JAMANI

THE DREAM WAS DIFFERENT on this occasion. All time had stopped dead. Was this the big adventure James had suspected awaited him in the moment of dying? Where was the afterlife? His eyes opened to darkness. His eyes closed to the same darkness. The smell of rotting flesh permeated the darkness. When he tried to move his hands and legs, heavy chains and manacles restrained him. He was bound fast to this black hole. He pulled on the chains to raise himself up and wake from this wicked dream. His head collided with a rough wooden ceiling only a few inches above him. A coffin lid? He banged his head again. Had he been buried alive? He could not breathe. His lungs

burned with the stench enveloping him. Now the black void pitched and rolled violently. He could feel the movement of other bodies around him, screaming and wailing in the nightmare. One rolled against him, a crushing weight on his right side. Then the abyss rolled again and more bodies on his left side clawed and flailed against their chains, smothering him. Lightning cracked, thunder boomed above, and slivers of light pierced down through the pinprick holes in the plankings and the hatches leading to the upper decks. In those briefest of illuminations, James could see people all around him, starving and dying. Their screams of terror were swallowed up by the next roar of thunder. James was not dead. That would have been a blessing. He was alive, chained belowdecks with the captured slaves on his own father's slave ship.

James had decided early in life that the phrase "Hell on earth" was an empty threat used by charlatans and priests to frighten their flocks. James had made a nuisance of himself asking his aunt Emily more than once after attending Sunday services if anyone could offer up even a scrap of scientific evidence that such a place existed.

He soon realized that people will believe anything and anyone promising relief from the suffering and injustices of living a mortal life. Better, James thought, to find the secret of immortality than to spend life investigating ways to relieve human suffering, the wages of aging, and the decay of dying. He could try to imagine the Heaven that these slaves must be conjuring under these most inhumane conditions to

give themselves any measure of hope. The island he dreamed of had to be more than a place in his imagination, more than a crutch he relied on in the same way Captain Creech used faith to justify crime. He would not entertain fairy tales about life after death and eternal Paradises in the sky, nor would his Neverland ever permit the enslaving of another. And James' Heaven would now never welcome his father or any of the men who profited from the selling of slaves. The Africans imprisoned in this hell must have included Kings and Queens and Lords, Princes and Sultanas—people of the highest honor and station in their lands. The brave men, women, and children struggling to survive on board this cursed ship were heroes in James' mind. James would carry their strength and their dignity burned into his heart for all time. He swore to himself that if he should ever cross His Lordship's path again in this life, he would bind his father in manacles and fetters and chain him in the hold of his own ship and let the wharf rats devour him. That would be justice!

James hardly recognized the voice that sprang from him loudly over the wailing as his own. The louder he bellowed, the more he liked the sound of his voice, and the more he liked his voice, the more enraged he became, until he thrashed at his chains like an inmate in a lunatic asylum. A hand black as night shot from the darkness and seized his arm, firmly pressing him back against the hard wooden shelf. James had been yanking against his chains so hard, the cold steel had cut into his skin. He was bleeding. A deep voice spoke from the void.

"Saburi, aki. Jasiri." The voice repeated the melodic phrase with calm assurance. *"Saburi, aki. Jasiri."*

The words were new to James, but he understood the intent. "Be calm, brother. Be brave." The darkness was so thick, the face of the slave chained next to him was featureless, but he was not screaming like the others around them. His voice revealed no fear. Two luminous objects appeared—their greenish glow originating from no light source James had ever encountered before. He thought he was hallucinating. The mysterious vision hovering before him resembled the glow of the moon but emanated from two rocks held in the powerful hands that had restrained him.

"Jamani." A face was revealed in the glow. *"Jamani,"* he said again. James understood the young African's meaning. Friend. James recognized him—the proud young warrior who had defied his captors and refused to cry out under the whips of the white men. He held the glowing rocks up to James' face and studied his pale skin, an odd shade of blue-green in the moonrock light. James started to speak, but the young warrior waved him off with a rattle of his chains and pointed to James' arms and wrists. They were bleeding . . . yellow. The warrior was fascinated by this strange-colored liquid leaking from James like candle wax. He reared back from James and jabbed him in the chest as if to see if he was in fact alive.

"Mauti?" The warrior mimicked choking himself and rolling his tongue to make his meaning clear. James shook his head.

"No. Not dead . . . different. I am James."

The warrior instinctively understood that James was in chains because he had tried to defend the Africans. He pointed to James' heart and repeated in his melodic accent, "James," then to his own chest with his clenched fist, "Azibo."

"Azibo . . ." James repeated the name and pointed to his new friend. Azibo nodded and offered the glowing rocks to James. They were cold to the touch, their luminescence welcome in the sea of darkness. Azibo produced two more from a pouch around his neck and set them on the shelf. They bumped and slid with each toss of the ship, giving the illusion of the eyes of some restless creature. Azibo revealed a small, rounded fruit with a coarse skin, like a coconut. The African bit off the tip and squeezed its juices onto James' wounds. The liquid stung, causing James to jerk back in protest; then suddenly, there was no pain at all. He held a moonrock down to his wrist. The yellow bleeding had stopped. The young warrior handed the fruit to James and gestured for him to drink—

"Nywa . . . ni . . . ni . . . nywa . . ."

"Drink . . . yes, well later, I think . . . Azibo."

James did not want to offend his friend, but he felt weak and sick and did not want to add to his present state of misery. The ship heeled wildly at an acute angle, causing bodies to slide until their chains were yanked taut. The screams of agony were unbearable. Azibo grabbed James' chains and held them tightly, preventing James from moving. With smothering force, the African jammed the strange fruit into James' mouth, holding it there, forcing him to take in some of the juice. James struggled only for the length of time it

took his taste buds to savor the nectar. Energy surged through his arms and legs. Where the chains and manacles dug into his flesh there was no pain as James felt the intoxicating sensation of being restored. The tossing of the *Sea Witch* no longer disoriented him. He was not even conscious of the ship's motions, as if all the elements were now under his own personal control—the power of the storm, the wind and the sea at his command.

Besides the surge of power he experienced throughout his body, the most startling effect of the nectar was to his vision. He could see in the dark! The masses of people filling the hold, crammed onto the shelves, and piled on top of one another were visible as if daylight had found its way below the decks. Colors did not exist, save for one—everything was bathed and outlined in a reddish hue. But he could see! He turned back to Azibo. The euphoria that swept over him, manifest in the gleam of his eyes, brought a wide-toothed grin to Azibo. The African pointed to his own eyes, then spread his fingers, pointing out to the world like a sorcerer casting his spell.

"Mng'ariza!"

"Bright eyes," he was saying. "Bright shining eyes." Azibo attempted to explain to James that they must use the shining eyes to find a way for his people to escape from this hell or they would all die. *"Mauti,"* Azibo repeated over and over again with grim tones, pointing in succession to his people stacked around the hold. Death. On Azibo's African island, he was free to herd his own cattle and learn the ways and wisdom of the native animals. Here there was

no freedom for the Africans—only *mauti* . . . death.

The novelty of his night sight turned quickly from an astonishing gift to a curse. James could see firsthand the anguish and terror in the faces of Azibo's kindred. Even when he closed his eyes to shut out the sight of them, their images lingered. The power of the nectar wore on for hours. James lay there cramped on the racks with almost two hundred others, James' blue-white hands and Azibo's blue-black hands linked by a common chain and a common purpose—escape.

Noises of the hatch opening in the deck head stirred the rows of legs and arms to life. The slaves raised their hands up to the streams of sunlight, shielding their eyes with one, begging for food and water with the other. James watched with Azibo as the coxswain, Starbuck, led the dregs of the crew down into the hold carrying whips and buckets of steaming gruel. The smell was so foul, it caused gagging among the Africans before they had even set eyes on the vile stuff. This was what the heavy iron pot had been used for—to prepare food for the slaves so they would not starve during the journey. The captives forced themselves to eat, but many immediately regurgitated the slop onto the floor.

Jolly R made his way along the rows, ladling out a cup of water for each. If any grabbed for more, the coxswain was there with a swift lick of his rod. Others carried the kind of short quirt normally reserved for exciting extra speed from a horse. Two lifeless bodies were unhooked from the chains

and raised on halyards up from the hold, through the hatch, and onto the main deck. The captives who cried out for their loved ones were beaten where they lay on the racks.

Azibo seethed a quiet curse on the men who would do these things to his people. James remained fixed on the coxswain, who wore keys around his neck. Starbuck felt James' eyes boring into him.

"Now what's little Lord Bastard lookin' at? Gone native, have ye'? I'm thinkin' you want to go cannibal on me, don't you, lad?"

James remained silent, letting the others draw closer. Jolly R knew that look in King Jas.'s eyes.

"*Mauti,*" James spat at the coxswain.

"The blue devil's already speaking the lingo. Well knock me dead," Starbuck replied.

"That can be arranged." James was never more sinister than when he was most polite.

"Feed him quick, now. He looks hungry." The coxswain sneered.

"For your blood." James licked his lips and rattled his chains, howling like a wolf on the hunt.

Azibo picked up on James' taunt and joined him. The other warriors, looking to Azibo, followed his lead and added their animal yowls to the demonstration. Jolly R marveled at James' uncanny ability to raise the spirits of these poor souls, inciting them against the authority that had enslaved them. He could easily have been rallying the Oppidans against the Collegers in the Wall Game.

Jolly R watched the crew back away, as fearful as the racks of Africans who gnashed their teeth and cackled like hyenas.

Infuriated, the coxswain marched down the row of shelves, lashing indiscriminately at the screeching captives. The Africans responded by hurling their gruel at their tormentors and refusing to eat. The coxswain reared back to strike James with his rod when Jolly R grabbed the man's arm, staying his blow.

"You want some of this sting too, scug?" Starbuck threatened the boy.

"No, sir, begging your pardon, sir, but the Captain doesn't want any marks on the bastard when he returns him to England." Jolly darted a glance at James, who smiled back at him.

"Good form, O.E.," he said under his breath.

"'E's never gonna see England again!" The coxswain brought his rod slamming hard across the bottoms of James' feet. The only reaction he roused from King Jas. was his impudent, superior smile. Starbuck struck again.

"Scream, you scug bastard. What kind of freakish sort are you? Scream!"

Jolly R grabbed for the coxswain's arm. The man wheeled and pummeled the Oppidan with repeated blows. Azibo moved with the grace and swiftness of a panther. Grabbing the beam above him with his hands, he raised his manacled feet just enough to scissor them around the coxswain's neck. With his powerful legs, he yanked the

coxswain back against the rack and was choking the life out of him with his locked ankles—

A single pistol report boomed through the hold, silencing the Africans. Mr. Blood stood on the deck ladder peering into the gloom. Smee was right behind him, along with the second mate and the two burly, armed thugs always in Blood's company.

"Mr. Starbuck. What's the cozening here? Someone doesn't like your cooking?"

The coxswain wrenched away from Azibo's choke hold, barely able to speak.

"It's these two here. The white bastard and this black one. They got 'em all refusin' to eat." Mr. Blood eyed James and Azibo from the steps, refusing to descend any farther into the stench.

"Of course. Who else would it be? Bring those two topside."

Jolly R looked at James, fearing what was to come. Starbuck lifted the key from his neck chain and released James' and Azibo's links to the main chain holding the captives to the shelves. Blood's two mates held James and Azibo at gunpoint as they were dragged off the shelf. Both young men could barely stand, much less walk, having been chained to the rack for hours.

"Oh, and Mr. Starbuck." Blood paused at the hatch. "If these consignees refuse to eat, they will starve and die, our profits will fall, and you will end up in a Bristol jail where I found you."

Climbing to the upper deck was an unexpectedly painful effort for James. Several times he dropped to his knees and then pulled himself up again to go on. Azibo tottered but somehow stayed upright. No one helped them, but instead lorded it over them, threatening with whips and firearms. When they reached the gun deck, it was Mr. Smee who insisted the two provocateurs be allowed to have a drink of water. The scrumpy nonconformist ushered Jolly R and his water bucket straight to James and Azibo in spite of Starbuck's protest. Both drank gratefully.

"You know what I wish, Jolly?" asked James when his thirst was quenched.

"I can think of a ripping few good ones that might prove useful about now."

"I wish Electra were here." James whistled, mimicking his pet, the spider. "I'd send her after Mr. Blood and then the Captain. She could drop right down on his neck while he's praying and give him a bit of the various. The end."

Jolly's spirits rose. King Jas. was full of fight and still plotting.

Of Electra's fate James had no knowledge. The last he had seen of his venomous pet was the night of his duel at the guillotine with Arthur Darling, which seemed a million years ago. He remembered he had dispatched the spider to deliver his note of challenge in a spun web, waiting for Darling to return to his room. Electra must have assumed her upside-down perch on the ceiling and waited for the vision of Darling and Rupert Wainwright to appear in her eight obsidian eyes. She

might then have pounced, biting them with her fangs until she had subdued them both or was stomped to death. Revenge was instinctive in the society of arachnids.

But Electra was not like the rest of her genus. She had a mind and a will of her own. She did not fancy ending up being stuck to the bottom of Arthur Darling's boot heel. And like Jolly, she was a devoted follower of King Jas. So she returned to James' empty garret room. All her kindred had been freed by James, so nothing remained there for the venerable *Lasiodora*. She followed the waterspout down to the next floor. A survey of Jolly R's room revealed that his belongings had been packed into a trunk and were ready for shipment back to his father's estate. When Jolly R opened his trunk to grab some clothes on his flight to sea, he found Electra, her eight hairy legs curled into her thorax in what could be called the undertaker's position. Jolly R was far more emotional at this discovery than he would ever have expected. Here this uncommonly intelligent spider, faithful like a good hunting hound, had had the good sense to secret herself away in Jolly R's luggage in the hope of being reunited with Jas., only to go eight toes up en route and arrive expired.

Looking at James bound in chains, emaciated and weak yet still combating his captors, Jolly did not have the pluck to tell him about the passing of Electra. He had carefully packed the dead spider into a tobacco tin and brought the tin with him to sea for some reason he could not decipher. Perhaps it was for good luck, or to bury her at sea.

"James—"

"This has the ring of a confession, Jolly. Save it. I have to remedy the current situation and I do not need your heart bleeding all over me."

Jolly breathed a strange sigh of relief as Mr. Blood had him moved to the side. Blood signaled to a crewman, who ladled up a bowl of the gruel from the iron pot on the main deck.

"Now, let's examine the situation." Blood directed the foul food to be held in front of James' face.

"I'm still not hungry."

"If you do not partake, then your native friend here will not. And that means none of the others will either. I've seen it happen. These primitives would rather starve to death than go to the plantations. Where they receive food, clothing, shelter, medical attention—"

Azibo had heard enough. He kicked the bowl of gruel into the air, spattering Mr. Blood's Royal Navy jacket.

"Make him eat or throw him overboard."

Blood's thugs seized James and held him as Azibo was grabbed from behind. Sailors tried to force open Azibo's mouth, so the feeder could attempt to shovel food down his throat. Azibo locked his jaws tightly, his teeth impossible to pry open. James called out in a commanding voice, challenging Blood.

"I am a citizen of England. A bastard, yes, but an important bastard! As many issues as I have with our current Queen, I am freeborn. And so is this man. I will bring charges of murder against you and every man jack on this

ship if he does not survive this voyage."

Mr. Blood chortled, not remotely concerned with James' hollow threat.

"Yes, I am sure you will. Right after you learn to fly. Let me demonstrate how free your friend is."

Blood ordered Starbuck to wrap a leather thong around Azibo's forehead and lash him to the mizzenmast.

"Ever seen how they feed the monkeys in the London Zoo when they refuse to eat? Hmmm?"

James struggled and fought in vain, knowing his friend was doomed to suffer another unspeakable offense.

"Speculum oris."

Mr. Blood signaled to Mr. Smee, who immediately tried to shrink into the deck and will himself invisible.

"Is that right-minded thinking, Mr. Blood? I'm not even sure I can put me hands on the particular instrument. Bit messy, that approach. Perhaps if I spoon some sugar onto a nice bun, we could solve this quandary."

"You're either with us or you're against us, Mr. Smee. I suggest you make up your mind."

The larger of Blood's two thugs grabbed the little man up under one arm, snatched his leather bag from around his shoulders, and tossed it on the deck. Mr. Blood directed Jolly R with his birch rod to fetch the bag. Jolly picked it up as if the bag contained a king cobra.

"The speculum. You do know what that is, don't you, boy?"

Jolly drew out a metal instrument shaped like tongs. He

held it up tentatively. Blood snagged it from his hands and presented it in front of Azibo and James.

"Time to feed the monkey."

James watched, horrified, as Blood forced the blades of the tongs into Azibo's mouth along the sides of the man's cheeks. Azibo clenched tighter, staring defiantly at Mr. Blood. The thumbscrew on the side of the instrument provided Mr. Blood all the leverage he needed. With each turn of the screw, the blades of the tongs were spread wider, forcing the African's mouth open. In this manner the last claim of power a slave had over his own body was removed. The coxswain fed Azibo until his mouth was full. Even then, the defiant African warrior refused to swallow in spite of the pain he was suffering from the pressure on his jaw by the cruel speculum oris.

"Be done with this. Over the side with him!" Blood made a dismissive gesture with his hand and turned his back on the whole affair.

"Noooooo! Murderer!" James tore at his chains, his commanding voice filled with hatred. Coxswain Starbuck and his sailors held Azibo fast as he was unchained.

"Perhaps you would like to join him, Master James?"

Smee sputtered his way across the deck in a rare moment of courage that would not be forgotten by James or Jolly R.

"Begging your extreme pardon, but according to maritime law, this is mur-murd—butchery. Any crewman who stands witness to this act could be found guilty of murder by the courts of England." Smee dug in his many pockets until he

found a well-worn pamphlet, which he began to thumb through. Crewmen stood about the deck, completely baffled.

"Is that right, Mr. Blood?" a sailor called out from the ratlines.

"That means being hung out to dry at Tilbury Point till our bones are picked clean. Just like they done to Cap'n Kidd," Pegleg Bumboo offered up as he pantomimed hanging himself. Uneasy voices whispered and muttered around the deck. James observed this break in ranks. The crew were not all men without consciences.

"Mr. Smee is right!" James called out. "If you let this happen, then you are all murderers in the eyes of the law!"

Mr. Blood took this in stride, assuring the men that there was no murder here. He made the argument that the "consignee" was refusing to eat, an act of suicide, which was against the laws of God.

"I'm sure the Captain can quote chapter and verse what the Good Book has to say about the taking of one's own life. Is this not a sin?" The more easily swayed of the crew see-sawed their allegiance back to Mr. Blood.

"This is not murder! We are sparing this human being the slow painful death of starvation. This is a merciful end we send him to!"

James and Jolly R watched in horror as Starbuck and the thugs dragged Azibo across the deck to the bulwark to shove him overboard.

Smee and several of the crew raised their voices in protest. Another voice shouted out an alarm.

"Sail! Sail!"

Mr. Toon's hail from way up in the crow's nest was a most timely interruption. He pointed off the starboard beam, a detectable note of glee in his voice.

"Off the starboard beam! She's heading right for us!"

Everyone herded to the starboard side of the ship to see the sight. James was never so glad to see another sail.

"She's English! I know she is!" James had no way of knowing this, but any ruse that thwarted Blood gave Azibo a few more minutes to live. With all attention drawn to the approaching ship, James was able to beckon Jolly R to his side.

"Don't say a word. Just move your head yes or no. Does anyone other than Starbuck have a key to all the chains?"

His loyal Oppidan swiveled his head no. James studied the coxswain as the thugs dragged the African back to the mast, where Starbuck pulled his keys from around his neck and locked the man's chains fast.

"That key is our only chance, Jolly. You have to get your hands on it."

Jolly R felt his gut twist and turn as he looked at the imposing coxswain, a brace of revolvers in his belt, barbed sword, and no less than three daggers hidden about him, one dangling from his neck along with the keys.

"Right," Jolly said. "Then what?"

James offered his most arrogant and confident smile.

"Fortune and glory, scug. Fortune and glory."

CHAPTER TWENTY-TWO

FORTUNE AND GLORY

MR. BLOOD STUDIED THE SHIP through his spy-glass. He did not like what he saw. The Union Jack flew from the fantail. A British man-o'-war bearing down on them less than two miles away. Signal ensigns were raised.

"She's on to you, isn't she, Mr. Blood?" In spite of the chains, James suddenly felt he had the upper hand. He yelled this out to the crew, causing a ripple of dissension among them. Mr. Blood glared at James.

"That won't change your destiny, Master James. I will see to that."

Mr. Blood ordered that James be chained to the mast

with Azibo, then climbed to the quarterdeck, followed by Starbuck, for a better view. They spoke in undertones so as not to be heard by the rest of the crew.

"She's faster, Mr. Starbuck. She'll overtake us in an hour. We'll have to lighten our load." He did not have to explain himself further. Starbuck nodded grimly, understanding what must be done.

"How much weight, sir?"

"Bring up four score to start. We'll lose them."

"Aye, sir."

Starbuck assembled a dozen crewmen, including the thugs, and descended belowdecks to carry out the macabre mission. The plan was not lost on James. He wagged his head at Jolly, urging him to act. Jolly R took a deep breath, hoping it would not be his last, and followed the coxswain and his detail below.

"Mr. Smee!" Blood summoned Smee to the quarterdeck. Smee had been watching Starbuck head below with the same growing suspicion James and many of the crew shared. If the Sea Witch were intercepted with a hold full of slaves, then they would all stand trial as slavers, down to the lowliest seaman. The laws prohibiting slavery passed by the House of Commons and the House of Lords carried stiff penalties against slave traders, involving both fines and imprisonment. But murder? Under the laws of England this crime was punishable by death.

"Inform the Captain that we are being pursued by a man-o'-war under the British ensign—they have signaled us to drop our sails and heave to. I suspect the ship is hunting

slavers. Port and starboard batteries will stand ready for battle if we cannot outrun them."

Smee hesitated, wanting to know more. He took to cleaning his spectacles, trying to find a way to ask.

"If I might venture, what if the Captain orders us to drop our sails and give it up?"

Mr. Blood remained fixed on the man-o'-war through his spyglass. His voice was cold and matter-of-fact.

"Then tell the Captain he should prepare to pray for the souls of these heathens when we . . . set them free."

Smee trembled right up his spine at the quartermaster's words and was summoning his courage to protest when Azibo's voice rang out—

"Uhuru! Uhuru!" Azibo continued to repeat the word at the top of his powerful voice. It was not a plea for mercy. He was not begging. His pride was too great for such an act. James could see this in Azibo's face. This was the courage of a great warrior calling out to his people.

"What is he saying? Does anyone know the language?" James called out to sailors around him.

Down in the hold the poor Africans being roused by Starbuck and his detail with whips and rods reacted to the stirring cry. Several whispered the word. *"Uhuru."*

"Shut them up! Get 'em above!" Starbuck commanded as he moved along a low shelf unlocking slaves from the main chain. Jolly R could hear the fear in the coxswain's voice. The crew forced the selected slaves off their racks under the whip and rod.

"Tell me when we get to eighty, boy!" The coxswain

pushed Jolly R down the row ahead of him. Jolly counted loudly. They had reached fifty-three. His Eton education had brought him to this moment in his life, being the only one on the grim detail who could count, right next to the man with the key that could free James. Jolly's sweat came from fear as much as the stale air in the hold.

"*Uhuruuuuuuu!*" Azibo continued to yell.

The sailor with the hollow wooden leg, now less full of bumboo rum than at the beginning of the voyage, hobbled close to James, pretending to check his bonds. James wheedled the man for information.

"I heard them primitives spoutin' the same gibberish on a slaver a few years back," he offered. "Right before the Cap'n heaved the sick ones overboard. One of the old Boucan, a Gold Coaster who'd been trapping the poor devils, said it's their lingo for 'freedom.'"

Freedom. Azibo was calling to his gods to let him die a free man. James took up the cry.

Two cannons reported from the distance, punctuating their cries. Two plumes of sea mushroomed only two hundred yards away from the *Sea Witch*. The British man-o'-war had closed to less than a mile away and had set off two of their cannons.

The first of the Africans were herded onto the main deck. Mr. Blood stood firm on the quarterdeck tracking the pursuing ship through his spyglass.

"Ready the starboard batteries!"

Gunners finished loading the nine starboard cannons and levered them into position.

"Aye, sir, powdered and primed," Cyclops, the one-eyed master gunner, reported. Muffled shouts from the Africans belowdecks echoed Azibo's cry for freedom.

" . . . Eighty . . . ," Jolly R practically whispered, regretting ever having learned what came after seventy-nine.

The young girl hiding as far onto the rack as she could fold herself clutched a doll carved from dark wood. Lion-mane strands had been added for hair. And two tiny uncut gems were embedded in the doll's face for eyes. Both sets of eyes were looking right at Jolly R. As frightened as the girl was, there were no tears in those dark, gleaming eyes. Only loathing. Others of her people echoed Azibo's cry for freedom around them as they were dragged up the hold stairs to the main deck. Of the crew, now only Jolly R and the coxswain remained in the hold.

"Letting the little wench make you all wobbly with those eyes, scug? A cobra'll do the same thing." Starbuck grabbed the doll from her hands and dug out the diamonds with the dagger dangling about his neck.

"I fancy these'll make my choppers all sparkly and nice," Starbuck said, baring a worn and crooked set of teeth. He held one diamond to his gold front tooth for show, laughing at the poor girl.

Jolly R watched helplessly as the crude coxswain held the doll up in front of the child and snapped its head off. Hate burned from her eyes.

"C'mon, wench. Let's see how big a splash you make, eh?" He grabbed her by the ankle manacles. The girl jolted at his touch and began to kick at the coxswain, making it

impossible for him to unlock her chains. Jolly R stared at the key dangling around Starbuck's neck. He was frozen, unable to move. The child's eyes burned into him as if she could sense his thoughts, and could see inside his mind that he wanted to act, that he wanted to help.

"Noooooo!" Jolly's voice summoned all his hatred for the coxswain. He grabbed the key chain hanging around the man's neck and pulled it tight. The surprise and desperation of Jolly's move drove the two slamming into the racks. Jolly tangled his hands in the key chain, refusing to let go. Starbuck slapped him repeatedly across the face as he fumbled for his dagger.

"Puling spawn! I'll end you—"

Starbuck raised his dagger to plunge it into Jolly R when a heavy chain struck the man across the back of his head with a noise that sounded like a ripe melon being split open. The coxswain stared at Jolly R with a quizzical expression on his face; then his eyes rolled back into his head and he crumpled on top of Jolly, flattening him to the floor of the hold. The man's eyes bulged and his horrid mouth gasped his last. Jolly R kicked and pushed until he managed to free himself. A large African woman shook her bloody chains angrily at Jolly R and reared back to bash him the same as she had the coxswain when the girl spoke:

"Katu! Mama yangu. Jamani. Jamani." The child pointed emphatically, shaking her head no to her mother. Jolly R seized the key and stood up slowly as he unlocked the woman's chains and then her daughter's.

"Whatever you said, I hope it's not 'Off with his head.'" He smiled. Jolly showed his further alignment with their cause by handing the coxswain's dagger to the mother and his cutlass to the African man chained next to her.

"*Jamani*," Jolly R repeated again and again as he began unlocking the remaining slaves. Even the weakest came to life as the chains fell away. "*Uhuru*" rang through their ranks as they pulled themselves off the confining racks.

Cannons suddenly roared as the *Sea Witch* loosed a broadside. The entire ship bucked with the recoil. Now the fire was returned as the frightened Africans huddled in the darkness. Jolly R heard the screaming of the incoming rounds splitting the air. He unlocked the rest of the chains as quickly as he could.

A round from the man-o'-war tore through the foreward staysail and splintered the mast. Rigging and canvas crashed onto the deck. Sailors immediately swarmed the debris with axes and blades, chopping away the lines. James looked up at the mast he and Azibo were chained to. Theirs could be the next.

"Fire!" Master gunner Cyclops spread both his arms and waved them forward as the cannons roared down the line with a return fusillade. The entire ship rocked on its beam as the guns shuddered. The man-o'-war still remained a good distance off. Mr. Blood was getting all the speed he could, but it was not enough. The Africans brought up from the hold sat huddled in the center of the deck under guard. With each cannonade their anxiety

increased. Azibo kept calling to them, *"Uhuru,"* and *"Ujabari,"* which James would later learn was Azibo's word for "courage."

"Run the plank on the port bow!" Mr. Blood sent his thugs hurrying past James and Azibo, carrying the thirty-foot heavy oak plank as if it were a splinter.

"Wise decision, Mr. Blood," James called out in his most sardonic voice, "so the prying eyes of the man-o'-war can't see your murderous deeds."

Sailors ran the thick plank out on the port side, out of view of the approaching British ship.

"I shall enjoy seeing you follow your new friend to a watery grave, Master James," said Mr. Blood as his thugs unchained Azibo from the mast. The leader reared and roared like a wild beast, riling up his tribespeople. But the thugs kept his chains stretched, forcing his arms behind him, keeping him tightly under control.

Mr. Smee stood in the Captain's quarters not knowing what to do. Only moments before, he had entered to alert Creech to the situation but found his voice catching in his throat when he laid eyes on the man. Captain Creech was prone in his berth, his hands folded in prayer but his face drawn taut in a frozen scream, his eyes wide open, fixed in a glassy stare. Unblinking. Unliving. His lips and neck were swollen and puffed out, the skin a sickly purplish hue. Poison! Smee had turned to go inform Mr. Blood but hesitated, thinking at any moment the Captain might snap

out of his dead sleep and berate Smee with an appropriate Bible verse. Smee ventured close enough to reach out and poke the Captain's bloated torso. The man was as hard as cold steel.

"Cap-cap-cap, Reverend Creech?"

A piercing whistle suddenly emitted from the man. Smee started back, tripping over himself at the sight of the fat, furry, eight-legged monster that trundled up on the Captain's chest and reared back on its haunches, baring its fangs and clacking its mandibles. Four pairs of large black eyes lined its head, and its thorax was covered in a bright-red fuzz with yellow dots that curved in the shape of a hook.

James' loyal arachnid had not expired after all! Electra! Alive and well. A stowaway on the *Sea Witch*! And now she was loose and on the hunt. The *Lasiodora*'s shrill whistle sent Smee backward to the cabin door. The beast hopped through the air and landed on the floor, heading right for Smee. Panicked, he fumbled for his whistle. As hard as he blew, no sound answered the piercing shrieks from Electra. Smee's mouth was too dry from fear.

Smee slammed the Captain's door, bracing himself against it as if he expected the feisty spider to burst right through the thick wood. Finally convinced the door was secure, he sought out Mr. Blood. But his words made no sense.

"A Mr. Spider . . . Blood. The Cap-cap-cap, the Reverend Creech is—" He was so scrambled, he walked right by James, who was screaming angrily in his chains—

" . . . De-de-de-de . . . expired. Gone. Poisoned." The little man finally got it out, thereby successfully ignoring the fact that Mr. Blood had forced Azibo onto the plank and the larger of the thugs was driving the proud warrior closer to the end with a trident. Azibo raged like a mad bull. He was not about to go to his death without a fight.

"You're next, Oppidan bastard!" Mr. Blood pushed right by Smee marching across the deck. Just as he reached midship, the hatch suddenly burst up, slamming into Blood and sending him spinning as the freed slaves poured onto the deck from the hold, swinging their chains about their heads and charging their captors. The surprise was complete. Slaves poured onto the gun deck and overran the battery and gunners in a matter of seconds. The mother of the young girl fought fiercely, knocking three of the gunners to the floor out cold. She raised her hand to strike again. Mr. Cyclops dropped his weapons and sank to his knees, awaiting the blow that would end him. It never came. The cries of "Azibo" turned her away.

A wall of Africans swinging chains and armed with cutlasses rushed the two hulking thugs at the plank. The big men were fierce fighters. The larger one swung his trident in great arcs, keeping his attackers at bay. This distraction gave Azibo the opportunity he needed. He lowered his head and charged back up the plank, driving his thick skull into the thug's lower spine. Before the slaver could turn around, Azibo head-butted the man in the back of his skull and dropped him to the deck. Azibo's tribesmen raised their tro-

phy above their heads and hurled the man overboard into the sea.

Jolly had reached James in the first seconds and was fumbling through links of chain to find the locks that held him.

"You might've come a shade quicker, Jolly."

"I forgot to stop counting at eighty."

James spotted a sailor above them on the ratlines taking aim at Azibo with a musket. James' cries were drowned out by the din. And then, sliding down the halyard from his perch in the crow's nest, Mr. Toon collided with the assailant and tumbled the man end over end into the ocean. Mr. Toon waved to James.

"I'm wi' you, Master James!"

Mr. Blood pulled himself erect again, shaking his head. All around him Africans had taken control of the *Sea Witch*. He watched as Azibo dispatched the one remaining thug with the captured trident and dropped the man to the deck to fight no more. Blood knew his time had come. Another round from the man-o'-war upended a cannon and ripped out a length of the bulwarks. He could only wonder what the British must think was going on, as their fire was no longer being returned by his gunners. He had one final task to perform before relinquishing his duties. Drawing his saber, the weapon of a true swordsman, he headed toward James, still chained to the mainmast. He would kill the insolent bastard.

"You!" Blood advanced across the deck toward James, his

saber slicing anyone who got in his way. "You!"

James watched the man bearing down on him like a great predatory bird.

"Get me loose, Jolly. Now would be good."

"If you could just hold still for a squidge—"

"I'm not Samson! These chains won't melt from my arms!"

"Bastard!" Blood contorted his face as his fury consumed him. The African who tried to attack him was slashed cleanly open, the cutting edge of the saber leaving a fatal wound.

"James?"

"Jolly?"

"You know that someday in the future when our foes might win?"

"What are you trying to tell me?"

Blood was on top of them preparing a stoccata slash right to James' face.

"I think you should know—this is *not* the day." Jolly R punctuated this news by yanking back James' chains, freeing him. James dodged to his right as the saber blade passed through his raven locks and buried itself in the mast. He yanked his hair loose with such force, he severed a long curl and watched it fall to the deck. James' eyes flashed immediately to that sinister red, like the eyes of a bat.

"I hope you're a better maestro di scherma than you are a barber, old man." James flung his severed locks at his nemesis.

James dodged to his right as the saber blade passed
through his raven locks and buried itself in the mast.

"Grab a blade and find out what you didn't learn in your quaint little fencing class at Eton," Blood challenged as he yanked the saber from the mast and pointed en garde.

Mr. Smee whistled to James and tossed him his shorter feder, a less elegant blade but just as lethal. The scrumpy nonconformist infuriated Blood.

"Smee? Not you too?"

"If he don't finish you, I got Johnny Corkscrew waiting for you." Smee waggled his serpentine dagger with dogged bravado.

Blood shoved the little man aside and attacked James immediately.

James deftly parried Blood's punta dritta thrust from the right, his punta rovescia from the left, and his ascendente to the head.

"Well done, bastard. You didn't learn that defense at Eton."

"One thing my illustrious slaver father did for his little bastard was make sure he could take care of himself." James attacked with a stunning combination of cuts and thrusts that left Mr. Blood defenseless.

"You know the Italian maestros well. But Viggiani and Grassi did not have a love for the drink like J. M. Waite. My deity of the sword. He never fought a duel sober," said Blood.

Mr. Toon joined Jolly R and several other crewmen and Africans, who surrounded the fighters like bystanders at a street brawl.

"Cut 'im, James!" Mr. Toon called out.

"Give him the blade, lad," Bumboo Pegleg urged from his perch on the bulwark.

Azibo pushed through the throng, ready with his purloined trident, yelling to his white friend to let him finish the fight. The duelists circled each other feinting and dodging, each feeling out the other's defenses.

"The British are coming, in case you'd forgotten," Blood said, toying with James. "The longer I dally with you, the closer they get. I'll end you with the great Marozzo's guardia di testa!"

Blood attacked, going for the kill, using his knowledge of the Italian sword masters. His coda de lunga slipped past James' guard and sliced him across the forearm, drawing blood. The crew reacted to the yellow ooze soaking James shirt. Azibo pounded the trident on the deck chanting, "Jabari! Jabari!" their word for God. Blood backed away, disturbed at the sight.

"What kind of thing are you?"

James smiled and countered with a sequence that backed Mr. Blood up the steps and onto the quarterdeck. James finished with his boot planted firmly on the hilt of Blood's blade. Blood stood completely disarmed and at James' mercy. The shouts went up again for James to run the blackguard through.

"That would be bad form, gents." James smiled at Blood, ever polite, and released his hold on his opponent's saber. Blood seized on James' good form. As he moved to

retrieve his weapon, he grabbed a gaff off a coil of line.

"James! The hook!" Jolly R bounded up the steps determined to stop the horror. Instead of picking up his sword, Blood slashed at James with the gaff hook. Jolly's warning had given James just the second he needed to turn, duck the vicious hook, and grab Blood's arm, fighting to keep the sharp point from gouging out his eye.

"Your good form will be the death of you."

"Someday—but not today. Jolly said so. Not today." James yanked Blood's torso around and now forced the hook with all his might toward Blood's gut.

"Give him the hook!" Mr. Toon yelled out.

"Give him the hook!" Jolly R pleaded the same.

"Gut the murdering devil!"

These last words came from Mr. Smee. All the years and indignities he had suffered being crimped into the service of Mr. Blood could be heard in his voice. James pressed the point of the hook closer. The two foes were so close, they could see their own reflections in each other's eyes.

"Go on. Kill me. You'll still be a bastard the rest of your life."

James hesitated, staring down at Smee and Jolly, Azibo and his people looking up to him, yelling in a cacophony of languages. "Kill!" Still James hesitated. Suddenly Blood snapped a small pistol from inside his jacket sleeve—

"Give him the hook! Give him the hook!"

James snapped from his brain lock and plunged the hook into Blood's abdomen, twisting it hard. Blood spewed an agonized laugh—"You can never change who you are, Bastard." Then he dropped the gun, breathed his last, and died.

A NEW FREEDOM

SILENCE FELL OVER THE ENTIRE SHIP. Azibo was the first to call out: *"Uhuru!"* James stood with the bloody hook still clutched in his hand. Slowly he raised the steel weapon over his head in triumph. Cheers went up. A reign of terror had been lifted.

But the celebration was short-lived, interrupted by a British cannonball tearing through the topsails on the mizzenmast. In the heat of the fight, no one had tended the helm. The *Sea Witch* was now drifting. The British man-o'-war was a half mile away and circling below the stern.

"She's in range, Master James." Mr. Toon raced up,

taking the helm, and tried to regain the wind in the remaining sails. "We lost too much canvas to run for it."

Azibo's people grew anxious again and began to wail. Azibo looked to James for some sign. Jolly R asked the question of the only person on the *Sea Witch* who had the command of the crew.

"What's going on in that mind of yours, King Jas.? Tell us what to do."

James looked at the faces of the crew and Azibo's people, all turned up to him on the quarterdeck. Fate had put him in command of the *Sea Witch*. "Surrender," he said. From the reaction of his shipmates, this was not the right answer.

"They'll send these poor blokes straight to prison till they can find out where they come from." Mr. Toon was adamant. "Most of them will die before the winter is over."

James was thinking out his plan as he watched the man-o'-war cross their stern.

"We're not really going to surrender," he said. "Just run up the white flag so they think we are and stop firing at us." James descended the steps to the main deck and approached Azibo. He looked the proud African in the eye and placed his hands on his shoulders.

"*Jamani?*"

"Yes. James *Jamani*," Azibo replied.

"James . . . *mauti*," James continued, using the word for death he had learned. He grabbed his own throat and mimed dying and collapsed to the deck. Then he jumped up

and repeated his performance even more dramatically.

"We all have to die!" James explained. "We all have to be sick from the plague and pretend we are dead."

Azibo got the message and began telling and showing his people how to pretend to be sick and dying.

"Master Cyclops," James addressed the master gunner on the gun deck in the throes of priming his remaining cannon. "Would you please ask your men to stand down?"

"We can still put up a good fight."

"Can you pretend to be sick and dying instead? Have your men stagger about as if they are all potty, then fall over dead?"

The old master gunner squinted at James with his one good eye.

"I believe I'm catching your drift, boy. You want them to think we're a ship full o' plague so they might be apt to leave us be."

"Good form. You are smarter than you look, aren't you, Master Cyclops?"

The master gunner grinned his crooked-toothed smile, accepting the backhanded compliment.

"I did a bit of theatrics in m' younger days," he said modestly.

James returned quickly to the main deck, where Jolly R was running up the white flag indicating surrender. He scanned the British man-o'-war with Blood's spyglass.

"They're holding their distance. Fly the plague ensign

as well, Jolly R. Let them think we are a sick ship." Jolly R
lit up at the ingenious idea.

"Topping swank, James."

"We need bodies . . . to hang up for the British to see.
Plague victims. . . ."

He stared across the deck at the crumpled form of Mr.
Blood. Mr. Smee was bent over him saying some last words.
Even a man like Blood deserved some final words. James
looked down at his hand and realized he was still carrying
the hook.

"I'll string him up for you," Mr. Toon called from the
helm, turning the wheel over to another crewman.

Jolly was fixed on the hook still clutched in his King's
hand. He reached out, beckoning for James to hand it over.

James waved him off brusquely. His knuckles had
turned white, as if his hand had been welded to the gleaming steel.

Mr. Toon tied a line around Mr. Blood's ankles and
hoisted the corpse, which swung upside-down from the aftmast yardarm. How ironic it was that Blood's dead eye
appeared no different in death from when he was alive.
James turned away. The main deck was now covered with
Azibo's people, in all manner of contorted positions feigning death. Azibo crawled about them, speaking assurances,
urging them to be *"mauti."*

Along the gunwales Master Cyclops and his gunners
were staggering about as if they had the fever, putting on
quite a show for the man-o'-war. The *Sea Witch* was looking

more like the ghost ship James had seen in their first days at sea. He could only hope their ruse was convincing.

Smee led James and Jolly R into the Captain's cabin but refused to approach Creech's body, still frozen stiff in his berth. He was quick to point out that he had never seen any plague like the Captain's. James probed Creech's swollen throat with the handle of his sword. The tissue was as hard as oakwood. So was his belly. Hard as stone. James recognized the repeated red-tainted bites all along the neck and face of the man.

"I'd be good and careful, Master James. When I went to inspect the Cap'n, this big mother of a spidery-doo come after me. Jumping like a ka-kang-kanga—a March hare it was. Practically flying, it was."

"That is precisely what killed him, Mr. Smee. The poisonous bites from a *Lasiodora* arachnid, I would venture." James had set his eyes on Jolly R, who looked everywhere but at his King.

"Did the spider make any unusual sounds?"

Smee seemed puzzled that young James should know so much.

"I'm not daft, mind you. Not yet. But the hairy thing whistled at me. It did. I'd swear on me mum's grave, if I had a mum."

James drilled Jolly R with his forget-me-nots, cradling the now ever-present hook in his folded arms.

"Jolly, my loyal Oppidan friend, did you forget to tell me something? Do we have a stowaway?"

Jolly did his best to explain about Electra's demise and how he had kept her remains in a tobacco tin.

"I've been meaning to tell you, Jas. Truthfully. I didn't have it in me. I brought the remains of Electra along with me. Why, I don't know. For luck, maybe."

James puckered up and whistled a shrill call. The answer came back instantly, like an echo. James whistled again. It was above them. Smee started as the furry eight-legged creature descended on her silky line of web and dropped onto James' hand.

"Electra!" The spider could not stop whistling and shrieking as she reared back and leaped through the air, speeding up James' arm and right up the side of his face to perch atop his dark curls like a crown.

"Now, gentlemen, our plague ship and crew is complete!"

From the deck of the man-o'-war the *Sea Witch* looked like a death ship. The deck was littered with the bodies of dead men. The Captain and a uniformed officer hung by their feet from the aftmast yardarm. A closer inspection of the Captain's face with the spyglass added to the horror. Bloated and bug-eyed he was, with his tongue swollen and black. And the lone helmsman lashed to the wheel was waving them off. He was so young. His long black curls hung about his face like a death veil. His skin was already deathly pale and bluing like a corpse.

Reluctantly, the British Captain closed his spyglass and turned to his first officer with an exceedingly long face.

"The *Sea Witch*. Poor devils. Down to a handful of men. Make a log entry to inform the Magistrate at Port-au-Prince. We'll let this prize sail on. The birds will pick their carrion clean. The sea will claim her in due course."

The Captain summoned the ship's chaplain to read an appropriate scripture. The man-o'-war tracked the *Sea Witch* for an hour and then broke off the pursuit and returned to its patrol along the middle crossing.

CHAPTER TWENTY-FOUR

THE PIRATE KING

JAMES REMAINED AT THE HELM feigning his slow death until the man-o'-war had turned away, and set a course heading south by southwest. Every time a sailor or an African broke from the masquerade and stood for a walkabout, he or she would instantly be admonished by Azibo or Mr. Smee. The scrumpy first mate added a newfound authority to his voice with the Captain and Mr. Blood dangling toes up from the yardarm. The stutter still plagued his speech, but now it was a commanding stutter. Crewmen listened and even obeyed the little man when he finally got around to saying what was on his mind.

"Mas-Mas-ster James. It appears as if—as if—as if

they're—" Smee managed to get the letter "g" out of his throat several times in an attempt to say "gone."

"We're free!" he finally blurted out.

The very concept was impossible to accept, even for the crew. Many had sailed under the tyrannical rule of the late Captain Creech and others like him for years. Some seamen had been conscripted into service and had no choice but to keep returning because their criminal records prevented them from crewing on the more legitimate merchant ships. Captain Creech liked his crews beholden to him for their livelihoods. By keeping lost men and boys crewing his ship, Creech had been assured that his illicit trade would not be questioned. If the truth were told, even Mr. Smee had a trail of questionable improprieties that had landed him in the Tower of London.

Azibo looked at James questioningly. James struck his kingly pose at the railing of the quarterdeck, overlooking the ship. All eyes were on him.

"You heard Mr. Smee," he said. "We're free! *Uhuru!*" James raised his hook in the air, triumphant. Cheers rose up from crew and Africans alike.

"Long live King Jas.!" Jolly R offered from the main deck.

The salute was echoed by several of the more liberated of the crew. The sailor with the bumboo-filled wooden leg stood on the bulwark and raised his peg leg in a drinker's toast. The master gunner, Mr. Cyclops, led his gunners to the yardarms, where the lifeless Captain Creech and Mr.

Blood hung, and released them into the sea. Another rousing cheer went up. But it was Mr. Toon who yelled down from the crow's nest words that would have a profound impact on young James Matthew Bastard all the rest of his days.

"Long live the Hook!"

James stared up at the hook raised in his hand, just catching the afternoon sun so the curved steel flashed brightly against the blue sky. The tribute rang through James' head, vibrating like a ship's bell.

"LONG LIVE THE HOOK!" More of the men took up the chant so that it echoed. "The Hook—the Hook—the Hook."

James paraded about the quarterdeck, pumping his arm up and down to the beat of—

"Hook—Hook—Hook—Hook—!" the Africans joining in now. James hopped up on the balustrade, balancing on the rail as he strutted the length of the quarterdeck.

Azibo began to clank and shake his chains in a rhythmic pattern. Many of his people joined the infectious clanking, making music with the very chains that had imprisoned them. Azibo sent up a tribal song in his mother tongue. The African voices blended with such purity and euphoria that Mr. Smee was moved to tears. Mr. Toon came down from his perch high above the main deck and, laughing and hollering with his shipmates, joined in the dance, trading steps with Azibo's people.

Jolly R weaved in and out of the throng with the coxswain's key, unlocking more chains and manacles and

repeating the word *"Uhuru."* One tall warrior lifted Jolly R up in the air, passing him to another and another before he was returned to the deck.

He was standing before the young girl from the hold. She smiled at him, the widest, happiest grin Jolly R had ever seen. Then she touched her hand to her heart and reached across and touched Jolly in the same spot.

"Uhuru. Jamani."

Jolly R flushed red. Pegleg Bumboo cackled from the bulwark, thumping his wooden leg on the rails.

"Hold on to your hat there, Jolly R. She is calling you 'friend.'" Bumboo added his concertina to the chains and melodic voices.

"Jamani yourself." Jolly R bowed, which sent the child into gales of laughter. She grabbed Jolly R by his key chain and pulled him into the tribal dance. Warriors and mothers, young and old circled around them, singing praise to the gods and the sea. James rocked back and forth on his heels, clapping his hands at the sight of Jolly R and the young girl spinning deliriously around the deck.

"Begging your pardon, Master James." Smee seemed distraught. "Spi—spi—oh, that furry thingy's on your head—"

Only then did James become aware of Electra. He could feel her gesticulating up and down on top of his locks to the African beats.

"Ah, Electra. My furry arachnid beauty."

James raised the hook up to his head. Electra whistled her approval and climbed on.

"I want you to meet our first mate, Electra. Mr. Smee. He is a fine, fit fellow. So be nice. I rely on him in all matters of importance."

Smee did not know whether to be flattered or run away. James delivered the furry beast to Smee's trembling shoulder, where she immediately stroked his gold earring with her thorny legs and hissed a loud whistle.

"She likes you. Good form, Smee."

Smee shook all over as Electra crawled up the side of his face and perched herself in the notch of his tricorn with a perfect view of the festivities. There had never been such a celebration aboard a slaver. Never before and not since.

And when the sun touched the sea's horizon and all the blues faded to purple, and when the banquet bread and all the Captain's stores had been shared with the freed Africans, the gravity of what had happened this day suddenly overwhelmed James, and he sank down exhausted on the deck.

"I killed a man today, Jolly R. I took another life."

Jolly had his boot off, rubbing lard on his blistered feet.

"Way I see it, King Jas., you saved a whole lot more."

"Is that supposed to make me feel better about what I have done this day?"

Jolly R thought long and hard. He did not have a good answer.

Azibo climbed the steps to the quarterdeck with three older warriors in the company of Smee and Mr. Toon.

"Azibo . . ."

"James . . ."

They bowed to each other. The reveling was over. Azibo was deeply serious, as were his escorts. He spoke slowly, trying to draw his words with his hands and gesturing to his people.

"From what I know of their language, the fellow wants to know what's to become of his people." Smee spoke without a stutter, rising to the weight and importance of the moment.

"Do we sail home to England?" Mr. Toon asked, acknowledging that James was now the Captain of the *Sea Witch*.

"England is not my home . . . Mr. Toon. We mutinied. That is treason and punishable by death. Correct, Mr. Smee? Not to mention the deaths of Mr. Blood, Mr. Starbuck, and four others killed in the takeover."

"We could throw ourselves on the mercy of the court, given the circumstances," Smee offered with little conviction.

James laughed at the idea of mercy in an English court.

"And what would happen to Azibo and his people?" James looked to Mr. Toon.

"Like I said . . . the fit ones would go to the Queen's farms until they could be shipped home, if that could be discovered. Most of them . . . they'd get consumption from the air and the rain. They'd die."

"Where do you want to go, Azibo?" James waved his

hook over their view of the Africans resting on the decks or watching the sun go down up on the masts. Women hovered around the iron pot, bathing the children with water warmed over a coal fire. James reached out his hand to Azibo and placed it on his strong shoulder, looking him square in the eye.

"*Makani,*" Azibo said.

The young warrior made a roof shape with his hands and drew a house in the air with his fingers.

"Home," James concluded. "Azibo needs to take his people home."

James cradled his hook, resting the point against his forehead deep in thought. "And we shall take them. How can we not?" he said after a moment.

"Aye, Captain. I'll tell the crew." Mr. Toon turned to leave. James gently hooked him on the shoulder and turned him back.

"Excuse me, Mr. Toon, but I'm hardly the Captain of this ship."

Mr. Toon looked young James in the eye, then turned to Smee, who offered no argument.

"If you're not, then who is . . . Cap'n James?"

"Captain Hook to you," answered James, trying it out.

Mr. Toon offered a proper salute and took his leave, calling to the men down on the main deck. James stood frozen at the rail, surveying every halyard, every crosstree, every mast, and every sail.

"Mr. Smee?"

"Aye, Captain?"

"Can we find Africa?"

"Easy as your mum's pie, Captain."

"I don't have a mother."

"Everybody's got one somewheres. I'll make way to set sail."

Electra chose this moment to abandon Mr. Smee and rejoin her new Captain.

The scrumpy man hurried down the steps, calling to the helmsman. James sagged against the rail. Electra crouched there, all eight of her eyes filled with multiple images of James.

"What are you looking at? How would you like to be a lab specimen, fur ball?" Electra whistled a scurrilous pattern that could only be taken as most obscene by another spider. James spun away from Electra, only to face Jolly R and Azibo standing side by side, neither able to suppress their grins. Azibo's mouth seemed as big as Jolly's head, his grin was so wide.

"How would you like to humor the hook?" James waggled his pointed weapon at them. Azibo waved Jolly R off and approached James with a serious face. He reached behind his neck and untied the thong holding the leather pouch. He poured the four moonrocks into James' palm, then folded their hands closed together around the treasures.

"*Maliki, jamani.*" "King and friend," he called James in his language. Then the warrior touched his open palm to James' chest, as his people did to show respect.

"Capp-tan . . . Jas. . . ." Azibo spoke the words carefully, trying to mimic the English pronunciation. He placed a forceful hand on the hook James held and raised it up between them.

"*Nahodha.* Capp-tan Jas. Hook . . ."

The young warrior saluted as he had seen Mr. Toon and Smee do. He continued to salute repeatedly and practice saying his friend's English name all the way down the steps and onto the main deck. At the first group of his people he came to, he called their attention to James on the quarter-deck and repeated the name again even more loudly. Then the big African taught the group to repeat the phrase in their singsong voices.

"I suppose it does have a nice ring to it. You'd never have to be James Matthew Bastard ever again," said Jolly R.

"That Oppidan died in a fire at Eton," James said.

"And Captain Hook was born at sea," said Jolly. "Take the name, Jas. It suits you. Think of the hook as Excalibur, King Arthur's magic sword."

James studied the hook as it caught the last rays of the sunset. He cradled the steel claw in his hand, weighing it.

"Jas. Hook." He savored the words, invoking the abbre-viation he had lifted from King Chas. II. "There is some-thing grand in the idea."

Jolly R watched his King and Captain standing on the fantail of the *Sea Witch*, fixed on the iron claw gripped tightly in his right hand. The wind kicked up around them. Below, his new crew, free Africans with free seamen, chanted

in at least three languages as they put their muscles to it and began raising the sails. Shouts echoed up the masts as sailors massed up the ratlines, monkeyed out onto the crosstrees, and released the flat-plaited gaskets, unfurling the main canvas.

The evening tidal winds billowed the canvas, snapping the surfaces taut. James could feel the ship come to life beneath his feet like a living giant rousing itself from a deep sleep. Mr. Toon called out the compass heading from the helm. Azibo beat the ship's drum and chanted a night song to keep them safe and make their journey swift and true.

"Yes . . . there is something grand in the idea . . . Captain."

Captain Jas. Hook regarded his Oppidan shipmate who had befriended him on his first day at Eton. It had been an awfully big adventure. And was most certainly about to get bigger.

"Good form, Jolly R. Topping swank good form."

One by one the stars winked to life overhead. Jas. Hook reared back on his heels and searched the evening sky for the blue star in Lyra. Ananova had said she would be waiting just below the second star to the right. There was this one particular island he would set sail for. He knew exactly what it looked like—every lagoon, every grain of sand, every magical plant and bird and beast. If he closed his eyes tight enough, he could almost see it. That lovely pool of shapeless colors suspended in the darkness. Then if he squeezed his eyes tighter still, the colors would become more vivid, so

vivid that with another squeeze they must go on fire. And just before they did, he would see the island—a place where dreams are born. . . .

Neverland . . .

"The end," whispered Captain Jas. Hook to his good friend Jolly R. "The end."

AUTHOR'S NOTE

All creative works require collaborators, mentors, and true friends. This book is no exception. And I would like to acknowledge those who have had a marked impact on my journey to this particular place. Most significantly, Sir J. M. Barrie, who crafted the venerable Captain Hook from his own life and his profound experience with the Llewellyn Davies boys, who gave him the spark of *Peter Pan*. Barrie's 1927 speech to the "First Hundred at Eton," titled "Hook at Eton," inspired the writing of this book and gave it a reason to exist. Captain Swarthy and Mr. Pilkington have definitely made their mark. I only hope I have served the evolution of Captain Hook well.

Mary Shelley, for her novel *The Last Man*, which set the stage, the language, and the life for young Hook at Eton.

Al Hart, my father, for supporting my writing muse with his patience and humor and his own brand of storytelling. Alice Hart, my mother, who dragged me kicking and screaming to the magical Jerome Robbins musical production of *Peter Pan* at Casa Mañana in Fort Worth, Texas, when I was eleven, and changed my life forever.

My friends at the Great Ormond Street Hospital for Children in London, Kit Palmer, Dona Selby, Nigel Clark, and Martin Sheehan; Sir Anthony Tippet, Sir Robert Clarke, Sir Robert Hall, and the Special Trustees, for entrusting me with the most treasured Barrie legacy.

Master illustrator, animator, and storyteller William Joyce, for his camaraderie, his inspirational conversations, and great days and nights in our hometown of Shreveport, Louisiana. Hey, Thomas

Wolfe was wrong. You can go home again. It's just different. And really cool. . . .

Laura Geringer, a wizardess of an editor, whose insight and unfathomable support can be found only in fairy tales and movies and, in this case, my novel. Brett Helquist, for giving his perfect illustrative vision to the words. Jill Santopolo and Lindsey Alexander for putting up with my endless changes. Robert Metz, for his meticulous pursuit of clarity for the existence of this novel. And Sterling Lord, my literary agent, who jumped in without knowing exactly why, and who remains the last great Gentleman in the entire publishing business.

My researchers and writing elves, Brian Suskind and Ashley Rudden; Stephani Cook, my friendly neighborhood editor; then there are the inspired spider wrangler, the many pixie dust suppliers, and Karl-Michael Emyrs, for his devotion to Barrie, and all that is and shall be the world of Peter Pan.

Albert and Elizabeth Watson, who believed even after Elvis had left the building. And to Miles Slater, for his perceptive conversations that taught me to hit singles and doubles instead of swinging for the fences all the time.

And, in the absence of ever being nominated for any prestigious cinema award, I would like to thank the following people for making my journey with Captain Hook from film to novel as much fun as a writer can have with those imaginary friends who keep me awake at night: Jon Levin, my devoted friend and advisor, who made it all happen via CAA; Stuart Rosenthal, my friend and counsel, whose advice and guidance keeps the boat afloat; Valerie Kerns, for the dedication and years devoted to making me embrace my storytelling neurosis; Nick Castle, for that first unforgettable flight to Neverland; Malia Scotch Marmo for believing in faeries; Caroline Goodall, for the first "Ballad of Captain Hook"; Dustin Hoffman, for giving Hook new life; Robin Williams, for the true Pan and friend he is; Bob Hoskins,

for inspiring me to write and write and write; John Napier and Anthony Powell, for showing me the powers of the imagination; Phil Collins, for his 24/7 soundtrack; and Steven Spielberg, for making it all come true.

David and Jan Crosby (and Django), for the magic voyages on the *Mayan* and the inspirations you are. Marsha, Zelda, Cody, Zak, Jack, Rosa and Linda, Jill, Lily, and Rachel and Bram, always my favorite crew, along with Chic and the Saxbe gang.

To those forces of nature, Judy, Jake, and Julia, the three J's in my life: Jake, my son, who at age six asked the magic question that led to *Hook*, and ultimately to this novel; Julia, my daughter, who always had the best lines and still does. Both write rings around mere mortals. And Judy, my bride, who has believed longer than most and remained devoted far beyond any reasonable or rational expectations. You are my pirate partner of my madness. You are and always will be my best story department.

This book is dedicated to my brother, David Hart, who left us way too soon and blessed me with this wisdom: Stop talking about all the things you are going to do in life and start doing them, because you don't have as much time as you think. I miss him every day. He is in every story I write. And to Michael Samuelson, a great philanthropist and humanitarian, who inspired my daughter to dedicate herself at a very young age to establishing the Peter Pan Birthday Club, which, like J. M. Barrie and GOSH, supports children's hospitals all over the world.

Thanks go to Cathy Rigby, for supporting our mission, and to my special PPCF Board members, with Maureen Lutz, Executive Director of the Peter Pan Children's Fund, for her dedication to educating, acknowledging, and inspiring young people to become philanthropists in support of children's hospitals just as Sir J. M. Barrie did with his gift of Peter Pan.

Let's see. Who is left? There is Peter Gent, my favorite writer and

king of the midnight e-mails . . . Ah, yes. Errol Flynn. Thank you for being my muse since I first watched *The Adventures of Robin Hood* on *Million Dollar Movie* one late Friday night on television in Fort Worth, Texas, in my glory days with all the Restless Hearts. Thanks, Mom and Dad, for letting me stay up late. . . .

After all, what would the world be like without Captain Hook?

Continued Happy Thoughts

J. V. Hart
New York
November 2004

EXTRAS

Capt. HOOK

A Never-Before-Seen Epilogue: Back to Africa

His eyes were blue forget-me-nots, burning like hot coals in the briny waters. His lungs were burning too, screaming for air. Jas. dared not open his mouth to breathe, or great waves of seawater would fill his lungs and he would drown. If he died, his death would, in Jolly R's words, "prematurely deprive the world of one of the greatest villainous saints in the history of evil." Jas. did not want the world to discover whether Jolly's words were true.

But was death the ultimate adventure? James had no time to think about such questions. He had to maintain his current course. The burning in his lungs and eyes would have to wait as he swam another fifty yards in the African coastal waters to the lagoon's shallows.

Ahead of him, Jas. could see Azibo pulling himself through the lagoon with powerful strokes. The moon reflected on the water like paint, spilling and spreading around the impressive gathering of swimmers. Azibo had assembled his strongest tribespeople for the two-mile swim from the *Sea Witch*, which lay hidden up the coast, offshore. The last hundred meters had to be swum underwater.

The young Masai warrior had made a pact with James: The *Sea Witch* would never carry another slave. Azibo was now a pirate, like the rest of James' crew. They were outlaws under the Queen's laws and could be hanged at the Bristol docks or condemned to rot in the London dungeons if they were caught. The price was high. James had taken a human life freeing others. He could never return to England.

The burning urge to breathe no longer gnawed the insides of his chest. James was suddenly at home in this liquid world. He rationalized that perhaps he did not need

EXTRAS

as much oxygen as his fellow humans, due to his yellow blood—a freakish oddity Jas. still had no explanation for. Someday a proper one would present itself—Jas. had no doubt—but . . . not today.

Perhaps he could swim far enough to reach his Neverland! He could taste it—the purity of the air, the freshness of the water! And Ananova would be there on Pandora, prancing in the gentle surf awaiting his arrival. James stared into the waters ahead, forcing his dream into focus. In a fleeting glimmer of moonlight, his island was there. Beckoning him to come! And Ananova! Just out of his reach! Air! He needed air! But there was none.

His lungs filled with water instead. James had stayed too long beneath the surface. In his oxygen-depleted euphoria, he was drowning. The demons that fueled his childhood fear of water now grabbed him and were pulling him down into the dark abyss, waiting to swallow him forever. . . .

Azibo's powerful hands grabbed James by his twisted curls and pulled him to the surface. When the young African had stopped swimming and turned back to signal it was time to surface, he saw his friend drowning and dived back under to save him.

Their heads broke the surface at the same time. James' starved gasps for air were muffled by Azibo's hands, cupped around his mouth so as not to alert the dogs in the Slavers' camp. James' black candle curls floated around his head like tentacles. He surveyed the coastline in the moonlight. This was not his Neverland. There were no mermaids. There were no mountains of exotic fruits and pure bleached sand. But he was alive.

"Thank you," James whispered in Azibo's tongue.

But no thanks were necessary. Captain Jas. Hook had

saved Azibo's life before—as well as his freedom. Now they returned to the Slavers' camp for one simple, powerful mission—payback. The Slavers, asleep on the shore, were about to learn a lesson in revenge.

Azibo signaled to his people, who spread out, swimming quietly toward the shore. James matched his African friend's strokes. He was relieved to see Mr. Toon at his other side. The midshipman had been the first of Mr. Blood's crew to throw his lot in with James' and join him in the "liberation" of the *Sea Witch*, as Mr. Toon politely referred to the mutiny. Jolly R's inability to swim had resigned him to wait on the ship with Mr. Smee and the others for James' signal to attack the Slavers.

A lone sentinel fire sputtered and crackled on the beach ahead. James could feel the sand beneath his feet. Quietly, the raiding party's legs began to churn, pushing against the lagoon's spongy floor, gaining momentum until, like wraiths rising from watery graves, James and Azibo's shadow army emerged from the moonlit waters and moved toward the encampment in silence.

Their war clubs were raised off their backs, each weapon decorated with personal symbols: prayers for strength in battle, warnings to foes, the marks of the warrior's tribe. James pulled out his own talisman. The gaff hook gleamed in his upraised hand, catching the moonbeams as he marched up the beach.

Many of the Slavers never rose from their mats before they were beaten and pummeled by the angry Africans who had come to mete out justice. James bolted through the array of thatched and mud huts like a banshee, his hook flashing as he cut and slashed the men who had kidnapped Azibo's people and sold them for a mountain of gold.

A mile away, at the mouth of the lagoon, the *Sea Witch* waited. Jolly R watched for the signal from his lookout perch high up on the mainmast. Intently, he studied the shore of the lagoon through Mr. Blood's spyglass. There it was: James' signal. A fiery plume lit the sky before the sound of the exploding powder stores echoed across the lagoon.

"Heavy at it, Mr. Smee! They made it!"

Mr. Smee took a moment to sigh, deeply relieved at this news, before taking action. Then, huffing his breath on his spectacles and giving them a wipe, he called down without a smidge of a stutter to the master gunner.

"Have at them, Mr. Winchester!"

Winchester delivered the command that began a chain reaction of explosions. The port-side battery boomed, sending a barrage of cannonballs across the lagoon. The pattern of splashes two-hundred yards offshore would not harm Azibo and Hook's raiding party, but the barrage wreaked havoc on the Slavers, who were trying to escape in jollyboats and canoes.

Azibo raced through the camp like a mad rhino, chopping open stockade gates with his war club, freeing Africans by the score. He searched the grateful faces rushing past him as they fled to freedom. But the one face he was looking for was not there. Finally, a voice cried out his name. Azibo's frantic search was over. The woman he had been praying to Enkai would still be alive raised her arms to him. His mother! Though injured, she rose and Azibo helped her out into the fresh air of freedom.

James witnessed Azibo's emotional reunion with his mother, his own heart breaking. How different would his life have been had he known his real mother? He watched as Azibo walked forward with his mother and proudly

presented her to James. James responded with a low bow of deep respect and spoke a proper Masai greeting. Azibo's mother wept and touched his long curls.

"En-kashomi," Azibo's mother said softly, *Family*. James understood. Azibo's people were freed and could now go home to their families. Capt. James Hook was still in search of his—

Jolly R arrived with the rest of the crew of the *Sea Witch* and promptly rounded up the remaining slavers. Azibo could hardly contain his people from pulling their former torturers apart. Jolly was particularly pleased with the little surprise he delivered to James with a mischievous grin.

"I saved this one for you, Jas. Just in case you might be feelin' merciful," he said.

A woman wrapped in the bright colors of Azibo's tribe hung her head, trying to hide. Smee, traditionally effete where women were concerned, angrily poked the woman with Johnny Corkscrew, herding her forward.

"Why don't you show the Cap'n your pretty face?" he taunted.

Before the enshrouded lady could protest, James curled his hook inside the woman's headdress and yanked it back. The young Captain was face to face with the Moor, the pock-marked, crater-faced slaver who had counted each piece of gold before handing over the pounds and pounds of flesh to be chained and imprisoned on the *Sea Witch*.

"You're giving these women a bad name, I'd say." James hardly needed to point out the sneer of hatred on Azibo's mother's face. Other women angrily joined in, jeering at the Moor and calling him names. Azibo's mum, aided by several other women, relieved the slaver of the colorful tribal clothing he was hiding in.

The Moor, outnumbered by righteously indignant mothers

EXTRAS

and daughters, remained defiant. "You!" he screamed at James. "You brought them back? Why?"

"I suppose I must have a soft spot for mothers. My friend here, Azibo—he just went through hell to get to his mum."

"He should've stayed there," the Moor spat.

"On that point, we disagree," James said, ever so politely. Then James placed the tip of his hook just inside the Moor's nostril and led him into the shallows. The mothers and other women wanted their revenge, but James had decided the slaver's fate. For his crimes against humanity, James ordered the Moor be set adrift in a jolly boat with a cask of fresh water, and no ale or weapon of any kind. Mr. Toon would see the man out of the lagoon until he caught the Gulf Stream, and then leave him. If the Moor was fortunate enough to be picked up by a merchant or warship, he was to deliver a message to its captain:

"Captain James Hook of the *Sea Witch* sends his compliments and a warning to Lord B: He will pay for all his injustices against his own flesh and blood, and the blood of others, with his own. Captain Hook suggests that Lord B sleep with one eye open, for he has been marked for judgment day."

Mr. Toon and Smee herded the slaver into the jollyboat and lashed him to the oarlocks, forcing him to row. Jolly R dropped the water keg on the Moor's toes as they pushed him adrift.

"You think you are God, boy? Do you?" the Moor screeched as he was guided into the lagoon.

James struck a confident pose, his hook and elbow cocked, and laughed.

"Someday, I might be God. . . ."

"But . . ." Jolly R chimed.

". . . but not today!!!" The two friends finished in unison. Mr. Smee, along with Mr. Toon and the rest of the crew of the *Sea Witch*, echoed their familiar phrase. Azibo joined in with a chant, praising Enkai. He hammered his war clubs together in a rhythmic cadence, praising James and calling him *"El-anjarie kuna! El-aeterani! El-appuroni!"* More of his warriors picked up the cry and began a slow, methodical dance through the encampment.

Mr. Smee and Mr. Toon joined in translation: "BROTHER—PIRATE—KING!"

Bammity bam!

"BROTHER! PIRATE! KING!"

Bammity bam!

"Got a feelin' that's gonna stick, King Jas.," Smee said with a wink.

"The End." Jolly R punctuated his agreement with Jas.' own phrase.

And Jas., the Pirate King, flashed his forget-me-not eyes and smiled.

Sultana Ananova's Letter to James

Dear James,

I am almost home. We have passed into the Aegean and will soon arrive in Crete, far away from you. But the distance doesn't mean I think of you any less. I dreamed last night that we were afloat on an iceberg that had found its way to warmer waters. And then our island of ice separated. We held hands as we floated along, talking and laughing and speaking of our dreams. But before we knew it, our hands no longer touched, and we drifted slowly apart, until we watched each other wave, you on your island and me on mine.

I do not want to lose you, James. I do not want to float so very far away. Whenever you need me, just look into the starry sky and know I am doing the same.

My island will be torn by conflict when I return. The coming revolution will place me in opposition to my family—especially my father. I see now that his rules and laws oppress any who do not agree with him. The revolutionaries say my youth is my enemy. But if I grow up to be like my father, then I would rather not grow up at all. There must be a way to remain forever young. Perhaps together we can find it.

Do you remember the story of Eurydice and Orpheus? When Orpheus went down into Hell to find the woman he loved, he was permitted to bring her back to the earthly world by Hades. But Hades made one condition: Orpheus was never to look upon her face again or he would lose her forever. Because of this, Eurydice began to cry. And when Orpheus turned to dry her tears, Hades pulled her back into the underworld. Eurydice's last words to Orpheus

were: "Love is standing in Hell with your arms open wide. . . ." I feel that way too.

Wherever you are in this world, James, I hope this letter finds you. Find my island so we can find yours.

Yours always,
Ananova

Letter to the *Eton Chronicle* from King Jas., Oppidan

Dear Editor,

Any Eton Blood of good form has by now been reeled and rocked by the news of the unfathomable Oppidan victory over the Collegers in the traditional St. Andrews Day Wall Game match, the first in the entire history of the game since its inception in the seventeenth century. With not even a smidge of modesty or humility, I am proud to say this historic match also resulted in the first goal scored by an Oppidan in over a century of play. Good form, Jolly R.

But what is the point of this violent, brutal competition? Bragging rights? A kingdom toppled? Death? Were it left to Arthur Darling, Colleger captain, I would no doubt have been left as a yellow smear of tissue and bone on the wall itself. When Harry VI founded Eton and this game arose, was it to educate Etonians to the hells of combat in the wars adults were waging? The wars we will hunger to ignite when we achieve the status of grown-up?

Compare the Wall Game to the ancient ball game of the Mayans and the Aztecs, called "Poc-ta-pok." According to recent archaeological findings at the Mayan city of Chiche'n Itza in Mexico by Sir James Wellington, warriors played this violent game in a huge arena, wearing armor and engaging in play for days until a victor emerged. As many as thirty thousand players once participated in a fortnight-long match. According to legend, the captain of the winning team would present his head to the losing captain, who would then decapitate the victor. Is this the epitome of good form?

It seems the Mayans considered this a direct and most speedy stairway to heaven, circumventing the thirteen

steps otherwise necessary to endure before reaching the ultimate reward.

I would propose that this is precisely what the Wall Game is lacking: a proper reward for winners and losers. A guillotine erected on the pitch for a good lopping and seeing a few heads roll would be far more satisfying and illuminating than stuffing ourselves with sweet sock and pudding. And certainly more civilized than the horrors of war.

For a final flourish and fanfare for all Eton Bloods, I would suggest that the heads of the participating Collegers and Oppidans be displayed along the top of the wall as a proper tribute to the heroics and great traditions that shall ever place Eton at the pinnacle of civilized education.

If death is the ultimate adventure, according to Aristotle, then what is the Wall Game, really, without the ultimate reward?

Let it be known that Jas. Hook will gladly provide the guillotine, if Arthur Darling will provide his head.

To die will be an awfully big adventure.

Floreat Etona,
King Jas.

The Rules Of The Wall Game

Length of Game: The games of St. Andrew's Day and Ascension Day last two complete half-hours. The length of other games should be agreed between Umpires and opposing captains.

The Toss: The captain that wins the toss decides whether to play toward the Good or Bad Calx in the first half.

The Beginning: The first bully forms under the Ladder, the team playing toward the Good Calx having "heads."

Ten and Fifteen Yard Offences:
Furking: No player may intentionally move the ball backward, except in Calx

In Calx:
Good Calx: The bully is formed opposite where the ball becomes dead unless at a point beyond the Stone, in which case the bully is always formed under the Stone. If ten yards are given against the defenders within ten yards of the Stone, the bully shall be formed under the Stone.

A Shy: A shy is got when an attacking player touches the ball with his hand below the wrist (the ball being supported against the Wall, fully off the ground, by any player on his own team with any part of his leg below the knee), and claims the shy with the words "Got it!" The garden wall is considered a continuation of the Wall. The hands and feet of the player supporting the ball, the player touching it, and the ball itself must be fully inside the Calx line.

The player touching the ball must be facing his opponents or facing the door if the ball is against the garden wall. A player may also claim a shy in Good Calx if while within the Furrow he kicks the ball against the garden wall and catches the rebound before the ball touches the ground.

When a Shy Is Claimed: When a shy is claimed, the bully must stop moving at once and break as instructed by the Umpire. The Umpire calls "Shy!" if he is happy that the claim is a fair one. If the defending side continues to play after the Umpire has told them to stop and, in the opinion of the Umpire, prevents a shy being claimed, the Umpire shall award a penalty shy.

Penalty Shy: No player on the defending side within the Furrow may deliberately attempt to prevent or obstruct the toucher from throwing the ball. Nor may the defending side continue to play if the toucher calls "Got it!" In each case, the toucher shall be allowed a penalty shy at goal during which all the players on both sides must be within the Furrow and behind the thrower. A goal scored in this way is a penalty goal.

Summary of Scoring:
Thrown Goal: 10 points
Kicked Goal or Penalty Goal: 5 points
Shy but no Goal: 1 point

These are some of the official rules of the Wall Game. To see the complete rules, please visit www.etoncollege.com

EXTRAS

A Map of Capt. Hook's Journey

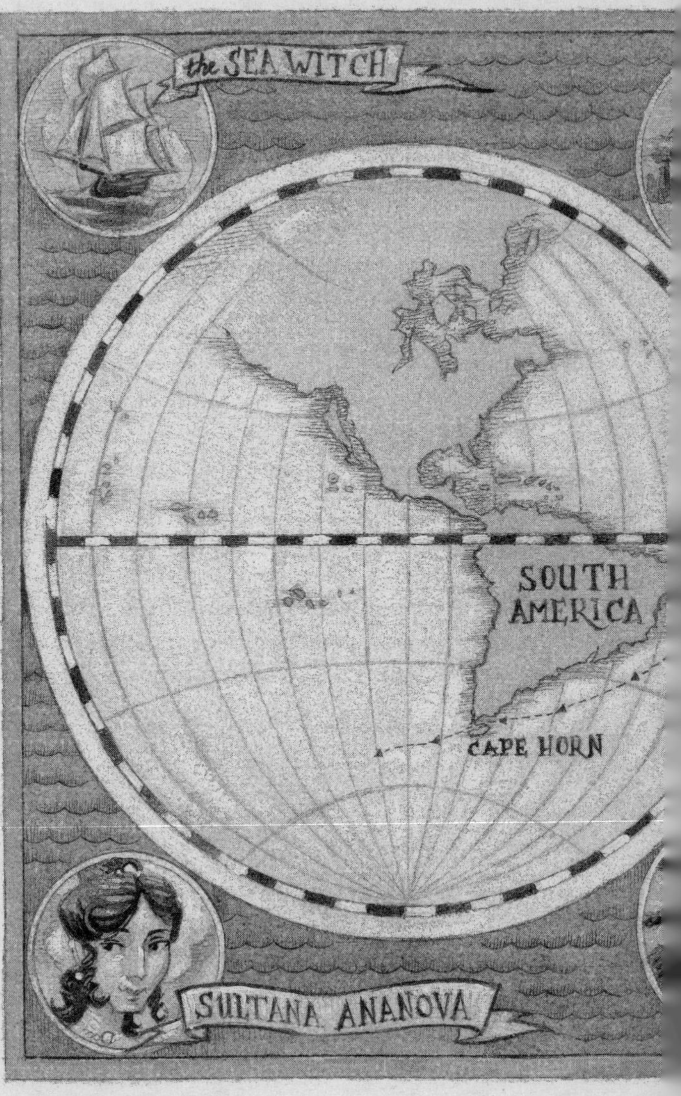

the SEA WITCH
SOUTH AMERICA
CAPE HORN
SULTANA ANANOVA

sequel, *Capt. Hook: Pirate King*

the MEPHISTOPHELES

ENGLAND

THYRA

AFRICA

IVORY COAST

CONGO

THE VOYAGES OF

Capt. Jas. Hook

EXTRAS

To learn more about Captain Hook, Peter Pan,
author J. V. Hart, and illustrator Brett Helquist,
visit www.thecaptainhookbook.com.

STOP.

You're reading the wrong way.

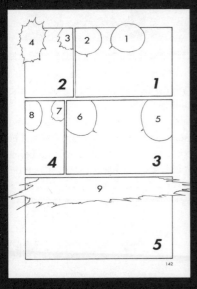

In keeping with the original Japanese comic format, this book reads from right to left—so action, sound effects and word balloons are completely reversed to preserve the orientation of the original artwork.

Check out the diagram shown here to get the hang of things, and then turn to the other side of the book to get started!

Behind the Scenes!!

STORY AND ART BY BISCO HATORI

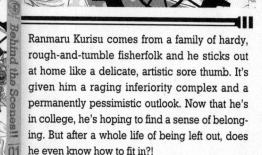

Ranmaru Kurisu comes from a family of hardy, rough-and-tumble fisherfolk and he sticks out at home like a delicate, artistic sore thumb. It's given him a raging inferiority complex and a permanently pessimistic outlook. Now that he's in college, he's hoping to find a sense of belonging. But after a whole life of being left out, does he even know how to fit in?!

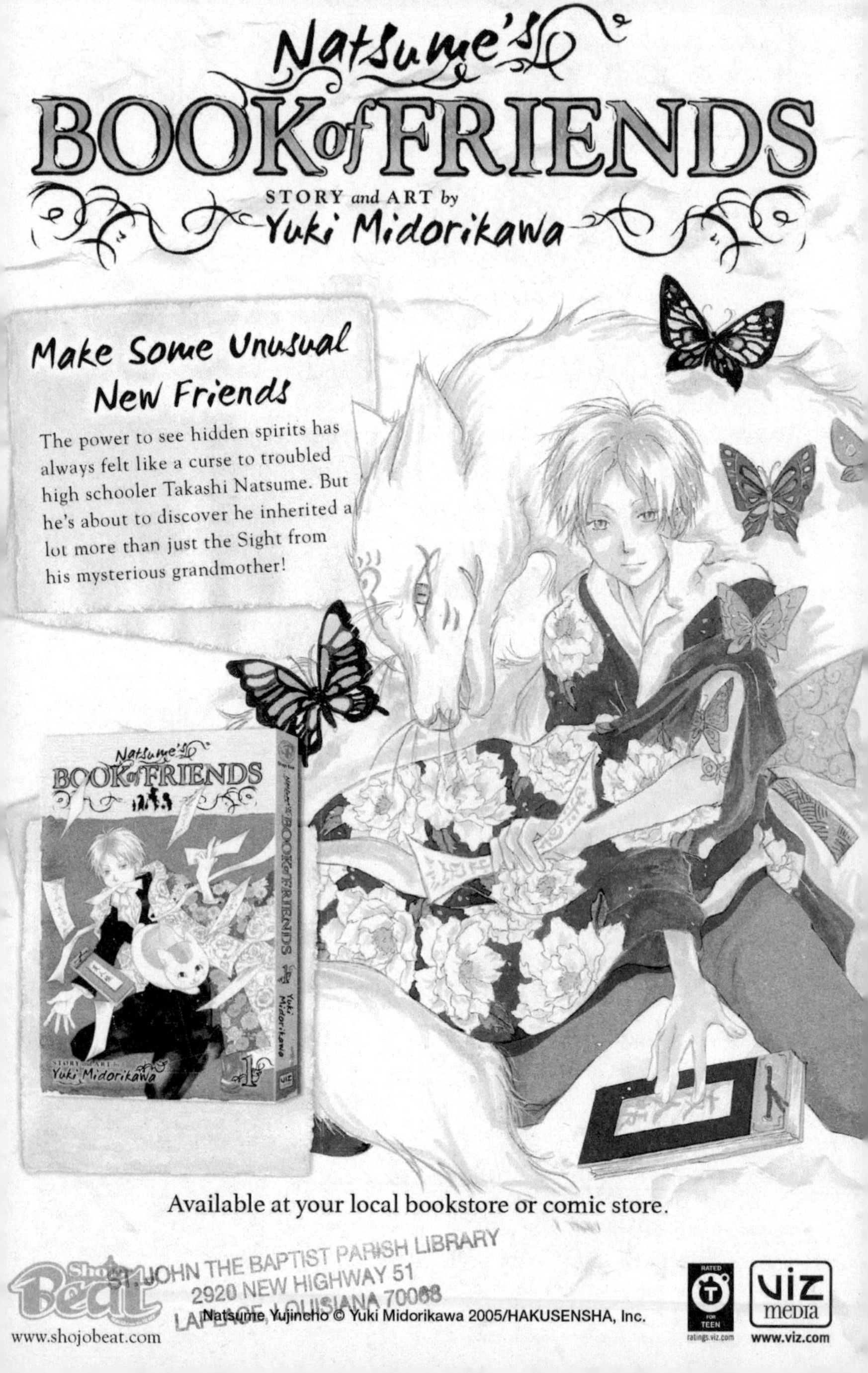
Natsume's BOOK of FRIENDS
STORY and ART by
Yuki Midorikawa
Make Some Unusual New Friends
The power to see hidden spirits has always felt like a curse to troubled high schooler Takashi Natsume. But he's about to discover he inherited a lot more than just the Sight from his mysterious grandmother!
Natsume's BOOK of FRIENDS
STORY and ART by
Yuki Midorikawa
Available at your local bookstore or comic store.
Shojo Beat
www.shojobeat.com
Natsume Yujincho © Yuki Midorikawa 2005/HAKUSENSHA, Inc.
RATED T FOR TEEN
ratings.viz.com
VIZ media
www.viz.com

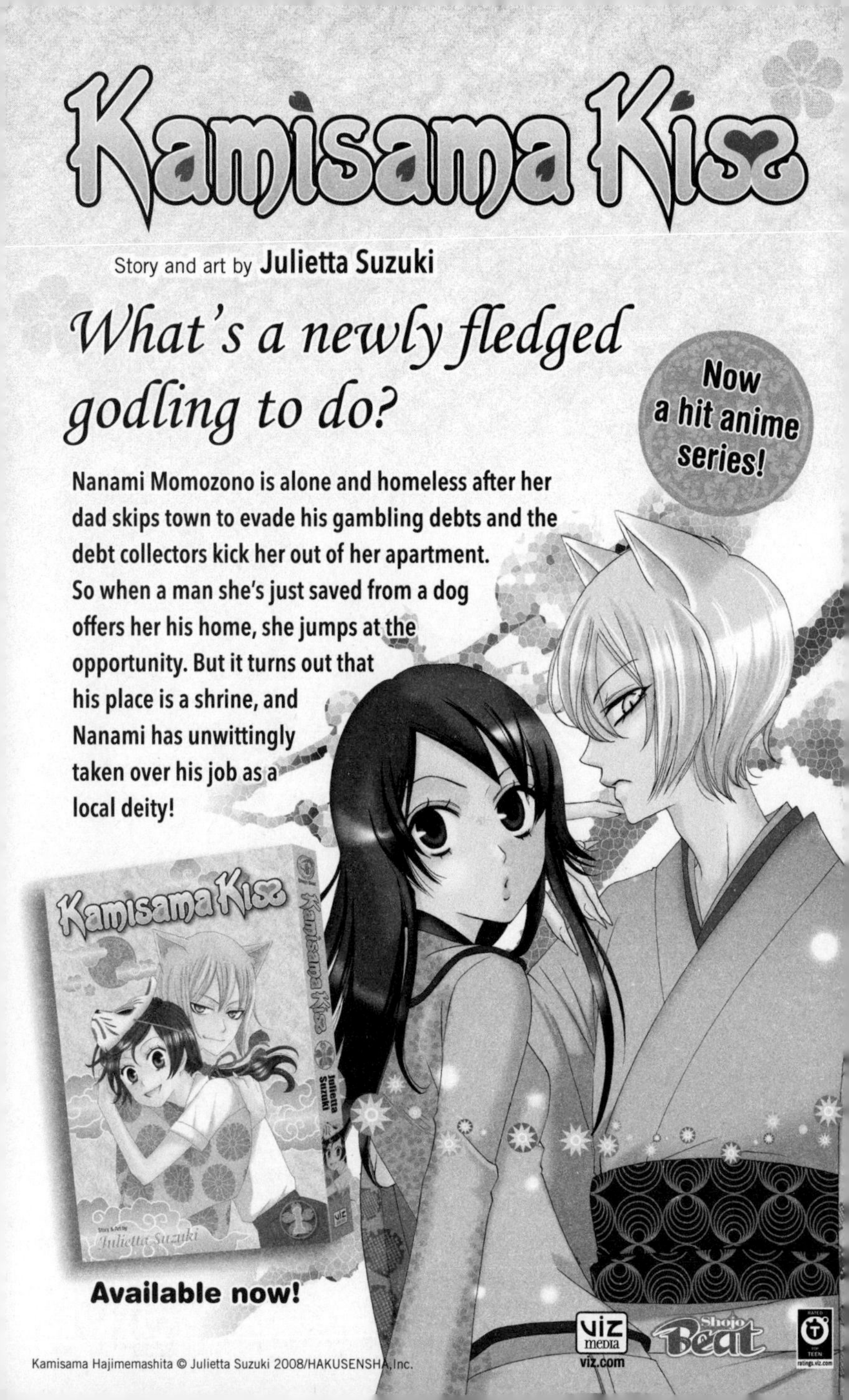
Kamisama Kiss
Story and art by Julietta Suzuki
What's a newly fledged godling to do?
Now a hit anime series!
Nanami Momozono is alone and homeless after her dad skips town to evade his gambling debts and the debt collectors kick her out of her apartment. So when a man she's just saved from a dog offers her his home, she jumps at the opportunity. But it turns out that his place is a shrine, and Nanami has unwittingly taken over his job as a local deity!
Kamisama Kiss
Julietta Suzuki
Available now!
viz media
viz.com
Shojo Beat
Kamisama Hajimemashita © Julietta Suzuki 2008/HAKUSENSHA, Inc.

IDOL dreams

STORY & ART BY ARINA TANEMURA

At age 31, office worker Chikage Deguchi feels she missed her chances at love and success. When word gets out that she's a virgin, Chikage is humiliated and wishes she could turn back time to when she was still young and popular. She takes an experimental drug that changes her appearance back to when she was 15. Now Chikage is determined to pursue everything she missed out on all those years ago—including becoming a star!

Nino Arisugawa, a girl who loves to sing, experiences her first heart-wrenching goodbye when her beloved childhood friend, Momo, moves away. And after Nino befriends Yuzu, a music composer, she experiences another sad parting! With music as their common ground and only outlet, how will everyone's unrequited loves play out?

ANONYMOUS NOISE

Story & Art by
Ryoko Fukuyama

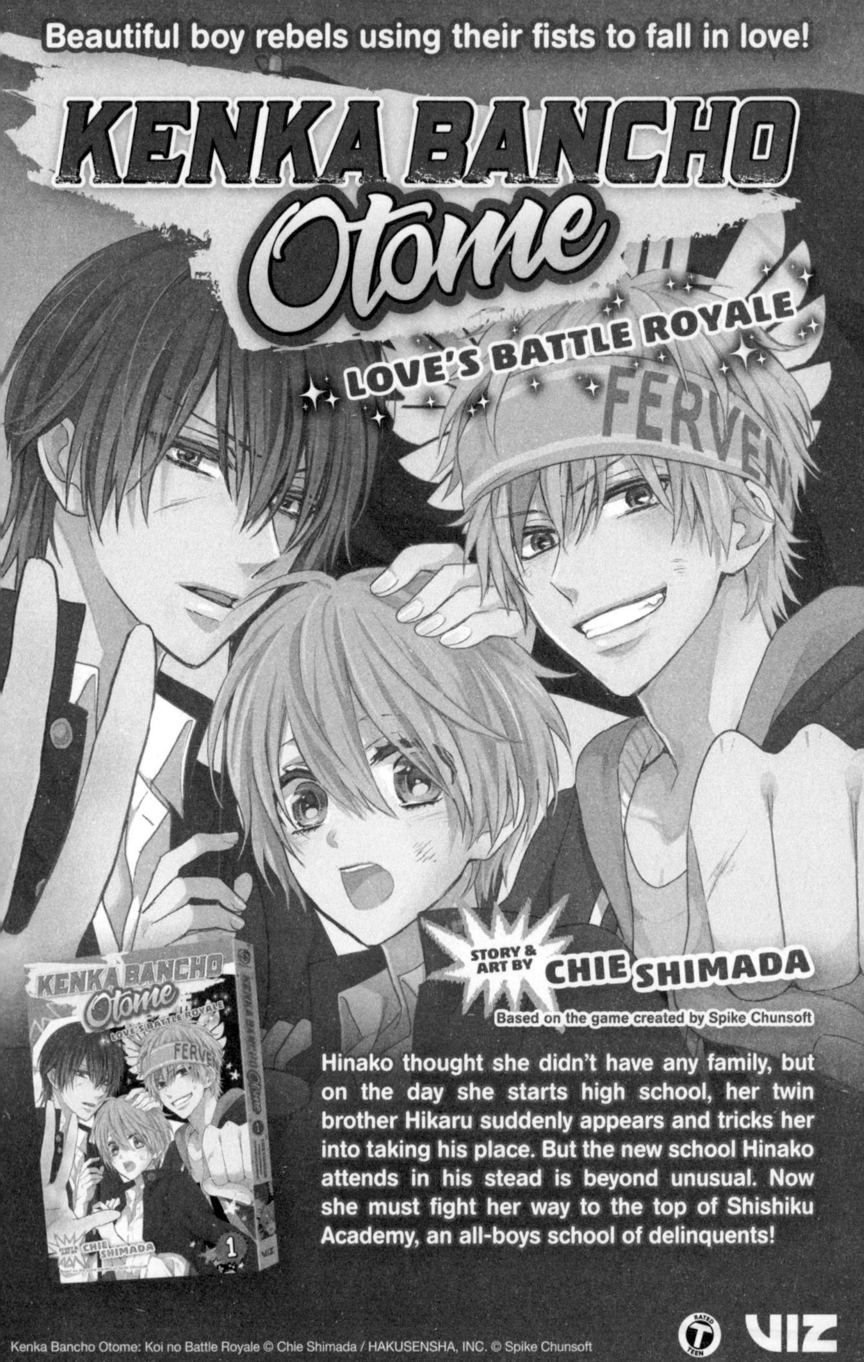
Beautiful boy rebels using their fists to fall in love!
KENKA BANCHO Otome
LOVE'S BATTLE ROYALE
FERVEN
STORY & ART BY CHIE SHIMADA
Based on the game created by Spike Chunsoft
Hinako thought she didn't have any family, but on the day she starts high school, her twin brother Hikaru suddenly appears and tricks her into taking his place. But the new school Hinako attends in his stead is beyond unusual. Now she must fight her way to the top of Shishiku Academy, an all-boys school of delinquents!
RATED T TEEN
VIZ

Takane &*Hana

VOLUME 12
SHOJO BEAT EDITION

STORY & ART BY **YUKI SHIWASU**

ENGLISH ADAPTATION **Ysabet Reinhardt MacFarlane**
TRANSLATION **JN Productions**
TOUCH–UP ART & LETTERING **Annaliese Christman**
DESIGN **Shawn Carrico**
EDITOR **Amy Yu**

Takane to Hana by Yuki Shiwasu
© Yuki Shiwasu 2018
All rights reserved.
First published in Japan in 2018 by HAKUSENSHA, Inc., Tokyo.
English language translation rights arranged with HAKUSENSHA, Inc., Tokyo.

Printed in the U.S.A.

Published by VIZ Media, LLC
P.O. Box 77010
San Francisco, CA 94107

10 9 8 7 6 5 4 3 2 1
First printing, December 2019

viz.com   shojobeat.com

Since I thought there weren't many
covers with Takane looking happy...

—YUKI SHIWASU

Born on March 7 in Fukuoka Prefecture, Japan,
Yuki Shiwasu began her career as a manga artist
after winning the top prize in the Hakusensha Athena
Newcomers' Awards from *Hana to Yume* magazine. She
is also the author of *Furou Kyoudai* (Immortal Siblings),
which was published by Hakusensha in Japan.

The Durian Guy

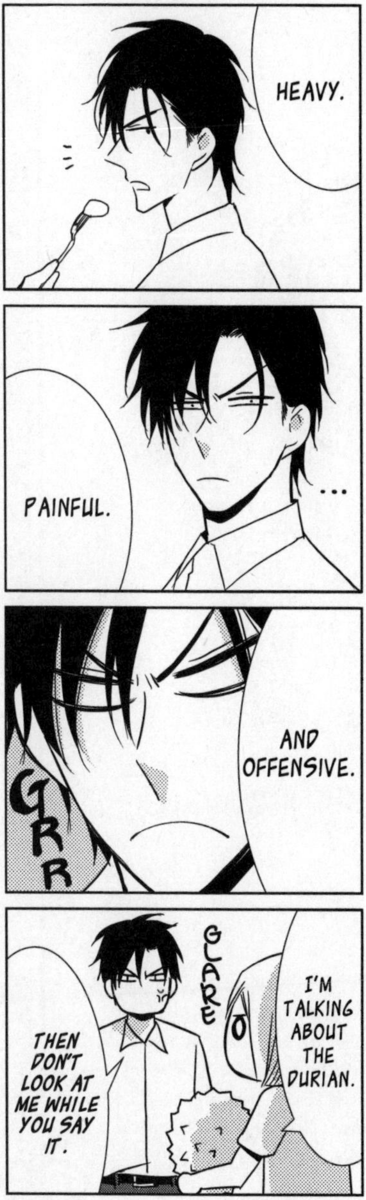
HEAVY.
...
PAINFUL.
AND OFFENSIVE.
GRR
I'M TALKING ABOUT THE DURIAN.
GLARE
THEN DON'T LOOK AT ME WHILE YOU SAY IT.